Cover photos from
www.cottages4you.co.uk

The original Farm Holiday Guide to
Coast & Country Holidays
in Britain

Farms, Hotels, Guest Houses, Self-catering, Caravans and Camping and Country Inns

For Contents see pages 2-3
Index of towns/ counties see page 311-314

Contents

Guide to Tourist Board Ratings 6
Readers' Offer Vouchers 7-40
Family-friendly Pubs and Inns 257-261
Pet-friendly Pubs and Inns..................262-275
Website Directory 277-310
Index of Towns/Counties 311-314

ENGLAND

BOARD

Bedfordshire 44
Buckinghamshire 44
Cambridgeshire 45
Cheshire 45
Cornwall 47
Cumbria 55
Derbyshire...59
Devon..61
Dorset 69
Essex 74
Gloucestershire 75
Hampshire 79
Herefordshire.....................................81
Isle of Wight 83
Kent...84
Lancashire 85
Leicestershire & Rutland 86
Lincolnshire..87
Norfolk..89
Northamptonshire 92
Northumberland.................................92
Oxfordshire 94
Shropshire 95
Somerset 99
Staffordshire 106
Suffolk 107
Sussex 108
Tyne & Wear 110
Warwickshire 110
Wiltshire 113
Worcestershire................................115
East Yorkshire 117
North Yorkshire 117
South Yorkshire 122

SELF-CATERING

Buckinghamshire 125
Cheshire 126
Cornwall 127
Cumbria 135
Derbyshire..142
Devon..144
Dorset 151
Durham 155
Gloucestershire 156
Herefordshire..................................157
Isle of Wight 158
Kent..159
Lancashire 160
Lincolnshire.....................................161
Norfolk..163
Northumberland..............................164
Nottinghamshire 167
Oxfordshire 168
Shropshire 169
Somerset 171
Staffordshire 174
Suffolk 175
East Sussex....................................177
West Sussex...................................178
Warwickshire 179
Worcestershire................................180
North Yorkshire 183
West Yorkshire 186

CARAVANS & CAMPING 189

Contents

SCOTLAND

BOARD
Aberdeen, Banff & Moray 195
Angus & Dundee 196
Argyll & Bute 197
Ayrshire & Arran 198
Dumfries & Galloway 200
Dunbartonshire 201
Fife 202
Highlands 203
Lanarkshire 205
Perth & Kinross 206
Stirling & The Trossachs 207
Scottish Islands(Skye) 207

SELF-CATERING
Aberdeen, Banff & Moray 210
Angus & Dundee 211
Argyll & Bute 212
Ayrshire & Arran 216
Borders 217
Dumfries & Galloway 219
Dunbartonshire 220
Edinburgh & Lothians 221
Fife 221
Highlands (North) 223
Highlands (South) 223
Lanarkshire 226
Morayshire 227
Perth & Kinross 227

CARAVANS & CAMPING 229

WALES

BOARD
Anglesey & Gwynedd 235
North Wales 237
Pembrokeshire 238
Powys 240

SELF-CATERING
Anglesey & Gwynedd 244
North Wales 247
Ceredigion 248
Pembrokeshire 249
Powys 251

CARAVANS & CAMPING 252

IRELAND

SELF-CATERING
CO. Clare 252

COUNTRY INNS

England / Scotland / Wales 253

© FHG Guides Ltd 2007
ISBN 1 85055 389 0
978-1-85055-389-2

Maps: ©MAPS IN MINUTES™ 2006. ©Crown Copyright,
Ordnance Survey Northen Ireland 2006 Permit No. NI 1675.

Typeset by FHG Guides Ltd, Paisley.
Printed and bound in Malaysia by Imago

Distribution. Book Trade: ORCA Book Services, Stanley House,
3 Fleets Lane, Poole, Dorset BH15 3AJ
(Tel: 01202 665432; Fax: 01202 666219)
e-mail: mail@orcabookservices.co.uk
Published by FHG Guides Ltd., Abbey Mill Business Centre,
Seedhill, Paisley PA1 ITJ (Tel: 0141-887 0428 Fax: 0141-889 7204).
e-mail: admin@fhguides.co.uk

The Original Farm Holiday Guide to Coast & Country Holidays
is published by FHG Guides Ltd,
part of Kuperard Group.

Cover design: FHG Guides
Cover pictures supplied by www.cottages4you.co.uk

Country Holidays

BRITAIN'S FAVOURITE COTTAGE HOLIDAYS

We offer the widest choice of holiday cottages, including the *ideal* one for you

With over 4,000 VisitBritain graded cottages throughout the UK, you're sure to find the ideal one for you. And as many of our properties also accept pets none of your family need miss out.

Look & book: **www.ch2007.co.uk**
For your free copy of our 2007 brochure call: **0870 608 4960**

Discover Britain...
...at its most beautiful

What more perfect place could there be to experience the beauty and variety of British landscape than from your very own rural retreat.

For more information, check availability and to book securely:

English Country Cottages
www.ecc2006.co.uk
0870 192 0399

Scottish Country Cottages
www.scc06.co.uk
0870 608 6529

Welcome holiday cottages

Whether you're looking for lots of outdoor adventure, something snug and romantic or a perfect location for the whole family, you'll find a great range of suitable properties at down to earth prices with Welcome

- Unbeatable prices
- No hidden extras

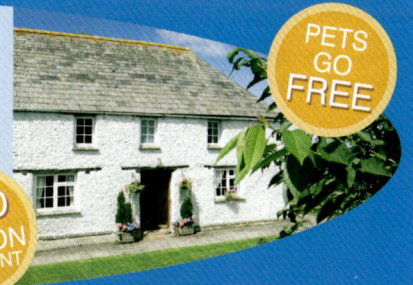

PETS GO FREE

TWO PERSON DISCOUNT

Check availability and book securely online – www.welcome2007.co.uk
Call for a 2007 brochure on – 0870 192 0847

Ratings & Awards

For the first time ever the AA, VisitBritain, VisitScotland, and the Wales Tourist Board will use a single method of assessing and rating serviced accommodation. Irrespective of which organisation inspects an establishment the rating awarded will be the same, using a common set of standards, giving a clear guide of what to expect. The RAC is no longer operating an Hotel inspection and accreditation business.

Accommodation Standards: Star Grading Scheme

Using a scale of 1-5 stars the objective quality ratings give a clear indication of accommodation standard, cleanliness, ambience, hospitality, service and food, This shows the full range of standards suitable for every budget and preference, and allows visitors to distinguish between the quality of accommodation and facilities on offer in different establishments. All types of board and self-catering accommodation are covered, including hotels, B&Bs, holiday parks, campus accommodation, hostels, caravans and camping, and boats.

VisitBritain and the regional tourist boards, **enjoyEngland.com**, **VisitScotland** and **VisitWales**, and **the AA** have full details of the grading system on their websites

The more stars, the higher level of quality

★★★★★
exceptional quality, with a degree of luxury

★★★★
excellent standard throughout

★★★
very good level of quality and comfort

★★
good quality, well presented and well run

★
acceptable quality; simple, practical, no frills

National Accessible Scheme

If you have particular mobility, visual or hearing needs, look out for the National Accessible Scheme. You can be confident of finding accommodation or attractions that meet your needs by looking for the following symbols.

Typically suitable for a person with sufficient mobility to climb a flight of steps but would benefit from fixtures and fittings to aid balance

Typically suitable for a person with restricted walking ability and for those that may need to use a wheelchair some of the time and can negotiate a maximum of three steps

Typically suitable for a person who depends on the use of a wheelchair and transfers unaided to and from the wheelchair in a seated position. This person may be an independent traveller

Typically suitable for a person who depends on the use of a wheelchair in a seated position. This person also requires personal or mechanical assistance (eg carer, hoist).

FHG READERS' OFFER 2007

LEIGHTON BUZZARD RAILWAY
Page's Park Station, Billington Road,
Leighton Buzzard, Bedfordshire LU7 4TN
Tel: 01525 373888
e-mail: info@buzzrail.co.uk
www.buzzrail.co.uk

One FREE adult/child with full-fare adult ticket
Valid 11/3/2007 - 28/10/2007

NOT TO BE USED IN CONJUNCTION WITH ANY OTHER OFFER

FHG READERS' OFFER 2007

BEKONSCOT MODEL VILLAGE & RAILWAY
Warwick Road, Beaconsfield,
Buckinghamshire HP9 2PL
Tel: 01494 672919
e-mail: info@bekonscot.co.uk
www.bekonscot.com

One child FREE when accompanied by full-paying adult
Valid February to October 2007

NOT TO BE USED IN CONJUNCTION WITH ANY OTHER OFFER

FHG READERS' OFFER 2007

BUCKINGHAMSHIRE RAILWAY CENTRE
Quainton Road Station, Quainton,
Aylesbury HP22 4BY
Tel & Fax: 01296 655720
e-mail: bucksrailcentre@btopenworld.com
www.bucksrailcentre.org

One child FREE with each full-paying adult
Not valid for Special Events

NOT TO BE USED IN CONJUNCTION WITH ANY OTHER OFFER

FHG READERS' OFFER 2007

THE RAPTOR FOUNDATION
The Heath, St Ives Road,
Woodhurst, Huntingdon, Cambs PE28 3BT
Tel: 01487 741140 • Fax: 01487 841140
e-mail: heleowl@aol.com
www.raptorfoundation.org.uk

TWO for the price of ONE
Valid until end 2007 (not Bank Holidays)

NOT TO BE USED IN CONJUNCTION WITH ANY OTHER OFFER

A 70-minute journey into the lost world of the English narrow gauge light railway. Features historic steam locomotives from many countries.
PETS MUST BE KEPT UNDER CONTROL AND NOT ALLOWED ON TRACKS

Open: Sundays and Bank Holiday weekends 11 March to 28 October. Additional days in summer.

Directions: on A4146 towards Hemel Hempstead, close to roundabout junction with A505.

Be a giant in a magical miniature world of make-believe depicting rural England in the 1930s.
"A little piece of history that is forever England."

Open: 10am-5pm daily mid February to end October.

Directions: Junction 16 M25, Junction 2 M40.

A working steam railway centre. Steam train rides, miniature railway rides, large collection of historic preserved steam locomotives, carriages and wagons.

Open: Sundays and Bank Holidays April to October, plus Wednesdays in school holidays 10.30am to 5.30pm.

Directions: off A41 Aylesbury to Bicester Road, 6 miles north west of Aylesbury.

Birds of Prey Centre offering audience participation in flying displays which are held 3 times daily. Tours, picnic area, gift shop, tearoom, craft shop.

Open: 10am-5pm all year except Christmas and New Year.

Directions: follow brown tourist signs from B1040.

SACREWELL FARM & COUNTRY CENTRE
Sacrewell, Thornhaugh,
Peterborough PE8 6HJ
Tel: 01780 782254
e-mail: info@sacrewell.fsnet.co.uk
www.sacrewell.org.uk

One child FREE with one full paying adult
Valid from March 1st to October 1st 2007

FHG READERS' OFFER 2007
K·U·P·E·R·A·R·D

NOT TO BE USED IN CONJUNCTION WITH ANY OTHER OFFER

GEEVOR TIN MINE
Pendeen, Penzance,
Cornwall TR19 7EW
Tel: 01736 788662 • Fax: 01736 786059
e-mail: bookings@geevor.com
www.geevor.com

TWO for the price of ONE or £3.75 off a family ticket
Valid 02/01/2007 to 20/12/2007

FHG READERS' OFFER 2007
K·U·P·E·R·A·R·D

NOT TO BE USED IN CONJUNCTION WITH ANY OTHER OFFER

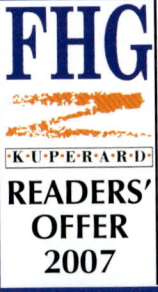

TAMAR VALLEY DONKEY PARK
St Ann's Chapel, Gunnislake,
Cornwall PL18 9HW
Tel: 01822 834072
e-mail: info@donkeypark.com
www.donkeypark.com

50p OFF per person, up to 6 persons
Valid from Easter until end October 2007

FHG READERS' OFFER 2007
K·U·P·E·R·A·R·D

NOT TO BE USED IN CONJUNCTION WITH ANY OTHER OFFER

NATIONAL SEAL SANCTUARY
Gweek, Helston,
Cornwall TR12 6UG
Tel: 01326 221361
e-mail: seals@sealsanctuary.co.uk
www.sealsanctuary.co.uk

TWO for ONE - on purchase of another ticket of
equal or greater value. Valid until December 2007.

FHG READERS' OFFER 2007
K·U·P·E·R·A·R·D

NOT TO BE USED IN CONJUNCTION WITH ANY OTHER OFFER

Farm animals, 18th century watermill and farmhouse, farm artifacts, caravan and camping, children's play areas. Restaurant and gift shop.	**Open:** all year. 9.30am to 5pm 1st March -30th Sept 10am-4pm 1st Oct to 28th Feb **Directions:** signposted off both A47 and A1.

FHG GUIDES, ABBEY MILL BUSINESS CENTRE, PAISLEY PA1 1TJ • www.holidayguides.com

Geevor is the largest mining history site in the UK in a spectacular setting on Cornwall's Atlantic coast. Guided underground tour, many surface buildings, museum, cafe, gift shop. Free parking.	**Open:** daily except Saturdays 10am to 4pm **Directions:** 7 miles from Penzance beside the B3306 Land's End to St Ives coast road

FHG GUIDES, ABBEY MILL BUSINESS CENTRE, PAISLEY PA1 1TJ • www.holidayguides.com

Cornwall's only Donkey Sanctuary set in 14 acres overlooking the beautiful Tamar Valley. Donkey rides, rabbit warren, goat hill, children's playgrounds, cafe and picnic area. New all-weather play barn.	**Open:** Easter to end Oct: daily 10am to 5.30pm. Nov to March: weekends and all school holidays 10.30am to 4.30pm **Directions:** just off A390 between Callington and Gunnislake at St Ann's Chapel.

FHG GUIDES, ABBEY MILL BUSINESS CENTRE, PAISLEY PA1 1TJ • www.holidayguides.com

Britain's leading grey seal rescue centre	**Open:** daily (except Christmas Day) from 10am **Directions:** from A30 follow signs to Helston, then brown tourist signs to Seal Sanctuary.

FHG GUIDES, ABBEY MILL BUSINESS CENTRE, PAISLEY PA1 1TJ • www.holidayguides.com

FHG READERS' OFFER 2007

CARS OF THE STARS MOTOR MUSEUM
Standish Street, Keswick,
Cumbria CA12 5HH
Tel: 017687 73757
e-mail: cotsmm@aol.com
www.carsofthestars.com

One child free with two paying adults
Valid during 2007

NOT TO BE USED IN CONJUNCTION WITH ANY OTHER OFFER

FHG READERS' OFFER 2007

ESKDALE HISTORIC WATER MILL
Mill Cottage, Boot, Eskdale,
Cumbria CA19 1TG
Tel: 019467 23335
e-mail: david.king403@tesco.net
www.eskdale.info

Two children FREE with two adults
Valid during 2007

NOT TO BE USED IN CONJUNCTION WITH ANY OTHER OFFER

FHG READERS' OFFER 2007

CRICH TRAMWAY VILLAGE
Crich, Matlock
Derbyshire DE4 5DP
Tel: 01773 854321 • Fax: 01773 854320
e-mail: enquiry@tramway.co.uk
www.tramway.co.uk

One child FREE with every full-paying adult
Valid during 2007

NOT TO BE USED IN CONJUNCTION WITH ANY OTHER OFFER

FHG READERS' OFFER 2007

THE BIG SHEEP
Abbotsham, Bideford,
Devon EX39 5AP
Tel: 01237 472366
e-mail: info@thebigsheep.co.uk
www.thebigsheep.co.uk

Admit one child FREE with each paying adult
Valid during 2007

NOT TO BE USED IN CONJUNCTION WITH ANY OTHER OFFER

A collection of cars from film and TV, including Chitty Chitty Bang Bang, James Bond's Aston Martin, Del Boy's van, Fab1 and many more.

PETS MUST BE KEPT ON LEAD

Open: daily 10am-5pm. Open February half term, 1st April to end November, also weekends in December.

Directions: in centre of Keswick close to car park.

The oldest working mill in England with 18th century oatmeal machinery running daily.

DOGS ON LEADS

Open: 11am to 5pm April to Sept. (may be closed Saturdays).

Directions: near inland terminus of Ravenglass & Eskdale Railway or over Hardknott Pass.

A superb family day out in the atmosphere of a bygone era. Explore the recreated period street and fascinating exhibitions. Unlimited tram rides are free with entry. Play areas, woodland walk and sculpture trail, shops, tea rooms, pub, restaurant and lots more.

Open: daily April to October 10 am to 5.30pm, weekends in winter.

Directions: eight miles from M1 Junction 28, follow brown and white signs for "Tramway Museum".

"England for Excellence" award-winning family entertainment park. Highlights: hilarious shows including the famous sheep-racing and the duck trials; the awesome Ewetopia indoor adventure playground for adults and children; brewery; mountain boarding; great local food.

Open: daily, 10am to 6pm April - Oct Phone for Winter opening times and details.

Directions: on A39 North Devon link road, two miles west of Bideford Bridge.

13

FHG
·K·U·P·E·R·A·R·D·
READERS' OFFER 2007

DEVONSHIRE COLLECTION OF PERIOD COSTUME
Totnes Costume Museum,
Bogan House, 43 High Street,
Totnes,
Devon TQ9 5NP

FREE child with a paying adult with voucher
Valid from Spring Bank Holiday to end of Sept 2007

NOT TO BE USED IN CONJUNCTION WITH ANY OTHER OFFER

FHG
·K·U·P·E·R·A·R·D·
READERS' OFFER 2007

CREALY ADVENTURE PARK
Sidmouth Road, Clyst St Mary, Exeter,
Devon EX5 1DR
Tel: 0870 116 3333 • Fax: 01395 233211
e-mail: fun@crealy.co.uk
www.crealy.co.uk

FREE superkart race or panning for gold.
Height restrictions apply. Valid until 31/10/07.
Photocopies not accepted. One voucher per person.

NOT TO BE USED IN CONJUNCTION WITH ANY OTHER OFFER

FHG
·K·U·P·E·R·A·R·D·
READERS' OFFER 2007

KILLHOPE LEAD MINING MUSEUM
Cowshill, Upper Weardale,
Co. Durham DL13 1AR
Tel: 01388 537505
e-mail: killhope@durham.gov.uk
www.durham.gov.uk/killhope

One child FREE with full-paying adult
Valid April to October 2007 (not Park Level Mine)

NOT TO BE USED IN CONJUNCTION WITH ANY OTHER OFFER

FHG
·K·U·P·E·R·A·R·D·
READERS' OFFER 2007

AVON VALLEY RAILWAY
Bitton Station, Bath Road, Bitton,
Bristol BS30 6HD
Tel: 0117 932 5538
e-mail: info@avonvalleyrailway.org
www.avonvalleyrailway.org

One FREE child with every fare-paying adult
Valid May - Oct 2007 (not 'Day Out with Thomas' events)

NOT TO BE USED IN CONJUNCTION WITH ANY OTHER OFFER

Themed exhibition, changed annually, based in a Tudor house. Collection contains items of dress for women, men and children from 17th century to 1980s, from high fashion to everyday wear.	**Open:** Open from Spring Bank Holiday to end September. 11am to 5pm Tuesday to Friday. **Directions:** centre of town, opposite Market Square. Mini bus up High Street stops outside.

FHG GUIDES, ABBEY MILL BUSINESS CENTRE, PAISLEY PA1 1TJ • www.holidayguides.com

Maximum fun, magic and adventure. An unforgettable family experience, with Tidal Wave log flume, rollercoaster, Queen Bess pirate ship, techno race karts, bumper boats, Vicorian carousel, animal handling, and huge indoor and outdoor play areas. The South-West's favourite family attraction!	**Open:** Summer: daily 10am to 5pm High season: daily 10am to 7pm Winter (Nov-March): Wed-Sun 10am -5pm **Directions:** minutes from M5 J30 on the A3052 Sidmouth road, near Exeter

FHG GUIDES, ABBEY MILL BUSINESS CENTRE, PAISLEY PA1 1TJ • www.holidayguides.com

Voted 'Most Family-Friendly Museum 2004' and 'Most Welcome Experience 2005', Killhope is Britain's best preserved lead mining site, with lots to see and do. Underground Experience is something not to be missed.	**Open:** April 1st to October 31st 10.30am to 5pm daily. **Directions:** alongside A689, midway between Stanhope and Alston in the heart of the North Pennines.

FHG GUIDES, ABBEY MILL BUSINESS CENTRE, PAISLEY PA1 1TJ • www.holidayguides.com

The Avon Valley Railway offers a whole new experience for some, and a nostalgic memory for others. **PETS MUST BE KEPT ON LEADS AND OFF TRAIN SEATS**	**Open:** Steam trains operate every Sunday, Easter to October, plus Bank Holidays and Christmas. **Directions:** on the A431 midway between Bristol and Bath at Bitton.

FHG GUIDES, ABBEY MILL BUSINESS CENTRE, PAISLEY PA1 1TJ • www.holidayguides.com

FHG K·U·P·E·R·A·R·D
READERS' OFFER 2007

NOAH'S ARK ZOO FARM
Failand Road, Wraxall,
Bristol BS48 1PG
Tel: 01275 852606 • Fax: 01275 857080
e-mail: info@noahsarkzoofarm.co.uk
www.noahsarkzoofarm.co.uk

One FREE child for each group of 4 or more persons
Valid until October 2007 (closed in winter)

NOT TO BE USED IN CONJUNCTION WITH ANY OTHER OFFER

FHG K·U·P·E·R·A·R·D
READERS' OFFER 2007

CIDER MUSEUM & KING OFFA DISTILLERY
21 Ryelands Street,
Hereford HR4 0LW
Tel: 01432 354207 • Fax: 01432 371641
e-mail: enquiries@cidermuseum.co.uk
www.cidermuseum.co.uk

50p reduction on entry fee
Valid during 2007

NOT TO BE USED IN CONJUNCTION WITH ANY OTHER OFFER

FHG K·U·P·E·R·A·R·D
READERS' OFFER 2007

MUSEUM OF KENT LIFE
Lock Lane, Sandling, Maidstone,
Kent ME14 3AU
Tel: 01622 763936 • Fax: 01622 662024
e-mail: enquiries@museum-kentlife.co.uk
www.museum-kentlife.co.uk

Two tickets for the price of one (cheapest ticket FREE)
Valid from March to November 2007

NOT TO BE USED IN CONJUNCTION WITH ANY OTHER OFFER

FHG K·U·P·E·R·A·R·D
READERS' OFFER 2007

QUEX MUSEUM, HOUSE & GARDENS
Quex Park,
Birchington
Kent CT7 0BH
Tel: 01843 842168 • Fax: 01843 846661
e-mail: pcmuseum@btconnect.com

QUEX MUSEUM.HOUSE GARDENS
The Powell-Cotton Collection

One adult FREE with each full-paying adult on
presentation of voucher. Valid until 31 December 2007

NOT TO BE USED IN CONJUNCTION WITH ANY OTHER OFFER

Fantastic 'hands-on' adventure zoo farm for all ages and all weathers. 80 different species from chicks and lambs to camels and rhinos. New indoor and outdoor mazes (longest in world and educational). Family-friendly cafe and shop.	**Open:** from February half-term to end October 10.30am to 5pm Mon to Sat. Check open days on website **Directions:** on B3128 between Bristol and Clevedon or Exit 19/20 M5

Discover the fascinating history of cider making. There is a programme of temporary exhibitions and events plus free samples of Hereford cider brandy.	**Open:** April to Oct 10am to 5pm; Nov to March 11am to 3pm. Closed Sun and Mon excluding Bank Holiday weekends. **Directions:** situated west of Hereford off the A438 Hereford to Brecon road.

Kent's award-winning open air museum is home to a collection of historic buildings which house interactive exhibitions on life over the last 150 years.	**Open:** seven days a week from February to start November, 10am to 5pm. **Directions:** Junction 6 off M20, follow signs to Aylesford.

World-ranking Museum incorporating Kent's finest Regency house. Gardens with peacocks, woodland walk, walled garden, maze and fountains. Children's activities and full events programme. Tearoom and gift shop. Full events programme.	**Open:** mid-March-Nov: Sun-Thurs 11am-5pm (House opens 2pm). Winter: Sundays 1-3.30pm (Museum and Gardens only). **Directions:** A2 to Margate, on entering Birchington turn right at church into Park Lane; Powell-Cotton Museum signposted.

FHG READERS' OFFER 2007

DOCKER PARK FARM
Arkholme, Carnforth,
Lancashire LA6 1AR
Tel & Fax: 015242 21331
e-mail: info@dockerparkfarm.co.uk
www.dockerparkfarm.co.uk

One FREE child per one paying adult (one voucher per child)
Valid from January to December 2007

NOT TO BE USED IN CONJUNCTION WITH ANY OTHER OFFER

FHG READERS' OFFER 2007

NATIONAL FISHING HERITAGE CENTRE
Alexandra Dock, Grimsby
N.E. Lincs DN31 1UZ
Tel: 01472 323345 • Fax: 01472 323555
nfhc@nelincs.gov.uk
www.nelincs.gov.uk

One child FREE with every paying adult.
Valid until August 2007 (not Bank Holidays)

NOT TO BE USED IN CONJUNCTION WITH ANY OTHER OFFER

FHG READERS' OFFER 2007

SKEGNESS NATURELAND SEAL SANCTUARY
North Parade, Skegness,
Lincolnshire PE25 1DB
Tel: 01754 764345
e-mail: natureland@fsbdial.co.uk
www.skegnessnatureland.co.uk

Free entry for one child when accompanied by
full-paying adult. Valid during 2007.

NOT TO BE USED IN CONJUNCTION WITH ANY OTHER OFFER

FHG READERS' OFFER 2007

DINOSAUR ADVENTURE PARK
Weston Park, Lenwade, Norwich,
Norfolk NR9 5JW
Tel: 01603 876310 • Fax: 01603 876315
e-mail: info@dinosaurpark.co.uk
www.dinosaurpark.co.uk

50p off standard admission prices for up to six people
Valid until end of October 2007

NOT TO BE USED IN CONJUNCTION WITH ANY OTHER OFFER

We are a working farm, with lots of animals to see and touch. Enjoy a walk round the Nature Trail or refreshments in the tearoom. Lots of activities during school holidays.	**Open:** Summer: daily 10.30am- 5pm. Winter: weekends only 10.30am-4pm. **Directions:** Junction 35 off M6, take B6254 towards Kirkby Lonsdale, then follow the brown signs.

FHG GUIDES, ABBEY MILL BUSINESS CENTRE, PAISLEY PA1 1TJ • www.holidayguides.com

Sign on as a crew member for an incredible journey of discovery that will take you to the edge of disaster and the extremes of the elements to witness at first hand the depths of human endurance. Plot your course, take the wheel in the Skipper's Wheelhouse, study maps and charts, try the radio, send a Morse Code message - and lots more.	**Open:** Apr-Oct: Mon-Fri 10am to 5pm, Sat-Sun 10.30am-5.30pm. Please phone for winter opening hours. **Directions:** A180 Corporation Road towards Sainsbury's.

FHG GUIDES, ABBEY MILL BUSINESS CENTRE, PAISLEY PA1 1TJ • www.holidayguides.com

Well known for rescuing and rehabilitating orphaned and injured seal pups found washed ashore on Lincolnshire beaches. Also: penguins, aquarium, pets' corner, reptiles, Floral Palace (tropical birds and butterflies etc).	**Open:** daily from 10am. Closed Christmas/Boxing/New Year's Days. **Directions:** at the north end of Skegness seafront.

FHG GUIDES, ABBEY MILL BUSINESS CENTRE, PAISLEY PA1 1TJ • www.holidayguides.com

It's time you came-n-saurus for a monster day out of discovery, adventure and fun. Enjoy the adventure play areas, dinosaur trail, secret animal garden and lots more.	**Open:** Please call for specific opening times or see our website. **Directions:** 9 miles from Norwich, follow the brown signs to Weston Park from the A47 or A1067

FHG GUIDES, ABBEY MILL BUSINESS CENTRE, PAISLEY PA1 1TJ • www.holidayguides.com

FHG · KUPERARD · READERS' OFFER 2007

THE COLLECTORS WORLD OF ERIC ST JOHN-FOTI
Hermitage Hall, Downham Market,
Norfolk PE38 0AU
Tel: 01366 383185 • Fax: 01366 386519
www.collectors-world.org

50p off adult admission - 25p off child admission
Valid during 2007

NOT TO BE USED IN CONJUNCTION WITH ANY OTHER OFFER

FHG · KUPERARD · READERS' OFFER 2007

THE TALES OF ROBIN HOOD
30 - 38 Maid Marian Way,
Nottingham NG1 6GF
Tel: 0115 9483284 • Fax: 0115 9501536
e-mail: robinhoodcentre@mail.com
www.robinhood.uk.com

One FREE child with full paying adult per voucher
Valid from January to December 2007

NOT TO BE USED IN CONJUNCTION WITH ANY OTHER OFFER

FHG · KUPERARD · READERS' OFFER 2007

NEWARK AIR MUSEUM
The Airfield, Winthorpe, Newark,
Nottinghamshire NG24 2NY
Tel: 01636 707170
e-mail: newarkair@onetel.com
www.newarkairmuseum.co.uk

Party rate discount for every voucher (50p per person
off normal admission). Valid during 2007.

NOT TO BE USED IN CONJUNCTION WITH ANY OTHER OFFER

FHG · KUPERARD · READERS' OFFER 2007

DIDCOT RAILWAY CENTRE
Didcot,
Oxfordshire OX11 7NJ
Tel: 01235 817200 • Fax: 01235 510621
e-mail: didrlyc@globalnet.co.uk
www.didcotrailwaycentre.org.uk

One child FREE when accompanied by full-paying adult
Valid until end 2007 except during Day Out With Thomas events

NOT TO BE USED IN CONJUNCTION WITH ANY OTHER OFFER

The collections of local eccentric Eric St John-Foti (Mr Norfolk Punch himself!) on view and the Magical Dickens Experience. Two amazing attractions for the price of one. Somewhere totally different, unique and interesting.	**Open:** 11am to 5pm (last entry 4pm) Open all year. **Directions:** one mile from town centre on the A1122 Downham/Wisbech Road.

FHG GUIDES, ABBEY MILL BUSINESS CENTRE, PAISLEY PA1 1TJ • www.holidayguides.com

Travel back in time with Robin Hood and his merry men on an adventure-packed theme tour, exploring the intriguing and mysterious story of their legendary tales of Medieval England. Enjoy film shows, live performances, adventure rides and even try archery! Are you brave enough to join Robin on his quest for good against evil?	**Open:** 10am-5.30pm, last admission 4.30pm. **Directions:** follow the brown and white tourist information signs whilst heading towards the city centre.

FHG GUIDES, ABBEY MILL BUSINESS CENTRE, PAISLEY PA1 1TJ • www.holidayguides.com

A collection of 70 aircraft and cockpit sections from across the history of aviation. Extensive aero engine and artefact displays.	**Open:** daily from 10am (closed Christmas period and New Year's Day). **Directions:** follow brown and white signs from A1, A46, A17 and A1133.

FHG GUIDES, ABBEY MILL BUSINESS CENTRE, PAISLEY PA1 1TJ • www.holidayguides.com

See the steam trains from the golden age of the Great Western Railway. Steam locomotives in the original engine shed, a reconstructed country branch line, and a re-creation of Brunel's original broad gauge railway. On Steam Days there are rides in the 1930s carriages.	**Open:** Sat/Sun all year; daily 23 June to 2 Sept + school holidays. 10am-5pm weekends and Steam Days, 10am-4pm other days and in winter. **Directions:** at Didcot Parkway rail station; on A4130, signposted from M4 (Junction 13) and A34

FHG GUIDES, ABBEY MILL BUSINESS CENTRE, PAISLEY PA1 1TJ • www.holidayguides.com

FHG READERS' OFFER 2007

THE HELICOPTER MUSEUM
The Heliport, Locking Moor Road,
Weston-Super-Mare BS24 8PP
Tel: 01934 635227 • Fax: 01934 645230
e-mail: office@helimuseum.fsnet.co.uk
www.helicoptermuseum.co.uk

One child FREE with two full-paying adults
Valid from April to October 2007

NOT TO BE USED IN CONJUNCTION WITH ANY OTHER OFFER

FHG READERS' OFFER 2007

EXMOOR FALCONRY & ANIMAL FARM
Allerford, Near Porlock, Minehead,
Somerset TA24 8HJ
Tel: 01643 862816
e-mail: exmoor.falcon@virgin.net
www.exmoorfalconry.co.uk

10% off entry to Falconry Centre
Valid during 2007

NOT TO BE USED IN CONJUNCTION WITH ANY OTHER OFFER

FHG READERS' OFFER 2007

TROPIQUARIA
Washford Cross, Watchet
Somerset TA23 0QB
Tel: 01984 640688 • Fax: 01984 641105
e-mail: info@tropiquaria.co.uk
www.tropiquaria.co.uk

One FREE child per full paying adult
(one child per voucher). Valid during 2007

NOT TO BE USED IN CONJUNCTION WITH ANY OTHER OFFER

FHG READERS' OFFER 2007

FLEET AIR ARM MUSEUM
RNAS Yeovilton, Ilchester,
Somerset BA22 8HT
Tel: 01935 840565
e-mail: enquiries@fleetairarm.com
www.fleetairarm.com

One child FREE with full paying adult
Valid during 2007 except Bank Holidays

NOT TO BE USED IN CONJUNCTION WITH ANY OTHER OFFER

The world's largest helicopter collection - over 70 exhibits, includes two royal helicopters, Russian Gunship and Vietnam veterans plus many award-winning exhibits. Cafe, shop. Flights. **PETS MUST BE KEPT UNDER CONTROL**	**Open:** Wednesday to Sunday 10am to 5.30pm. Daily during school Easter and Summer holidays and Bank Holiday Mondays. November to March: 10am to 4.30pm **Directions:** Junction 21 off M5 then follow the propellor signs.

FHG GUIDES, ABBEY MILL BUSINESS CENTRE, PAISLEY PA1 1TJ • www.holidayguides.com

Falconry centre with animals - flying displays, animal handling, feeding and bottle feeding - in 15th century NT farmyard setting on Exmoor. Also falconry and outdoor activities, hawk walks and riding.	**Open:** 10.30am to 5pm daily **Directions:** A39 west of Minehead, turn right at Allerford, half a mile along lane on left.

FHG GUIDES, ABBEY MILL BUSINESS CENTRE, PAISLEY PA1 1TJ • www.holidayguides.com

Animal and adventure park where you can hold snakes and tarantulas in the Tropical Hall. Visit the Aquarium, Puppet Theatre and Radio Museum. Play on our two full-size pirate ships and indoor playcastle.	**Open:** daily Easter-Sept 10am-6pm. Sept - end Oct: 11am-5pm; Nov - Easter: weekends and school holidays. **Directions:** on A39 between Williton and Minehead. Look for tall pirate ship masts. Buses: 14, 28, 38.

FHG GUIDES, ABBEY MILL BUSINESS CENTRE, PAISLEY PA1 1TJ • www.holidayguides.com

Europe's largest naval aviation collection with over 40 aircraft on display, including Concorde 002 and Ark Royal Aircraft Carrier Experience. Situated on an operational naval air station.	**Open:** open daily April to October 10am-5.30pm; November to March 10am-4.30pm (closed Mon and Tues). **Directions:** just off A303/A37 on B3151 at Ilchester. Yeovil rail station 10 miles.

FHG GUIDES, ABBEY MILL BUSINESS CENTRE, PAISLEY PA1 1TJ • www.holidayguides.com

FHG READERS' OFFER 2007
K·U·P·E·R·A·R·D

ANIMAL FARM ADVENTURE PARK
Red Road, Berrow, Burnham-on-Sea
Somerset TA8 2RW
Tel: 01278 751628 • Fax: 01278 751633
info@afap.fsnet.co.uk
www.animal-farm.co.uk

*TWO admissions for the price of ONE.
Valid until end 2007*

NOT TO BE USED IN CONJUNCTION WITH ANY OTHER OFFER

FHG READERS' OFFER 2007
K·U·P·E·R·A·R·D

PARADISE PARK & GARDENS
Avis Road, Newhaven,
East Sussex BN9 0DH
Tel: 01273 512123 • Fax: 01273 616000
e-mail: enquiries@paradisepark.co.uk
www.paradisepark.co.uk

*Admit one FREE adult or child with one adult
paying full entrance price. Valid during 2007*

NOT TO BE USED IN CONJUNCTION WITH ANY OTHER OFFER

FHG READERS' OFFER 2007
K·U·P·E·R·A·R·D

YESTERDAY'S WORLD
High Street, Battle, E. Sussex TN33 0AQ
Tel: 01424 775378 (24hr info)
Enquiries/bookings: 01424 893938
e-mail: info@yesterdaysworld.co.uk
www.yesterdaysworld.co.uk

*One child FREE when accompanied by one
full-paying adult. Valid until end 2007*

NOT TO BE USED IN CONJUNCTION WITH ANY OTHER OFFER

FHG READERS' OFFER 2007
K·U·P·E·R·A·R·D

AMERICAN ADVENTURE GOLF
Fort Fun, Royal Parade,
Eastbourne, East Sussex BN22 7LU
Tel: 01323 642833
e-mail: fortfuneb@aol.com
www.fortfun.co.uk

*One FREE game of golf with every full-paying customer
(value £3). Valid April-Oct 2007 before 12 noon only*

NOT TO BE USED IN CONJUNCTION WITH ANY OTHER OFFER

Stay and play all day at Somerset's top all-weather family day out. Cuddle pets and baby animals, mega playbarn with 3 levels of fun and exciting giant slides! Acres of friendly animals to meet and feed, farm walks, massive play park with trampolines, free train rides and lots, lots more! See website for event days.

Open: 10am-5.30pm daily all year except 24-26 December.

Directions: from M5 J22 head for Berrow/Brean; follow Animal Farm signs.

FHG GUIDES, ABBEY MILL BUSINESS CENTRE, PAISLEY PA1 1TJ • www.holidayguides.com

---

Discover 'Planet Earth' for an unforgettable experience. A unique Museum of Life, Dinosaur Safari, beautiful Water Gardens with fish and wildfowl, plant houses, themed gardens, Heritage Trail, miniature railway. Playzone includes crazy golf and adventure play areas. Garden Centre and Terrace Cafe.

Open: open daily, except Christmas Day and Boxing Day.

Directions: signposted off A26 and A259.

FHG GUIDES, ABBEY MILL BUSINESS CENTRE, PAISLEY PA1 1TJ • www.holidayguides.com

---

The past is brought to life at one of the South East's best loved family attractions. 100,000+ nostalgic artefacts, set in a charming 15th century house and country garden. New attractions and tearooms.

Open: 9.30am to 6pm (last admission 4.45pm, one hour earlier in winter). Closing times may vary – phone or check website.

Directions: just off A21 in Battle High Street opposite the Abbey.

FHG GUIDES, ABBEY MILL BUSINESS CENTRE, PAISLEY PA1 1TJ • www.holidayguides.com

---

18-hole American Adventure Golf set in ⅓ acre landscaped surroundings. Played on different levels including water features.

Open: April until end October 10am until dusk.

Directions: on the seafront ¼ mile east of Eastbourne Pier.

FHG GUIDES, ABBEY MILL BUSINESS CENTRE, PAISLEY PA1 1TJ • www.holidayguides.com

FHG READERS' OFFER 2007
K·U·P·E·R·A·R·D

WILDERNESS WOOD
Hadlow Down, Near Uckfield,
East Sussex TN22 4HJ
Tel: 01825 830509 • Fax: 01825 830977
e-mail: enquiries@wildernesswood.co.uk
www.wildernesswood.co.uk

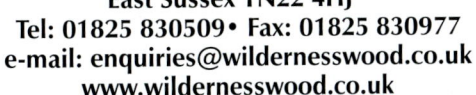

one FREE admission with a full-paying adult
Valid during 2007 (not for Special Events)

NOT TO BE USED IN CONJUNCTION WITH ANY OTHER OFFER

FHG READERS' OFFER 2007
K·U·P·E·R·A·R·D

WASHINGTON WETLAND CENTRE
Pattinson, Washington,
Tyne & Wear NE38 8LE
Tel: 0191 416 5454
e-mail: info.washington@wwt.org.uk
www.wwt.org.uk

One FREE admission with full-paying adult
Valid from 1st Jan to 30th Sept 2007

NOT TO BE USED IN CONJUNCTION WITH ANY OTHER OFFER

FHG READERS' OFFER 2007
K·U·P·E·R·A·R·D

HATTON COUNTRY WORLD FARM VILLAGE
Dark Lane, Hatton, Near Warwick,
Warwickshire CV35 8XA
Tel: 01926 843411
e-mail: hatton@hattonworld.com
www.hattonworld.com

Admit one child FREE with one full-paying adult day ticket.
Admission into Shopping Village free. Valid during 2007

NOT TO BE USED IN CONJUNCTION WITH ANY OTHER OFFER

FHG READERS' OFFER 2007
K·U·P·E·R·A·R·D

STRATFORD BUTTERFLY FARM
Swan's Nest Lane, Stratford-upon-Avon
Warwickshire CV37 7LS
Tel: 01789 299288 • Fax: 01789 415878
e-mail: sales@butterflyfarm.co.uk
www.butterflyfarm.co.uk

Admit TWO for the price of ONE
Valid until 31/12/2007

NOT TO BE USED IN CONJUNCTION WITH ANY OTHER OFFER

Wilderness Wood is a unique family-run working woodland in the Sussex High Weald. Explore trails and footpaths, enjoy local cakes and ices, try the adventure playground. Many special events and activities. Parties catered for.	**Open:** daily 10am to 5.30pm or dusk if earlier. **Directions:** on the south side of the A272 in the village of Hadlow Down. Signposted with a brown tourist sign.

Conservation site with 100 acres of stunning wetland and woodland, home to rare wildlife. Waterside cafe, play area, gift shop.	**Open:** every day except Christmas Day **Directions:** signposted from A19, A195, A1231 and A182.

Two attractions side-by-side. Hatton Farm Village has fun for the whole family, with animals, demonstrations and adventure play. Hatton Shopping Village has 25 craft and gift shops, an antiques centre, a factory-style store, and two restaurants. Free parking.	**Open:** daily 10am to 5pm. Open until 4pm Christmas Eve; 11am-4pm 27 Dec-1st Jan incl; closed Christmas Day & Boxing Day. **Directions:** 5 minutes from M40 (J15), A46 towards Coventry, then just off A4177 (follow brown tourist signs).

Wander through a tropical rainforest with a myriad of multicoloured butterflies, sunbirds and koi carp. See fascinating animals in Insect City and view deadly spiders in perfect safety in Arachnoland.	**Open:** daily except Christmas Day. 10am-6pm summer, 10am-dusk winter. **Directions:** on south bank of River Avon opposite Royal Shakespeare Theatre. Easily accessible from town centre, 5 minutes' walk.

FHG KUPERARD READERS' OFFER 2007

AVONCROFT MUSEUM
Stoke Heath,
Bromsgrove,
Worcestershire B60 4JR
Tel: 01527 831363 • Fax: 01527 876934
www.avoncroft.org.uk

One FREE child with one full-paying adult
Valid from March to November 2007

NOT TO BE USED IN CONJUNCTION WITH ANY OTHER OFFER

FHG KUPERARD READERS' OFFER 2007

YORKSHIRE DALES FALCONRY & WILDLIFE CONSERVATION CENTRE
Crow's Nest, Giggleswick, Near Settle LA2 8AS
Tel: 01729 822832• Fax: 01729 825160
e-mail: info@falconryandwildlife.com
www.falconryandwildlife.com

One child FREE with two full-paying adults
Valid until end 2007

NOT TO BE USED IN CONJUNCTION WITH ANY OTHER OFFER

FHG KUPERARD READERS' OFFER 2007

WORLD OF JAMES HERRIOT
23 Kirkgate, Thirsk,
North Yorkshire YO7 1PL
Tel: 01845 524234
Fax: 01845 525333
www.worldofjamesherriot.org

Admit TWO for the price of ONE (one voucher per transaction only). Valid until October 2007

NOT TO BE USED IN CONJUNCTION WITH ANY OTHER OFFER

FHG KUPERARD READERS' OFFER 2007

EMBSAY & BOLTON ABBEY STEAM RAILWAY
Bolton Abbey Station, Skipton,
North Yorkshire BD23 6AF
Tel: 01756 710614
e-mail: embsay.steam@btinternet.com
www.embsayboltonabbeyrailway.org.uk

One adult travels FREE when accompanied by a full fare paying adult (does not include Special Event days). Valid during 2007.

NOT TO BE USED IN CONJUNCTION WITH ANY OTHER OFFER

A fascinating world of historic buildings covering 7 centuries, rescued and rebuilt on an open-air site in the heart of the Worcestershire countryside. **PETS ON LEADS ONLY**	**Open:** July and August all week. March to November varying times, please telephone for details. **Directions:** A38 south of Bromsgrove, near Junction 1 of M42, Junction 5 of M5.

FHG GUIDES, ABBEY MILL BUSINESS CENTRE, PAISLEY PA1 1TJ • www.holidayguides.com

All types of birds of prey exhibited here, from owls and kestrels to eagles and vultures. Special flying displays 12 noon, 1.30pm and 3pm. Bird handling courses arranged for either half or full days. **GUIDE DOGS ONLY**	**Open:** 10am to 4.30pm summer 10am to 4pm winter **Directions:** on main A65 trunk road outside Settle. Follow brown direction signs.

FHG GUIDES, ABBEY MILL BUSINESS CENTRE, PAISLEY PA1 1TJ • www.holidayguides.com

Visit James Herriot's original house recreated as it was in the 1940s. Television sets used in the series 'All Creatures Great and Small'. There is a children's interactive gallery with life-size model farm animals and three rooms dedicated to the history of veterinary medicine.	**Open:** daily. Easter-Oct 10am-5pm; Nov-Easter 11am to 4pm **Directions:** follow signs off A1 or A19 to Thirsk, then A168, off Thirsk market place

FHG GUIDES, ABBEY MILL BUSINESS CENTRE, PAISLEY PA1 1TJ • www.holidayguides.com

Steam trains operate over a 4½ mile line from Bolton Abbey Station to Embsay Station. Many family events including Thomas the Tank Engine take place during major Bank Holidays.	**Open:** steam trains run every Sunday throughout the year and up to 7 days a week in summer. 10.30am to 4.30pm **Directions:** Embsay Station signposted from the A59 Skipton by-pass; Bolton Abbey Station signposted from the A59 at Bolton Abbey.

FHG GUIDES, ABBEY MILL BUSINESS CENTRE, PAISLEY PA1 1TJ • www.holidayguides.com

FHG READERS' OFFER 2007
K·U·P·E·R·A·R·D

MUSEUM OF RAIL TRAVEL
Ingrow Railway Centre, Near Keighley,
West Yorkshire BD22 8NJ
Tel: 01535 680425
e-mail: admin@vintagecarriagestrust.org
www.vintagecarriagestrust.org • www.museumofrailtravel.co.uk

"ONE for ONE" free admission
Valid during 2007 except during special events (ring to check)

NOT TO BE USED IN CONJUNCTION WITH ANY OTHER OFFER

FHG READERS' OFFER 2007
K·U·P·E·R·A·R·D

THE COLOUR MUSEUM
Perkin House, PO Box 244, Providence Street,
Bradford BD1 2PW
Tel: 01274 390955 • Fax: 01274 392888
e-mail: museum@sdc.org.uk
www.colour-experience.org

TWO for ONE
Valid during 2007

NOT TO BE USED IN CONJUNCTION WITH ANY OTHER OFFER

FHG READERS' OFFER 2007
K·U·P·E·R·A·R·D

THACKRAY MUSEUM
Beckett Street, Leeds LS9 7LN
Tel: 0113 244 4343
Fax: 0113 247 0219
e-mail: info@thackraymuseum.org
www.thackraymuseum.org

TWO for ONE on the purchase of a full adult ticket
Valid until July 2007 excluding Bank Holidays

NOT TO BE USED IN CONJUNCTION WITH ANY OTHER OFFER

FHG READERS' OFFER 2007
K·U·P·E·R·A·R·D

EUREKA! THE MUSEUM FOR CHILDREN
Discovery Road, Halifax,
West Yorkshire HX1 2NE
Tel: 01422 330069
e-mail: info@eureka.org.uk
www.eureka.org

243 - £6.50 ticket
244 - £1.95 ticket

One child FREE with one adult paying full price.
Valid Saturdays and Sundays only during 2007

NOT TO BE USED IN CONJUNCTION WITH ANY OTHER OFFER

A fascinating display of railway carriages and a wide range of railway items telling the story of rail travel over the years.

ALL PETS MUST BE KEPT ON LEADS

Open: daily 11am to 4.30pm

Directions: approximately one mile from Keighley on A629 Halifax road. Follow brown tourist signs

FHG GUIDES, ABBEY MILL BUSINESS CENTRE, PAISLEY PA1 1TJ • www.holidayguides.com

---

The Colour Museum is unique. Dedicated to the history, development and technology of colour, it is the ONLY museum of its kind in Europe. A truly colourful experience for both kids and adults, it's fun, it's informative and it's well worth a visit.

Open: Tuesday to Saturday 10am to 4pm (last admission 3.30pm).

Directions: just off Westgate on B6144 from the city centre to Haworth.

FHG GUIDES, ABBEY MILL BUSINESS CENTRE, PAISLEY PA1 1TJ • www.holidayguides.com

---

The Thackray Museum has been England's Visitor Attraction of the Year and is a fantastic day out, transporting you into a living experience of health and medicine, past, present and future. Experience life as a character in the Victorian Slums of 1840, where you will be flabbergasted at the incredible lotions and potions once offered as cures, then see how this has evolved into modern medicine. Then step inside the human body in the interactive Life Zone!

Open: daily 10am till 5pm, closed 24th-26th + 31st Dec and 1st Jan.

Directions: from M621 follow signs for York (A64), then follow brown tourist signs. From the north, take A58 towards city, then follow brown tourist signs.

FHG GUIDES, ABBEY MILL BUSINESS CENTRE, PAISLEY PA1 1TJ • www.holidayguides.com

---

The UK's first and foremost museum for children under 11, where hundreds of interactive exhibits let them make fascinating discoveries about themselves and the world around them.

Open: daily 10am to 5pm (closed 24-26 December)

Directions: next to Halifax railway station, five minutes from J24 M62

FHG GUIDES, ABBEY MILL BUSINESS CENTRE, PAISLEY PA1 1TJ • www.holidayguides.com

FHG READERS' OFFER 2007

THE GRASSIC GIBBON CENTRE
Arbuthnott, Laurencekirk,
Aberdeenshire AB30 1PB
Tel: 01561 361668
e-mail: lgginfo@grassicgibbon.com
www.grassicgibbon.com

TWO for the price of ONE entry to exhibition (based on full adult rate only). Valid during 2007 (not groups)

NOT TO BE USED IN CONJUNCTION WITH ANY OTHER OFFER

FHG READERS' OFFER 2007

STORYBOOK GLEN
Maryculter,
Aberdeen
Aberdeenshire AB12 5FT
Tel: 01224 732941
www.storybookglenaberdeen.co.uk

10% discount on all admissions
Valid until end 2007

NOT TO BE USED IN CONJUNCTION WITH ANY OTHER OFFER

FHG READERS' OFFER 2007

OBAN RARE BREEDS FARM PARK
Glencruitten, Oban,
Argyll PA34 4QB
Tel: 01631 770608
e-mail: info@obanrarebreeds.com
www.obanrarebreeds.com

20% DISCOUNT on all admissions
Valid during 2007

NOT TO BE USED IN CONJUNCTION WITH ANY OTHER OFFER

FHG READERS' OFFER 2007

INVERARAY JAIL
Church Square, Inveraray,
Argyll PA32 8TX
Tel: 01499 302381 • Fax: 01499 302195
e-mail: info@inverarayjail.co.uk
www.inverarayjail.co.uk

One child FREE with one full-paying adult
Valid until end 2007

NOT TO BE USED IN CONJUNCTION WITH ANY OTHER OFFER

Visitor Centre dedicated to the much-loved Scottish writer Lewis Grassic Gibbon. Exhibition, cafe, gift shop. Outdoor children's play area. Disabled access throughout.	**Open:** daily April to October 10am to 4.30pm. Groups by appointment including evenings. **Directions:** on the B967, accessible and signposted from both A90 and A92.

FHG GUIDES, ABBEY MILL BUSINESS CENTRE, PAISLEY PA1 1TJ • www.holidayguides.com

28-acre theme park with over 100 nursery rhyme characters, set in beautifully landscaped gardens. Shop and restaurant on site.	**Open:** 1st March to 31st October: daily 10am to 6pm; 1st Nov to end Feb: Sat/Sun only 11am to 4pm **Directions:** 6 miles west of Aberdeen off B9077

FHG GUIDES, ABBEY MILL BUSINESS CENTRE, PAISLEY PA1 1TJ • www.holidayguides.com

Rare breeds of farm animals, pets' corner, conservation groups, tea room, woodland walk in beautiful location	**Open:** 10am to 6pm mid-March to end October **Directions:** two-and-a-half miles from Oban along Glencruitten road

FHG GUIDES, ABBEY MILL BUSINESS CENTRE, PAISLEY PA1 1TJ • www.holidayguides.com

19th century prison with fully restored 1820 courtroom and two prisons. Guides in uniform as warders, prisoners and matron. Remember your camera!	**Open:** April to October 9.30am-6pm (last admission 5pm); November to March 10am-5pm (last admission 4pm) **Directions:** A83 to Campbeltown

FHG GUIDES, ABBEY MILL BUSINESS CENTRE, PAISLEY PA1 1TJ • www.holidayguides.com

FHG READERS' OFFER 2007
K·U·P·E·R·A·R·D

SCOTTISH MARITIME MUSEUM
Harbourside, Irvine,
Ayrshire KA12 8QE
Tel: 01294 278283
Fax: 01294 313211
www.scottishmaritimemuseum.org

TWO for the price of ONE
Valid from April to October 2007

NOT TO BE USED IN CONJUNCTION WITH ANY OTHER OFFER

FHG READERS' OFFER 2007
K·U·P·E·R·A·R·D

JEDFOREST DEER & FARM PARK
Mervinslaw Estate, Camptown, Jedburgh,
Borders TD8 6PL
Tel: 01835 840364
e-mail: mervinslaw@ecosse.net
www.aboutscotland.com/jedforest

One FREE child with two full-paying adults
Valid May/June and Sept/Oct 2007

NOT TO BE USED IN CONJUNCTION WITH ANY OTHER OFFER

FHG READERS' OFFER 2007
K·U·P·E·R·A·R·D

SCOTTISH SEABIRD CENTRE
The Harbour, North Berwick,
East Lothian EH39 4SS
Tel: 01620 890202 • Fax: 01620 890222
e-mail: info@seabird.org
www.seabird.org

20% OFF any admission
Valid until 1st October 2007

NOT TO BE USED IN CONJUNCTION WITH ANY OTHER OFFER

FHG READERS' OFFER 2007
K·U·P·E·R·A·R·D

THE SCOTTISH MINING MUSEUM
Lady Victoria Colliery, Newtongrange,
Midlothian EH22 4QN
Tel: 0131-663 7519 • Fax: 0131-654 0952
visitorservices@scottishminingmuseum.com
www.scottishminingmuseum.com

One child FREE with full-paying adult
Valid January to December 2007

NOT TO BE USED IN CONJUNCTION WITH ANY OTHER OFFER

Scotland's seafaring heritage is among the world's richest and you can relive the heyday of Scottish shipping at the Maritime Museum.

Open: 1st April to 31st October - 10am-5pm

Directions: situated on Irvine harbourside and only a 10 minute walk from Irvine train station.

Working farm with visitor centre showing rare breeds, deer herds, ranger-led activities, and walks. Birds of prey displays and tuition. Corporate activities. Shop and cafe.

Open: daily Easter to August 10am to 5.30pm; Sept/Oct 11am to 4.30pm.

Directions: 5 miles south of Jedburgh on A68.

Get close to Nature with a visit to this award-winning Centre. With panoramic views across islands and sandy beaches, the area is a haven for wildlife. Live cameras zoom in close to see wildlife including gannets, puffins and seals. Wildlife boat safaris, new Environmental Zone and Flyway.

Open: daily from 10am

Directions: from A1 take road for North Berwick; near the harbour; Centre signposted.

---

visitscotland 5-Star Attraction with two floors of interactive exhibitions, a 'Magic Helmet' tour of the pithead, re-created coal road and coal face, and new Big Stuff tour. Largest working winding engine in Britain.

Open: daily. Summer: 10am to 5pm (last tour 3.30pm). Winter: 10am to 4pm (last tour 2.30pm)

Directions: 5 minutes from Sherrifhall Roundabout on Edinburgh City Bypass on A7 south

FHG READERS' OFFER 2007
K·U·P·E·R·A·R·D

BO'NESS & KINNEIL RAILWAY
Bo'ness Station, Union Street,
Bo'ness, West Lothian EH51 9AQ
Tel: 01506 822298
e-mail: enquiries.railway@srps.org.uk
www.srps.org.uk

FREE child train fare with one paying adult/concession. Valid 31st March-31st Oct 2007. Not Thomas events or Santa Steam trains

NOT TO BE USED IN CONJUNCTION WITH ANY OTHER OFFER

FHG READERS' OFFER 2007
K·U·P·E·R·A·R·D

MYRETON MOTOR MUSEUM
Aberlady,
East Lothian
EH32 0PZ
Tel: 01875 870288

*One child FREE with each paying adult
Valid during 2007*

NOT TO BE USED IN CONJUNCTION WITH ANY OTHER OFFER

FHG READERS' OFFER 2007
K·U·P·E·R·A·R·D

GLASGOW SCIENCE CENTRE
50 Pacific Quay
Glasgow
G51 1EA
Tel: 0871 540 1000
www.glasgowsciencecentre.org

£1 off entry to Science Mall or IMAX Cinema (not valid for feature-length films; not with group tickets). Valid until 30/5/2007

NOT TO BE USED IN CONJUNCTION WITH ANY OTHER OFFER

FHG READERS' OFFER 2007
K·U·P·E·R·A·R·D

SPEYSIDE HEATHER GARDEN & VISITOR CENTRE
Speyside Heather Centre, Dulnain Bridge,
Inverness-shire PH26 3PA
Tel: 01479 851359 • Fax: 01479 851396
e-mail: enquiries@heathercentre.com
www.heathercentre.com

*FREE entry to 'Heather Story' exhibition
Valid during 2007*

NOT TO BE USED IN CONJUNCTION WITH ANY OTHER OFFER

Steam and heritage diesel passenger trains from Bo'ness to Birkhill for guided tours of Birkhill fireclay mines. Explore the history of Scotland's railways in the Scottish Railway Exhibition. Coffee shop and souvenir shop.	**Open:** weekends April to October, daily July and August. **Directions:** in the town of Bo'ness. Leave M9 at Junction 3 or 5, then follow brown tourist signs.

FHG GUIDES, ABBEY MILL BUSINESS CENTRE, PAISLEY PA1 1TJ • www.holidayguides.com

On show is a large collection, from 1899, of cars, bicycles, motor cycles and commercials. There is also a large collection of period advertising, posters and enamel signs.	**Open:** March-November - open daily 11am to 4pm. December-February - weekends 11am to 3pm or by special appointment. **Directions:** off A198 near Aberlady. Two miles from A1.

FHG GUIDES, ABBEY MILL BUSINESS CENTRE, PAISLEY PA1 1TJ • www.holidayguides.com

Hundreds of interactive exhibits, live science shows and Scotland's only IMAX cinema - a great day out whatever the weather!	**Open:** 10am-6pm 7 days until 28/10/06. From 29/10/06 to 30/3/2007 open 10am-6pm Tues-Sun. **Directions:** J24 M8, J21 M77. Nearest Underground: Cessnock. Train - Exhibition Centre.

FHG GUIDES, ABBEY MILL BUSINESS CENTRE, PAISLEY PA1 1TJ • www.holidayguides.com

Award-winning attraction with unique 'Heather Story' exhibition, gallery, giftshop, large garden centre selling 300 different heathers, antique shop, children's play area and famous Clootie Dumpling restaurant.	**Open:** all year except Christmas Day. **Directions:** just off A95 between Aviemore and Grantown-on-Spey.

FHG GUIDES, ABBEY MILL BUSINESS CENTRE, PAISLEY PA1 1TJ • www.holidayguides.com

FHG KUPERARD READERS' OFFER 2007

NEW LANARK WORLD HERITAGE SITE
New Lanark Mills, Lanark,
Lanarkshire ML11 9DB
Tel: 01555 661345 • Fax: 01555 665738
e-mail: visit@newlanark.org
www.newlanark.org

One FREE child with one full price adult
Valid until 31st October 2007

NOT TO BE USED IN CONJUNCTION WITH ANY OTHER OFFER

FHG KUPERARD READERS' OFFER 2007

LLANBERIS LAKE RAILWAY
Gilfach Ddu, Llanberis,
Gwynedd LL55 4TY
Tel: 01286 870549
e-mail: info@lake-railway.co.uk
www.lake-railway.co.uk

One pet travels FREE with each full fare paying adult
Valid Easter to October 2007

NOT TO BE USED IN CONJUNCTION WITH ANY OTHER OFFER

FHG KUPERARD READERS' OFFER 2007

PILI PALAS - BUTTERFLY PALACE & NATURE WORLD
Menai Bridge
Isle of Anglesey LL59 5RP
Tel: 01248 712474
e-mail: info@pilipalas.co.uk
www.pilipalas.co.uk

One child FREE with two adults paying full entry price
Valid March to October 2007

NOT TO BE USED IN CONJUNCTION WITH ANY OTHER OFFER

FHG KUPERARD READERS' OFFER 2007

FELINWYNT RAINFOREST CENTRE
Felinwynt, Cardigan,
Ceredigion SA43 1RT
Tel: 01239 810882/810250
e-mail: dandjdevereux@btinternet.com
www.butterflycentre.co.uk

TWO for the price of ONE (one voucher per party only)
Valid until end October 2007

NOT TO BE USED IN CONJUNCTION WITH ANY OTHER OFFER

A beautifully restored cotton mill village close to the Falls of Clyde. Explore the fascinating history of the village, try the 'Millennium Experience', a magical ride which takes you back in time to discover what life used to be like.

Open: 11am-5pm daily. June-August 10.30am-5pm daily. Closed Christmas Day and New Year's Day.

Directions: 25 miles from Glasgow and 35 miles from Edinburgh; well signposted on all major routes.

FHG GUIDES, ABBEY MILL BUSINESS CENTRE, PAISLEY PA1 1TJ • www.holidayguides.com

---

A 60-minute ride along the shores of beautiful Padarn Lake behind a quaint historic steam engine. Magnificent views of the mountains from lakeside picnic spots.

DOGS MUST BE KEPT ON LEAD AT ALL TIMES ON TRAIN

Open: most days Easter to October. Free timetable leaflet on request.

Directions: just off A4086 Caernarfon to Capel Curig road at Llanberis; follow 'Country Park' signs.

FHG GUIDES, ABBEY MILL BUSINESS CENTRE, PAISLEY PA1 1TJ • www.holidayguides.com

---

Visit Wales' top Butterfly House, with Bird House, Snake House, Ant Avenue, Tropical Hide, shop, cafe, adventure playground, indoor play area, picnic area, nature trail etc.

Open: March to end Oct: 10am - 5.30pm daily; Nov/Dec 11am-3pm

Directions: follow brown and white signs when crossing to Anglesey; one-and-a- half miles from Bridge

FHG GUIDES, ABBEY MILL BUSINESS CENTRE, PAISLEY PA1 1TJ • www.holidayguides.com

---

Mini-rainforest full of tropical plants and exotic butterflies. Personal attention of the owner, Mr John Devereux. Gift shop, cafe, video room, exhibition. Suitable for disabled visitors. WTB Quality Assured Visitor Attraction.

PETS NOT ALLOWED IN TROPICAL HOUSE ONLY

Open: daily Easter to end October 10.30am to 5pm

Directions: West Wales, 7 miles north of Cardigan off Aberystwyth road. Follow brown tourist signs on A487.

FHG GUIDES, ABBEY MILL BUSINESS CENTRE, PAISLEY PA1 1TJ • www.holidayguides.com

39

FHG KUPERARD READERS' OFFER 2007

NATIONAL CYCLE COLLECTION
Automobile Palace, Temple Street,
Llandrindod Wells, Powys LD1 5DL
Tel: 01597 825531
e-mail: cycle.museum@powys.org.uk
www.cyclemuseum.org.uk

TWO for the price of ONE
Valid during 2007 except Special Event days

NOT TO BE USED IN CONJUNCTION WITH ANY OTHER OFFER

FHG KUPERARD READERS' OFFER 2007

RHONDDA HERITAGE PARK
Lewis Merthyr Colliery, Coed Cae Road,
Trehafod, Near Pontypridd CF37 7NP
Tel: 01443 682036
e-mail: info@rhonddaheritagepark.com
www.rhonddaheritagepark.com

Two adults or children for the price of one when accompanied by a full paying adult. Valid until end 2007 for full tours only. Not valid on special event days/themed tours.

NOT TO BE USED IN CONJUNCTION WITH ANY OTHER OFFER

Looking for Holiday Accommodation?

FHG
KUPERARD

for details of hundreds of
properties throughout the UK
visit our website on

www.holidayguides.com

Journey through the lanes of cycle history and see bicycles from Boneshakers and Penny Farthings up to modern Raleigh cycles. Over 250 machines on display

PETS MUST BE KEPT ON LEADS

Open: 1st March to 1st November daily 10am onwards.

Directions: brown signs to car park. Town centre attraction.

FHG GUIDES, ABBEY MILL BUSINESS CENTRE, PAISLEY PA1 1TJ • www.holidayguides.com

---

Make a pit stop whatever the weather! Join an ex-miner on a tour of discovery, ride the cage to pit bottom and take a thrilling ride back to the surface. Multi-media presentations, period village street, children's adventure play area, restaurant and gift shop. Disabled access with assistance.

Open: Open daily 10am to 6pm (last tour 4pm). Closed Mondays Oct - Easter, also Dec 25th to 2nd Jan incl.

Directions: Exit Junction 32 M4, signposted from A470 Pontypridd. Trehafod is located between Pontypridd and Porth.

FHG GUIDES, ABBEY MILL BUSINESS CENTRE, PAISLEY PA1 1TJ • www.holidayguides.com

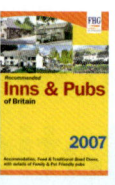

FHG Guides 2007

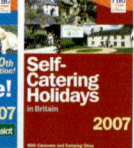

Autumn Edition

- Recommended COUNTRY HOTELS
- Recommended INNS & PUBS
- BED & BREAKFAST STOPS • CHILDREN WELCOME!
- The Original FHG Guide to COAST & COUNTRY HOLIDAYS
- CARAVAN & CAMPING HOLIDAYS GUIDE
- BRITAIN'S BEST Leisure & Relaxation Holidays
- THE GOLF GUIDE Where to Play / Where to Stay
- PETS WELCOME!
- Recommended SHORT BREAK HOLIDAYS in Britain
- SELF CATERING HOLIDAYS in Britain

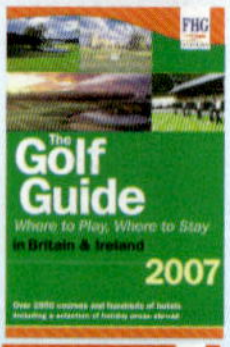

Summer Edition

Available from bookshops or larger newsagents

FHG Guides Ltd.
Abbey Mill Business Centre,
Seedhill, Paisley PA1 ITJ
www.holidayguides.com

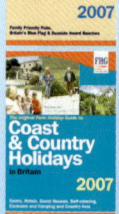

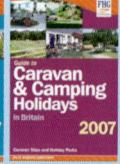

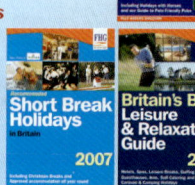

Foreword

As its name suggests **The Original Farm Holiday GUIDE TO COAST & COUNTRY HOLIDAYS** offers an excellent selection of holiday accommodation, mostly situated in the countryside or near the sea. There's something to suit everyone, from hotels and B&Bs, to self-catering and caravan holidays, and a selection of Country Inns and Pubs. The entries are well written, with a full description of the facilities, and there is usually an indication of rates. We usually advise if children and pets are welcome, and whether the premises are suitable for disabled guests. Visitors can expect a warm welcome, clean comfortable accommodation, and good wholesome food.

No holiday is complete without exploring the surrounding area, and you will usually find some general information within the entries to help you plan ahead. Our Readers' Offer Vouchers (pages 7-40) may save you some money on family outings and, should you wish to stops for a meal or snack, our Family Friendly Pubs and Inns (pages 257-261) and Pet Friendly Pubs and Inns (pages 262-275) supplements list a range of establishments which make an extra effort to cater for parents and children, or for those who wish to bring their dog.

Anne Cuthbertson, **Editor**

Canal at Newbury, Berkshire. Picture courtesy of Berkshire Tourism

ENGLAND and WALES Counties

NORTH WALES
1. Denbighshire
2. Flintshire
3. Wrexham

SOUTH WALES
4. Swansea
5. Neath and Port Talbot
6. Bridgend
7. Rhondda Cynon Taff
8. Merthyr Tydfil
9. Vale of Glamorgan
10. Cardiff
11. Caerphilly
12. Blaenau Gwent
13. Torfaen
14. Newport
15. Monmouthshire

©MAPS IN MINUTES™ 2006

England

Photos: North Hill Farm, Church Stretton, Shropshire   Swaledale Watch, Caldbeck, Cumbria   Home Farm House, Chipping Campden, Gloucestershire

Board

Bedfordshire

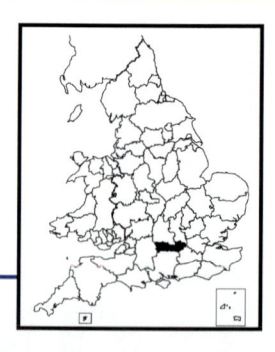

Bedford

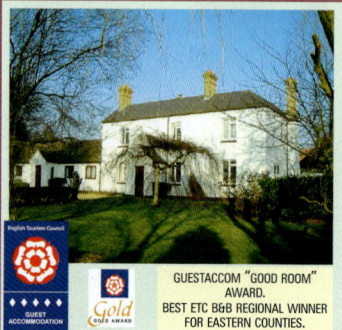

Tranquil welcoming atmosphere on attractive arable farm.
Set well back off A1 giving quiet, peaceful seclusion yet within easy reach of the RSPB, the Shuttleworth Collection, the Greensand Ridge Walk, Grafham Water and Woburn Abbey. Cambridge 22 miles, London 50 miles.

All rooms have tea/coffee making facilities, all have bathroom en suite and some are on the ground floor.
There is a separate guests' sitting room with TV. Family room.
Dogs welcome by arrangement. No smoking. Most guests return!
Prices from £32.50 per person per night.

Mrs M. Codd, Highfield Farm, Tempsford Road, Sandy, Bedfordshire SG19 2AQ
Tel: 01767 682332; Fax: 01767 692503
e-mail: margaret@highfield-farm.co.uk
website: www.highfield-farm.co.uk

GUESTACCOM "GOOD ROOM" AWARD.
BEST ETC B&B REGIONAL WINNER FOR EASTERN COUNTIES.

Buckinghamshire

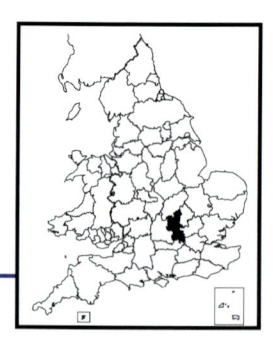

Aylesbury

Poletrees Farm

This working family farm provides spacious, comfortable Bed & Breakfast accommodation for couples and individuals, whether on an overnight visit or longer.
• Non-smoking
• En suite bedrooms with colour TV and tea/coffee tray

The Burnwode Jubilee Way cuts through the farm, and there are many places of historic interest in the area.

Ludgershall Road, Brill, Near Aylesbury, Bucks HP18 9TZ • Tel & Fax: 01844 238276
www.country-accom.co.uk/poletrees-farm
Self-catering also available in 2 cottages in courtyard.

Cambridgeshire

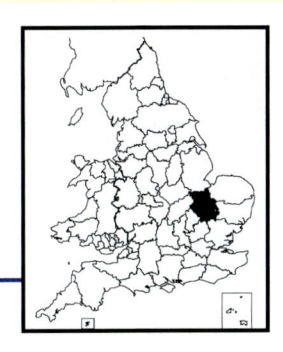

Bedford

Sharps Farm *Bed & Breakfast*
Twentypence Road, Wilburton, Ely CB6 3PU

A charming tranquil setting awaits you along with friendly hospitality in our family home. Situated in open countryside and ideally placed to visit the surrounding historic sites of Cambridge, Ely and Newmarket. Two en suite ground floor rooms and one double on the first floor with private bathroom all have TV, radio alarm, tea/coffee making facilities and hairdryers. A delicious English breakfast is served in our garden room using eggs from our free range chickens. Evening meal by arrangement. Special diets catered for. Disabled facilities. Non-smoking. Ample parking. B&B from £27 per person.

Tel: 01353 740360 • e-mail: sharpsfarm@yahoo.com • www.sharpsfarm.co.uk

Cheshire

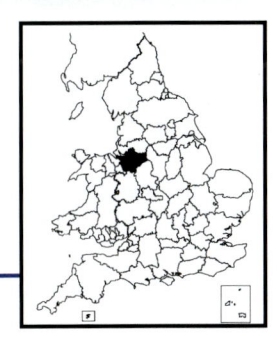

Congleton

- Wooded walks and beautiful views.
- Meet a whole variety of pets and farm animals on this friendly working farm.
- One double and one triple room, both en suite.
- Your comfort is our priority and good food is a speciality.
- Generous scrummy breakfasts and traditional evening meals.
- A true taste of the countryside!

Bed and Breakfast £28 to £35
optional Evening Meal from £15. Brochure on request.
Mrs Sheila Kidd, Yew Tree Farm, North Rode, Congleton
CW12 2PF • Tel: 01260 223569
e-mail: yewtreebb@hotmail.com

www.yewtreebb.co.uk

46 CHESHIRE   Hyde (near Manchester), Malpas, Nantwich, Tarporley **BOARD**

Needhams Farm

e-mail: charlotte@needhamsfarm.co.uk
www.needhamsfarm.co.uk

AA Guest Accommodation ♦♦♦

A cosy 16th century farmhouse set in peaceful, picturesque surroundings by Werneth Low Country Park and the Etherow Valley, which lie between Glossop and Manchester. The farm is ideally situated for holidaymakers and businessmen, especially those who enjoy peace and quiet, walking and rambling, golfing and riding, as these activities are all close by. At Needhams Farm everyone, including children and pets, receives a warm welcome. Good wholesome evening meals available Monday to Thursday. Friday/Saturday/Sunday by arrangement. Residential licence and Fire Certificate held • Open all year.
Bed and Breakfast from £25 single, £40 double; Evening Meal £8.
Mrs Charlotte R. Walsh, Needhams Farm, Uplands Road, Werneth Low, Gee Cross, Near Hyde SK14 3AG
Tel: 0161 368 4610 • Fax: 0161-367 9106

Mill House

Higher Wych, Malpas, Cheshire SY14 7JR

Modernised mill house on the Cheshire/Clwyd border in a quiet valley, convenient for visiting Chester, Shrewsbury and North Wales. The house is centrally heated and has an open log fire in the TV lounge. Bedrooms have washbasins, radio and tea-making facilities. Two bedrooms have en suite shower and WC. Open January to November. Prices from £22 per person per night. Self-catering accommodation also available.

Tel: 01948 780362 • Fax: 01948 780566

email: angela@videoactive.co.uk • www.millhouseandgranary.co.uk

NANTWICH Mrs Jean E. Callwood, Lea Farm, Wrinehill Road, Wybunbury, Nantwich CW5 7NS (01270 841429; Fax: 01270 841030).
Charming farmhouse set in landscaped gardens, where peacocks roam, on 150 acre family farm. Spacious bedrooms, colour TVs, electric blankets, radio alarm and tea/ coffee making facilities. Centrally heated throughout. Family, double and twin bedrooms, en suite facilities. Luxury lounge, dining room overlooking gardens. Pool/snooker; fishing in well stocked pool in beautiful surroundings. Bird watching. Help feed the birds and animals. Near Stapeley Water Gardens, Bridgemere Garden World, also Nantwich, Crewe, Chester, the Potteries and Alton Towers.
Rates: Bed and Breakfast from £24-£27 per person. Children half price. Weekly terms available.
• Working farm. • Children welcome. • Dogs welcome if kept under control.
AA ★★★
e-mail: contactus@leafarm.freeserve.co.uk   www.leafarm.co.uk

Haycroft Farm
Bed and Breakfast

AA ★★★★ FARMHOUSE

A traditional working farm with an unspoilt Listed farmhouse built on the site of an ancient medieval settlement. Within easy reach of Chester, Wrexham and Shrewsbury. Double/twin rooms with private bathroom, family bedroom with en suite. TV/radios, tea/coffee, hairdryer. Non-Smoking.
Single room from £35; Double from £60, Twin from £60 and Family room from £70.
Haycroft Farm, Peckforton Hall Lane, Spurstow, Tarporley, Cheshire CW6 9TF
Tel/Fax: 01829 260389 • Mobile: 07801 550530
e-mail: richard.a.spencer@talk21.co.uk
www.haycroftfarm.co.uk

Caravan Site
Mown field • 16amp hook-ups • Children and Dogs Welcome.
Toilet • Batteries Charged • £9 per night • Tents £7 per night

BOARD   CORNWALL 47

Cornwall

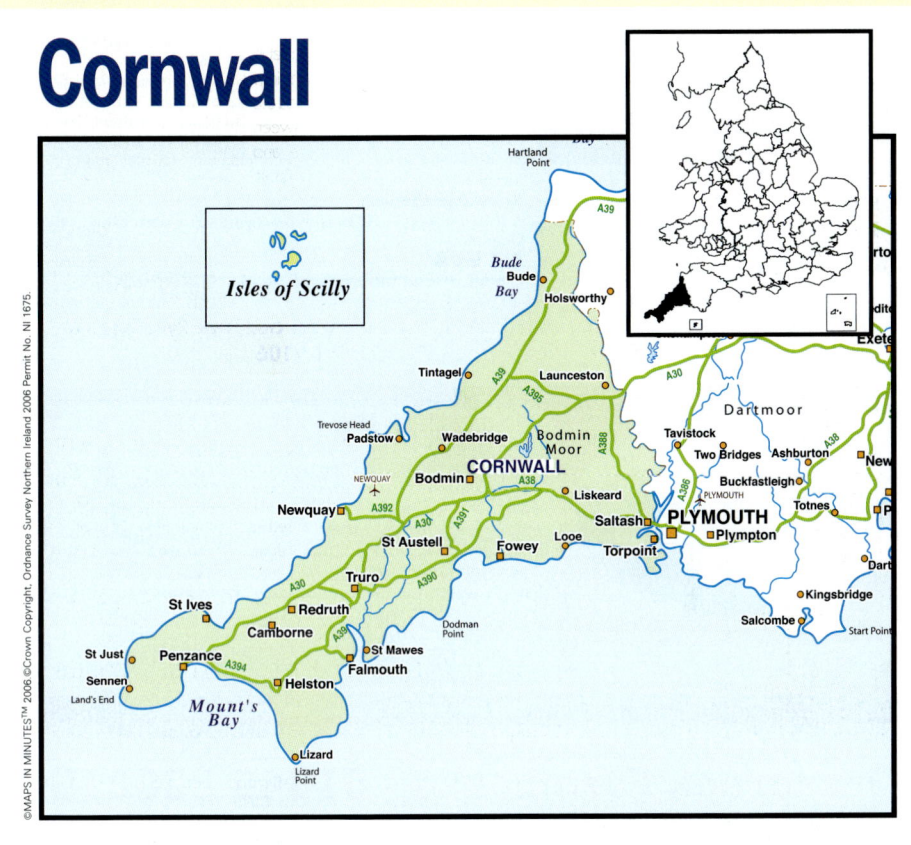

Cornwall receives most of its visitors over the summer months, exploring the beautiful beaches and indulging in the exceptional clotted cream teas - but the county has much to offer besides the Cornish pastie and the traditional bucket and spade holiday. The "shoulder" and winter months offer opportunities for the discerning visitor which may go unnoticed in the annual stampede to the beaches. There are villages boasting curious and ancient names - Come To Good, Ting Tang, London Apprentice and Indian Queens, often sporting parish churches, ancient graveyards and distinctive crosses which reveal their early Christian history. Wayside crosses, holy wells and Celtic stone circles are reminders that the Cornish are true Celts - it was they who embossed the headlands with cliff forts to repel marauders.

To discover more about life in the Iron Age there are numerous settlements to visit, for example Castle an Dinas, one of the largest preserved hill forts in Cornwall. Alternatively Chysauster Ancient Village is a deserted Roman village comprising eight well-preserved houses around an open court. More up-to-date is St Michael's Mount with its 14th century castle, or Prideaux Place, a stunning Elizabethan House, and Lanhydrock, the National Trust's most visited property in Cornwall, which was once the residence of a local family whose wealth came from tin mining.

A useful index of towns/counties appears on pages 311-314

48 CORNWALL
Boscastle, Bude BOARD

BOSCASTLE Mrs Paula Perfili, Trefoil Farm, Camelford Road, Boscastle PL35 0AD (01840 250606).
Set in own grounds (parking). En suite accommodation; tea/coffee, TV in rooms. Overlooking Boscastle village, with views of coast and Lundy Island; close to sandy beaches, surfing. Three miles Tintagel, King Arthur Country. Haven for walkers. Two minutes' walk to local 16th century inn, with real ales and good food.
Rates: from £28pppn.
• Non-smoking. • No pets. • No children. • Open Easter to end October.
ETC ♦♦♦
e-mail: trefoil.farm@tiscali.co.uk

www.thisisnorthcornwall.com

Trehane Farmhouse

Our traditional farmhouse is in a magnificent position overlooking the sea and the wild rugged coastline of North Cornwall. It is in a peaceful and secluded position, yet close to the Coastal Path and hidden coves. Guests can enjoy plenty of wholesome, fresh, local food, home-made bread, and exciting vegetarian dishes. There are two pretty, en suite rooms with views over the fields to the sea. Sarah's interest in art is reflected in the original paintings, ceramics and art works around the house, and the area is a delight for artists and writers. Brochure available.
2004 TASTE OF THE WEST BRONZE AWARD.
Sarah James, Trehane Farmhouse, Trevalga, Boscastle PL35 0EB

Tel: 01840 250510
e-mail: james_sarah@btconnect.com

Trencreek Farmhouse - 01840 230219

Comfortable farmhouse offering homely and relaxed family atmosphere. Situated in quiet and peaceful surroundings yet within easy reach of Crackington Haven. Well placed for easy access to coastal and countryside walks. Family, double and twin-bedded rooms, most en suite, all with tea/coffee making facilities. Two comfortable lounges. Games room. Separate diningroom. Generous portions of freshly prepared, home-cooked farmhouse food.
Children welcome, special rates for unders 12s.
Spring and Autumn breaks available. Non-smoking. 
**Margaret and Richard Heard,
Trencreek Farmhouse, St Gennys, Bude EX23 0AY**

West Nethercott Farm, North Cornwall

Personal attention and a warm welcome await you on this dairy and sheep farm. Watch the cows being milked, scenic farm walks. Short distance from sandy beaches, surfing and the rugged North Cornwall coast. Ideal base for visiting any part of Devon or Cornwall. We are located in Cornwall though our postal address is Devon. The traditional farmhouse has four bedrooms, two en suite; diningroom and separate lounge with TV. Plenty of excellent home cooking. Access to the house at anytime. Bed and Breakfast from £22-£27, Evening Meal available. Children under 12 years reduced rates. Weekly terms available. 
Mrs Pearl Hopper, West Nethercott Farm, Whitstone, Holsworthy (Devon) EX22 6LD • 01288 341394
e-mail: pearl@westnethercott.fsnet.co.uk

BOARD Bude   **CORNWALL 49**

Langaton Farm

Whitstone Holsworthy EX22 6TS
Tel: 01288 341215

Mrs Margaret Short

Traditional working farm set in the quiet countryside, eight miles from the market town of Holsworthy and six miles from the coast at Bude with its sandy beaches. Help to feed the calves and chickens and make friends with the farm dogs and cats. Play area for children. Close to local 18-hole golf course, swimming pool, horse riding, local park and bowling green, and Tamar Lakes for birdwatching. Two bedrooms, one suitable for a family, with an en suite shower room, the other has a double bed and en suite shower. Both rooms have a TV and hospitality tray; cot and high chair available. Central heating and log fires.

Bed and Breakfast from £24pppn, children under 12 half price. Weekly rate from £150.

e-mail: langatonfarm@hotmail.com • www.langaton-farm-holidays.co.uk

Situated on the Devon/Cornwall border six miles from the surfing beaches at Bude and Widemouth Bay, we are ideally placed for touring both Devon and Cornwall. Guests are welcome to wander on our 205 acre mixed farm. Three large and tastefully furnished family rooms sleeping up to four - two rooms en suite, and all are south facing and enjoy views of the surrounding farmland. Children are especially welcome - cot, highchair and free babysitting available. Full English breakfast served daily; ample four course meal available. Numerous sandy beaches nearby and the picturesque villages of Clovelly and Tintagel are within half an hour's drive. **Open from March to November. B&B from £22 per person.**

Mrs Sylvia Lucas, Elm Park Farmhouse Bed & Breakfast, Bridgerule, Holsworthy, Devon EX22 7EL • 01288 381231

Bears and Boxes

Friendly, comfortable accommodation is available in our cottage situated in a peaceful, rural Area of Outstanding Natural Beauty on Cornwall's Heritage Coast, a few minutes' walk from the spectacular Coastal Path. All rooms are equipped with hostess tray, TV and other luxuries; all are en suite. Cot and high chair available. Lounge, reading room and dining room for guests' use. Safe bathing, very good surfing, sea and fly fishing, horse riding, golf and trekking within easy reach; Widemouth Bay, Bude and Boscastle a short drive away.

Evening meals by arrangement • No smoking
Pets welcome by arrangement • Open all year
B&B from £29.50pppn.

Robert & Francoise Holmes, Bears & Boxes Country Guest House, Dizzard, St Gennys, Near Bude EX23 0NX • Tel: 01840 230318
www.bearsandboxes.com

Note

All the information in this guide is given in good faith in the belief that it is correct. However, the publishers cannot guarantee the facts given in these pages, neither are they responsible for changes in ownership or facilities that may take place after the date of going to press.

Readers should always satisfy themselves that the facilities they require are available and that the terms, if quoted, still apply.

Edge of Bodmin Moor

Are you looking for peace and relaxation? Come and stay on our small sheep farm and unwind in a unique setting off the beaten track. An ideal base for walking, or touring around Cornwall. Just 1.5 miles from the A39 Atlantic Highway. Enjoy a day out on Bodmin Moor, or at the Eden Project, cycle the Camel Trail, walk the Coastal Paths, surf at Polzeath, Bude or Newquay, or visit one of the many golf clubs. The family, including our dogs and cats, offer a relaxing atmosphere and warm welcome. Ground floor bedrooms. Dogs by arrangement. Good pubs and restaurants nearby.

Higher Trezion
Tresinney, Advent,
Camelford PL32 9QW
Tel: 01840 213761
E-mail: higher.trezion@btinternet.com
www.highertrezion.co.uk

Wringford Down

Family friendly hotel set in 4 acres of Cornish countryside

Located on the Rame peninsula in an Area of Outstanding Natural Beauty with tiny Cornish fishing villages, dramatic cliff top walks and secluded sandy bays.

Great facilities for all ages:
- Family suites
- Bar & restaurant
- Covered, heated pool
- Tennis court
- Indoor & outdoor play areas
- Two caravans available
- Ball pool, bouncy castle
- Pool & table tennis
- Childcare on-site
- Shetland ponies & other animals

Tel: 01752 822287 www.cornwallholidays.co.uk

Rosemullion Hotel

Gyllyngvase Hill, Falmouth TR11 4DF • 01326 314690 • Fax: 01326 210098

Built as a gentleman's residence in the latter part of the 19th century, Rosemullion Hotel offers you a holiday that is every bit as distinctive as its Tudor appearance. Rosemullion is a house of great character and charm, appealing strongly to the discerning guest. The emphasis is very much on that rarest of commodities in today's world – peace. That is why we do not cater for children and do not have a bar of our own. A family-owned hotel continually being refurbished and updated to first class accommodation. Fully centrally heated with 13 bedrooms, some with glorious views over the bay. Large parking area.

Non-smoking • B&B £27.50 to £29.50pppn inclusive of VAT.
e-mail: gail@rosemullionhotel.demon.co.uk
www.SmoothHound.co.uk/hotels/rosemullion.html

Rocklands

"Rocklands" is situated overlooking part of Cornwall's superb coastline and enjoys uninterrupted sea views. The Lizard is well known for its lovely picturesque scenery, coastal walks and enchanting coves and beaches, as well as the famous Serpentine Stone which is quarried and sold locally. Open Easter to October. Generations of the Hill family have been catering for visitors on the Lizard since the 1850s. Three bedrooms with sea views, two en suite, tea/coffee making facilities and electric heaters; sittingroom with TV and video; sun lounge; diningroom with separate tables. Children and well trained pets welcome.

Bed and Breakfast £23pppn, en suite £25pppn; reductions for children under 10 years.

**Mrs D. J. Hill, "Rocklands", The Lizard,
Near Helston TR12 7NX • Tel: 01326 290339**

BOARD Launceston, Liskeard, Looe   **CORNWALL 51**

Hurdon Farm
Launceston PL15 9LS
01566 772955

Elegant Listed 18th century farmhouse, idyllically tucked away amidst our 400 acre mixed working farm. Centrally positioned on Devon/Cornwall border, it is ideally located for exploring the many attractions in both counties. Near the Eden Project.

Six luxurious and spacious en suite bedrooms, all with colour TV, radio, tea/coffee facilities and central heating. Comfortable guests' lounge. Superb English breakfasts and delicious four-course dinners, freshly prepared and cooked by arrangement, are served at separate tables in the dining room.

Open May till November • B&B from £24.

AA Guest Accommodation

Nebula Hotel
27 Higher Lux Street, Liskeard
PL14 3JU 01579 343989

Relax in your home from home friendly hotel. Old English atmosphere in a Grade II Listed building. Unwind by our large granite fireplace in the lounge area with licensed bar. Six spacious comfortable en suite rooms, single, double, twin and family, all with TV and tea/coffee facilities. Large car park. Liskeard is ideally placed to tour Cornwall and Plymouth. Near the moors, coast, gardens, golf courses, Eden Project and museums. Enjoy! Book the whole hotel (sleeps 15) and use it as your home in a relaxing atmosphere. Terms from £30.
SOUTH WEST TOURISM, CORNWALL TOURIST BOARD

e-mail: info@nebula-hotel.com
www.nebula-hotel.com

Little Larnick Farm
Pelynt, Looe, Cornwall PL13 2NB

Telephone:
01503 262837   *Silver SILVER AWARD*

Little Larnick is situated in a sheltered part of the West Looe river valley. Walk to Looe from our working farm and along the coastal path to picturesque Polperro. The character farmhouse and barn offers twin and double en suite rooms. The bedrooms are superbly equipped and decorated to a high standard. Our newly renovated barn offers three self-contained bedrooms with their own lounge areas. Cycling shed, drying room and ample parking. No pets. No smoking. Bed and Breakfast from £26- £31. Open all year. Contact: **Mrs Angela Eastley**.

e-mail: littlelarnick@btclick.com
www.littlelarnick.co.uk

• Bake Farm •
Pelynt, Looe, Cornwall PL13 2QQ
Tel: 01503 220244

This is an old farmhouse, bearing the Trelawney Coat of Arms (1610), situated midway between Looe and Fowey. Two double and one family bedroom, all en suite and decorated to a high standard, have tea/coffee making facilities and TV. Sorry, no pets, no smoking. Open from March to October. A car is essential for touring the area, ample parking. There is much to see and do here – horse riding, coastal walks, golf, National Trust properties, the Eden Project and Heligan Gardens are within easy reach. The sea is only five miles away and there is shark fishing at Looe.

Bed and Breakfast from £24 to £27. Brochure available on request.

52 CORNWALL Mevagissey, Mullion, Newquay, Padstow **BOARD**

Lancallan is a large 17th century farmhouse on a working 700-acre dairy and beef farm in a beautiful rural setting, one mile from Mevagissey. We are close to Heligan Gardens, lovely coastal walks and sandy beaches, and are well situated for day trips throughout Cornwall. Also six to eight miles from the Eden Project (20 minutes' drive). Enjoy a traditional farmhouse breakfast in a warm and friendly atmosphere. Accommodation comprises one twin room and two double en suite rooms (all with colour TV and tea/coffee facilities); bathroom, lounge and diningroom.
Terms and brochure available on request. SAE please.

Mrs Dawn Rundle, Lancallan Farm, Mevagissey, St Austell PL26 6EW
Tel & Fax: 01726 842284
e-mail: dawn@lancallan.fsnet.co.uk • www.lancallanfarm.co.uk

MULLION Mrs Joan Hyde, Campden House, The Commons, Mullion TR12 7HZ (01326 240365).
Campden House offers comfortable accommodation in a peaceful setting with large gardens and a beautiful sea view. It is within easy reach of Mullion, Polurrian and Poldhu Coves, and is ideally situated for exploring the beautiful coast and countryside of the Lizard. Mullion golf course is less than one mile away. All seven bedrooms have handbasin with hot and cold water and comfortable beds; some rooms are en suite. There is a large sun lounge, TV lounge with colour TV and a large dining room. Guests have access to the lounges, bedrooms and gardens at all times.
Rates: Bed and Breakfast from £20 to £25 (en suite).
• Children and pets welcome.

Take a break in the heart of Cornwall

A warm and friendly welcome awaits you at Pensalda. Situated on the main A3058 road, an ideal location from which to explore the finest coastline in Europe. Close to airport and the Eden Project. Double and family rooms available, all en suite, all with TV, tea/coffee making facilities, including two chalets set in a lovely garden. Fire certificate • Large car park • Licensed • Central heating • Non-smoking.
Bed and Breakfast from £23 • Special offer breaks November to March (excluding Christmas and New Year).

Karen and John, Pensalda Guest House, 98 Henver Road, Newquay TR7 3BL
Tel & Fax: 01637 874601 • e-mail: karen_pensalda@yahoo.co.uk
www.pensalda-guesthouse.co.uk

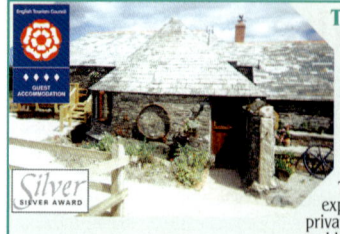

TREWITHEN FARMHOUSE is a renovated Cornish Roundhouse, set in a large garden and situated on a working farm enjoying country and coastal views. The picturesque town of Padstow with its pretty harbour and narrow streets with famous fish restaurants is only three miles away. St Merryn Parish boasts seven beautiful sandy beaches and bays. Also coastal walks, golf, fishing and horse riding on neighbouring farm. Hire a bike or walk along the Camel Trail cycle and footpath - winding for 18 miles along the River Camel. Eden Project 20 miles.

The accommodation has been tastefully decorated to complement the exposed beams and original features. All bedrooms are en suite or have private bathrooms, TVs and hot drink facilities.

• Parking • Full English breakfast • TV lounge.
• Bed and Breakfast from £25 to £30 per person per night.
• Winter weekend breaks available.
• Non-smoking.

Mrs Sandra May,
Trewithen Farm, St Merryn,
Near Padstow PL28 8JZ
01841 520420
www.trewithenfarmhouse.co.uk

KERRIS MANOR FARM
Kerris, Penzance TR19 6UY
Tel: 01736 731198

Linda & Alan Sunderland

A member of Penzance & District Tourism Association, we welcome you to our friendly B&B accommodation in a superb location. Grade II Listed Manor house with two double bedrooms, lounge/dining room with cosy woodburner and a full range of usual facilities. Enjoy a traditional, full English breakfast cooked on the Aga or choose from our interesting menu, full of local produce. Peaceful, relaxing countryside setting, a perfect base for exploring the wild and exciting far west! Ample parking. Open all year. Non-smoking. Brochure and details on request.

e-mail: linda.sunderland@btinternet.com • www.kerrismanorfarm.co.uk

Camilla House
12 Regent Terrace, Penzance TR18 4DW • Tel & Fax: 01736 363771

Award-winning Regency Townhouse overlooking Penzance seafront, within short distance of rail and bus terminals. Relax on your short break in a friendly and totally non-smoking environment that exudes subtle quality from the furnishings and decor. Start the day with a wide range of breakfast options using fresh local produce then, after a long day exploring the delights of West Cornwall, relax in the bar and enjoy a good malt or glass of wine. Extra services include wireless broadband internet access throughout; detailed travel arrangements; car & bike hire; guided tours; personalised itineraries; picnic hamper loan and restaurant bookings.

Bed & Breakfast from £30-£40pppn. Open all year.
Short Breaks available October to April, details on request.

RAC Sparkling Diamond
RAC Warm Welcome
AA ♦♦♦♦

e-mail: enquiries@camillahouse.co.uk • www.camillahouse.co.uk

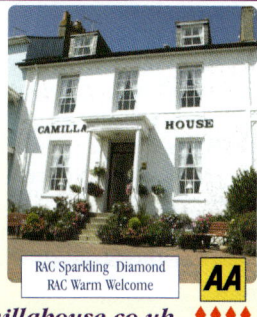

Penventon
— PARK HOTEL —

Redruth, West Cornwall TR15 1TE • Telephone: 01209 20 3000
e-mail: manager@penventon.com • www.penventon.com

Long established Superior Country House Hotel
in acres of Private Parkland. Central for touring.
Award Winning Restaurant, Health and Leisure Spa.

Many Special Offers • AA ★★★ *High Quality*

Tregilgas Farm
Gorran, St Austell PL26 6ND

Come and enjoy the warm, friendly atmosphere of our large detached farmhouse, in a quiet spot, off the beaten track, with rolling fields and peaceful countryside. Tastefully decorated, en suite rooms, lounge. Delicious breakfasts. Ideal for the Lost Gardens of Heligan, Eden Project. Open all year except Christmas and New Year. Pets by arrangement. Children welcome. Contact: Mrs D. Clemes

Tel: 01726 842342 • Mobile: 07789 113620 • e-mail: dclemes88@aol.com

TRENONA FARM Ruan High Lanes, Truro, Cornwall TR2 5JS

Enjoy a relaxing stay on this mixed farm, on the unspoilt Roseland Peninsula midway between Truro and the Eden Project at St Austell. Victorian farmhouse with four guest bedrooms, all of which are double/family rooms with colour TV, mini-fridges, tea/coffee making facilities and are either en suite or with private bathroom. Separate TV lounge and dining room, together with gardens and a patio. Brochure available. Children welcome. Pets welcome by arrangement.

Open March to November.

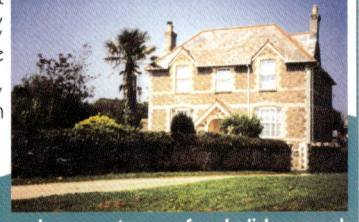

Tel: 01872 501339 • e-mail:info@trenonafarmholidays.co.uk • www.trenonafarmholidays.co.uk

A Listed Georgian farmhouse on a working dairy farm, in a quiet location overlooking wooded valleys. Tastefully decorated and centrally heated throughout, offering one double and one twin room, both en suite with TV, radio, hairdryer and beverage trays. Full English breakfast, using mainly local produce, is served in the traditional style diningroom. Special diets by prior arrangement. Comfortable lounge with TV/video. Large garden with outstanding views for relaxing. Static caravan also available.

Mrs E. Hodge, Pengelly Farm, Burlawn, Wadebridge PL27 7LA • Tel: 01208 814217
e-mail: hodgepete@hotmail.com • www.pengellyfarm.co.uk

An ideal walking, touring and cycling base, only six miles from the coast, with sailing, surfing, golf, riding and coastal walks; Camel Trail, the Saints' Way and Pencarrow House nearby. The Eden Project 35 minutes' drive, Padstow 20 minutes, Wadebridge one and a half miles, with shopping, pubs, restaurants, leisure facilities and The Camel Trail.

Looking for holiday accommodation?
for details of hundreds of properties throughout the UK including comprehensive coverage of all areas of Scotland try:

www.holidayguides.com

Cumbria

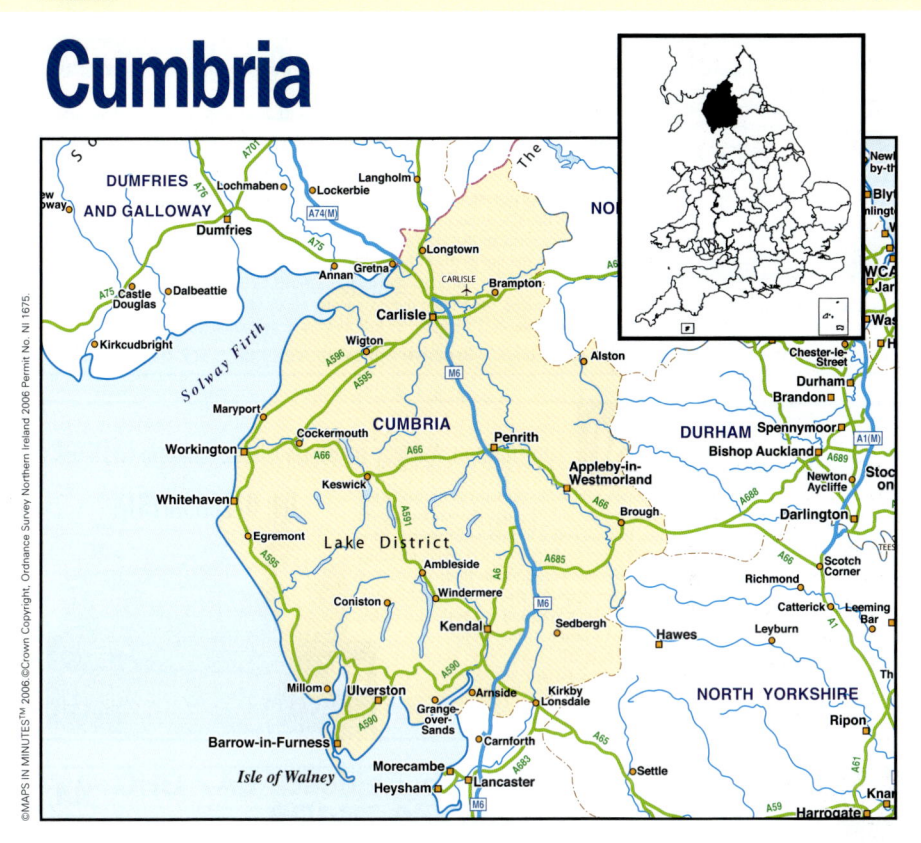

Cumbria - The Lake District is often described as the most beautiful corner of England, and it's easy to see why 15 million visitors head here every year. It is a place of unrivalled beauty, with crystal clear lakes, bracken-covered mountains, peaceful forests, quiet country roads and miles of stunning coastline.

At the heart of Cumbria is the Lake District National Park. Each of the lakes that make up the area has its own charm and personality: Windermere, England's longest lake, is surrounded by rolling hills; Derwentwater and Ullswater are circled by craggy fells; England's deepest lake, Wastwater, is dominated by high mountains including the country's highest, Scafell Pike. For those who want to tackle the great outdoors, Cumbria offers everything from rock climbing to fell walking and from canoeing to horse riding – all among stunning scenery.

Cumbria has many delightful market towns, historic houses and beautiful gardens such as Holker Hall with its 25 acres of award-winning grounds. There are many opportunities to sample local produce, such as Cumbrian fell-bred lamb, Cumberland Sausage, and trout and salmon plucked fresh from nearby lakes and rivers.

Cumbria is a county of contrasts with a rich depth of cultural and historical interest in addition to stunning scenery. Compact and accessible, it can offer something for every taste.

When making enquiries please mention FHG GUIDES

56 CUMBRIA   Ambleside, Appleby-in-Westmorland, Caldbeck **BOARD**

Broadview Guest House • Lake Road, Ambleside LA22 0DN

Broadview is a quality, friendly, non-smoking guest house in the heart of the Lake District. A short stroll from the centre of the village and Lake Windermere at Waterhead, Broadview is perfect for a holiday or a short break, whether as a base for touring or exploring the fells on foot. There are 6 comfortable guest rooms, (doubles, twins and a room that sleeps 3), most en suite or with private bathroom. All have TV, DVD, tea/coffee making facilities, mini-fridge, bathrobes, fluffy towels and hairdryer, along with the little extras to make your stay more comfortable. There is a king-size four-poster room for that extra special romantic break. The Broadview breakfast will set you up for the day, with local meats, free-range eggs and home-made breads. Vegetarian, vegan and most special diets catered for by prior arrangement. Drying facilities, maps, guides and packed lunches can be provided; free parking during your stay. Please visit our website, e-mail or phone for more information and details of our special offers. Rates £25-£40pppn. *We look forward to welcoming you to Broadview soon.*

www.broadviewguesthouse.co.uk • enquiries@broadviewguesthouse.co.uk • Tel: 015394 32431

Broom House   Long Marton, Appleby-in-Westmorland, Cumbria CA16 6JP

Welcome to Broom House, nestled in peaceful seclusion with open views of the Eden Valley countryside and the Pennines beyond. Through the window, as you relax with tea and home made scones, you will notice the old parish church, cows and sheep grazing, countless wild rabbits and perhaps even a kingfisher feeding from the bird-table. Come and rest and be pampered. We lie three-quarters of a mile from the main A66 road between Appleby and Penrith, within easy reach of the Lake District, Borders, Hadrian's Wall and the Yorkshire Dales. Good home cooking, en suite facilities. A warm welcome awaits.

Tel: 01768 361318

Open all year (except Christmas and New Year).
Single £25-£35 Double/Twin £27-£35
Children 10 years and over.   Non-Smoking
www.broomhouseappleby.co.uk

Swaledale Watch, Whelpo, Caldbeck CA7 8HQ
Tel & Fax: 016974 78409

Mixed farm of 300 acres situated in beautiful countryside within the Lake District National Park. Central for Scottish Borders, Roman Wall, Eden Valley and the Lakes. Primarily a sheep farm (everyone loves lambing time). Visitors are welcome to see farm animals and activities. Many interesting walks nearby or roam the peaceful Northern fells. Enjoyed by many Cumbrian Way walkers. Very comfortable accommodation with excellent breakfasts. All rooms have private facilities. Central heating. Tea making facilities. We are a friendly Cumbrian family and make you very welcome. Bed and Breakfast from £22 to £28. Contact: **Mr and Mrs A. Savage**

e-mail: nan.savage@talk21.com
www.swaledale-watch.co.uk

Looking for holiday accommodation?

for details of hundreds of properties
throughout the UK including
comprehensive coverage of all areas of Scotland try:

www.holidayguides.com

BOARD Cockermouth, Dent, Keswick   CUMBRIA 57

Mosser Heights

Tel: 01900 822644
e-mail: AmandaVickers1@aol.com

Mosser, Cockermouth, Cumbria CA13 0SS

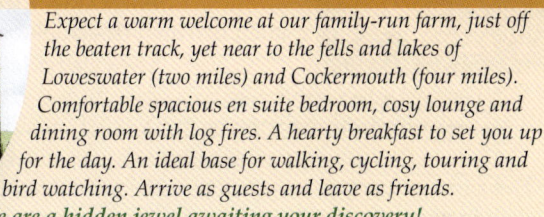

Expect a warm welcome at our family-run farm, just off the beaten track, yet near to the fells and lakes of Loweswater (two miles) and Cockermouth (four miles). Comfortable spacious en suite bedroom, cosy lounge and dining room with log fires. A hearty breakfast to set you up for the day. An ideal base for walking, cycling, touring and bird watching. Arrive as guests and leave as friends.

We are a hidden jewel awaiting your discovery!

The Old Homestead

The Old Homestead is a sympathetically renovated, award-winning, 16thC Cumbrian longhouse. Situated in the Vale of Lorton in peaceful countryside, with a backdrop of the Lakeland fells and easy access to the unspoilt Western Lakes. The accommodation has contemporary style, yet retains and complements the historical features. All 10 bedrooms are en suite, with underfloor heating throughout. Simple oak and leather furniture sits comfortably beneath ancient oak beams. This is the perfect location for walkers and cyclists, and has amenities nearby for riding, fishing, golf and outdoor pursuits. Also suitable for groups and large family bookings.

Byresteads Farm, Cockermouth CA13 9TW
Tel: 01900 822223 • Allan & Christine Watson

Enjoy the warmth of Cumbria
e-mail: info@byresteads.co.uk
www.byresteads.co.uk

The GEORGE & DRAGON

Main Street, Dent, Cumbria LA10 5QL

Idyllic rural village setting, on Dales Way Footpath, Pennine Cycle Way and Settle-Carlisle Railway.
Hiking – Cycling – Golfing – Pony trekking – Fishing
B&B from £39.00 per room. All rooms en suite.
2 bars + restaurant. Local brewery - Dent real ales.
Home-cooked food available 2pm to 9.30pm.
Family-friendly – Children welcome – Pets welcome
Contact: 01539 625256
e-mail: mail@thegeorgeanddragondent.co.uk
www.dentbrewery.co.uk

Springs Farm Guesthouse

Springs Farm, Springs Road, Keswick CA12 4AN
Tel: 017687 72144/72546 • mobile: 07816 824253
Fax: 017687 72546 • e-mail: info@springsfarmcumbria.co.uk

Charming family-run farm guesthouse offering warm comfortable accommodation with good food and friendly atmosphere as standard. Three en suite rooms with wonderful views of surrounding meadows and mountains make this working dairy farm the ideal location for families and a perfect base for walkers and cyclists; secure lock up area for bikes, drying facilities and packed lunches are available. The peaceful location is only a 10-minute walk from town. Disabled access. Stair lift available. Our small farm shop offers locally produced goods and gifts, ice cream and hot and cold drinks.

www.springsfarmcumbria.co.uk

Contact: Mrs A Hutton or Ms H.C. Hutton.

58 CUMBRIA Patterdale, Penrith, Windermere **BOARD**

Deepdale Hall Farmhouse
Patterdale, Penrith CA11 0NR
Tel: 017684 82369
e-mail: brown@deepdalehall.freeserve.co.uk
www.deepdalehall.co.uk

17th century Lakeland farmhouse on working hill farm with stunning mountain views. An ideal base for walking, touring the Lakes, or just relaxing in a beautiful setting. Close to Lake Ullswater with steamer cruises, boats and many other activities. Oak beams • Log fires • Aga-cooked breakfast • Ample parking • Open Feb-Dec. Self-catering also available in spacious 2-bedroom barn conversion (ETC 4 Stars)

Pallet Hill Farm

Pallet Hill Farm is pleasantly situated two miles from Penrith, four miles from Ullswater, with easy access to the Lake District, Scottish Borders and Yorkshire Dales.
• Good farmhouse food and hospitality with personal attention.
• An ideal place to spend a relaxing break.
• Golf club, swimming pool, pony trekking in the area.
• Double, single and family rooms; Children welcome.
• Sorry, no pets. • Car essential, parking.
• Open Easter to November.

Bed and Breakfast £15 (reduced weekly rates), reduced rates for children.

Penrith, Cumbria CA11 0BY
Tel: 017684 83247

Greenah Crag, Troutbeck, Penrith CA11 0SQ (017684 83233)

Enjoy a relaxing break at Greenah Crag, a 17th century former farmhouse peacefully located in the Lake District National Park, 10 miles Keswick, eight miles from M6.
Ideal for exploring Northern Lakes and Western Pennines.

Two doubles en suite, and one twin with washbasin.
Guests' sittingroom with woodburning stove • Full breakfast.
Excellent choice of pubs within three miles • Regret no pets, no smoking.

Please telephone for brochure.
Bed and Breakfast from £23 per person.

e-mail: greenahcrag@lineone.net
www.greenahcrag.co.uk

Meadow Cottage
Tel: 01539 821269
www.meadow-cottage.net

Sandra and David Lennon extend a warm welcome to guests who stay at Meadow Cottage. Set in one and a half acres, this old Lakeland cottage has spectacular views and is the ideal location when visiting this beautiful region. All bedrooms are en suite, have tea and coffee facilities and colour TV. We provide Aga-cooked vegetarian or English breakfasts. Some five miles from Lake Windermere, the popular heart of the Lake District, we are conveniently placed for touring, walking or cycling exploration. A flexible service is provided in this non-smoking guest house. Please enquire for details. Prices from £28 per person.

Mr and Mrs D. Lennon, Meadow Cottage, Ratherheath Lane, Crook, Kendal LA8 8JX

BOARD Ashbourne, Glossop DERBYSHIRE 59

Derbyshire

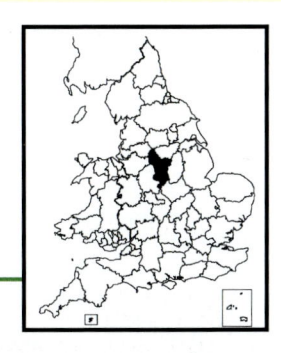

Turlow Bank

Hognaston, Ashbourne, Derbyshire DE6 1PW
Tel & Fax: 01335 370299
e-mail: turlowbank@w3z.co.uk
www.turlowbank.co.uk

AA ♦♦♦♦♦

Recently renovated early 19th century farmhouse in a quiet location, surrounded by glorious views. Spacious guest lounge with log fire; double bedroom with private bathroom, king-size bedroom en suite, central heating throughout. Full English breakfast, vegetarians catered for. Pub meals available locally, restaurant and cafe nearby. A step away from walking country and Carsington Water is only a short walk, where water sports, bird watching and cycling are available. Convenient for all attractions of the Peak District. *Bed and Breakfast from £35 to £55 pppn.*

Near Dovedale and Manifold Valley • B&B and Self-catering

On a working farm in quiet countryside, within easy reach of Alton Towers, stately homes and places of historic interest. Ideal touring centre.

• **B&B** – 4 double/twin rooms (3 en suite); dining/sitting room with TV. Tea/coffee making; full central heating; open fire. Terms from £30pppn; reduced rates for children; cot and high chair available.

• **Self-catering** – Cottage (sleeps 7), two farmhouses (sleep 12), River Lodge (sleeps 5). Sitting rooms and dining rooms (kitchen/diner in cottage). Electric cookers, fridges, washing machine and dryer. All have open fires. Car essential; nearest shops 3 miles. Phone. Pets permitted. **ETC ★★★★**

Details from Mrs M.A. Richardson, Throwley Hall Farm, Ilam, Near Ashbourne, Derbyshire DE6 2BB
Tel: 01538 308202/308243 • www.throwleyhallfarm.co.uk
e-mail: throwleyhall@talk21.com or throwley@btinternet.com

Graham and Julie Caesar
Windy Harbour Farm Hotel
Woodhead Road, Glossop SK13 7QE
01457 853107

Situated in the heart of the Peak District on the B6105, approximately one mile from Glossop town centre and adjacent to the Pennine Way. All our bedrooms are en suite, with outstanding views of Woodhead and Snake Passes and the Longdendale Valley is an ideal location for all outdoor activities. A warm welcome awaits you in our licensed bar and restaurant serving a wide range of excellent home-made food.

60 DERBYSHIRE

Glossop, Matlock, Melbourne **BOARD**

A Country House Hotel in the Heart of The Peak District

THE WIND IN THE WILLOWS

The Wind in the Willows Country House Hotel
Derbyshire Level, Glossop, Derbyshire SK13 7PT
Tel: 01457 868001 • Fax: 01457 853354
e-mail: info@windinthewillows.co.uk
www.windinthewillows.co.uk

MATLOCK Mr Joe Lomas, Middlehills Farm Bed and Breakfast, Grange Mill, Matlock DE4 4HY (01629 650368).
We know the secret of contentment - we live in the most picturesque part of England. Share our good fortune, breathe the fresh air, absorb the peace, feast your eyes on the beautiful scenery that surrounds our small working farm, with our pot bellied pig who just loves to have her ears scratched, and Bess and Ruby who are ideal playmates for children of all ages. Retire with the scent of honeysuckle and waken to the aroma of freshly baked bread and sizzling bacon then sample the delights of the Peak District and Derbyshire Dales such as Dovedale, Chatsworth and Haddon Hall.
• Working farm.

Ivy House Farm is a small arable working farm. The farmhouse, converted in 2000, has three double bedrooms and we have also converted our redundant cowsheds into three ground floor double/twin bedrooms, all of which are en suite, with tea/coffee making facilities and TV. There is lots to do and see in the area, such as Calke Abbey, ski slopes, Alton Towers, motor racing at Donington Park, not forgetting the National Forest. Children are welcome, but we are strictly non-smoking. Ample off-road parking.
Bed and Breakfast from £32.

Ivy House Farm Guesthouse, Stanton-by-Bridge, Derby DE73 7HT
Tel: 01332 863152
e-mail: mary@guesthouse.fsbusiness.co.uk   www.ivy-house-farm.com

Silver SILVER AWARD

Publisher's note

While every effort is made to ensure accuracy, we regret that FHG Guides cannot accept responsibility for errors, misrepresentations or omissions in our entries or any consequences thereof. Prices in particular should be checked.
We will follow up complaints but cannot act as arbiters or agents for either party.

Devon

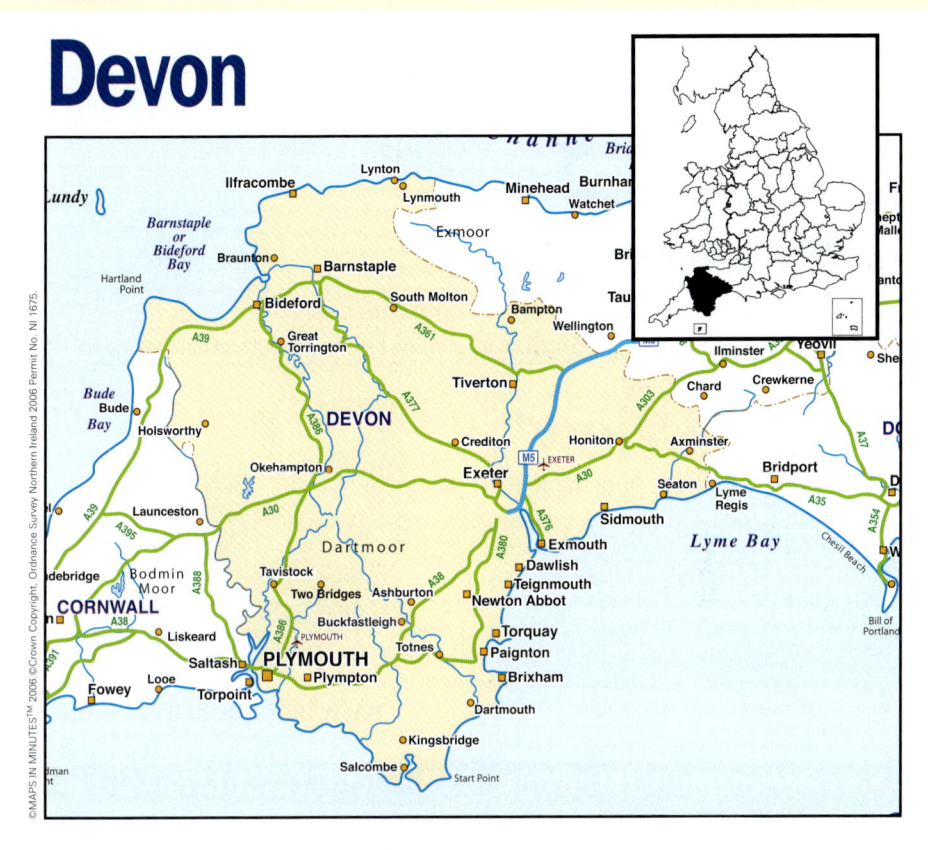

Devon is unique, with two different coastlines: bare rugged cliffs, white pebble beaches, stretches of golden sands, and the Jurassic Coast, England's first natural World Heritage Site. Glorious countryside: green rolling hills, bustling market towns and villages, thatched, white-washed cottages and traditional Devon longhouses. Wild and wonderful moorland: Dartmoor, in the south, embraces wild landscapes and picture-postcard villages; Exmoor in the north combines breathtaking, rugged coastline with wild heather moorland. Step back in time and discover historic cities, myths and legends, seafaring characters like Drake and Raleigh, and settings for novels by Agatha Christie and Conan Doyle.

Devon is home to an amazing and diverse range of birds. Enjoy special organised birdwatching trips, perhaps on board a RSPB Avocet Cruise or a vintage tram. Devon is the walking county of the South West – imagine drifts of bluebells lit by dappled sunlight, the smell of new mown hay, the sound of the sea, crisp country walks followed by a roaring fire and hot 'toddies'! If pedal power is your choice, you will discover exciting off-road cycling, leisurely afternoon rides, and challenging long distance routes such as the Granite Way along Dartmoor, the Grand Western Canal and the coastal Exmouth to Budleigh Circuit.

Please mention **FHG Guides** when making enquiries about accommodation featured in these pages

62 DEVON
Barnstaple, Bideford BOARD

HAXTON DOWN FARM
Bratton Fleming, Barnstaple EX32 7JL
Tel & Fax: 01598 710275

Traditional country living on a working farm set in spectacular surroundings, close to the coast, Exmoor and so many places to visit you will be spoilt for choice. This 16th-18th century farmhouse offers comfort, charm and warmth to make a relaxing base. En suite rooms with TV, tea making facilities, radio, hairdryer etc. Guest lounge with TV, DVD and CD player, and cosy wood burner for cooler evenings. Dining room with separate tables with wide choice of breakfast and dinner dishes. There is a wide selection of inns and restaurants in the area. Whatever your holiday tastes, North Devon has a lot to offer. Open mid April to mid November. Children and pets welcome. Parking. Prices from £22 to £25 pppn, Evening Meal £10.

e-mail: haxtondown@tiscali.co.uk • www.haxton-down-farm-holidays.co.uk

"Valley View"
Guineaford, Marwood, Barnstaple EX31 4EA

"Valley View" is a bungalow set in 320 acres of farmland which visitors are free to enjoy. The farm, situated 3½ miles from Barnstaple, near Marwood Hill Gardens and Arlington Court, produces lamb and is home to Helenbrie Miniature Shetland ponies. Accommodation comprises two bedrooms each containing a double and single bed. Bed and Breakfast from £20. Children are welcomed, half-price for those under 12 years. Babysitting free of charge. Pets by arrangement. Car essential – parking. Open all year.

Tel: 01271 343458
www.helenbriestud.co.uk

Near Barnstaple • Farmhouse B&B • Tel & Fax: 01271 858230

Our family working farm of 240 acres, with a pedigree herd of suckler cows and sheep, is situated in a small rural village between Barnstaple and Torrington, the Tarka Trail and Rosemoor Gardens. Six miles to the nearest beaches. Double room en suite, twin bedroom also available. Guest lounge with TV and tea/coffee making facilities. Good farmhouse cooking.
Ample parking • No pets • Non-smoking

B&B from £20. Reduced rates for children under 12; weekly terms on request.

Mrs J. Ley, West Barton, Alverdiscott, Near Barnstaple, Devon EX31 3PT

Riversford Hotel
Limers Lane, Bideford, Devon EX39 2RG

Riversford is beautifully situated in its own mature gardens, with stunning views across the River Torridge. The bustling port of Bideford is ten minutes' walk away, while a gentle stroll along a leafy woodland path will lead you to the fishing village of Appledore. Our restaurant has earned a fine reputation for some superb dishes, with local seafood a speciality. Traditional English breakfast. All rooms are en suite with colour TV, tea/coffee making facilities, direct-dial telephone and full central heating. Four-poster suites available.

Tel: 01237 474239 • Fax: 01237 421661
e-mail: Riversford@aol.com
www.Riversford.co.uk

The South Devon Hotel with a Different Outlook...

- Family Friendly
- 66 En suite Bedrooms
- Indoor & Outdoor Pools
- Magnificent Sea Views
- Relaxation Therapies
- Fitness Room
- Hairdresser
- Tennis
- Snooker
- Table Tennis
- Licensed Bars
- Extensive Lounges
- 19 Acres of Grounds

Langstone Cliff Hotel

Dawlish • South • Devon • EX7 0NA

Telephone 01626 868000

e-mail: cch@langstone-hotel.co.uk

www.langstone-hotel.co.uk/cch

RAC ★★★ Hotel   AA Hotel

West Titchberry Farm

Situated on the rugged North Devon coast, West Titchberry is a traditionally run stock farm, half a mile from Hartland Point. The South West Coastal Path skirts around the farm making it an ideal base for walkers.

The three guest rooms comprise an en suite family room; one double and one twin room, both with wash basins. All rooms have colour TV, radio, hairdryer, tea/coffee making facilities; bathroom/toilet and separate shower room on the same floor. Outside, guests may take advantage of a sheltered walled garden and a games room for the children. Sorry, no pets.

Hartland village is 3 miles away, Clovelly 6 miles, Bideford and Westward Ho! 16 miles and Bude 18 miles.

Tel & Fax: 01237 441287

B&B from £20–£25pppn • Evening meal £12 • Children welcome at reduced rates for under 12s • Open all year

Mrs Yvonne Heard, West Titchberry Farm, Hartland Point, Near Bideford EX39 6AU

Crowborough Farmhouse

Open all year • Rest and Relax in North Devon

A beautifully quiet and secluded old farmhouse, Crowborough is only 2 miles from the seaside village of Croyde, 4 miles from Saunton Championship Golf Course, and just 8 minutes' walk from Georgeham village. Enjoy exploring the nearby beaches, coastal walks and North Devon countryside, return to the peace and quiet that Crowborough offers, freshen up, then take a leisurely walk to one of the two excellent inns (good food, wine and ale) in the village.

Three bedrooms • Two bathrooms • Breakfast/sitting room with TV • Wood Burner in winter • No children or pets • Tariff: from £30 pppn.

Georgeham, Braunton, North Devon EX33 1JZ

Tel: Audrey Isaac 01271 891005 • www.crowboroughfarm.co.uk

Enjoy a peaceful break in beautiful countryside. Close to the Exe Estuary and Powderham Castle, and only two miles to the nearest sandy beach. Take a stroll to the village (only half a mile) to discover many eating places, or a little further to some specially recommended ones. Birdwatching, golf, fishing, racing, etc. all nearby and centrally situated for exploring all the lovely countryside and coastline in the area. Good shopping in Exeter. Comfortable rooms, guests' lounge, English breakfast. Nice garden. Plenty of parking. NON- SMOKING. Personal service and a 'home from home' atmosphere. Bed and Breakfast from £22pppn; weekly rates available.

Stile Farm

Starcross, Exeter EX6 8PD
Tel & Fax: 01626 890268
www.stile-farm.co.uk

HONITON Mrs June Tucker, Yard Farm, Upottery, Honiton EX14 9QP (01404 861680).

A most attractively situated working farm. The house is a very old traditional Devon farmhouse located just three miles east of Honiton and enjoying a superb outlook across the Otter Valley. Enjoy a stroll down by the River Otter which runs through the farmland. Try a spot of trout fishing. Children will love to make friends with our two horses. Lovely seaside resorts 12 miles, swimming pool, adventure park and garden near by. Traditional English breakfast, colour TV, washbasin, heating, tea/coffee facilities in all rooms.

Rates: Bed and Breakfast £18 to £22. Reductions for children.
• Working farm.

BOARD Ivybridge, Kingsbridge   DEVON 65

Venn Farm

Enjoy a rural retreat at Venn, which is only three miles from the dual carriageway. We are 20 minutes from beaches and South Dartmoor is visible from the farm. There are two family bedrooms, and a separate garden cottage which has two twin ground floor bedrooms overlooking a large pond. We also have self-catering for eight, four and two persons, again with ground floor bedrooms.

DISABLED CATEGORY 2 ACCESSIBILITY.

Mrs P. Stephens, Venn Farm, Ugborough, Ivybridge PL21 0PE • 01364 73240
www.SmoothHound.co.uk/hotels/vennfarm

Mrs M. Newsham, Marsh Mills, Aveton Gifford, Kingsbridge TQ7 4JW • 01548 550549

Georgian Mill House, overlooking the River Avon, with mill pond, mill leat and duck pond. Small farm with friendly animals. Peaceful and secluded, just off A379, Kingsbridge four miles, Salcombe 7 miles, Plymouth 17 miles, Dartmoor 8 miles. Bigbury Bay and Bantham beach with beautiful golden sands are nearby, or enjoy a walk along our unspoilt river estuary, or the miles of beautiful South Devon coastal paths.

One double and one double/twin room, both en suite with tea/coffee facilities, room heaters and colour TV. Breakfast in the sun lounge or your own dining/sitting room. Beautiful gardens, ample parking.
- Bed and Breakfast from £25pppn.
- Self-catering, sleeps 2/3, also available; dogs welcome.
- Phone, SAE or e-mail for enquiries or brochure.

e-mail: newsham@marshmills.co.uk • www.marshmills.co.uk

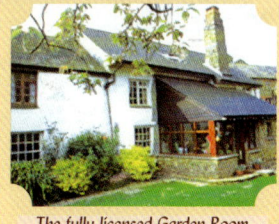

You and your family can be assured of a warm welcome from Anne Rossiter.

For **B&B** the farmhouse offers a choice of tastefully decorated family, double, twin or single rooms, all en suite, centrally heated and equipped with tea/coffee making facilities and TV. This is a non-smoking zone.

For **Self-Catering** there are two and three bedroomed cottages, with fully equipped kitchens, colour TV/video, night storage heaters and beautiful stone-built fireplaces. They have large gardens, perfect for children and parents alike.

The fully licensed Garden Room Restaurant provides tasty traditional home cooking with fresh quality produce. Large and small functions can be catered for in a friendly, relaxed atmosphere.

BURTON FARMHOUSE Galmpton, Kingsbridge TQ7 3EY
Tel: 01548 561210 • Fax: 01548 562257
e-mail: anne@burtonfarm.co.uk • www.burtonfarmhouse.co.uk

Please note

All the information in this book is given in good faith in the belief that it is correct. However, the publishers cannot guarantee the facts given in these pages, neither are they responsible for changes in policy, ownership or terms that may take place after the date of going to press. Readers should always satisfy themselves that the facilities they require are available and that the terms, if quoted, still apply.

ROCK HOUSE HOTEL
Lynmouth, North Devon EX35 6EN
Tel: 01598 753508

Share the magic of living at the water's edge in a Grade II Listed building which stands alone at the harbour entrance. Offering peace and tranquillity, it is the perfect place to relax. All rooms have sea views, are centrally heated, en suite, with TV, hairdryer, alarm clock and tea/coffee making facilities. Fresh ingredients used in all meals; vegetarian and special diets catered for. Superb wine list. Fully licensed bar. Putting, tennis and numerous woodland, coastal and riverside walks nearby. Explore the Heritage Coast by boat; ideal for birdwatching. Visit the Valley of Rocks and Doone Valley; the heart of Exmoor is only a short journey away by car or bus.

e-mail: enquiries@rock-house.co.uk
www.rock-house.co.uk

Great Sloncombe Farm
Moretonhampstead Devon TQ13 8QF
Tel: 01647 440595

Share the magic of Dartmoor all year round while staying in our lovely 13th century farmhouse full of interesting historical features. A working mixed farm set amongst peaceful meadows and woodland abundant in wild flowers and animals, including badgers, foxes, deer and buzzards. A welcoming and informal place to relax and explore the moors and Devon countryside. Comfortable double and twin rooms with en suite facilities, TV, central heating and coffee/tea making facilities. Delicious Devonshire breakfasts with new baked bread.

Open all year~No smoking~Farm Stay UK
e-mail: hmerchant@sloncombe.freeserve.co.uk • website: www.greatsloncombefarm.co.uk

COOKSHAYES
33 Court Street, Moretonhampstead TQ13 8LG
Tel/Fax: 01647 440374
E-mail: cookshayes@aol.com • www.cookshayes.co.uk

Elegant, mid-Victorian country guest house with ornamental garden. All rooms have colour TV, tea/coffee making facilities, central heating, hairdryers and seating; six rooms en suite. Ground floor and non-smoking rooms available. The guest house is situated on the edge of Dartmoor and is an excellent centre for touring, walking and fishing. Secure parking.
Bed and Breakfast from £22.50 pppn.

AA ♦♦♦

Mrs Rosemary Ward,
Parsonage Farm,
Iddesleigh, Winkleigh,
Devon EX19 8SN
Tel: 01837 810318
e-mail: roseward01@yahoo.co.uk
www.parsonage-farm-devon.co.uk

A warm welcome awaits you at our family-run organic dairy farm, situated approximately one mile from the picturesque village of Iddesleigh. There is an excellent 15th century inn called The Duke of York and the market town of Hatherleigh is three miles away. The Tarka Trail passes through our farmyard, and 400m of salmon/trout fishing is available on the farm boundary. An ideal, peaceful haven for touring Devon and Cornwall. Accommodation consists of a two-bedroom family suite and a double room, both with private bathroom, tea/coffee making facilities, central heating and colour TV. Guests are able to relax in the lounge or our large walled garden. There is a games room for guests, with snooker and table tennis. B&B from £25 pppn. Open Easter–October. No smoking and no pets. Reductions for children and weekly bookings.

LOWER PINN FARM
Peak Hill, Sidmouth EX10 0NN
Tel: 01395 513733
e-mail: liz@lowerpinnfarm.co.uk • www.lowerpinnfarm.co.uk

19th century built farmhouse on the World Heritage Jurassic Coast, two miles west of the unspoilt coastal resort of Sidmouth and one mile to the east of the pretty village of Otterton. Ideally situated for visiting many places, and for walking, with access to coastal path.

Comfortable, centrally heated en suite rooms with colour television and hot drink making facilities. Guests have their own keys and may return at all times throughout the day. Good hearty breakfast served in the dining room. Ample off-road parking. Children and pets welcome. Lower Pinn is a no smoking establishment. Open all year.

Bed and Breakfast from £25 to £30

TIVERTON Mrs L. Arnold, The Mill, Lower Washfield, Tiverton EX16 9PD (01884 255297).
A warm welcome awaits you at our converted mill, beautifully situated on the banks of the picturesque River Exe. Close to National Trust's Knightshayes Court and on the route of the Exe Valley Way. Easy access to both the north and south coasts, Exmoor and Dartmoor. Only two miles from Tiverton. Relaxing and friendly atmosphere with delicious farmhouse fare. En suite bedrooms with TV and tea/coffee making facilities.
Rates: Bed and Breakfast from £26.
e-mail: arnold5@washfield.freeserve.co.uk
www.washfield.freeserve.co.uk

Hornhill
Tel: 01884 253352
Exeter Hill, Tiverton, Devon EX16 4PL
e-mail: hornhill@tinyworld.co.uk
www.hornhill-farmhouse.co.uk

Excellent B&B accommodation situated at the top of a hill with panoramic views overlooking the beautiful Exe valley, only 10 minutes from the M5 yet amidst the peace and quiet of the countryside. Ideal base from which to explore Devon and the surrounding area, including Exeter, Exmoor, Dartmoor and several National Trust properties. The three bedrooms, one a four-poster room, have either private or en suite facilities. One room is on the ground floor and suitable for the 'not so able'.
Full English or Continental breakfast available. From £32 single, £55 double/twin. Dinner by prior arrangement.

LEONARD HOUSE Farmhouse B&B
Come and share our lovely family farmhouse just five minutes from Junction 27 of the M5, and close to the coast. Golf courses, canal walks, cycle routes, city and towns are all within easy reach. Accommodation is in en suite family, double and twin rooms with TV, tea and coffee facilities. Guests have their own lounge/diningroom/conservatory and there is a lovely garden to relax in. Children of all ages welcome. Non-smoking.

Mrs S. Quick, Leonard House, Near Sampford Peverell,
Tiverton EX16 7EL
Tel/Fax: 01884 820881 • Mobile: 078136 18607
e-mail: sue.quick1@btinternet.com

B&B from £25pppn
Family room £70 per night

Aveland Hotel

A family run, licensed hotel in a quiet level location close to Cary Park. A short walk to St Marychurch Village and Babbacombe Downs with panoramic views across Lyme Bay. An ideal location for holidays, short breaks and many attractions in the area.

- AA 4 Star Guest Accommodation
- Licensed
- All rooms en-suite
- Evening meal optional
- Children welcome
- Car park and gardens
- Non Smoking Silver Award
- All major credit cards accepted

Aveland Road, Babbacombe, Torquay, Devon, TQ1 3PT
Tel/Minicom: 01803 326622 email: avelandhotel@aol.com
Website: www.avelandhotel.co.uk

Callisham Farm B&B

Meavy, Near Yelverton PL20 6PS
Tel/Fax: 01822 853901

Rustic charm in rural Devon countryside

Esme Wills and her family extend a warm welcome to their guests all year round. Feel at home in one of the three comfortable en suite bedrooms, with tea/coffee tray, clock radio and TV. Relax in the warm and cosy guests' lounge. A superb English breakfast is the perfect beginning to the day; vegetarian and special diets catered for on request. With easy access to rolling moorland, Callisham is a perfect base for riding, fishing, golf, and touring the beautiful coasts of Devon and Cornwall. In the nearby village of Meavy, the Royal Oak offers a selection of real ales and fine food; other pubs within a mile and a half; Plymouth 12 miles.

www.callisham.co.uk • esme@callisham.co.uk

Useful Guidance for Guests and Hosts

Every year literally thousands of holidays, short breaks and overnight stops are arranged through our guides, the vast majority without any problems at all. In a handful of cases, however, difficulties do arise about bookings, which often could have been prevented from the outset.

It is important to remember that when accommodation has been booked, both parties – guests and hosts – have entered into a form of contract. We hope that the following points will provide helpful guidance.

Guests

- When enquiring about accommodation, be as precise as possible. Give exact dates, numbers in your party and the ages of any children.
- State the number and type of rooms wanted and also what catering you require – bed and breakfast, full board etc. Make sure that the position about evening meals is clear – and about pets, reductions for children or any other special points.
- Read our reviews carefully to ensure that the proprietors you are going to contact can supply what you want. Ask for a letter confirming all arrangements, if possible.
- If you have to cancel, do so as soon as possible. Proprietors do have the right to retain deposits and under certain circumstances to charge for cancelled holidays if adequate notice is not given and they cannot re-let the accommodation.

Hosts

- Give details about your facilities and about any special conditions. Explain your deposit system clearly and arrangements for cancellations, charges etc. and whether or not your terms include VAT.
- If for any reason you are unable to fulfil an agreed booking without adequate notice, you may be under an obligation to arrange suitable alternative accommodation or to make some form of compensation.

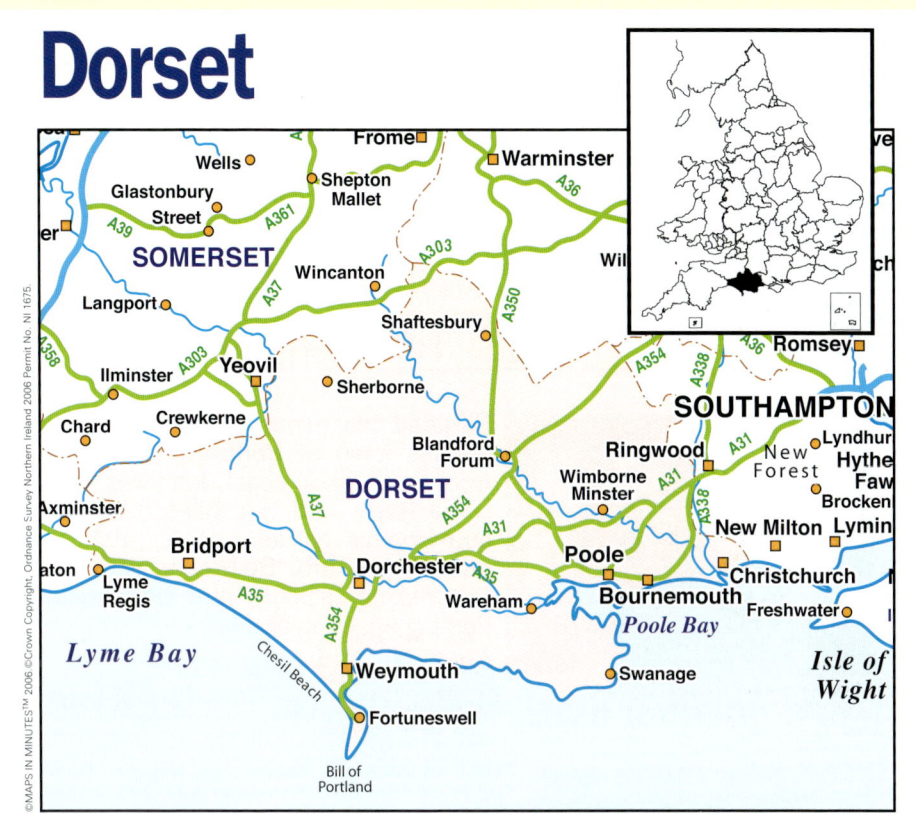

Dorset

Sandbanks, Dorset. Picture courtesy of Poole Tourism

70 DORSET — Bridport, Cerne Abbas, Charmouth, **BOARD**

Frogmore Farm — Chideock, Bridport DT6 6HT

Set in the rolling hills of West Dorset, enjoying splendid sea views, our delightful 17th century farmhouse offers comfortable, friendly and relaxing accommodation. An ideal base from which to ramble the many coastal and country footpaths of the area (nearest beach Seatown one-and-a-half miles) or tour by car the interesting places of Dorset and Devon. Bedrooms with en suite shower rooms, TV and tea making facilities. Guests' dining room and cosy lounge with woodburner. Well behaved dogs welcome. Open all year; car essential. Bed and Breakfast from £25. Brochure and terms free on request from Mrs Sue Norman.

Tel: 01308 456159

Situated ten minutes' walk from the market town of Bridport, two miles from the Jurassic coast, ten miles from Lyme Regis and ten miles from the sub-tropical gardens at Abbotsbury near Weymouth. Bedrooms with TV, tea making facilities and washbasin. Parking space available.

Mrs K.E. Parsons, 179 St Andrews Road, Bridport • 01308 422038

CERNE ABBAS Mrs T. Barraclough, Magiston Farm, Sydling St Nicholas, Dorchester DT2 9NR (01300 320295).

Magiston is a 400-acre working farm with a comfortable 17th century cob and brick farmhouse set deep in the heart of Dorset. Large garden with river. Half-an-hour's drive from coast and five miles north of Dorchester. The farmhouse comprises double, twin and single bedrooms including a twin on the ground floor. Delicious evening meals served. Central heating. Please write or telephone for further details.

Rates: Bed and Breakfast from £20 per person per night. Evening Meal, three courses £12.00.
- Working farm. • Children over 10 years and pets welcome.
- Open January to December.

ETC ♦♦♦

Cardsmill Farm Holidays

Whitchurch Canonicorum, Charmouth, Bridport, Dorset DT6 6RP
Tel & Fax: 01297 489375 • e-mail: cardsmill@aol.com
website: www.farmhousedorset.com

Stay on a real working family farm in the Marshwood Vale, an Area of Outstanding Natural Beauty. Enjoy country walks to the village, coast and around farm and woods. Watch the daily milking, see baby calves and lambs, and seasonal activities here on this 590 acre farm. En suite family, double and twin rooms available, with CTV, tea/coffee trays. Also available, three large, rural, quiet farmhouses. Each has private garden, double glazed conservatory and ample parking. **TAPHOUSE** has 6 bedrooms, 3 bathrooms, lounge, 22'x15' kitchen/diner. **COURTHOUSE FARMHOUSE** and **DAIRY** each have 4 bedrooms and 2 or 3 bathrooms. Games room, parking, separate gardens. All have C/H, dishwasher, washing machine and very well equipped kitchen/diner/lounge. All available all year for long or short stays. Brochure available, or check the website.

B&B £24–£30pppn

BOARD Dorchester, Lulworth Cove, Poole   DORSET **71**

This country house with its friendly and homely atmosphere welcomes you to the heart of Hardy's Wessex. Central for touring the many places of interest that Dorset has to offer, including Corfe Castle, Lyme Regis, Dorchester, Weymouth, Lulworth Cove, etc. Lovely country walks and many local attractions. Two double rooms, one single, en suite or separate bathroom. TV lounge, dining room. Large garden. Open all year. Central heating. Car essential, ample parking. Bed and Breakfast from £25. Take A35 from Dorchester, we are the last house at the western edge of the village.

Nethercroft
Winterbourne Abbas, Dorchester DT2 9LU

Mrs V.A. Bradbeer
Tel: 01305 889337
e-mail: v.bradbeer@ukonline.co.uk

ETC ♦♦♦♦ **CHURCHVIEW GUEST HOUSE**
Winterbourne Abbas, Dorchester, Dorset DT2 9LS   Tel/Fax: 01305 889296

Our 17th century Guest House, noted for warm hospitality, delicious breakfasts and evening meals, makes an ideal base for touring beautiful West Dorset. Our character bedrooms are comfortable and well-appointed. Meals, served in our beautiful dining room, feature local produce, with relaxation provided by two attractive lounges and licensed bar. Hosts, Jane and Michael Deller, are pleased to give every assistance, with local information to ensure a memorable stay. Short breaks available. Non-smoking.

Terms: Bed and Breakfast: £30 – £38; Dinner, Bed and Breakfast: £46 – £57.
e-mail: stay@churchview.co.uk • www.churchview.co.uk

Cromwell House Hotel
Lulworth Cove, Dorset

Catriona and Alistair Miller welcome guests to their comfortable family-run hotel, set in secluded gardens with spectacular sea views. Situated 200 yards from Lulworth Cove, with direct access to the Jurassic Coast. A heated swimming pool is available for guests' use from May to October. Accommodation is in 20 en suite bedrooms, with TV, direct-dial telephone, and tea/coffee making facilities; most have spectacular sea views. There is disabled access and a room suitable for disabled guests. Self-catering cottages available. Restaurant, bar wine list.

B&B from £40. Two nights DB&B (fully en suite) from £114 per person. Off-peak mid week breaks all year except Christmas.

Cromwell House Hotel, Lulworth Cove, Dorset BH20 5RJ
Tel: 01929 400253/400332 • Fax: 01929 400566
ETC/AA/RAC ★★

Built in 1892, **HOLLY HEDGE FARM** is situated next to Bulbury Woods Golf Course, set in 11 acres of wood and grassland adjacent to lake. We are just 15 minutes away from the Purbecks, the beach and the forest. The area is ideal for walking or cycling and Poole Quay and Harbour are also nearby.

Accommodation comprises two double/family rooms, one twin and one single, all with en suite showers, colour TV, tea/coffee making facilities, radio alarms and central heating. Cottage available.

- *Prices for a single room £35 per night, double £60 per night.*
- *Open all year round for summer or winter breaks.*
- *Full English or Continental breakfast served.*

Mrs Stephenson
Holly Hedge Farm
Bulbury Lane, Lytchett Matravers,
Poole, Dorset BH16 6EP
Tel: 01929 459688

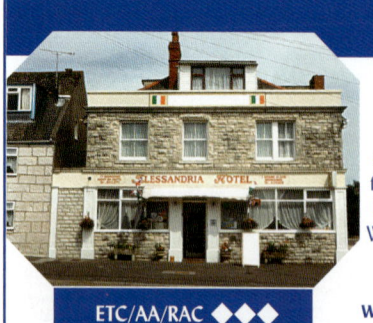

Alessandria Hotel
71 Wakeham, Easton, Portland DT5 1HW

This former 18th century inn is situated in a quiet location. Comfortable accommodation; 15 bedrooms, most en suite; some with sea view; colour TV, tea/coffee; free parking. Ground floor rooms. 4 spacious en suite family rooms. Children welcome. Bed and Breakfast at reasonable prices. Vegetarians catered for. Warm and friendly hospitality. Same owner/manager for 16 years.

Tel: 01305 822270/820108
Fax: 01305 820561
www.s-h-systems.co.uk/hotels/alessand.html

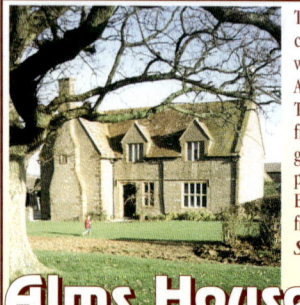

ETC/AA/RAC ♦♦♦

Alms House Farm

This charming old farmhouse was a monastery during the 16th century, restored in 1849 and is now a Listed building. A family-run working dairy farm, 140 acres overlooking the Blackmoor Vale. Accommodation is in three comfortable en suite rooms with colour TV and tea/coffee making facilities. Diningroom with inglenook fireplace, lounge with colour TV, for guests' use at all times. Also garden and lawn. Plenty of reading material and local information provided for this ideal touring area. Bed and Breakfast from £27. Excellent evening meals in all local inns nearby. Situated six miles from Sherborne with its beautiful Abbey and Castle.

SAE for further details. Mrs Jenny Mayo

Hermitage, Holnest, Sherborne, Dorset DT9 6HA
Tel and Fax: 01963 210296

SHERBORNE (NEAR) Mrs Susan Stretton, Beech Farm, Sigwells, Charlton Horethorne, Near Sherborne, Dorset DT9 4LN (Tel & Fax: 01963 220524).

Comfortable farmhouse with relaxed atmosphere on our 137 acre dairy farm, with beef and horses. A peaceful area on the Somerset/Dorset border with wonderful views of Corton Beacon. Four miles from the old abbey town of Sherborne, six miles from Wincanton, and just two miles off the A303. The farmhouse offers a double room en suite, a twin room, guest bathroom and an attic family room, all with TV and tea/coffee trays.

Rates: Bed and Breakfast £20 per person, less 10% for two or more nights.

• Pets and horses by arrangement. • Open all year except Christmas.

e-mail: stretton@beechfarmsigwells.freeserve.co.uk

Pennhills Farm

Pennhills Farmhouse, set in 100 acres of unspoiled countryside, is situated one mile from the village of Shillingstone in the heart of the Blackmore Vale, an ideal peaceful retreat, short break or holiday. It offers spacious comfortable accommodation for all ages; children welcome, pets by arrangement. One downstairs bedroom. All bedrooms en suite with TV and tea/coffee making facilities, complemented by traditional English breakfast with home produced bacon and sausages. Vegetarians catered for. Good meals available locally. Brochure sent on request. A warm and friendly welcome is assured from your host Rosie Watts. From £26 per person.

Mrs Rosie Watts, Pennhills Farm, Sandy Lane,
Off Lanchards Lane, Shillingstone, Blandford DT11 0TF
Tel: 01258 860491

BOARD Sturminster Newton, Swanage, Tolpuddle　　　　　　　DORSET 73

Lower Fifehead Farm

Fifehead St Quinton, Sturminster Newton DT10 2AP
Tel: 01258 817335 (Lower Fifehead)
Tel: 01258 817896 (Honeysuckle House)

Both properties ★★★★

B&B £22-£30pppn

Come and have a relaxing holiday at Lower Fifehead Farm, staying in our lovely Listed farmhouse (pictured here), mentioned in Dorset books for its architectural interest, or in our new farmhouse called Honeysuckle House, actually on the farm, set within fields with outstanding views. We offer in both excellent breakfasts and tea/coffee making; Honeysuckle House also offers evening meals.

Both farmhouses have guest lounges for you to relax in. We are within easy reach of the coast and all Dorset's beauty spots; excellent walking, riding and fishing can be arranged.

For Lower Fifehead Farm contact Mrs Jill Miller, for Honeysuckle House contact Mrs Jessica Miller

Downshay Farm

A Victorian Purbeck stone farmhouse, on a working farm in the heart of the beautiful Isle of Purbeck.
Family room en suite and one double with private shower room close by, both with colour TV and tea/coffee making facilities.
Steam railway within walking distance, coastal path and sandy beaches three miles away.
Excellent pubs and restaurants found locally.
Open February 1st to November 30th.
Bed and Breakfast from £20 per person.

Tel: 01929 480316
e-mail: downshayfarm@tiscali.co.uk
www.downshayfarm.co.uk

Haycrafts Lane, Harmans Cross
Swanage, Dorset BH19 3EB

THE LIMES HOTEL

◆◆◆◆

A warm welcome awaits everyone at the Limes Hotel, only a few hundred yards from wonderful coastal walks and beach, surrounded by the unspoilt Purbeck Hills. En suite rooms with colour TV and hospitality trays. Pets come free!
• Car Park • Licensed Bar
• Families, Pets and Groups Welcome
• Open all Year for Bed and Breakfast

48 Park Road, Swanage, Dorset BH19 2AE
Tel: 01929 422664
info@limeshotel.net
www.limeshotel.net

TOLPUDDLE HALL
Tel: 01305 848986

Tolpuddle, Near Dorchester DT2 7EW

An historic house in village centre in an Area of Outstanding Natural Beauty, not far from the coast. Convenient for Bournemouth, Poole, Dorchester, Weymouth, Isle of Purbeck and many small market towns and villages. Centre for local interests e.g., birdwatching, walking, local history, Thomas Hardy, the Tolpuddle Martyrs, etc.

*Two double, one family, one twin and two single bedrooms, all with TV • Full English breakfast
Tea/coffee making, TV sitting room
Small kitchen available to residents
Open all year • Pets welcome except high season*

From £20pp. Weekly rate available.

Essex

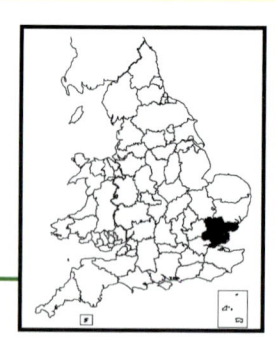

Earls Hall Farm
Clacton on Sea, Essex CO16 8BP
Tel: 01255 820458
Excellent base for the Essex Sunshine Coast. Ideal for birdwatching, beaches, woodland walks and exploring East Anglia. Non-smoking. Open all year.

Pond House Bed & Breakfast
Victorian farmhouse with one double (king-size) and one twin room, both en suite. Guests' sitting room.
Rates per night from £52 double, from £35 single.
VisitBritain SILVER AWARD.

Pond Cottage Self Catering Holidays
Cosy cottage annexe, very well equipped, with full central heating. Sleeps four in one king-size double and one twin room, both en suite. Terms from £200 - £450 per week. Short breaks available.

Contact Mrs Brenda Lord • e-mail: brenda_lord@farming.co.uk • www.earlshallfarm.info

Seven Arches Farm
Georgian farmhouse set in large garden close to the ancient town of Colchester. The farm extends to 100 acres and supports both arable crops and cattle. Private fishing rights on the River Colne, which runs past the farmhouse.
This is a good location for visits to North Essex, Dedham and the Stour Valley which have been immortalised in the works of John Constable, the landscape painter.

- Children and pets welcome.
- Open all year.
- Static caravan on caravan site also available.

◆ Bed and Breakfast from £30
◆ Evening Meal from £5
◆ Twin room £50
◆ Family room en suite

Mrs Jill Tod, Seven Arches Farm,
Chitts Hill, Lexden, Colchester CO3 9SX
01206 574896

Rye Farm
Rye Farm is a 17th century moated farmhouse. It enjoys a quiet location adjacent to Abberton Reservoir. Ideal for a relaxing break.
A good base for exploring Colchester with its castle and museums, Colchester Zoo, Mersea Island, Layer Marney Towers, Beth Chatto Gardens, Maldon and Constable Country. 30 mins from the coast; 50 mins from Stansted Airport/Harwich Port.
B&B from £55 double and £35 single.

Two comfortable en suite rooms, with central heating, TV/DVD, tea and coffee making facilities, fridge, hairdryer, clock/radio/CD player.
• Non-smoking •

Rye Lane, Layer De La Haye,
Colchester CO2 0JL

Contact: Virginia Bunting.
Phone: 01206 734350/07976 524276
e-mail: peter@buntingp.fsbusiness.co.uk
www.buntingp.fsbusiness.co.uk

BOARD Bath   **GLOUCESTERSHIRE 75**

Gloucestershire

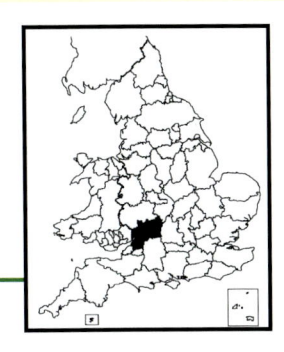

Gloucestershire, in an enviable position west of London between Bath, Oxford and Stratford-on-Avon, has style, elegance, charm…..and cheese rolling. The funkiest Farmers' Markets, happening hotels and, once a year, a mad scramble down the steepest slope to catch a cheese or two.

The county is best known for the Cotswolds, but the area includes The Royal Forest of Dean, Cheltenham, Tewkesbury and Gloucester.

In recent years the Cotswolds area has reinvented itself. Forget twee B&Bs and chintzy hotels, the Cotswolds is now a hotspot of chic hotels, award-winning designer farm shops and entertaining farmers' markets. Liz Hurley, Hugh Grant, Kate Moss, Kate Winslet and Sam Mendes have recently moved to the area and it's easy to see why. The Cotswolds offer space and escape in a beautiful environment and that's exactly what's on offer to visitors too.

Nearby, the Royal Forest of Dean is the last great English broadleaf forest, formerly a hunting ground for the kings of England. Nowadays it's emerging as a great destination for adrenaline sports and activity breaks, all against the backdrop of acres of woodland and nature reserves. It's one of the most colourful corners of England - daffodils, green shoots and bluebells in spring, and gold in Autumn.

POOL FARM
Bath Road, Wick, Bristol BS30 5RL
Tel: 0117 937 2284

Welcome to our 350 year old Grade II Listed farmhouse on a working farm. On A420 between Bath and Bristol and a few miles from Exit 18 of M4, we are on the edge of the village, overlooking fields, but within easy reach of pub, shops and golf club. We offer traditional Bed and Breakfast in one family and one twin room with tea/coffee facilities and TV; guest lounge. Central heating. Ample parking. Open all year except Christmas. Terms from £22.

Bredons Norton, Chipping Campden BOARD

Meadows Home Farm

Home Farm is a family-run working farm set in the small unspoilt village of Bredons Norton, in the heart of the Cotswolds. The farm has been designated an Area of Outstanding Natural Beauty. This is an excellent base for touring the Cotswolds, Worcester, Cheltenham and the Malverns. Superb walking country.
Meadows Home Farm, Bredons Norton, Tewkesbury GL20 7HA • Tel: 01684 772322
www.meadowshomefarm.co.uk

Two rooms are available for B&B. One is a double room with en suite bathroom; the other is also en suite and has a double and single bed. Both are tastefully furnished, with central heating, tea/coffee making and TV. A full English breakfast is served, with bacon and sausages from the farm shop. There is a beautiful garden and patio area, as well as a TV lounge. Local pubs are available for evening meals.

Self-catering also available in Stable Cottage (sleeps 4/5)

'Brymbo' ETC ♦♦♦♦
Honeybourne Lane, Mickleton, Chipping Campden, Gloucestershire GL55 6PU
Tel: 01386 438890 • Fax: 01386 438113
e-mail: enquiries@brymbo.com • www.brymbo.com

A warm and welcoming farm building conversion with large garden in beautiful Cotswold countryside, ideal for walking and touring.

All rooms are on the ground floor, with full central heating. The comfortable bedrooms all have colour TV and tea/coffee making facilities. Sitting room with open log fire. Breakfast room. Children and dogs welcome. Parking. Two double, two twin, one family. Bathrooms: three en suite, two private or shared. Bed and Breakfast: single £27 to £42; double £45 to £60. Brochure available. Credit Cards accepted.
Close to Stratford-upon-Avon, Broadway, Chipping Campden and with easy access to Oxford and Cheltenham.

A warm and friendly welcome awaits you at our completely refurbished 15th century Grade II Listed farmhouse, in the heart of this beautiful village. Spacious beamed rooms, inglenook fireplace in dining room where a full English breakfast is served. Large private car park at rear. All bedrooms are en suite and have coffee/tea making facilities, TV, radio and hairdryer.

Accommodation comprises one double, two twin and one family suite consisting of a single and a double room en suite. Sorry no pets allowed in the house. Non-smoking. No children under 12.

Terms per night: from £65 per double-bedded suite, 2 persons sharing. More than two nights from £50. Twin-bedded rooms are £55 or single occupancy £40. Family room for 3 persons sharing £80.

Veronica Stanley, Home Farm House, Ebrington, Chipping Campden GL55 6NL
Tel & Fax: 01386 593391 • e-mail: willstanley@farmersweekly.net
www.homefarminthecotswolds.co.uk

Silver SILVER AWARD

Publisher's note

While every effort is made to ensure accuracy, we regret that FHG Guides cannot accept responsibility for errors, misrepresentations or omissions in our entries or any consequences thereof. Prices in particular should be checked.
We will follow up complaints but cannot act as arbiters or agents for either party.

BOARD Fairford, Gloucester (near)   **GLOUCESTERSHIRE 77**

Tel & Fax: 01452 840224

Quality all ground floor accommodation. "Kilmorie" is Grade II Listed (c1848) within conservation area in a lovely part of Gloucestershire. Double, twin, family or single bedrooms, all having tea tray, colour TV, radio, mostly en suite. Very comfortable guests' lounge, traditional home cooking is served in the separate dining room overlooking large garden. Perhaps walk waymarked farmland footpaths which start here. Children may "help" with our pony, and our free range hens. Rural yet perfectly situated to visit Cotswolds, Royal Forest of Dean, Wye Valley and Malvern Hills. Children over five years. No smoking, please. Ample parking.

Bed and Full English Breakfast from £21 per person.

S.J. Barnfield, "Kilmorie Smallholding", Gloucester Road, Corse, Staunton, Gloucester GL19 3RQ
e-mail: sheila-barnfield@supanet.com

'Severn Bank' is a large country house set in riverside gardens, four miles west of Gloucester. Ideally situated for touring nearby Forest of Dean, Severn Vale, Cotswolds and Malverns, and is a recommended viewpoint for the Severn Bore tidal wave. The area is rich in history and packed with intriguing places of interest, from caves to castles.

We have three large double/twin or family en suite rooms, all with tea and coffee making facilities, own TV and hairdryer. We serve a healthy buffet breakfast of fresh fruits, cereals, breads etc. Sorry, no pets.

All rooms non-smoking.
£60 per room per night.

Mrs Carter, 'Severn Bank', Minsterworth GL2 8JH
Tel: 01452 750146 • www.severn-bank.com

Looking for Holiday Accommodation?

FHG
KUPERARD

for details of hundreds of properties throughout the UK visit our website

www.holidayguides.com

78 GLOUCESTERSHIRE Moreton-in-Marsh, Stow-on-the-Wold, Winchcombe, **BOARD**

Snowshill Hill Estate
Bed & Breakfast Accommodation
Snowshill Hill, Moreton-in-Marsh GL56 9TH
Tel: 01386 853959 • Fax: 01386 853416

TOURISM EXCELLENCE AWARDS 2006-2007

GUEST ACCOMMODATION ★★★★★

SILVER AWARD

High standard accommodation offering a comfortable, self-contained, independent dwelling. All rooms en suite; thoughtfully and tastefully furnished.
Working farm, beautiful countryside.
Walking and cycling. Ideal for small groups.
All ground floor accommodation.
Separate sitting room/dining room with woodburner.
Breakfasts using local produce.
Broadway and Chipping Campden - 4 miles.
South West Tourism's Excellence Award
Best B&B Finalist 2006/07.

e-mail: snowshillhill@aol.com • www.broadway-cotswolds.co.uk/snowshillhill.html
www.cotswoldsbreakfast.com/accommodation/snowshill-hill-estate.html

STOW-ON-THE-WOLD Robert Smith and Julie-Anne, Corsham Field Farmhouse, Bledington Road, Stow-on-the-Wold GL54 1JH (01451 831750; Fax: 01451 832247).
A traditional farmhouse with spectacular views of Cotswold countryside. Quiet location one mile from Stow. Ideally situated for exploring all Cotswold villages including Bourton-on-the-Water, Broadway, Burford and Chipping Campden. Within easy reach of Cheltenham, Oxford and Stratford-upon-Avon; also places of interest such as Blenheim Palace, Warwick Castle and many National Trust houses and gardens. Family, twin and double bedrooms; mostly en suite. TV, tea tray and hairdryer in all rooms. Relaxing guest lounge/dining room. Excellent pub food five minutes' walk away.
Rates: Bed and Full English Breakfast from £24 (reductions for children).
• Children welcome. • Open all year.
ETC/AA ◆◆◆
e-mail: farmhouse@corshamfield.co.uk   www.corshamfield.co.uk

---

Ireley is an 18th century farmhouse located in the heart of gentle countryside, one-and-a-half miles from Winchcombe and within easy reach of Cheltenham, Gloucester, Stratford-upon-Avon and Worcester.

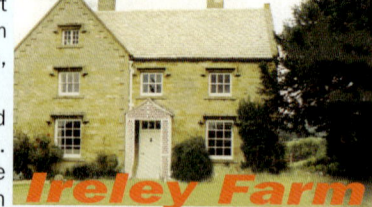

The cosy yet spacious guest rooms (one double and two twin) offer either en suite or private bathroom. Relax in the evening beside a traditional open fire and in the morning enjoy a delicious English breakfast. Families are welcome, to enjoy the unique atmosphere of this working farm.

Ireley Farm

Mrs Margaret Warmington, Ireley Farm, Broadway Road, Winchcombe GL54 5PA
Tel: 01242 602425 • e-mail: warmingtonmaggot@aol.com

B&B from £25 per person.

BOARD 79

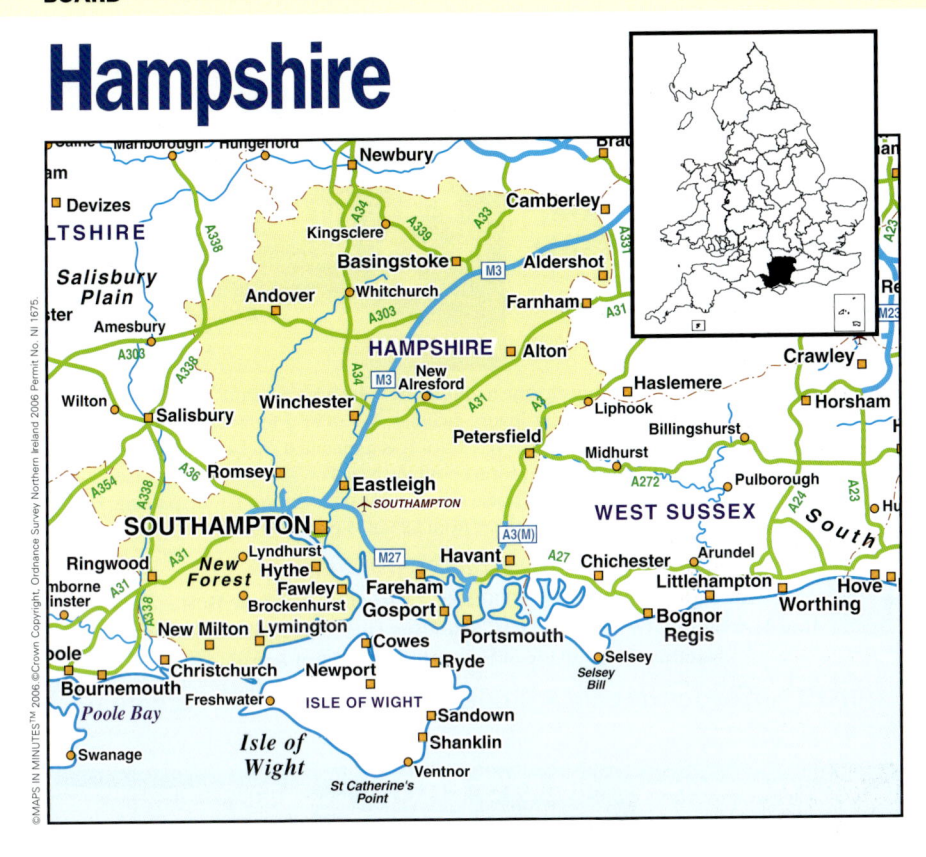

Hampshire

New Forest Ponies. Photo: Joe Low

Efford Cottage

Everton, Lymington, Hampshire SO41 0JD

Tel: 01590 642315
Fax: 01590 641030

Guests receive a warm and friendly welcome to our home, which is a spacious Georgian cottage. All rooms are en suite with many extra luxury facilities. We offer a four-course, multi-choice breakfast with homemade bread and preserves. Patricia is a qualified chef and uses our home-grown produce. An excellent centre for exploring both the New Forest and the South Coast, with sports facilities, fishing, bird watching and horse riding in the near vicinity. Private parking. Dogs welcome. Sorry, no children. Bed and Breakfast from £25–£35 pppn. Mrs Patricia J. Ellis.

Winner of "England For Excellence 2000"
FHG Diploma 1997/1999/2000/2003 / Michelin / Welcome Host
Awards Achieved: Gold Award / RAC Sparkling Diamond & Warm Welcome
Nominated Landlady of Year & Best Breakfast Award.

e-mail: effordcottage@aol.com • www.effordcottage.co.uk

MAYS FARM

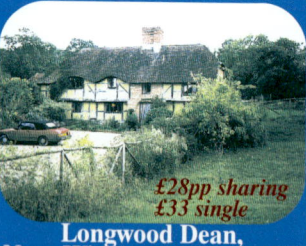

Twelve minutes' drive from Winchester, (the 11th century capital city of England), Mays Farm is set in rolling countryside on a lane which leads from nowhere to nowhere. The house is timber framed, originally built in the 16th century and has been thoroughly renovated and extended by its present owners, James and Rosalie Ashby.

£28pp sharing
£33 single

**Longwood Dean,
Near Winchester SO21 1JS
www.englishbandb.com**

There are three guest bedrooms, (one double, one twin and one either), each with a private bathroom or shower room. Dining room with open log fire and views over terrace and garden. Ducks, geese, chickens and goats make up the two-acre "farm". Booking is essential. Please phone or fax for details.

Tel: 01962 777486
Fax: 01962 777777 (office hours)

Note

All the information in this guide is given in good faith in the belief that it is correct. However, the publishers cannot guarantee the facts given in these pages, neither are they responsible for changes in ownership or facilities that may take place after the date of going to press.
Readers should always satisfy themselves that the facilities they require are available and that the terms, if quoted, still apply.

Herefordshire

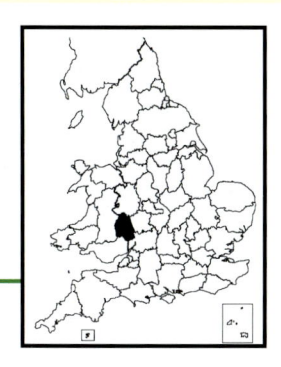

Herefordshire lies on the border with Wales, but is merely a stone's throw from Birmingham, Bristol, the Cotswolds and Cardiff. Green countryside, meandering rivers and acres of traditional cider orchards make up the landscape of this most rural of counties. It is home to the Hereford breed of cattle and has since become recognised for the standard of its local food and drink.

Hereford, a traditional Cathedral City but with the feel of a market town, offers visitors an interesting array of shops, cafes and bistros. The Norman Cathedral is home to the world famous Mappa Mundi, the oldest map of the world, and to the largest Chained Library in the world. The five market towns (Bromyard, Kington, Ledbury, Leominster and Ross-on-Wye) all offer something different to delight the visitor, and the 'Black and White Village' Trail explores a group of villages with beautiful half-timbered houses, cottages and country inns.

There is something for everyone – tranquil gardens, inviting tea-rooms, castles and historic houses, and of course, plenty of fresh country air in which to try canoeing, cycling, pony trekking, or maybe a good walk along one of the many long distance trails that intersect the county, including the recently opened Herefordshire Trail.

Looking for holiday accommodation?

for details of hundreds of properties throughout the UK including comprehensive coverage of all areas of Scotland try:

www.holidayguides.com

Free or reduced rate entry to
Holiday Visits and Attractions – see our
READERS' OFFER VOUCHERS on pages 7-40

Moor Court Farm
Bed and Breakfast

Discover this beautiful 15th century timber-framed farmhouse with its spacious gardens. Set in its own 500 acres, we are easy to find, yet ideally located for access to the local towns of Hereford, Ledbury, Leominster, Bromyard, Ross-on-Wye, Ludlow and Malvern, with the Wye Valley, Black Mountains, Brecon Beacons and the Malvern Hills only a short drive away.

Guests will enjoy spacious en suite bedrooms including a four-poster room, all of which are beautifully furnished. Separate dining room and guests' lounge - ideal for family groups to unwind together at the end of an eventful day. Centrally heated throughout to ensure a comfortable stay. Fabulous catering using fine local ingredients and a variety of local wines. Healthy and wholesome breakfast.

Open all year. Terms from £25 per person based on two sharing, £27 single. Evening meal from £15.
Self-catering holiday cottage also available (sleeps 5).

Moor Court Farm B&B, Stretton Grandison, Ledbury HR8 2TP Tel: 01531 670408

Mrs Jenny Davies
Holgate Farm
Kingsland
Leominster HR6 9QS
Tel: 01568 708275

Set amidst the beautiful North Herefordshire countryside on a family-run stock and arable farm, this attractive 17th Century farmhouse offers a warm, friendly welcome. Within easy reach of the Welsh border country, Hereford, Leominster and Ludlow. Spacious and well appointed bedrooms with tea and coffee trays. Guests' own bathroom and sitting room. Open all year except Christmas and New Year. This is a no smoking house.

B&B £22.50pppn, single room £25.
Reductions for children.

Thatch Close, Llangrove, Ross-on-Wye HR9 6EL

Secluded, peaceful, comfortable Georgian farmhouse, yet convenient for A40, M4 and M50. Our three lovely bedrooms, all en suite, have magnificent views over the unspoilt countryside. Relax in the visitors' lounge or sit in the shade of mature trees in our garden. You may be greeted by our dog or free flying parrot. Terms from £30 per person (sharing). Please telephone or e-mail for brochure.
Wildlife Action Gold Award.

Mrs M.E. Drzymalski (01989 770300)

e-mail: info@thatchclose.co.uk • website: www.thatchclose.co.uk

Isle of Wight

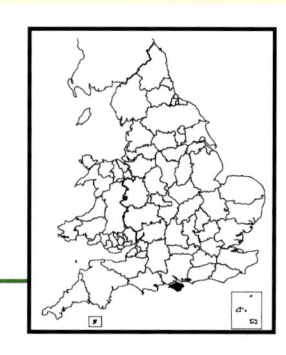

The Isle of Wight has several award-winning beaches, including Blue Flag winners, all of which are managed and maintained to the highest standard. Sandown, Shanklin and Ryde offer all the traditional delights; or head for Compton Bay where surfers brave the waves, fossil hunters admire the casts of dinosaur footprints at low tide, kitesurfers leap and soar across the sea and paragliders hurl themselves off the cliffs

Newport is the commercial centre of the Island with many famous high street stores and plenty of places to eat and drink. Ryde has a lovely Victorian Arcade lined with shops selling books and antiques. Cowes is great for sailing garb and Godshill is a treasure chest for the craft enthusiast. Lovers of fine food will enjoy the weekly farmers' markets selling home-grown produce and also the Garlic Festival held annually in August.

Many attractions are out of doors to take advantage of the Island's milder than average temperatures. However, if it should rain, there's plenty to choose from. There are vineyards offering wine tasting, cinemas, theatres and nightclubs as well as sports and leisure centres, a bowling alley and an ice skating rink, home to the Island's very own ice hockey team – the Wight Raiders.

The Island's diverse terrain makes it an ideal landscape for walkers and cyclists of all ages and abilities. Pony trekking and beach rides are also popular holiday pursuits and the Island's superb golf courses, beautiful scenery and temperate climate combine to make it the perfect choice for a golfing break.

Frenchman's Cove
ALUM BAY OLD ROAD, TOTLAND, ISLE OF WIGHT PO39 0HZ

Our delightful family-run guesthouse is set amongst National Trust downland, not far from the Needles and safe sandy beaches. Ideal for ramblers, birdwatchers, cyclists and those who enjoy the countryside. We have almost an acre of grounds. Cots and high chairs are available. All rooms are en suite, with colour TV and tea/coffee making facilities. Guests can relax in the attractive lounges. Also available is the Coach House, a well appointed self-catering apartment (ETC 3 Stars) for two adults and two children. No smoking. No pets.

Please contact Sue or Chris Boatfield for details.
Tel: 01983 752227 • www.frenchmanscove.co.uk

Kent

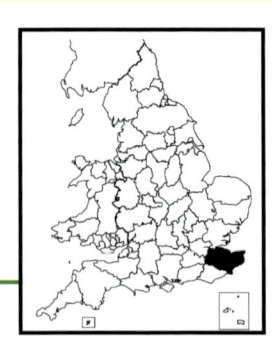

Upper Ansdore

Beautiful secluded Listed Tudor farmhouse with various livestock, situated in an elevated position with far-reaching views of the wooded countryside of the North Downs. The property overlooks a Kent Trust Nature Reserve, is five miles south of the cathedral city of Canterbury and only 30 minutes' drive to the ports of Dover and Folkestone. The accommodation comprises one family, three double and one twin-bedded rooms. All have shower and WC en suite and tea making facilities. Dining/sitting room, heavily beamed with large inglenook. Pets welcome. Car essential.

Tel: 01227 700672

Bed and Breakfast from £27.50 per person. Credit cards accepted.
Mr and Mrs R. Linch, Upper Ansdore, Duckpit Lane, Petham, Canterbury CT4 5QB
e-mail: rogerd@talktalk.net • www.upperansdore.co.uk

Great Field Farm

Stelling Minnis, Canterbury, Kent CT4 6DE
Tel: 01227 709223

Situated in beautiful countryside, our spacious farmhouse provides friendly, comfortable accommodation.
• Full central heating and double glazing.
• Traditional breakfasts cooked on the Aga.
• Courtesy tray and colour TV in each suite/bedroom.
• Cottage suite with its own entrance.
• Both Annexe suite and new detached ground floor "Sunset Lodge" ideal for B&B and self-catering.
• Ample off-road parking.
• Good pub food nearby. • Non-smoking establishment.

**Bed and Breakfast from £25 per person;
Ask about reductions for children.**

Bed & Breakfast • Self-Catering • www.great-field-farm.co.uk

Bleriot's ••• Dover

A Victorian residence set in a tree-lined avenue, in the lee of Dover Castle. Within easy reach of trains, bus station, town centre, ferries and cruise terminal. Channel Tunnel approximately 10 minutes' drive. Off-road parking. We specialise in one night 'stop-overs' and mini-breaks. Single, double, twin and family rooms with full en suite. All rooms have colour TV, tea and coffee making facilities, and are fully centrally heated. Full English breakfast served from 7am. Reduced rates for room only. Open all year. MasterCard and Visa accepted.

Bed and Breakfast £24 to £28 per person per night.
Mini-Breaks January to April and October to December £21 per person per night.

**Bleriot's, 47 Park Avenue, Dover CT16 1HE • Tel: 01304 211394
e-mail: info@bleriots.net • www.bleriots.net**

Lancashire

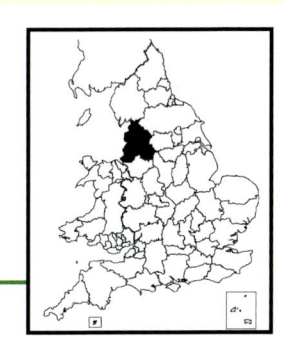

Rakefoot Farm
Chaigley, Near Clitheroe BB7 3LY
VisitBritain ★★★★
VisitBritain ★★★/★★★★

Tel: (Chipping) 01995 61332 or 07889 279063 • Fax: 01995 61296
e-mail: info@rakefootfarm.co.uk • website: www.rakefootfarm.co.uk

Family farm in the beautiful countryside of the Ribble Valley in the peaceful Forest of Bowland, with panoramic views. Ideally placed for touring Coast, Dales and Lakes. 9 miles M6 Junction 31a. Superb walks, golf and horse riding nearby, or visit pretty villages and factory shops. Warm welcome whether on holiday or business, refreshments on arrival.

BED AND BREAKFAST or SELF-CATERING in 17th century farmhouse and traditional stone barn conversion. Wood-burning stoves, central heating, exposed beams and stonework. Most bedrooms en suite, some ground floor. Excellent home cooked meals, pubs/restaurants nearby. Indoor games room, garden and patios. Dogs by arrangement. Laundry. **Past winner of NWTB Silver Award for Self-catering Holiday of the Year.**

B&B £20 - £32.50pppn sharing, £20 - £37.50pn single
S/C four properties (3 can be internally interlinked)
£100 - £595 per property per week. Short breaks available.

Sandy Brook Farm,
52 Wyke Cop Road, Scarisbrick, Southport PR8 5LR

Bill and Wendy Core offer a homely, friendly atmosphere at Sandy Brook, a small working farm situated three-and-a-half miles from the seaside resort of Southport and five miles from the historic town of Ormskirk. Motorways are easily accessible, and the Lake District, Trough of Bowland, Blackpool and North Wales are within easy reach. Six en suite bedrooms with colour TV and tea/coffee making facilities. Room available for disabled guests. Open all year except Christmas. Bed and Breakfast from £19. Reductions for children. Weekly terms on request.

ETC ◆◆◆
NWTB SILVER AWARD WINNER "PLACE TO STAY" FARMHOUSE CATEGORY

01704 880337 • www.sandybrookfarm.co.uk
e-mail: sandybrookfarm@lycos.co.uk

Visit the FHG website
www.holidayguides.com
for details of the wide choice of accommodation featured in the full range of FHG titles

Leicestershire and Rutland

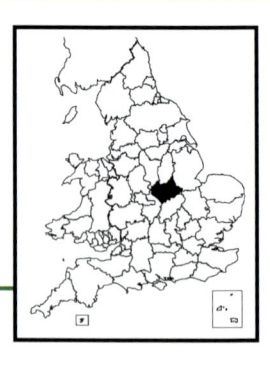

THE Old Rectory

Belton-in-Rutland, Oakham LE15 9LE
Tel: 01572 717279 • Fax: 01572 717343

Guest accommodation. Victorian country house and guest annexe in charming village overlooking Eyebrook valley and rolling Rutland countryside. Comfortable and varied selection of rooms, mostly en suite, with direct outside access. Prices from £25 per person per night including breakfast. Small farm environment (horses and sheep) with excellent farmhouse breakfast. Public House 100 yards. Lots to see and do: Rutland Water, castles, stately homes, country parks, forestry and Barnsdale Gardens. Non-smoking. Self catering also available.

e-mail: bb@iepuk.com   www.theoldrectorybelton.co.uk

Grange Farm Bed & Breakfast

Enjoy friendly hospitality at our 460-acre working farm, in peaceful open countryside. Our spacious stone farmhouse offers tasteful decor, elegant dining room (log fire), large conservatory, and extensive gardens. Excellent farmhouse breakfast, including local produce, fresh fruit and home-made preserves. Close to Rutland, Barnsdale Gardens, Uppingham, Oakham, Stamford (Burghley House) and Rockingham Speedway.

Non-smoking. TV and tea/coffee in all rooms. One en suite family room, one en suite double, and one double/twin with private bathroom.
Double from £27.50pppn, single from £35pn.

Mrs Sue Reading, Grange Farm, Seaton, Uppingham, Rutland LE15 9HT
Tel: 01572 747664 • Mobile: 07748 527469
e-mail: david.reading@farmline.com
www.SmoothHound.co.uk/hotels/grangefarm

Looking for holiday accommodation?
for details of hundreds of properties throughout the UK visit:

www.holidayguides.com

Lincolnshire

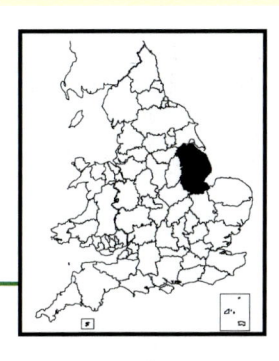

An early 18th century Listed farmhouse with spacious en suite bedrooms and original beamed ceilings. Enjoy a generous farmhouse breakfast using fresh local produce. Centrally located for five 'Bomber Country' museums, championship golf at Woodhall Spa, antiques at Horncastle and local fishing. Historic pubs nearby serving excellent evening meals. Within easy reach of the east coast and the Lincolnshire Wolds. One double and one twin bedroom. Central heating, tea and coffee facilities and colour TV.
Open all year except Christmas • No smoking
Children welcome • B&B from £20pp;
reductions for three days or more.

Mrs C. Whittington, High House Farm, Tumby Moorside, Near Coningsby, Boston PE22 7ST • Tel: 01526 345408 • e-mail: HighHousefarm@aol.com

Other specialised holiday guides from FHG

Recommended **INNS & PUBS** OF BRITAIN
Recommended **COUNTRY HOTELS** OF BRITAIN
Recommended **SHORT BREAK HOLIDAYS** IN BRITAIN
The bestselling and original **PETS WELCOME!**
The **GOLF GUIDE,** *Where to Play, Where to Stay* IN BRITAIN & IRELAND
COAST & COUNTRY HOLIDAYS
SELF-CATERING HOLIDAYS IN BRITAIN
BED & BREAKFAST STOPS
CARAVAN & CAMPING HOLIDAYS
CHILDREN WELCOME! Family Holiday & Days Out Guide
BRITAIN'S BEST LEISURE & RELAXATION GUIDE

Published annually: available in all good bookshops or direct from the publisher:
FHG Guides, Abbey Mill Business Centre, Seedhill, Paisley PA1 1TJ
Tel: 0141 887 0428 • Fax: 0141 889 7204
• E-mail: admin@fhguides.co.uk • Web: www.holidayguides.com

Baumber Park

Spacious elegant farmhouse in quiet parkland setting, on a mixed farm. Large plantsman's garden, wildlife pond and grass tennis court. Fine bedrooms with lovely views, period furniture, log fires and books. Central in the county and close to the Lincolnshire Wolds, this rolling countryside is little known, quite unspoilt, and ideal for walking, cycling or riding. Championship golf courses at Woodhall Spa. Well located for historic Lincoln, interesting market towns and many antique shops. Enjoy a relaxing break, excellent breakfasts, and a comfortable, homely atmosphere.

2 Doubles, 1 twin room. All en suite or private bathroom.
Bed and Breakfast from £29.

Mrs C.E. Harrison, Baumber Park, Baumber, Near Horncastle LN9 5NE
01407 578425 • Fax: 01507 578417 • mobile: 07977 722776
www.baumberpark.com

Bed & Breakfast at No. 19 West Street
Kings Cliffe, Near Stamford, Peterborough PE8 6XB
Tel: 01780 470365 • Fax 01780 470623

A beautifully restored 500-year-old Listed stone house, reputedly one of King John's Hunting Lodges, situated in the heart of the stone village of Kings Cliffe on the edge of Rockingham Forest. Both the double and twin rooms have their own private bathrooms, and there is colour TV and a welcome tray in each. In the summer breakfast can be served on the terrace overlooking a beautiful walled garden. Off-street parking is behind secure gates. Within 10 miles there are seven stately homes, including Burghley House famous for the Horse Trials, Rutland Water, and the beautiful old towns of Stamford and Oundle. Open all year.

A non-smoking house • Bed and Breakfast from £25 per person • Proprietor: Jenny Dixon
e-mail: kjhl_dixon@hotmail.com • www.kingjohnhuntinglodge.co.uk

---

**Mrs S. Evans, Willow Farm,
Thorpe Fendykes, Wainfleet,
Skegness PE24 4QH
Tel: 01754 830316
Email: willowfarmhols@aol.com
Website: www.willowfarmholidays.co.uk**

In the heart of the Lincolnshire Fens, Willow Farm is a working smallholding with free range hens, goats, horses and ponies. Situated in a peaceful hamlet with abundant wildlife, ideal for a quiet retreat – yet only 15 minutes from the Skegness coast, shops, amusements and beaches.
Also 1 bedroom self-catering Cottage available from 2006.

Bed and Breakfast is provided in comfortable en suite rooms from £20 per person per night, reductions for children (suppers and sandwiches can be provided in the evening on request). Rooms have tea and coffee making facilities and a colour TV and are accessible to disabled guests. Also one bed self-catering cottage available from 2006. Friendly hosts! Ring for brochure.

Please note

All the information in this book is given in good faith in the belief that it is correct. However, the publishers cannot guarantee the facts given in these pages, neither are they responsible for changes in policy, ownership or terms that may take place after the date of going to press. Readers should always satisfy themselves that the facilities they require are available and that the terms, if quoted, still apply.

BOARD Diss

NORFOLK 89

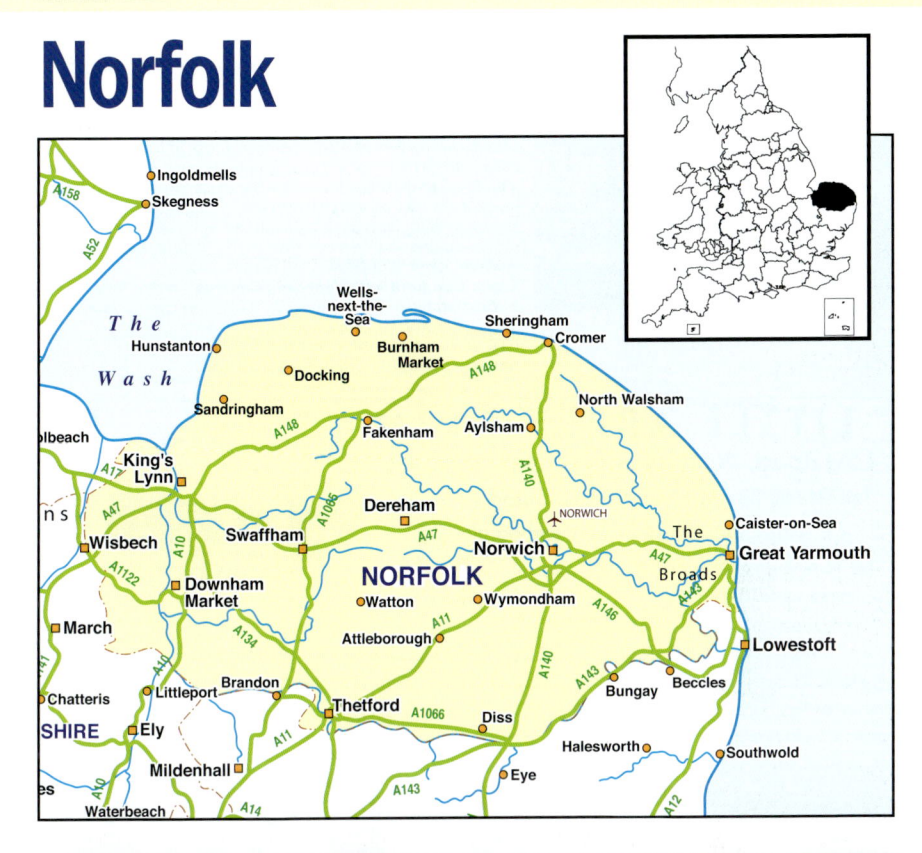

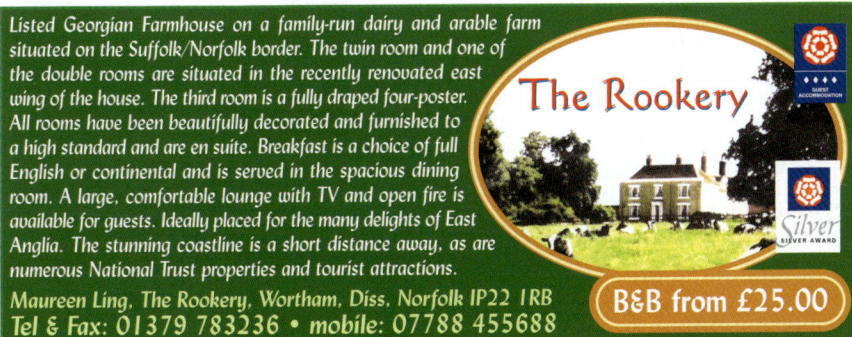

Norfolk

The Rookery

Listed Georgian Farmhouse on a family-run dairy and arable farm situated on the Suffolk/Norfolk border. The twin room and one of the double rooms are situated in the recently renovated east wing of the house. The third room is a fully draped four-poster. All rooms have been beautifully decorated and furnished to a high standard and are en suite. Breakfast is a choice of full English or continental and is served in the spacious dining room. A large, comfortable lounge with TV and open fire is available for guests. Ideally placed for the many delights of East Anglia. The stunning coastline is a short distance away, as are numerous National Trust properties and tourist attractions.

Maureen Ling, The Rookery, Wortham, Diss, Norfolk IP22 1RB
Tel & Fax: 01379 783236 • mobile: 07788 455688

B&B from £25.00

The FHG Directory of Website Addresses

on pages 277-310 is a useful quick reference guide for holiday accommodation with e-mail and/or website details

FHG
K·U·P·E·R·A·R·D

HOLT Mrs Lynda Mack, Hempstead Hall, Holt NR25 6TN (01263 712224).

Enjoy a relaxing holiday with a friendly atmosphere in our 19th century flint farmhouse, beautifully set on a 300 acre arable farm with ducks, donkey and large gardens. Close to the north Norfolk coast and its many attractions. Take a ride on the steam train or a boat trip to Blakeney Point Seal Sanctuary. Spot the wild deer or the barn owl on the circular walk through our conservation award-winning farm to Holt Country Park. Large en suite family room, double with private bathroom. Colour TV, tea/coffee facilities. Large lounge with log burning stove.

Rates: B&B from £28 per person. Children's reductions.
• Working farm. • Non-smoking. • Children over 8 years only, please. • Sorry, no pets indoors.
ETC ★★★★, *FARM STAY UK MEMBER.*
www.broadland.com/hempsteadhall

LITTLE ABBEY FARM
Low Road, Pentney, King's Lynn PE32 1JF
Tel: 01760 337348 • www.littleabbeyfarm.co.uk
enquiries@littleabbeyfarm.co.uk

This is a traditional working farm offering bed and breakfast accommodation in an annexe to the main farmhouse. One twin and two double rooms available, all on one level on the ground floor and comfortably furnished in country-style pine. There is a guests' lounge with TV, DVD and wood burning fire. Evening Meals are available. Ample parking. The farm is situated close to Sandringham, King's Lynn and the Norfolk coast, and there is a good range of footpaths for walkers. All rooms are non-smoking. Sorry, no pets. **Contact:** Mrs D. Howlett.

Greenacres Farmhouse
Woodgreen, Long Stratton, Norwich NR15 2RR

Period 17th century farmhouse on 30 acre common with ponds and natural wildlife, 10 miles south of Norwich (A140). The beamed sittingroom with inglenook fireplace invites you to relax. A large sunny dining room encourages you to enjoy a leisurely traditional breakfast. All en suite bedrooms (two double/twin) are tastefully furnished to complement the oak beams and period feature and TV, with tea/coffee facilities and TV. Full size snooker table and all-weather tennis court for guests' use. Jo is trained in therapeutic massage, aromatherapy and reflexology and is able to offer this to guests who feel it would be of benefit. Come and enjoy the peace and tranquillity of our home. Bed and Breakfast from £25. Reductions for two nights or more. Non-smoking.

Tel: 01508 530261 • website: www.abreakwithtradition.co.uk

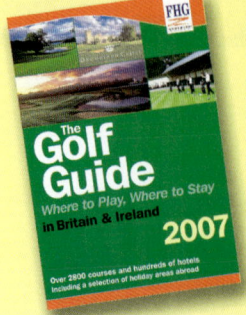

The Golf Guide · 2007
Where to Play, Where to Stay

Available from most booksellers, **The Golf Guide, Where to Play, Where to Stay** covers details of every UK golf course – well over 2800 entries – for holiday or business golf. Hundreds of hotel entries offer convenient accommodation, with accompanying details of the courses – the 'pro', par score, length and more. Including holiday golf in Ireland, France, Portugal, Spain, the USA, South Africa and Thailand.

Only £9.99 from booksellers or direct from the publishers: FHG Guides, Abbey Mill Business Centre, Seedhill, Paisley PA1 1TJ (postage charged outside UK)

BOARD Norfolk Broads (Neatishead), Norwich, Wymondham   NORFOLK **91**

NORFOLK BROADS (NEATISHEAD) Alan and Sue Wrigley, Regency Guest House, The Street, Neatishead, Near Norwich NR12 8AD (Tel & Fax: 01692 630233).
An 18th century guest house in picturesque, unspoilt village in heart of Broadlands. Personal service top priority - same owners for 28 years. Long established name for very generous English Breakfasts. 20 minutes from medieval city of Norwich and six miles from coast. Ideal base for touring East Anglia - a haven for wildlife, birdwatching, cycling and walking holidays. Number one centre for Broads sailing, fishing and boating. Guesthouse, holder of "Good Care" award for high quality services, has three bedrooms (king-size double or twin en suite, double en suite, and standard king-size or twin), individually Laura Ashley-style decorated and tastefully furnished with TV and tea/coffee making facilities. Two main bathrooms. Separate tables in beamed ceiling breakfast room. Guests' sittingroom. Parking. Fire Certificate held. There are two good eating places within walking distance of guest house.
Rates: Bed and Breakfast from £26. Reduced rates on stays of more than one night.
• Pets welcome. • Cot, babysitting. • Open all year
AA/ETC ♦♦♦♦ ETC *SILVER AWARD.*
e-mail: regencywrigley@btopenworld.com   www.regencyguesthouse.com
www.go2norfolk.co.uk

Wensum Valley Hotel, Golf & Country Club
Norwich, Norfolk

Golf & Leisure Breaks from just £65.00 pppn
Two 18 hole golf courses
Leisure Centre with Health & Beauty Salon
Set in 350 acres of the beautiful Wensum Valley ...
... The perfect location to relax & unwind.
Tel: 01603 261012
www.wensumvalleyhotel.co.uk

WYMONDHAM Mrs Joy Morter, Home Farm, Morley, Wymondham NR18 9SU (01953 602581).
Comfortable accommodation set in four acres, quiet location, secluded garden. Conveniently situated off A11 between Attleborough and Wymondham, an excellent location for Snetterton and only 20 minutes from Norwich and 45 minutes from the Norfolk Broads. Accommodation comprises two double rooms and one twin-bedded room, all with TV, tea/coffee facilities and central heating.
Rates: Bed and Breakfast from £27 to £30 per person per night.
• Children over five years old welcome. • Sorry no animals
• Non-smoking.

Looking for holiday accommodation?
for details of hundreds of properties
throughout the UK visit:

www.holidayguides.com

Northamptonshire

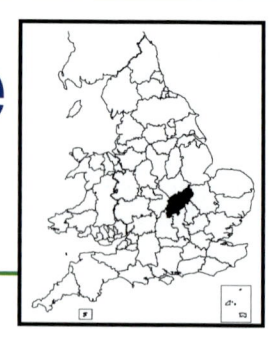

Kettering

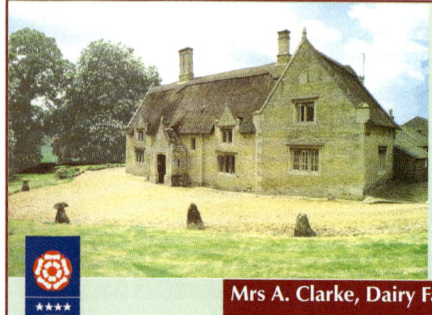

ENJOY A HOLIDAY in our comfortable 17th century farmhouse with oak beams and inglenook fireplaces. Four-poster bed now available. Peaceful surroundings, large garden containing ancient circular dovecote. Dairy Farm is a working farm situated in a beautiful Northamptonshire village just off the A14, within easy reach of many places of interest or ideal for a restful holiday. Good farmhouse food and friendly atmosphere. Open all year, except Christmas. Bed and Breakfast from £28 to £38 (children under 10 half price); Evening Meal £17.

Mrs A. Clarke, Dairy Farm, Cranford St Andrew, Kettering NN14 4AQ
Telephone: 01536 330273

Northumberland

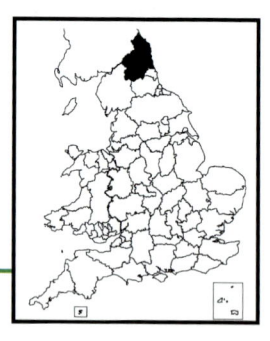

Haltwhistle

Saughy Rigg Farm
info@saughyrigg.co.uk
www.saughyrigg.co.uk

- High quality en suite rooms
- Delicious home-cooked food
- Open to non-residents
- Pets and families welcome

From £25pppn

Saughy Rigg Farm, Twice Brewed, Haltwhistle, Northumberland NE49 9PT • Tel: 01434 344120

BOARD Hexham, Kirkwhelpington, Otterburn, Seahouses **NORTHUMBERLAND** 93

❖ Struthers Farm ❖
Catton, Allendale, Hexham NE47 9LP

Struthers Farm offers a warm welcome in the heart of England, with many splendid local walks from the farm itself. Panoramic views. Situated in an area of outstanding beauty. Double/twin rooms, en suite bathrooms, central heating. Good farmhouse cooking. Ample safe parking. Come and share our home and enjoy beautiful countryside. Near Hadrians Wall (½ hour's drive). Children welcome, pets by prior arrangement. Open all year. Bed and Breakfast from £25; Optional Evening Meal from £12.50.

Contact Mrs Ruby Keenleyside ❖ **01434 683580**

Horncastle Farm B&B

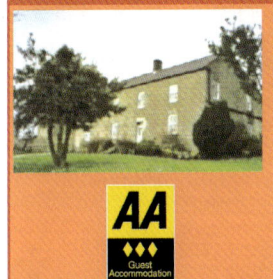

A traditional family stock farm with stunning views across the rolling countryside. Set in 307 acres, we offer comfortable accommodation decorated to a high standard with use of separate guest sitting/TV room. Organic meats for breakfast, large well stocked garden. Ideally situated for touring Northumbrian/ Scottish Borders. Open all year except April and Christmas. Children welcome. No smoking. B&B £25pp.

Mrs Susan Pittendrigh, Horncastle Farm,
Kirkwhelpington NE19 2RA
Tel: 01830 540247 • mobile: 07721 639775

Otterburn Tower Country House Hotel & Restaurant
Otterburn NE19 1NT • 01830 520620

Dating back to a cousin of William the Conqueror, this AA ★★★ hotel possesses a unique blend of history and comfort. The food is prepared from fresh local produce wherever possible - often from the owners' farm. Each bedroom is en suite with its own piece of history. Ideal for relaxing, exploring the coast, Kielder Water, Alnwick Castle or perhaps learning to quad bike or shoot clay pigeons. Explore the wild valley of Redesdale - only a short trip from the Scottish Borders.

Special midweek breaks - 25% discount.
Dinner, Bed & Breakfast £85 pppn.
Christmas and New Year special two-night breaks - ask for brochure.

e-mail: info@otterburntower.com
www.otterburntower.com

Wyndgrove House

A warm and friendly welcome awaits you at Wyndgrove House. Quietly situated within short walking distance of the sea front. Newly refurbished, comfortable rooms all with en suite facilities. Four poster, double, family and ground floor twin rooms available. *No smoking*. Vegetarian breakfast on request. Perfectly located for the beautiful coast and countryside with its many historic castles. Ideally based for birdwatching, walking, golfing, diving, horse riding and cycling. By boat you can visit Holy Island and the Farne Islands, with colonies of seals and seabirds.
Short drive to Bamburgh and Alnwick. B&B from £30 pppn.

Paul and Donna, Wyndgrove House, 156 Main Street, Seahouses NE68 7UA • 01665 722855

Oxfordshire

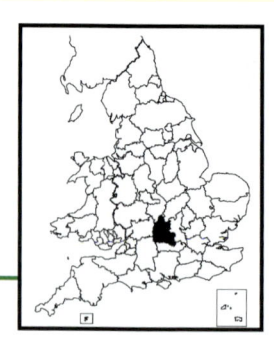

THE OLD BAKERY
Skirmett, Near Henley-on-Thames RG9 6TD

This welcoming family house is situated on the site of an old bakery, seven miles from Henley-on-Thames and Marlow; half-an-hour from Heathrow and Oxford; one hour from London. It is in the Hambleden Valley in the beautiful Chilterns, with many excellent pubs selling good food nearby. Excellent village pub in Skirmett within easy walking distance. One double en suite, one twin-bedded room and one double with use of own bathroom. All with TV and tea making facilities. Open all year. Parking for five cars (car essential). Children and pets welcome.

Bed and Breakfast from £30 single; £60 double, £75 en suite.

e-mail: lizzroach@aol.com
Tel: 01491 638309 • Office: 01491 410716
Fax: 01491 638086

Conifer Lodge

New, luxury stone house on the outskirts of Oxford, only 2 miles frequent bus service to the city centre, yet situated in the peace and quiet of the countryside.

Central heating in all rooms • Double glazed throughout • Colour TV • Large garden and patio • Parking

B&B from £35 per person - business persons welcome.
No cancellations accepted within 7 days of booking.

**Conifer Lodge, 159 Eynsham Road, Oxford OX2 9NE
Tel: 01865 862280 • www.smoothhound.co.uk/oxford**

Fords Farm
Ewelme, Wallingford OX10 6HU
Tel: 01491 839272
e-mail: fordsfarm@callnetuk.com

500-acre mixed farm, arable, beef and sheep. Attractive farmhouse set in historic part of village with famous church almshouses and school. Peaceful surroundings with good walks and good selection of pubs nearby. Easy access to Henley, Oxford, Reading, Windsor, Heathrow and London. Friendly and comfortable atmosphere. Two twin rooms and one double room. No smoking. *Contact Marlene Edwards*

Shropshire

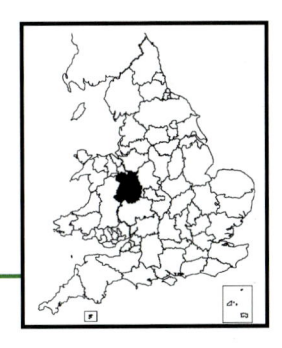

Shropshire is perhaps less well-known than other English counties. This is despite being the birthplace of Charles Darwin, home to the world's first iron bridge (now a World Heritage Site), having not one, but two of the finest medieval towns in England, inspiring the creation of the modern Olympics, and being the kingdom of the real King Arthur. After all, Shropshire is easy enough to find and get to from almost anywhere. (Hint: just north of Birmingham or south of Manchester depending on your direction of travel, and sitting snugly on the Welsh borders).

It may also come as a surprise to find out just how much is on offer. There are plenty of indoor and outdoor attractions, so the weather isn't a problem either. In Ironbridge, you can step into the past at the Ironbridge Gorge Museums where you'll find 10 museums to visit, all following the history of the Industrial Revolution. For retail therapy at its best, small independent shops can be found in all its market towns, full of those special 'somethings' you were looking for and even some things you weren't.

Shrewsbury is the beautiful county town, and home (naturally enough) to the Shrewsbury Summer Season – packed with over 200 events including the Shrewsbury Flower Show and the Cartoon Festival. There is also the Darwin Festival to celebrate the town's most famous son, and the foot-tapping Folk Festival. Ludlow, a medieval town, once the seat of the Welsh parliament, and now famed equally for its events and food, is also full of surprises. The Ludlow Festival is an annual two week gathering of actors, musicians, singers, entertainers, and generally some blooming interesting people to keep you rather amused.

All in all, Shropshire has a surprising amount to offer. So take the Shropshire option – for a great day out, fresh clean air and no jams (except those the W.I. make!).

Rectory Farm

Woolstaston, Church Stretton SY6 6NN
Tel: 01694 751306
e-mail: rectory.farm@btconnect.com
www.stmem.com/rectoryfarm

Rectory Farm is a beautiful half-timbered farmhouse which happily combines unspoilt, ancient charm with first class modern accommodation in the heart of the Shropshire highlands.

Three comfortable bedrooms: one double and two twin-bedded, each with colour TV and a well appointed en suite bathroom. All give panoramic views of the countryside. Tea/coffee facilities in rooms. Guests may also relax in the spacious oak-beamed lounge and cosy television room. No dogs or children under 12.

"The Best Bed & Breakfast in the Cotswolds & the Welsh Marches"
The Worldwide Bed & Breakfast Association

Explore beautiful countryside ✱ Historic houses and gardens ✱ Castles & Hill Forts ✱ Shrewsbury ✱ Ludlow ✱ Ironbridge ✱ Horse riding ✱ Golf ✱ Rambling ✱ Bird watching

96 SHROPSHIRE   Church Stretton **BOARD**

Lovely 17th century farmhouse in peaceful village amidst the beautiful South Shropshire Hills, an Area of Outstanding Natural Beauty. The farmhouse is full of character and all rooms have heating and are comfortable and spacious. The bedrooms are either en suite or private bathroom with hairdryers, tea/coffee making facilities, patchwork quilts and colour TV. There is a lounge with colour TV and inglenook fireplace. Children welcome. We are a working farm, centrally situated for visiting Ironbridge, Shrewsbury and Ludlow, each being easily reached within half an hour. Touring and walking information is available for visitors. Bed and full English Breakfast from £24pppn. Non-smoking. Open all year excluding November, December and January.

Mrs Mary Jones, Acton Scott Farm, Acton Scott, Church Stretton SY6 6QN • Tel: 01694 781260
Fax: 0870-129 4591 • e-mail: fhg@actonscottfarm.co.uk • www.actonscottfarm.co.uk

Rooms with a view... North Hill Farm
Cardington, Church Stretton SY6 7LL
Tel: 01694 771532

AA ♦♦♦♦

Bed and Breakfast accommodation in the beautiful Shropshire hills, one mile from Cardington village. Quiet, rural setting with plenty of wildlife. Ideal walking and riding country. Rooms have wonderful views with TV & hot drinks tray. Great local pubs. Well behaved dogs and horses welcome. Bed and full English breakfast from £25 per person. En suite courtyard room £30 per person. Dogs £2 per night. Non-Smoking.

Mrs Chris Brandon-Lodge
e-mail: cbrandon@btinternet.com • www.virtual-shropshire.co.uk/northhill/

Malt House Farm

Olde worlde beamed farmhouse situated amidst spectacular scenery at the lower slopes of the Long Mynd Hills. We are a working farm producing beef cattle and sheep. One double bedroom and one twin, both with en-suite bathroom, colour TV, hairdryer and tea tray. Good farmhouse cooking is served in the dining room. Private guests' sitting room.
Non-smoking • Regret no children or pets

AA ♦♦♦ Guest Accommodation

Bed and Breakfast from £25pppn • Evening meal from £15 per person

Malt House Farm, Lower Wood, Church Stretton SY6 6LF
Tel: 01694 751379 • Proprietor: Mrs Lyn Bloor

Court Farm

Our traditional family farm is situated in the peaceful and secluded hamlet of Gretton, in an Area of Outstanding Natural Beauty.
Here you can escape the pressures of modern life in our Grade II Listed 17th century home; relax in front of a log fire or enjoy the setting of our country garden.
Accommodation comprises one double room and one twin room, both en suite.
We are within easy reach of Shrewsbury, Ironbridge, Ludlow and Bridgnorth.

Non-smoking. Bed and Breakfast from £27.50 per person.
Open all year except Christmas. Awaiting Inspection.

Mrs Alison Norris, Court Farm, Gretton, Church Stretton SY6 7HU • 01694 771219

BOARD Craven Arms, Ludlow, Newport, Oswestry   SHROPSHIRE 97

SPRINGHILL FARM is a working farm in an idyllic situation on the Offa's Dyke footpath in glorious South Shropshire countryside with panoramic views over hills and valleys. Walks from the front door. This is a place to relax and unwind away from the pressures of life. Close by are Ludlow, Church Stretton, Ironbridge. All rooms en suite. Evening meals are provided.

Ingrid Evans, Springhill Farm, Clun, Craven Arms SY7 8PE
Tel & Fax: 01588 640337

Relax in our early 19th century farmhouse, with many original features, oak stairs lead to comfortable rooms (one en suite, another planned), all with TV, tea/coffee making facilities and views over the beautiful, unspoilt countryside. Large attractive garden. Approximately two miles from the A49 and within easy reach of Ludlow, National Trust Properties, gardens and lovely villages. Private carp fishing. Walk by the river, sample local foods. Combine your visit with the Ludlow Festival or one of its many other events. AA ★★★

B&B from £24 per person per night.
Evening meal - check price and availability. Non-smoking.
Pets by arrangement. Children over six years welcome.

**Mrs Rachel Edwards, Haynall Villa,
Little Hereford, Near Ludlow SY8 4BA • Tel & Fax: 01584 711589
e-mail: rachelmedwards@hotmail.com • www.haynallvilla.co.uk**

Sambrook Manor
Sambrook, Newport TF10 8AL

Sambrook is a quiet, pretty village set in picturesque countryside close to the Shrops/Staffs border and within easy reach of Lilleshall sports centre, H.A.A.C., Ironbridge, Shrewsbury, Stafford and the Potteries. The charming historic Listed manor house (1702 AD) offers comfortable bedrooms, all en suite with TV and tea tray, and a relaxing lounge and conservatory, which opens on to a large garden. Full English breakfast cooked to your individual taste. Close to the Shropshire Union Canal and the national cycle network and with easy access to the Midlands motorway network. Local pub/restaurant within walking distance, also local fishing and horse riding. Stabling available and many accessible bridle paths. Private on-site parking. Boot room and cycle shelter. B&B Double/Twin £25, Single £30, reduction for children.

www.sambrookmanor.com

Tel: 01952 550256 • mobile: 07811 915535

TOP FARM HOUSE Knockin, Near Oswestry SY10 8HN

Full of charm and character, this beautiful 16th century Grade 1 Listed black and white house is set in the delightful village of Knockin. Enjoy the relaxed atmosphere and elegant surroundings of this special house with its abundance of beams. Sit in the comfortable drawing room where you can read, listen to music, or just relax with a glass of wine (please feel free to bring your own tipple). Hearty breakfasts from our extensive menu are served in the lovely dining room which looks out over the garden. The large bedrooms are all en suite, attractively decorated and furnished. All have tea/coffee making facilities, colour TV, etc. Convenient for the Welsh Border, Shrewsbury, Chester and Oswestry. Friendly hosts and great atmosphere. Bed and Breakfast from £27.50 to £35.

Telephone: 01691 682582
E-mail: p.a.m@knockin.freeserve.co.uk

Ratings & Awards

For the first time ever the AA, VisitBritain, VisitScotland, and the Wales Tourist Board will use a single method of assessing and rating serviced accommodation. Irrespective of which organisation inspects an establishment the rating awarded will be the same, using a common set of standards, giving a clear guide of what to expect. The RAC is no longer operating an Hotel inspection and accreditation business.

Accommodation Standards: Star Grading Scheme

Using a scale of 1-5 stars the objective quality ratings give a clear indication of accommodation standard, cleanliness, ambience, hospitality, service and food, This shows the full range of standards suitable for every budget and preference, and allows visitors to distinguish between the quality of accommodation and facilities on offer in different establishments. All types of board and self-catering accommodation are covered, including hotels, B&Bs, holiday parks, campus accommodation, hostels, caravans and camping, and boats.

The more stars, the higher level of quality

★★★★★
exceptional quality, with a degree of luxury

★★★★
excellent standard throughout

★★★
very good level of quality and comfort

★★
good quality, well presented and well run

★
acceptable quality; simple, practical, no frills

VisitBritain and the regional tourist boards, **enjoyEngland.com**, **VisitScotland** and **VisitWales**, and **the AA** have full details of the grading system on their websites

National Accessible Scheme

If you have particular mobility, visual or hearing needs, look out for the National Accessible Scheme. You can be confident of finding accommodation or attractions that meet your needs by looking for the following symbols.

Typically suitable for a person with sufficient mobility to climb a flight of steps but would benefit from fixtures and fittings to aid balance

Typically suitable for a person with restricted walking ability and for those that may need to use a wheelchair some of the time and can negotiate a maximum of three steps

Typically suitable for a person who depends on the use of a wheelchair and transfers unaided to and from the wheelchair in a seated position. This person may be an independent traveller

Typically suitable for a person who depends on the use of a wheelchair in a seated position. This person also requires personal or mechanical assistance (eg carer, hoist).

BOARD

SOMERSET 99

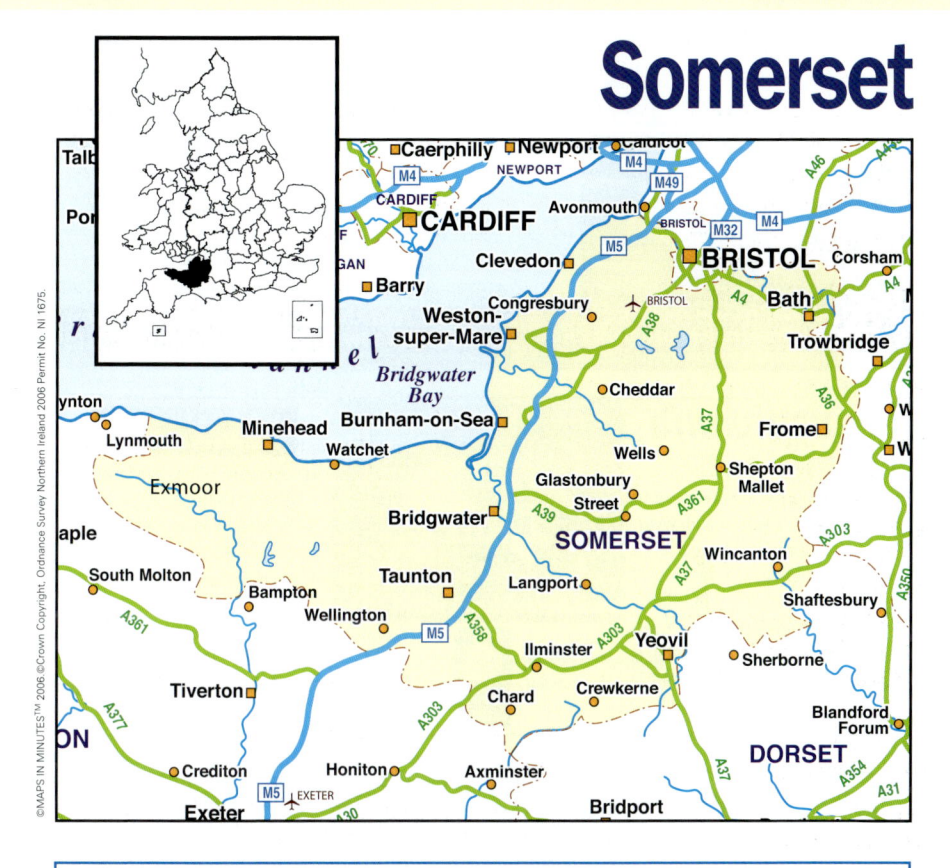

Somerset

Other specialised holiday guides from **FHG**

Recommended **INNS & PUBS** OF BRITAIN

Recommended **COUNTRY HOTELS** OF BRITAIN

Recommended **SHORT BREAK HOLIDAYS** IN BRITAIN

The bestselling and original **PETS WELCOME!**

The **GOLF GUIDE,** Where to Play, Where to Stay IN BRITAIN & IRELAND

COAST & COUNTRY HOLIDAYS

BED & BREAKFAST STOPS

CARAVAN & CAMPING HOLIDAYS

CHILDREN WELCOME! Family Holiday & Days Out Guide

BRITAIN'S BEST LEISURE & RELAXATION GUIDE

Published annually: available in all good bookshops or direct from the publisher:
FHG Guides, Abbey Mill Business Centre, Seedhill, Paisley PA1 1TJ
Tel: 0141 887 0428 • Fax: 0141 889 7204
• E-mail: admin@fhguides.co.uk • Web: www.holidayguides.com

SOMERSET — Ashbrittle, Bath, Bristol **BOARD**

On Devon/Somerset borders, 230 acre family-run farm with cattle, sheep, poultry and horses. Ideal for walking, touring Exmoor, Quantocks, both coasts and many National Trust properties. Pleasant farmhouse, tastefully modernised but with olde worlde charm, inglenook fireplaces and antique furniture, set in large gardens with lawns and flower beds in peaceful, scenic countryside. Two family bedrooms with private facilities and tea/coffee making. Large lounge, separate dining room offering guests every comfort. Noted for relaxed, friendly atmosphere and good home-cooking.

Bed and Breakfast from £25; Dinner £12 per person.
Reductions for children.

tel: 01398 361296
e-mail: lowerwestcott@aol.com
Brochure on request

Mrs Ann Heard, Lower Westcott Farm,
Ashbrittle, Wellington
Somerset TA21 0HZ

Pennsylvania Farm

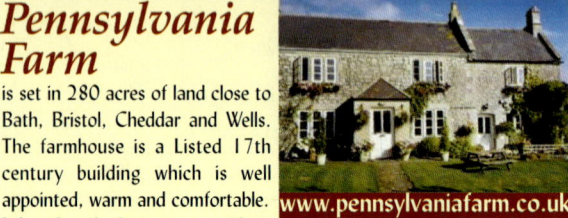

is set in 280 acres of land close to Bath, Bristol, Cheddar and Wells. The farmhouse is a Listed 17th century building which is well appointed, warm and comfortable. It has three bedrooms, two with en suite bathrooms (power showers), one with private bathroom; a cosy dining room and a pleasant sunny sitting room with log fire.

www.pennsylvaniafarm.co.uk

Wonderful farmhouse breakfasts available

SELF-CATERING available adjacent to the farmhouse in three lovely converted cottages with two bedrooms and their own kitchen and lounge (sleep four).

Mrs P Foster
Pennsylvania Farm
Newton-St-Loe, Bath BA2 9JD
Tel: 01225 314912

The Model Farm

Model Farm is situated two miles off the A37 in a hamlet nestling under the Dundry Hills. A working arable and beef farm in easy reach of Bristol, Bath, Cheddar and many other interesting places. The spacious accommodation is in two en suite rooms, one family and one double, with tea/coffee facilities. Separate dining room and lounge with colour TV for visitors. Private parking. Open all year (except Christmas and New Year). Bed and Breakfast from £25.

Mrs M. Hasell, The Model Farm, Norton Hawkfield, Pensford, Bristol BS39 4HA • 01275 832144
e-mail: margarethasell@hotmail.com • www.themodelfarm.co.uk

200-year old, comfy, warm farmhouse on working livestock farm, with open log fire in the guest lounge during the winter months. Central heating, TV, video. Bedrooms with TV and beverage trays. Double en suite, family room with private bathroom. Menu available, breakfasts cooked to order. B&B from £27, discounts for 3 days or more. Credit cards accepted. Regret no pets. Self catering also available.

For brochure contact: Josephine Smart
Leigh Farm, Pensford, Near Bristol BS39 4BA • Tel & Fax: 01761 490281
Bristol International Airport 10 miles approx.

BOARD Chard, Cocklake   **SOMERSET 101**

Keymer Cottage
Buckland St Mary, Chard TA20 3JF

Tel: 01460 234226
or 07940 051439
e-mail: keymercottage@tiscali.co.uk

A stone-built Victorian farmhouse, with inglenook, attractively furnished, offering friendly and comfortable hospitality. Good local eating venues and many places of interest in the area, including National Trust properties, cider mills, museums, gardens etc. It is one mile from the A303, five miles from Chard and Ilminster, and nine miles from Taunton, the county town. Exmoor, Dartmoor and the North Somerset coast are within easy reach and Lyme Regis is only 19 miles away. There is a guest sittingroom with colour TV and three bedrooms, either en suite or with private bathroom; tea making facilities. Non-smoking. Sorry, no children.

Bed and full English Breakfast from £22.50 per person per night.

Cricklake Farm
Bed & Breakfast on the Somerset Levels
**Cocklake, Wedmore, Somerset BS28 4HH
Tel: 01934 712736
Mobile: 07821 606046**

Cricklake Farm is a working dairy farm in a small rural hamlet, facing the beautiful Mendip Hills and surrounded by green fields and superb, unbroken views. 5 minutes from Cheddar Gorge. Bristol Airport 17 miles.
You will find a very warm, friendly welcome from hosts Christabelle and Phil Nicholls. The area is noted for its wealth of indoor and outdoor activities, including walking and cycling.

- *All rooms en suite, with hot drinks facility, hairdryer, TV, clock/radio.*
- *Luxurious dining room*
- *Delicious farmhouse breakfasts.*
- *Sorry, no pets.*

**www.cricklakefarm.the-cider-house.net
info@cricklakefarm.co.uk**

B&B £27.50-£30pppn twin/double • single £30-£40

Looking for holiday accommodation?
for details of hundreds of properties throughout the UK visit:

www.holidayguides.com

102 SOMERSET — Dulverton, Exmoor, Stogumber, Taunton **BOARD**

Marsh Bridge Cottage. This superb accommodation has been made possible by the refurbishment of this Victorian former gamekeeper's cottage on the banks of the River Barle. The friendly welcome, lovely rooms, delicious (optional) evening meals using local produce, and clotted cream sweets are hard to resist! Open all year, and in autumn the trees that line the river either side of Marsh Bridge turn to a beautiful golden backdrop. Just off the B3223 Dulverton to Exford road, it is easy to find and, once discovered, rarely forgotten. From outside the front door footpaths lead in both directions alongside the river. Fishing available.

Terms from £25 per person Bed and Breakfast or £41 per person Dinner, Bed and Breakfast.
Mrs Carole Nurcombe, Marsh Bridge Cottage, Dulverton TA22 9QG • 01398 323197

Springfield Farm
Ashwick Lane, Dulverton TA22 9QD

Wonderful hospitality and delicious food on our 270 acre sheep and cattle farm set within the Exmoor National Park. Peacefully situated a 1½ mile walk from the famous beauty spot of Tarr Steps, 4 miles from the market town of Dulverton (film location of 'The Land Girls'). Much wildlife including red deer on the farm. An ideal base for walking or touring Exmoor and North Devon coastal resorts. Riding and fishing nearby. Ample parking (garage by request). One double, on twin en suite, one double with private shower. Guests' lounge. No smoking in farmhouse, please. B&B from £25 per person per night. Evening meals (3 courses & tea/coffee, with 24 hours notice) £19. Reductions for stays of three nights or more. ETC ★★★★

Mrs P. Vellacott, • Tel & Fax: 01398 323722
e-mail: info@springfieldfarms.co.uk • www.springfieldfarms.co.uk

A Taste of Somerset...

Come and enjoy the beauty of Somerset for that relaxing break. Wick House is a charming old family house in the picturesque West Somerset village of Stogumber, in an area of outstanding beauty, where many country pursuits are available. We offer a friendly, informal atmosphere and high standard of accommodation. All bedrooms are en suite, with television and tea/coffee making facilities. A full English breakfast is served, evening meals by prior arrangement.
Disabled accommodation available • Children of all ages welcome

Tel: 01984 656422   Credit cards accepted
e-mail: sheila@wickhouse.fsbusiness.co.uk
www.wickhouse.fsbusiness.co.uk

Wick House
Brook Street, Stogumber, Somerset TA4 3SZ
Bed & Breakfast Accommodation

LOWER MARSH FARM
Kingston St Mary TA2 8AB
Tel & Fax: 01823 451331
e-mail: b&b@lowermarshfarm.co.uk
www.lowermarshfarm.co.uk

This delightful, family-run mixed farm, located at the foot of the Quantock Hills, provides luxurious, comfortable bedrooms, complemented by many extra facilities. Accommodation is all en suite, with tea/coffee facilities. Evening meals are available by arrangement and, like breakfast, are served in an attractive dining room. There is a guest lounge. Central heating throughout. Ample off road parking. No pets and no smoking.

Bed & Full English Breakfast
Double: from £60.00 • Single: from £30.00
Children: (12 Years & under) £12.00 Per Child Per Night

AA ★★★★ Guest Accommodation

The Falcon Hotel
Henlade, Taunton
TA3 5DH

You can always expect a warm welcome at this historic villa, with just the right blend of comfortable, spacious accommodation, friendly efficient staff and the personal attention of its family owners. Located one mile from the M5 motorway, it makes an ideal base for business stays, or as a touring centre for this attractive corner of the West Country. Facilities include ten en suite bedrooms with colour TV, tea/coffee making facilities, direct dial telephone, etc. Honeymoon suite, conference facilities, restaurant and ample parking. Superbly accessible to Quantock, Blackdown Hills, Exmoor, North and South Devon coasts. Our tariff is inclusive of a Full English Breakfast.

Tel: 01823 442502 • Fax: 01823 442670
www.hotelfalcon.co.uk
mail@hotelfalcon.co.uk

TAUNTON Bill Slipper, The Old Mill, Bishop's Hull, Taunton TA1 5AB (Tel & Fax: 01823 289732).
Relax and enjoy the hospitality in this Grade II Listed former Corn Mill, situated on the edge of a conservation village just two miles from Taunton. We have two lovely double bedrooms, The Mill Room with en suite facilities overlooking the weir pool, and The Cottage Suite with its own private bathroom, again with views over the river. Both rooms are centrally heated, with TV, generous beverage tray and thoughtful extras. Guests have their own lounge and dining area overlooking the river, where breakfast may be taken from our extensive breakfast menu amidst machinery of a bygone era.
Rates: Double en suite £27.50 pppn, double with private bathroom £25 pppn, single occupancy from £35 per night.
• We are a non-smoking establishment.
VisitBritain ★★★★★ *SILVER AWARD.*

FARTHINGS HOTEL & RESTAURANT
Hatch Beauchamp, Taunton TA3 6SG
Tel: 01823 480120 • Fax: 01823 481118
www.farthingshotel.co.uk
e-mail: info@farthingshotel.co.uk

Welcome to 'Farthings', an elegant Georgian hotel situated in the heart of the Somerset countryside in the historic village of Hatch Beauchamp. Set in three acres of peaceful gardens and overlooking the village green, it enjoys an enviable reputation for hospitality, comfort, pure relaxation and superb cuisine. All ten bedrooms are individual, spacious and en suite, tastefully decorated and furnished.

The hotel is an ideal base for visiting the many attractions just a short drive away. Within 30 minutes you can visit Wells Cathedral, Bath, Cheddar Gorge, Wookey Hole, the Mendips, Exmoor and both the North and South Devon coasts. Many National Trust and other heritage sites are also within easy reach.

Hungerford Farm is an attractive 13th century farmhouse on a family-run 350 acre farm with cattle, horses, free range chickens and ducks. We are situated in beautiful countryside on the edge of the Exmoor National Park. Ideal country for walking, riding or cycling. The medieval village of Dunster with its spectacular castle, mentioned in the Domesday Book, and the numerous attractions of Exmoor are all a short distance away. There is a good choice of local pubs within easy reach. Double and twin bedrooms with TV. Children welcome. Stabling available for visitors' horses. Dogs by arrangement. From £22 per person. Open February to November.

Hungerford Farm, Washford, Somerset TA23 0JZ
Tel: 01984 640285 • e-mail: sarah.richmond@virgin.net

'LANA'
Hollow Farm, Westbury-sub-Mendip,
Near Wells, Somerset BA5 1HH
Tel & Fax: 01749 870635
Mrs Sheila Stott
e-mail: Sheila@stott2366.freeserve.co.uk

Modern farmhouse on working farm. Comfortable family home in beautiful gardens with views of Somerset Levels and Mendips. Quiet location. Breakfast room for sole use of guests. Full English breakfast. Meals available at local pub five minutes' walk away. En suite rooms with fridge, hairdryer, tea/coffee making facilities, shaver point, colour TV and central heating. Non-smoking.

Terms £27pppn, reduced rates for 3 nights or more.

Honeysuckle Cottage, Worth, Near Wells

A recent barn conversion (sleeps 5) on small working farm in the heart of rural Somerset. Maintains 'olde worlde' charm while offering all modern amenities. The cottage has oil-fired central heating throughout and log-burning stove. One double en suite bedroom, plus one double with adjoining single sharing large bathroom. Spacious kitchen/dining/living room with TV/DVD, and French windows leading to large patio and raised garden looking onto Mendip Hills and surrounding countryside. Kitchen has double oven and hob, dishwasher, washing machine, microwave and large fridge freezer.
Honeysuckle Cottage is a strictly non-smoking cottage.

Details from **Mrs L. Law, Honeycroft Farm, Worth, Wells BA5 1LW**
Tel: 01749 678971 • e-mail: honeycroft2@aol.com

Double-Gate Farm
Godney, Near Wells BA5 1RX

An award-winning B&B on the banks of the River Sheppey. All bedrooms are en suite, attractively decorated and thoughtfully equipped. Breakfast in the farmhouse dining room or in the garden, the extensive menu offering local and home grown produce accompanied with home-made bread. An ideal base for exploring this pretty and interesting county. Children welcome. No smoking or pets. Self-catering also available. B&B from £30 to £32.50 per person.

**Tel: 01458 832217 • Fax: 01458 835612
e-mail: doublegatefarm@aol.com
www.doublegatefarm.com**

Free or reduced rate entry to Holiday Visits and Attractions – see our READERS' OFFER VOUCHERS on pages 7-40

FHG Guides

publish a large range of well-known accommodation guides.
We will be happy to send you details or you can use the order form at the back of this book.

FHG
K·U·P·E·R·A·R·D

BOARD Weston-Super-Mare, Wiveliscombe   SOMERSET **105**

Sunset Bay Hotel — 53 Beach Road,
Weston-Super-Mare BS23 1BH • 01934 623519

Small, family-run hotel enjoying an unrivalled position on the seafront, with superb views to Weston Bay and the Welsh coastline. A guest lounge on the first floor overlooks the bay, with games and books for the enjoyment of our guests.

Breakfast is served in the dining room/bar overlooking the beach and lawns, and though we do not provide evening meals, there is a menu of hot and cold snacks. Packed lunches can be supplied on request.

All rooms en suite, or with private bathroom, and TV, tea/coffee making facilities, hairdryers and towels are supplied in all rooms. Complimentary tray of tea and cakes on arrival.

Ideal for family holidays, weekend breaks, short breaks and holidays at any time of year. **Non-smoking**.

e-mail: relax@sunsetbayhotel.co.uk
www.sunsetbayhotel.co.uk

North Down Farm

In tranquil, secluded surroundings on the Somerset/Devon Border. Traditional working farm set in 150 acres of natural beauty with panoramic views of over 40 miles. M5 7 miles, Taunton 10 miles. All rooms tastefully furnished to high standard include en suite, TV, and tea/coffee facilities. Double, twin or single rooms available. Dining room and lounge with log fires for our guests' comfort; centrally heated and double glazed. Drying facilities. Delicious home produced food a speciality. Fishing, golf, horse riding and country sports nearby. Dogs welcome.

Bed and Breakfast from £29 pppn,
B&B and Evening Meal £225 weekly.
North Down Break: three nights B&B and Evening Meal £109 per person.
Jenny Cope, North Down Farm, Pyncombe Lane, Wiveliscombe,
Taunton TA4 2BL • Tel & Fax: 01984 623730
e-mail: jennycope@btinternet.com • www.north-down-farm.co.uk

English Tourism Council — Silver Award — Guest Accommodation

Useful Guidance for Guests and Hosts

Every year literally thousands of holidays, short breaks and overnight stops are arranged through our guides, the vast majority without any problems at all. In a handful of cases, however, difficulties do arise about bookings, which often could have been prevented from the outset.

It is important to remember that when accommodation has been booked, both parties – guests and hosts – have entered into a form of contract. We hope that the following points will provide helpful guidance.

Guests

- When enquiring about accommodation, be as precise as possible. Give exact dates, numbers in your party and the ages of any children.
- State the number and type of rooms wanted and also what catering you require – bed and breakfast, full board etc. Make sure that the position about evening meals is clear – and about pets, reductions for children or any other special points.
- Read our reviews carefully to ensure that the proprietors you are going to contact can supply what you want. Ask for a letter confirming all arrangements, if possible.
- If you have to cancel, do so as soon as possible. Proprietors do have the right to retain deposits and under certain circumstances to charge for cancelled holidays if adequate notice is not given and they cannot re-let the accommodation.

Hosts

- Give details about your facilities and about any special conditions. Explain your deposit system clearly and arrangements for cancellations, charges etc. and whether or not your terms include VAT.
- If for any reason you are unable to fulfil an agreed booking without adequate notice, you may be under an obligation to arrange suitable alternative accommodation or to make some form of compensation.

Staffordshire

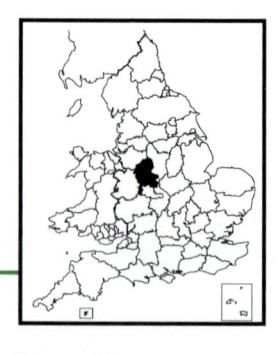

Mrs Helen Bonsall, Slindon House Farm,
Slindon, Eccleshall ST21 6LX • 01782 791237

Slindon House is set in a large attractive garden and offers excellent accommodation in comfortable, spacious and well equipped rooms on a working dairy, arable and sheep farm. Situated on the A519, between Junctions 14 and 15 of the M6, ideal for an overnight break or a longer stay to visit such local attractions as the Potteries, County Showground, Bridgemere, Trentham, Telford and Ironbridge. There is a good selection of local places to eat.

Regret no pets.
Terms from £30-£35 single, £25 per person double.

e-mail: bonsallslindonhouse@supanet.com

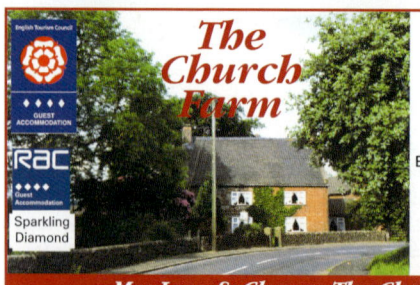

The Church Farm

Famous Alton Towers is just five and a half miles from our farm. The Churnet Valley, with steam railway, wildlife park, narrowboat trips, Nick Williams Pottery and a maze of footpaths, is a fifteen minute walk; truly a hidden paradise!
The Potteries and Peak District are within eight miles.
Having visited all of these, come and unwind in our spacious cottage garden or with a book by the log fire in winter.
Enjoy our beautifully furnished period farmhouse built in 1700 with many thoughtful additions for your comfort. Breakfast menu using own and local produce. En suite bedrooms with TVs and beverage making facilities. Totally non-smoking.
Tariff: Adults £25.00, Single £30.00, children 12 years and under £12.
"WHICH? GOOD BED & BREAKFAST GUIDE."

Mrs Jane S. Clowes, The Church Farm, Holt Lane, Kingsley,
Stoke-on-Trent ST10 2BA • Tel: 01538 754759
E-mail: thechurchfarm@yahoo.co.uk

Crowtrees Farm

200-year-old working family farm overlooking the Churnet Valley offering very comfortably furnished accommodation in four en suite bedrooms and family rooms in a converted barn.
Within easy reach of the Potteries, Peak District and Alton Towers (less than 3 miles). Non-smoking. Own entrance with access at any time.

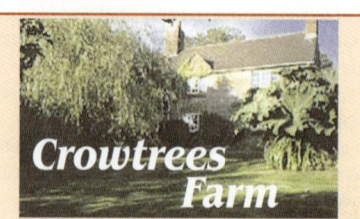

Bed and Breakfast from £24.
Special short breaks available.

Mrs D. Bickle, Crowtrees Farm,
Oakamoor, Stoke-on-Trent ST10 3DY
Tel & Fax: 01538 702260
e-mail: dianne@crowtreesfarm.co.uk
www.crowtreesfarm.co.uk

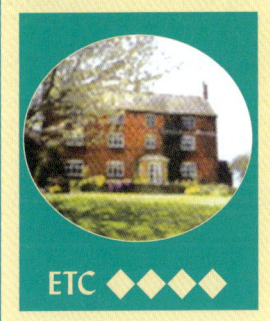

BOARD Uttoxeter   STAFFORDSHIRE/SUFFOLK **107**

Loxley Bank Farm
Loxley, Uttoxeter ST14 8QB
Tel: 01889 562467 • Mobile: 07976 401887

A Grade II traditional farmhouse on a working dairy farm, finished and maintained to a high standard. Peaceful, rural setting in the heart of the Staffordshire countryside. Easy and safe parking. Ideal for business persons and the discerning traveller. £32.50 to £45 per person.

e-mail: loxleybankfarm@uttoxeter.com

ETC ♦♦♦♦

Suffolk

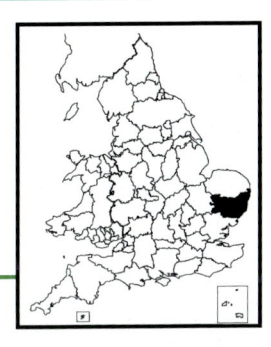

Framlingham

High House Farm   ETC ♦♦♦
Cransford, Framlingham, Woodbridge, Suffolk IP13 9PD
Tel: 01728 663461 * Fax: 01728 663409
e-mail: b&b@highhousefarm.co.uk
website: www.highhousefarm.co.uk

Exposed oak beams ♦ inglenook fireplaces ♦ one double room, en suite and one large family room with double and twin beds and private adjacent bathroom ♦ children's cots ♦ high chairs ♦ books ♦ toys ♦ outside play equipment ♦ attractive semi-moated gardens ♦ farm and woodland walks

Explore the heart of rural Suffolk, local vineyards, Easton Farm Park, Framlingham and Orford Castles, Parham Air Museum, Saxtead Windmill, Minsmere, Snape Maltings, Woodland Trust and the Heritage Coast.
Bed and Breakfast from £25. Reductions for children and stays of three nights or more.

Signposted on B1119, Fiddlers Hall is a 14th century, moated, oak-beamed farmhouse set in a beautiful and secluded position. It is two miles from Framlingham Castle, 20 minutes' drive from Aldeburgh, Snape Maltings, Woodbridge and Southwold. A Grade II Listed building, it has lots of history and character. The bedrooms are spacious; one has en suite shower room, the other has a private bathroom. Use of lounge and colour TV. Plenty of parking space. Lots of farm animals kept. Traditional farmhouse cooking. Bed and Breakfast terms from £65 per room.

Mrs Jennie Mann, Fiddlers Hall, Cransford, Near Framlingham, Woodbridge IP13 9PQ • 01728 663729 • www.fiddlershall.co.uk

SUFFOLK/SUSSEX

Stowmarket BOARD

STOWMARKET Mrs Mary Noy, Red House Farm, Station Road, Haughley, Near Stowmarket IP14 3QP (01449 673323; Fax: 01449 675413).
A warm welcome and homely atmosphere awaits you at our attractive farmhouse set in the beautiful surroundings of mid-Suffolk. Comfortably furnished bedrooms with en suite shower rooms, tea/coffee making facilities. One double, one twin and two single rooms. Central heating. Guests' own lounge with TV; dining room. Ideal location for exploring, walking, cycling and birdwatching.
Rates: Bed and Breakfast from £55-£60 per double/twin room; £35 to £45 per single room.
• Open all year. • No smoking. • No pets.
ETC ♦♦♦♦

e-mail: mary-n@tiscali.co.uk
www.farmstayanglia.co.uk

Sussex

FHG Guides

publish a large range of well-known accommodation guides.
We will be happy to send you details or you can use the order form at the back of this book.

FHG
KUPERARD

East Sussex

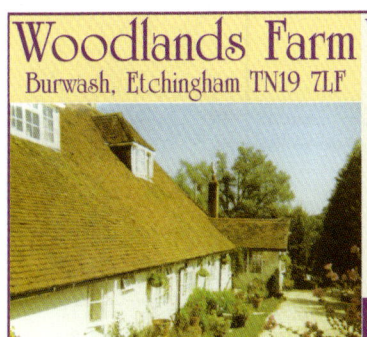

Woodlands Farm
Burwash, Etchingham TN19 7LF

Woodlands Farm stands one third of a mile off the road, surrounded by fields and woods. This peaceful and beautifully modernised 16th century farmhouse offers comfortable and friendly accommodation. Sitting/dining room; two bathrooms, one en suite, double or twin-bedded rooms (one has four-poster bed) together with excellent farm fresh food. This is a farm of 108 acres with a variety of animals and is situated within easy reach of 20 or more places of interest to visit and half an hour from the coast.

Open all year • Central heating • Literature provided to help guests. Children welcome • Dogs allowed if sleeping in owner's car. Parking • Evening Meal optional • Non-smoking.

Bed and Breakfast from £35 single to £60 double.
Telephone or SAE please • Mrs E. Sirrell • Tel & Fax: 01435 882794

e-mail: liz_sir@lineone.net
www.SmoothHound.co.uk/hotels/woodlands.html

Far End
139 Royal Parade, Eastbourne, East Sussex BN22 7LH
www.farendhotel.co.uk

From the moment you arrive you are assured of a warm welcome and real "home from home" atmosphere. Our centrally heated bedrooms with colour TV and tea/coffee making facilities are tastefully decorated, most have en suite facilities and sea views. Residents have their own lounge and private car park. Enjoy freshly prepared traditional home cooking. Special diets can be catered for. Credit cards accepted.

Tel: 01323 725666
Tim and Karen Camp

We are adjacent to the popular Princes Park with boating lake, lawns, bowling greens and pitch'n'putt, close by you can enjoy sailing, fishing, bowling, tennis and swimming. We are in easy reach of Beachy Head, the South Downs and Newhaven. We will be delighted to provide information on the many local attractions and services, and shall do our best to make your stay as memorable and pleasant as possible.

Bed and Breakfast from £23
Evening Meal available.
Low season short breaks.
Please call or write for colour brochure.

AA ★★★★

Note

All the information in this guide is given in good faith in the belief that it is correct. However, the publishers cannot guarantee the facts given in these pages, neither are they responsible for changes in ownership or facilities that may take place after the date of going to press.
Readers should always satisfy themselves that the facilities they require are available and that the terms, if quoted, still apply.

The FHG Directory of Website Addresses

on pages 277-310 is a useful quick reference guide for holiday accommodation with e-mail and/or website details

FHG
KUPERARD

Tyne & Wear

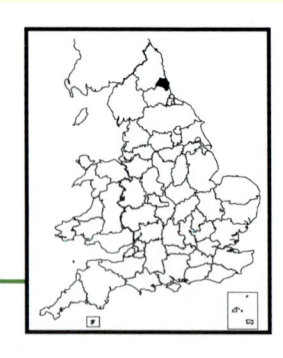

Newcastle-upon-Tyne

127 Osborne Road, Jesmond, Newcastle-upon-Tyne NE2 2TB
Tel: 0191-281 7711 • Fax: 0191-281 3369

This privately owned hotel is situated in a quiet location, but only minutes from the city centre. It has built up a reputation for good food and friendly, efficient service in a warm and congenial atmosphere. All bedrooms are en suite, with hospitality tray, direct-dial telephone, colour TV with satellite, and radio. There is a spacious cocktail lounge and a restaurant serving the best of modern and classic cuisine. Local attractions include the Metro Centre, Northumbria National Park, Holy Island and Bamburgh Castle. Single from £52.50, double from £79.50.

New Kent Hotel

Warwickshire

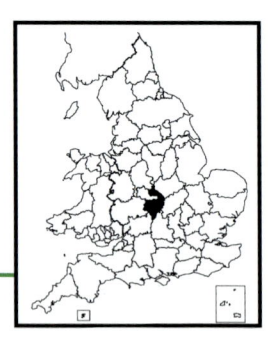

Coventry

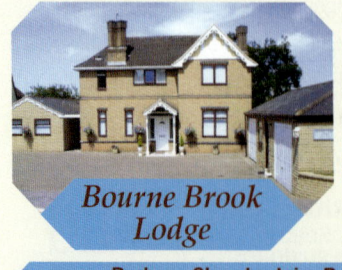

Experience the peace and tranquillity of our country house offering high standards of comfort and cleanliness in picturesque surroundings. En suite facilities in stone-built chalet rooms having colour TV and hostess tray. Private car park and gardens. Prices include full English breakfast. We are a non-smoking establishment. Telephone bookings only.
- Convenient for NEC, Forest of Arden and Belfry golf courses, Birmingham, Coventry and Stratford.
- Double/twin en suite £65 per room, single en suite £40, single with shared facilities £35.

Bourne Brook Lodge

Barbara Chamberlain, Bourne Brook Lodge, Mill Lane, Fillongley, Near Coventry CV7 8EE • 01676 541898 • www.bournebrooklodge.co.uk

BOARD Lighthorne, Stratford-upon-Avon **WARWICKSHIRE 111**

Church Hill Farm B&B

An idyllic Cruck farmhouse B&B (Grade II Listed and dating back to before the 15th century), close to Warwick, Stratford-upon-Avon and Royal Leamington Spa, Church Hill Farm is a 300-acre working farm with a warm and friendly welcome. It has been a family home for hundreds of years and contains fine antique furniture. There are three spacious bedrooms, all with en suite bathrooms.

- Good access from the M40 but in a rural location.
- Network of footpaths gives good countryside access.
- Centrally situated for Shakespeare Country and the Cotswolds.
- Hearty breakfasts using local produce. • Open all year.

Sue Sabin, Church Hill Farm, Lighthorne CV35 0AR • Tel: 01926 651251 • Fax: 01926 650339
www.churchhillfarm.co.uk • e-mail: sue@churchhillfarm.co.uk

STABLE CROFT

On the A422 halfway between Stratford and Banbury • Welcome to the peace and tranquillity of the countryside. Our bright, spacious ground floor bedrooms are new and purpose-built. Guests' own entrance and all modern facilities including fridge. Two village pubs in walking distance. Lovely country walks, golf, fishing and horse riding locally. Ideal base to explore the Cotswolds, Shakespearian Stratford, and Warwick with its fine castle. Prices include full English breakfast.

We are a non-smoking establishment

Double room (en suite bathroom) £60 per night.
Twin room (en suite shower room) £60 per night.
Single occupancy available £40 per night.

Pamela Emerson, Stable Croft, Green Lane, Oxhill CV35 0RB
Tel: 01295 680055 • Mobile 07792 105277
• www.stablecroft.co.uk

Other specialised holiday guides from FHG

Recommended **INNS & PUBS** OF BRITAIN
Recommended **COUNTRY HOTELS** OF BRITAIN
Recommended **SHORT BREAK HOLIDAYS** IN BRITAIN
The bestselling and original **PETS WELCOME!**
The **GOLF GUIDE,** Where to Play, Where to Stay IN BRITAIN & IRELAND
COAST & COUNTRY HOLIDAYS
SELF-CATERING HOLIDAYS IN BRITAIN
BED & BREAKFAST STOPS
CARAVAN & CAMPING HOLIDAYS
CHILDREN WELCOME! Family Holiday & Days Out Guide
BRITAIN'S BEST LEISURE & RELAXATION GUIDE

Published annually: available in all good bookshops or direct from the publisher:
FHG Guides, Abbey Mill Business Centre, Seedhill, Paisley PA1 1TJ
Tel: 0141 887 0428 • Fax: 0141 889 7204
• E-mail: admin@fhguides.co.uk • Web: www.holidayguides.com

Monks Barn Farm is situated 2 miles south of Stratford on the A3400. Dating back to the 16th century, the farm lies along the banks of the River Stour. Now modernised, it still preserves the old character, and offers first-class amenities; some accommodation is separate from the main house. Ground floor rooms available. Pleasant riverside walks to the village of Clifford Chambers. Centrally situated for visiting Stratford, Warwick and the Cotswolds. Three double, two twin, one family and one single room, most en suite. Children of all ages welcome. Non-smoking. B&B from £24-£26.50. Credit cards accepted.

ritameadows@btconnect.com
www.monksbarnfarm.com

Monks Barn Farm
Shipston Road, Stratford-upon-Avon,
Warwickshire CV37 8NA
Tel: 01789 293714 • Fax: 01789 205886

Holly Tree Cottage
Birmingham Road, Pathlow, Stratford-upon-Avon CV37 0ES
Tel & Fax: 01789 204461

Period cottage dating from 17th Century, with antiques, paintings, collection of porcelain, fresh flowers, tasteful furnishings and friendly atmosphere. Picturesque gardens, orchard, paddock and pasture with wildlife and extensive views over open countryside. Situated 3 miles north of Stratford-upon-Avon towards Henley-in-Arden on A3400. Rooms have television, radio/alarm, hospitality trays and hairdryers. Breakfasts are a speciality. Pubs and restaurants nearby. Ideally located for Theatre, Shakespeare Country, Heart of England, Cotswolds, Warwick Castle, Blenheim Palace and National Trust Properties. Well situated for National Exhibition Centre, Birmingham and National Agricultural Centre, Stoneleigh. Children welcome, pets by arrangement. Non-smoking. Bed and Breakfast from £29 per person.

e-mail: john@hollytree-cottage.co.uk • website: www.hollytree-cottage.co.uk

Looking for Holiday Accommodation?

FHG
K·U·P·E·R·A·R·D

for details of hundreds of properties throughout the UK visit our website

www.holidayguides.com

Wiltshire

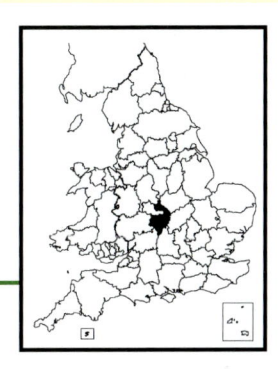

Wiltshire, in the south west of England, is known for the World Heritage Sites of Stonehenge and Avebury, two fascinating, magical stone circles dating back some 6,000 years. However, these famous icons are but a glimpse of what Wiltshire has to offer!

Wiltshire is ideally placed for visitors who arrive at London's airports (an hour's drive) or Bristol Airport (45 minutes' drive), and offers the best in country house hotels, top quality inns and B&B accommodation, and superb self-catering properties.

Wiltshire has a range of beautiful National Trust houses and gardens, including the world famous 18th century landscape garden and Palladian House at Stourhead, and The Courts at Bradford on Avon, a fascinating country garden, full of variety and colour. 'Capability' Brown, the industrious 18th century landscape gardener, has played a large part in the design of gardens at Bowood House, Longleat House and Elizabethan Corsham Court, with its splendid peacocks strutting about the grounds.

Another of Wiltshire's heritage treasures is the city of Salisbury with its medieval Cathedral whose spire is the tallest in England at 123 metres. It is surrounded by the magnificent Close, a gracious, spacious area of grassland, Georgian terraces, historic houses and museums.

Add to this mix a delightful variety of country towns and hidden villages and you have the mystery and magic that sums up what Wiltshire has to offer. There is also a comprehensive mix of events spread across the county, throughout the year.

Rates: from £26 per person.

e-mail: Dorothyboydsfarm@aol.com

BATH (NEAR) Mrs Dorothy Robinson, Boyds Farm, Gastard, Near Corsham SN13 9PT (Tel & Fax: 01249 713146).
Dorothy and Andrew Robinson warmly welcome guests to Boyds Farm which is a family-run working farm with a pedigree herd of Hereford Cattle. The farmhouse is a delightful 16th century Listed building surrounded by beautiful mature gardens. Near to Bath, Lacock, Bradford-on-Avon, Castle Combe, Stonehenge, etc. Accommodation comprises one double en suite, one family or twin with private bathroom and one double with private shower room, all well furnished with tea/coffee facilities, electric blankets, etc; guest lounge with log fire for cooler nights. Featured in the "Daily Express," "The Sunday Observer," and "Sunday Mail".

• Working farm.
ETC ♦♦♦♦♦ *SILVER AWARD*, *WELCOME HOST*.
www.SmoothHound.co.uk/hotels/boydsfarm.html

114 WILTSHIRE — Devizes, Malmesbury, Marlborough, Warminster **BOARD**

Welcome to Longwater. We offer good old-fashioned hospitality but with all the comfort and facilities of a modern home. Explore the beautiful cities of Bath and Salisbury, enjoy coarse fishing in our tranquil lake, play golf on the adjacent 18-hole course, or simply relax in our gardens or conservatory overlooking our picturesque lakes and parkland. Traditional farmhouse breakfast; local inns offer excellent dinners. All rooms en suite with tea/coffee facilities, fridge, TV, radio. Twin and double rooms and family room (children over 5 years); ground floor rooms. Wheelchair-friendly – Accessibility Level 2. Pets welcome. Brochure on request.

Longwater Farm Guest House
Erlestoke, Devizes SN10 5UE
Tel & Fax: 01380 830095

Enjoy traditional hospitality at our delightful farmhouse on a working farm just three miles from the historic town of Malmesbury with its wonderful Norman abbey and gardens and central for Cotswolds, Bath, Stratford, Avebury and Stonehenge.

Two attractive en suite bedrooms with delightful views, each with tea/coffee making facilities, colour TV and radio. Delicious full English breakfast served in our cosy dining room/lounge. Central heating throughout.

Bed and Breakfast from £27.50. Credit cards accepted. Non-smoking accommodation. Open all year.

Mrs Susan Barnes, Lovett Farm, Little Somerford, Near Malmesbury SN15 5BP
Tel & Fax: 01666 823268 • Mobile: 07808 858612
e-mail: sue@lovettfarm.co.uk • www.lovettfarm.co.uk

WERNHAM FARM
Clench Common, Marlborough, Wiltshire SN8 4DR
Tel: 01672 512236
e-mail: margglvsf@aol.com

This working farm is set in picturesque countryside on Wansdyke, off the A345. It is close to Marlborough, Avebury, Pewsey and the Kennet & Avon Canal.

Accommodation is available in two family bedrooms, one en suite and one with private bathroom.

Terms: £40 single, £55 double.

Five caravan and camping pitches are also available.

Spinney Farmhouse ~ Thoulstone, Chapmanslade, Westbury BA13 4AQ

Off A36, three miles west of Warminster; 16 miles from historic city of Bath. Close to Longleat, Cheddar and Stourhead. Reasonable driving distance to Bristol, Stonehenge, Glastonbury and the cathedral cities of Wells and Salisbury. Pony trekking and fishing available locally.

- Washbasins, tea/coffee-making facilities and shaver points in all rooms.
- Family room available. • Guests' lounge with colour TV.
- Central heating. • Children and pets welcome.
- Ample parking. • Open all year. • No smoking.

*Enjoy farm fresh food in a warm, friendly family atmosphere.
Bed and Breakfast from £23 per night. Reduction after 2 nights.
Evening Meal £12.*

Telephone 01373 832412 • Madeline Hoskins & Family

Worcestershire

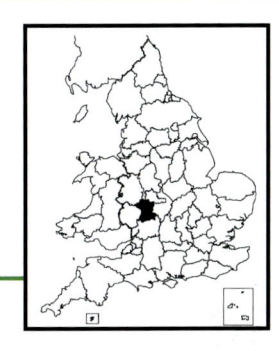

BRICKBARNS, a 200-acre mixed farm, is situated two miles from Great Malvern at the foot of the Malvern Hills, 300 yards from the bus service and one-and-a half miles from the train. The house, which is 300 years old, commands excellent views of the Malvern Hills and guests are accommodated in one double, one single and one family bedrooms with washbasins; two bathrooms, shower room, two toilets; sittingroom and diningroom. Children welcome and cot and babysitting offered. Central heating. Car essential, parking. Open Easter to October for Bed and Breakfast from £20 nightly per person. Reductions for children and Senior Citizens. Birmingham 40 miles, Hereford 20, Gloucester 17, Stratford 35 and the Wye Valley is just 30 miles.

Mrs J.L. Morris, Brickbarns Farm, Hanley Road, Malvern Wells WR14 4HY
Tel: 016845 61775 • Fax: 01886 830037

THE BARN HOUSE, Broadwas on Teme, Worcester WR6 5NS

Peaceful period property set in two acres of mature garden and surrounded by open countryside. The ground floor accommodation is immediately adjacent to the main house.

Rooms are en suite with tea/coffee making facilities, central heating, television and pleasant garden view. The comfortable guest lounge has a cosy log fire for winter months Terms from £25 twin/double or £30 single; full English or Continental breakfast is included. *Ample car parking. Open all year except Christmas and New Year.*

Mrs C. Wilesmith • Tel/Fax: 01886 888733
e-mail: info@barnhouse.online.co.uk • www.barnhouseonline.co.uk

Publisher's note

While every effort is made to ensure accuracy, we regret that FHG Guides cannot accept responsibility for errors, misrepresentations or omissions in our entries or any consequences thereof. Prices in particular should be checked.
We will follow up complaints but cannot act as arbiters or agents for either party.

Yorkshire

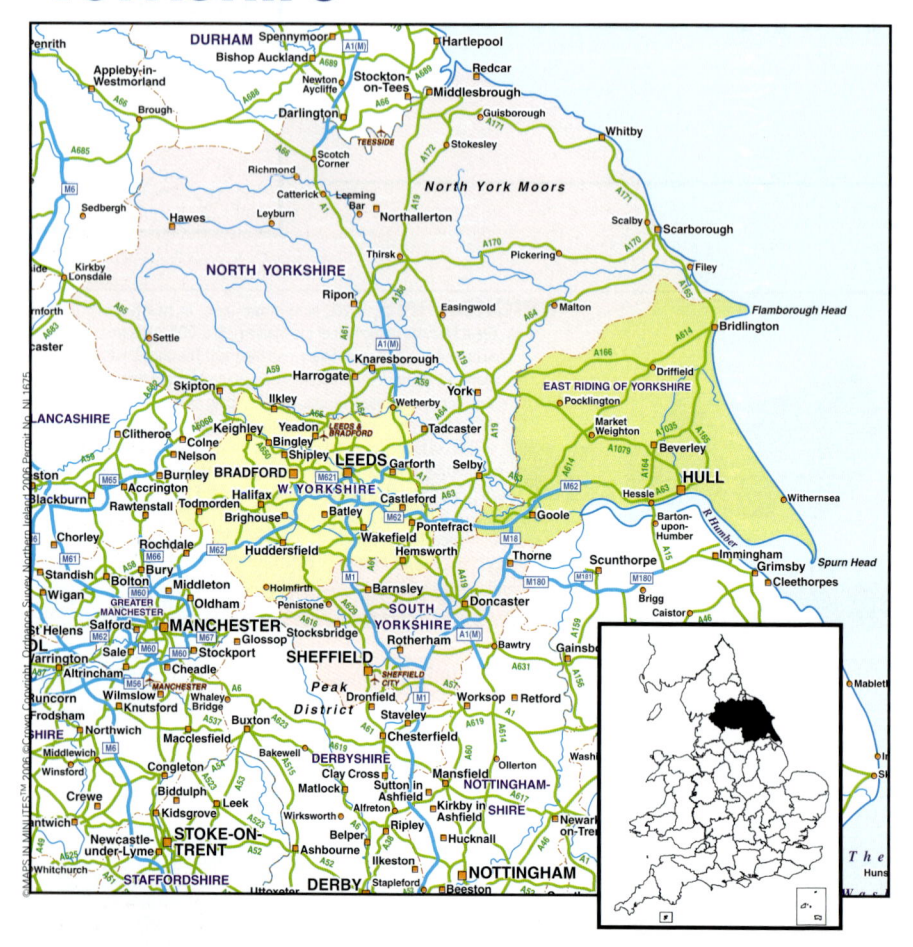

When making enquiries please mention FHG GUIDES

Looking for holiday accommodation?
for details of hundreds of properties throughout the UK visit:

www.holidayguides.com

East Yorkshire

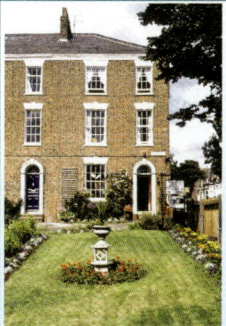

Rosebery House
1 Belle Vue, Tennyson Avenue, Bridlington YO15 2ET
Telephone: 01262 670336

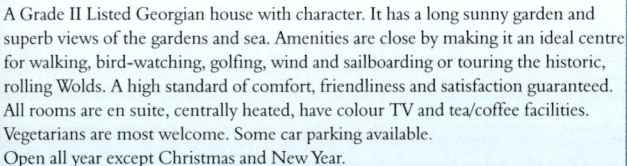

A Grade II Listed Georgian house with character. It has a long sunny garden and superb views of the gardens and sea. Amenities are close by making it an ideal centre for walking, bird-watching, golfing, wind and sailboarding or touring the historic, rolling Wolds. A high standard of comfort, friendliness and satisfaction guaranteed. All rooms are en suite, centrally heated, have colour TV and tea/coffee facilities. Vegetarians are most welcome. Some car parking available.
Open all year except Christmas and New Year.

Bed and Breakfast from £22.50 per person. Senior Supersaver Oct to June.

LIFE HILL FARM
www.lifehillfarm.co.uk

Gold Award

Enjoy peace, tranquillity, and views over the Yorkshire Wolds. Savour the rich variety of flora and fauna throughout the 500 acres, which are managed with particular regard for the environment. Lovely walking and riding countryside. Centrally located for the coast, York and Moors. Open all year. Non-smoking. All rooms en suite. Disabled facilities.
Self-catering accommodation also available.
**Contact: Andrew and Fay Grace
Life Hill Farm, Sledmere, Driffield YO25 3EY
Tel: 01337 236224
e-mail: info@lifehillfarm.co.uk**

North Yorkshire

Coverdale

Peacefully situated farmhouse away from the madding crowd.
B&B with optional Evening Meal • Home cooking.
Pets sleep where you prefer.
Ideally positioned for exploring the beautiful Yorkshire Dales.

**Mrs Julie Clarke, Middle Farm,
Woodale, Coverdale, Leyburn,
North Yorkshire DL8 4TY 01969 640271
e-mail: j-a-clarke@amserve.com**

www.yorkshirenet.co.uk/stayat/middlefarm/index.htm

Free or reduced rate entry to
Holiday Visits and Attractions – see our
READERS' OFFER VOUCHERS on pages 7-40

118 NORTH YORKSHIRE Danby. Glaisdale, Harrogate, Helmsley **BOARD**

ROWANTREE FARM is a family-run dairy farm situated in the heart of the North York Moors. Ideal walking and mountain biking area, with panoramic moorland views. Coast easily accessible. Our non-smoking home comprises one family room and one twin-bedded room, with private bathroom and private shower room, also full central heating, beverage tray, clock radio and hairdryer. Relax in our residents' lounge with colour TV/video. Ample car parking. 
- Children welcome; cot and high chair available.
- Good home cooking (vegetarians catered for), served in our separate dining room. Packed lunches available.
- B&B from £23; Evening Meal by prior arrangement.

Mrs L. Tindall, Rowantree Farm, Ainthorpe, Whitby YO21 2LE • 01287 660396
e-mail: krbsatindall@aol.com • www.rowantreefarm.co.uk

Red House Farm

Listed Georgian farmhouse featured in "Houses of the North York Moors". Completely refurbished to the highest standards, retaining all original features. Bedrooms have bath/shower/toilet, central heating, TV and tea making facilities. Excellent walks straight from the doorstep. Friendly farm animals – a few cows, horses, geese and pretty free-roaming hens. One-and-a-half acres of gardens, sitting-out areas. Magnificent views. Interesting buildings – Listed barns now converted to 3 holiday cottages. Games room with snooker table. Eight miles from seaside/Whitby. Village pub within walking distance. Stabling available for horses/dogs. Non-smoking.

Tom and Sandra Spashett, Red House Farm, Glaisdale, Near Whitby YO21 2PZ • Tel & Fax: 01947 897242
e-mail: spashettredhouse@aol.com
www.redhousefarm.com

Homely, comfortable, Christian accommodation. Spacious stone built bungalow in beautiful Nidderdale which is very central for touring the Yorkshire Dales; Pateley Bridge two miles, Harrogate 14 miles, Ripon nine miles. Museums, rocks, caves, fishing, bird watching, beautiful quiet walks, etc all nearby. En suite rooms (one twin, two double), TV. Private lounge. Tea making facilities available. Choice of breakfast. Evening meals available one mile away. Ample parking space on this working farm. Open Easter to end of October.

Mrs C.E. Nelson, Nidderdale Lodge Farm, Fellbeck, Pateley Bridge, Harrogate HG3 5DR • Tel: 01423 711677

Barn Close Farm

Rievaulx, Helmsley, North Yorkshire YO62 5LH

01439 798321

Mrs J. Milburn

BARN CLOSE FARM is nicely situated in the North York Moors National Park. This family farm in beautiful surroundings offers homely accommodation to holidaymakers all year round. Within easy reach of Rievaulx Abbey and many other places of interest, it is an ideal centre for tourists.
Pony trekking nearby.
Good walking terrain!
Highly commended for good food.
En suite double bedrooms; bathroom; toilets; sitting room and dining room.

Bed and Breakfast from £25 to £35, Evening Dinner £15.
"WHICH?" RECOMMENDED. "DAILY TELEGRAPH" RECOMMENDED.

BOARD Helmsley, Northallerton, Pickering,   NORTH YORKSHIRE 119

A large 18th century Grade II Listed farmhouse nestling on Easterside Hill and enjoying panoramic views. Ideal base for walking, touring, the coast and the city of York. Enjoy good food and a warm welcome in comfortable surroundings. All rooms have en suite facilities.

Bed and Breakfast from £30
Evening Meal from £17.
Children welcome.
Open all year except Christmas.

Mrs Sarah Wood, Easterside Farm, Hawnby, Helmsley YO62 5QT
01439 798277
www.eastersidefarm.co.uk

NORTHALLERTON Ann Saxby, Hallikeld House, Stokesley Road, Brompton, Northallerton DL6 2UE (01609 773613; Fax: 01609 770262; mobile: 077300 58807).
Two miles east of Northallerton in open countryside, ideal for travelling from coast to Dales. Easy access to A19 and A1. Central heating, lounge.
Rates: Bed and Breakfast from £18 per person per night.
e-mail: asaxby@supanet.com

Discover this unspoilt area on the edge of the North Yorkshire Moors and experience a relaxed, friendly atmosphere, with excellent home cooking.

All rooms are en suite and have central heating, hospitality trays and lots of little extras. There is a guests' dining room; and a lounge with log fire and colour TV.

Seavy Slack is only 10 minutes drive from the market town of Pickering, and is an ideal location for exploring the moors, coast and historic York.

Open all year except Christmas. B&B from £25 per person.

Mrs Anne Barrett, Seavy Slack, Stape,
PICKERING YO18 8HZ • 01751 473131

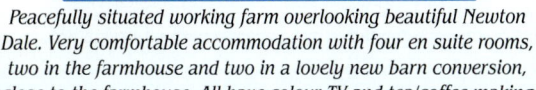

Farfields Farm

Peacefully situated working farm overlooking beautiful Newton Dale. Very comfortable accommodation with four en suite rooms, two in the farmhouse and two in a lovely new barn conversion, close to the farmhouse. All have colour TV and tea/coffee making facilities; one annexe has a small kitchenette. Lovely walks from the farm, with a bird's eye view of the steam train. Ideal base for exploring the city of York, moors, Dalby Forest, Heritage Coastline. Farfields Farm offers a warm welcome with a chance to relax and enjoy the peace and tranquillity within the magnificent National Park. Five minute stroll to local inn. £28-£33pppn.
Mrs E. Stead, Farfields Farm, Lockton, Pickering YO18 7NQ • Tel: 01751 460209
e-mail: stay@farfieldsfarm.co.uk • www.farfieldsfarm.co.uk

Readers are requested to mention this guidebook when making enquiries about accommodation.

120 NORTH YORKSHIRE — Robin Hood's Bay, Scarborough BOARD

ROBIN HOOD's BAY Mrs B. Reynolds, 'South View', Sledgates, Fylingthorpe, Whitby YO22 4TZ (01947 880025).
Pleasantly situated, comfortable accommodation in own garden with sea and country views. Ideal for walking and touring. Close to the moors, within easy reach of Whitby, Scarborough and many more places of interest. There are two double rooms, lounge and dining room. Parking spaces. Phone for further details.
Rates: Bed and Breakfast from £22, including bedtime drink.

Brinka House, 2 Station Square, Ravenscar, Scarborough YO13 0LU • 01723 871470

Situated in Ravenscar – midway between Scarborough and Whitby with stunning views across to Robin Hood's Bay and surrounded by the moors. The village boasts a variety of walks, cycle tracks, golf course, pony and llama trekking and a bus service that runs from the front door into town.

A warm welcome and tasty breakfast awaits everyone, vegetarians and special diets are catered for. We have a romantic double room with a large corner bath en suite, and a twin/family room en suite. All rooms have TV, drinks facilities and sea views.

Rates: £22.50 per person per night, £25 for single room.

www.brinkahousebedandbreakfast.co.uk

SCARBOROUGH Sue and Tony Hewitt, Harmony Country Lodge, Limestone Road, Burniston, Scarborough YO13 0DG (0800 2985840; Tel & Fax: 01723 870276).
DISTINCTIVELY DIFFERENT. Peaceful and relaxing retreat, octagonal in design and set in two acres of private grounds with 360° panoramic views of the National Park and sea. An ideal centre for walking or touring. Two miles from Scarborough and within easy reach of Whitby, York and the beautiful North Yorkshire countryside. Tastefully decorated en suite centrally heated rooms with colour TV and all with superb views. Attractive dining room, guest lounge and relaxing conservatory. Traditional English breakfast, including vegetarian. Licensed. Private parking facilities. Personal service and warm, friendly Yorkshire hospitality.
Rates: Bed and Breakfast from £25 to £36. Christmas packages.
• Non-smoking. • Children over 7 years welcome. • Spacious 5-berth caravan also available for self-catering holidays.
ETC ★★★★
e-mail: tony@harmonylodge.net   www.harmonylodge.net

Plane Tree Cottage Farm
Staintondale, Scarborough YO13 0EY
Telephone 01723 870796

This small sheep farm is situated in beautiful rural countryside, with stunning coastal views. The ideal spot to stay for visiting many places of interest, Scarborough, Whitby and the North York Moors, just to mention a few. We have two cats, sheep dogs and free range hens for the eggs used in our delicious breakfasts. Evening meals by arrangement only. One twin en suite, one double with separate bathroom. Also one ground floor double en suite. No smoking in house. Car essential. Bed and Breakfast from £25 per person per night. We also have one static caravan to let, with two bedrooms, shower room, kitchen and lounge. Wonderful sea views. Please phone for details.

AA ★★★

NORTH YORKSHIRE/SOUTH YORKSHIRE

YORK David and Katherine Leedham, York House, 62 Heworth Green, York YO31 7TQ (Tel & Fax: 01904 427070).
Receive a warm welcome at this family-run guesthouse. Enjoy breakfast in our attractive conservatory or outside on our beautiful patio. York House is approximately 10 minutes' walk from York Minster and is the perfect base for a visit to York or the surrounding areas. Rooms offer all the conveniences you could need for a relaxing and enjoyable stay. Some of the facilities offered: en suite shower or bath facilities, four-poster, double, twin, family and single rooms, tea/coffee making facilities, off-street parking, full English/vegetarian breakfast.
Rates: from £28 pppn
* Non-smoking. • Children welcome.
ETC ★★★★
e-mail: yorkhouse.bandb@tiscali.co.uk
www.yorkhouseyork.com

Robeanne House

Family B&B • Country location, 18 miles from historic York • Ideal for coast and Moors, racing, Beverley, Cycle Route 66 and Wolds Way • Beautiful country house and gardens • Also holiday cottage available • All rooms en suite • For bookings please contact
Jeanne Wilson, Robeanne House, Driffield Lane, Shiptonthorpe, York YO43 3PW
AA ★★★ *Awards for Comfort & Hospitality*
e-mail: robeannehouse@btconnect.com
www.robeannehouse.co.uk

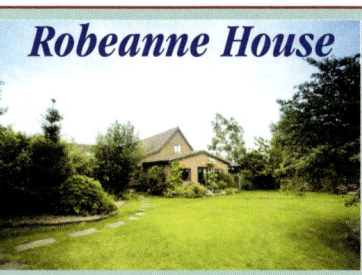

Tel: 01430 873312

Other specialised holiday guides from FHG

Recommended **INNS & PUBS** OF BRITAIN
Recommended **COUNTRY HOTELS** OF BRITAIN
Recommended **SHORT BREAK HOLIDAYS** IN BRITAIN
The bestselling and original **PETS WELCOME!**
The **GOLF GUIDE,** Where to Play, Where to Stay IN BRITAIN & IRELAND
COAST & COUNTRY HOLIDAYS
SELF-CATERING HOLIDAYS IN BRITAIN
BED & BREAKFAST STOPS
CARAVAN & CAMPING HOLIDAYS
CHILDREN WELCOME! Family Holiday & Days Out Guide
BRITAIN'S BEST LEISURE & RELAXATION GUIDE

Published annually: available in all good bookshops or direct from the publisher:
FHG Guides, Abbey Mill Business Centre, Seedhill, Paisley PA1 1TJ
Tel: 0141 887 0428 • Fax: 0141 889 7204
• E-mail: admin@fhguides.co.uk • Web: www.holidayguides.com

South Yorkshire

Padley Farm Bed & Breakfast

Dungworth Green, Sheffield S6 6HE
Tel: 0114 2851427

Padley Farm is situated to the west of Sheffield in the quiet village of Dungworth, near the Dam Flask reservoir. Although in the countryside, we are only 10 minutes from the centre of Sheffield. All rooms have scenic views, en suite facilities and TV with DVD. Ground floor rooms have easy access from the courtyard. Visitors can enjoy hearty meals at local pubs. See our website for directions, local amenities and price lists.

www.padleyfarm.co.uk
info@padleyfarm.co.uk

FHG
·K·U·P·E·R·A·R·D·

Visit the FHG website
www.holidayguides.com
for details of the wide choice of accommodation featured in the full range of FHG titles

Please note

All the information in this book is given in good faith in the belief that it is correct. However, the publishers cannot guarantee the facts given in these pages, neither are they responsible for changes in policy, ownership or terms that may take place after the date of going to press. Readers should always satisfy themselves that the facilities they require are available and that the terms, if quoted, still apply.

England

Strefford Hall, Craven Arms, Shropshire — *Island Cottage Holidays, Isle of Wight* — *Poletrees Farm, Aylesbury, Buckingham*

Self-Catering

Dales Holiday Cottages

Just what you've been looking for

Make sure your holiday is the most memorable ever. Trust Dales Holiday Cottages to find you the perfect cottage, in the most sublime of locations. There's something for everyone, just tell us what you want. We've got personally inspected cottages throughout Northern Britain for couples, groups & families. Pet lovers will always find something just right. And each one is full of character, with many located near great walks and wonderful country pubs. So whatever cottage you've got pictured in your mind, give us a call and let us help make it a reality.

For your choice of over 500 cottages
call **0870 909 9500** or visit **www.dalesholcot.com**

A60

Looking for Holiday Accommodation?

FHG
KUPERARD

for details of hundreds of properties throughout the UK visit our website

www.holidayguides.com

SELF-CATERING Aylesbury, Buckingham   BUCKINGHAMSHIRE 125

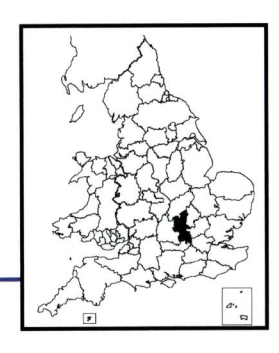

Buckinghamshire

Poletrees Farm

Two charming cottages in courtyard of working farm. They are beautifully furnished and well equipped, with private patios and farmland views.
- Each sleeps 4 • Disabled friendly with carer
- Non-smoking • Open April to September
- Village pubs within 2 miles

The Burnwode Jubilee Way cuts through the farm, and there are many places of historic interest in the area.

Ludgershall Road, Brill, Near Aylesbury, Bucks HP18 9TZ • Tel & Fax: 01844 238276
www.country-accom.co.uk/poletrees-farm
Farmhouse B&B also available.

Situated midway between the market towns of Buckingham and Brackley, close to Stowe Gardens and the Silverstone Circuit; an ideal touring base for Oxford and the Cotswolds. The farm courtyard is a delightfully peaceful spot, overlooking rolling countryside.

Three imaginatively converted traditional stone, timber and slate properties offer the very best in holiday accommodation amidst the peace of the English countryside. Huntsmill is a working, mainly arable farm, with many nature trails and walks.

Chris and Fiona Hilsdon, Huntsmill Farm, Shalstone, Buckingham MK18 5ND
Tel & Fax: 01280 704852 • mobile: 07973 386756
www.huntsmill.com

English Tourism Council ★★★★ SELF CATERING

Note

All the information in this guide is given in good faith in the belief that it is correct. However, the publishers cannot guarantee the facts given in these pages, neither are they responsible for changes in ownership or facilities that may take place after the date of going to press.

Readers should always satisfy themselves that the facilities they require are available and that the terms, if quoted, still apply.

Cheshire

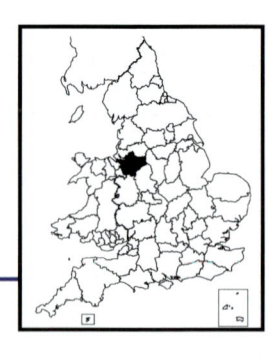

Bosley, Malpas SELF-CATERING

The Old Byre, Pye Ash Farm, Leek Road, Bosley, Macclesfield

The Old Byre at Pye Ash Farm is particularly well designed to suit two families wishing to spend their holidays together in the countryside. Set amongst the fields but only half a mile from Bosley Village, with its shop and a choice of two pubs, many walks can be taken from the farm, into the fields and woods. Bosley Minns overlooks the reservoir and forms part of the Gritstone Trail. Alton Towers is 15 miles away. All accommodation is on the ground floor, suitable for the less able visitor. The Cow Shed sleeps six and the Sheep Shed sleeps four, both have well equipped kitchen and shower room; rear porch with washing and drying facilities. Ample parking. ETC ★★★.

For further details please contact: Dorothy Gilman, Woodcroft, Tunstall Road, Bosley, Macclesfield SK11 0PB
Tel & Fax: 01260 223293
e-mail: dotgilman@hotmail.co.uk

The Granary
Higher Wych, Malpas, Cheshire SY14 7JR

Situated in a quiet valley with a small stream in the garden, The Granary is a self-contained bungalow adjacent to Mill House. Sleeps 4/5 in two double bedrooms. Kitchen/living area, shower and WC, TV and central heating. Cot and babysitting available. Convenient for visiting Chester, Shrewsbury and North Wales. Prices from £190 to £260 per week. B&B also available.

Tel: 01948 780362 • Fax: 01948 780566
email: angela@videoactive.co.uk
www.millhouseandgranary.co.uk

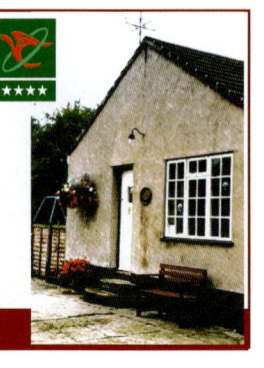

FHG **K·U·P·E·R·A·R·D**

Visit the FHG website
www.holidayguides.com
for details of the wide choice of accommodation featured in the full range of FHG titles

Cornwall

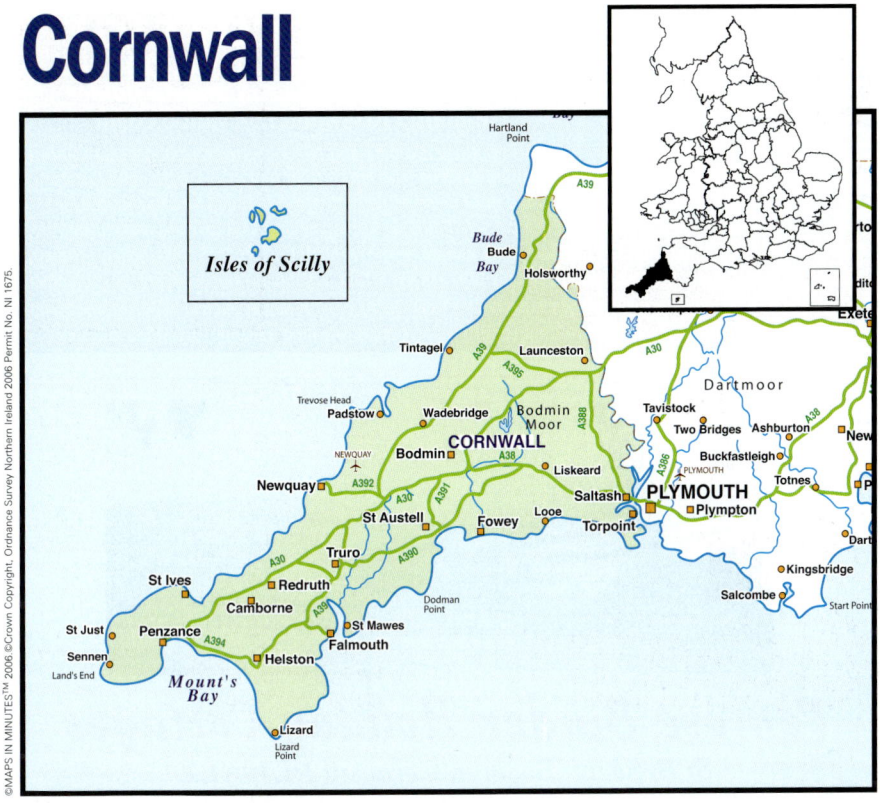

10 Things you didn't Know about Cornwall

- Using the South West Coast Path you can walk around the entire 400 km coast of Cornwall! The South West Coast Path is one of the UK's most spectacular walking routes and with over 4000 km of inland paths, Cornwall is a hikers' delight.
- Warmed by the Gulf Stream, Cornwall has a unique climate and many sub-tropical plant species thrive here. There are over 70 gardens open to the public, from large formal estate gardens such as Lanhydrock to rescued and restored treasures such as the Lost Gardens of Heligan.
- One of the UK's most visited attractions is located in Cornwall. The Eden Project attracts 1.5 million visitors each year and it provides an entertaining and educational insight into man's relationship with plants.
- Cornwall's heritage is rich in myth, folklore and legend. From strange Bronze Age stone monuments to King Arthur's famous castle at Tintagel. Cornwall's industrial heritage is also hugely important, so much so that a bid has been made to UNESCO for World Heritage Site status to help preserve these landscapes.
- Marazion near Penzance is the oldest town in Cornwall and it dates back to 1257. It is a popular destination for those visiting the mysterious island of St Michael's Mount. At low tide visitors can walk across to the mount from Marazion by means of a causeway.
- The first sighting of the approaching Spanish Armada was from Cornwall on July 19th 1588. Watchers on Halzephron Cliff watched the Armada as it approached Mounts Bay. Rumour has it that rather than fight they ran and hid...
- Cornwall boasts some of Europe's finest surfing beaches and each year Newquay hosts a number of international surfing competitions. But if surfing isn't enough to get the adrenaline going, the growing sport of kite surfing is guaranteed to!
- You don't need to head to London for fine dining! With an increasing number of top national chefs beating a path to the county, visitors are spoilt for choice. Great pubs, stylish restaurants and beachside cafes all serving a fantastic choice of local cuisine.
- Cornwall has beaches to rival the Costa del Sol! The Porthminster Beach St Ives was recently voted the 3rd best beach in the world because of its great location, golden sands, Blue Flag status and great choice of bars/cafes.
- Outside London, Cornwall has the largest concentration of artists in the UK. It even has its very own Tate Gallery which occupies a spectacular position overlooking Porthmeor Beach in St Ives.

128 CORNWALL   Bodieve, Bodmin, Bude **SELF-CATERING**

CORNISH COTTAGE
Bodieve, Wadebridge, Cornwall PL27 6EG
Tel: 01208 813024 – Mrs Angela Holder
e-mail: crosswood32@yahoo.co.uk

Cornish Cottage is a 400 year old converted farmhouse, surrounded by sunny gardens with lawns front and rear + patio with furniture, in a quiet crescent with off-street parking, ideally situated for local safe bathing, surfing, sailing, cliff walking and cycling.

The accommodation comprises • well furnished lounge, with two-seater settee and three-seater sofabed, woodburner and night storage heater, TV and DVD player • fully equipped double-aspect kitchen/diner • 3 bedrooms with king-size/twin/full-size bunk beds • main bedroom with washbasin and night storage heater • bathroom with shower into bath • outhouse with fridge/freezer, washing machine, dryer and 2nd toilet.

Penrose Burden Holiday Cottages
St Breward, Bodmin, Cornwall PL30 4LZ
Tel: 01208 850277 / 850617; Fax: 01208 850915
www.penroseburden.co.uk

Situated within easy reach of both coasts and Bodmin Moor on a large farm overlooking a wooded valley with own salmon and trout fishing. These stone cottages with exposed beams and quarry tiled floors have been featured on TV and are award-winners. Home-made meals can be delivered daily. All are suitable for wheelchair users and dogs are welcomed.

Our cottages sleep from two to seven and are open all year.

Please write or telephone for a colour brochure.   Nancy Hall

Close to The Eden Project

Hilton Farm Holiday Cottages, Marhamchurch, Bude EX23 0HE
Tel & Fax: 01288 361521

Where coast meets countryside, in an Area of Outstanding Natural Beauty, the ideal place to make the most of Devon and Cornwall. Superb setting in 25 acres of ground. 16th century farmhouse, sleeps 10; three new luxury cottages and six fully equipped converted barn cottages. Superb heated outdoor swimming pool and jacuzzi, all-weather tennis court, activity area/play area/barbecue and picnic area; laundry facilities. Just two miles from sandy beaches; world-famous Eden Project 45 minutes' drive. Self-catering cottages open all year.
Contact: Fiona & Ian Goodman.

e-mail: ian@hiltonfarmhouse.freeserve.co.uk   website: www.hiltonfarmhouse.co.uk

SELF-CATERING Bude, Delabole, Falmouth, Fowey   CORNWALL 129

LOWER KITLEIGH COTTAGE — Week St Mary, Near Bude, Cornwall

Pretty, Listed farmhouse in unspoilt country near magnificent coast. Newly renovated with all conveniences, yet retaining its charm, it stands in a peaceful grassy garden with picnic table and own parking. The sitting room has period furniture, inglenook fireplace, free logs and colour TV. The fully equipped kitchen has fridge/freezer, double sink, electric cooker and washer/tumble dryer. Three bedrooms with panoramic views, cots, duvets. Well-controlled dogs allowed. Riding nearby, golf, safe beaches, surfing, Cornish Moors, markets, cliff walks. All electricity inclusive, and central heating ensures a cosy stay throughout the year. Prices from £275 to £650 weekly; reductions for part week. Sleeps seven plus cot.

Mr and Mrs T. Bruce-Dick, 114 Albert Street, London NW1 7NE Tel: 0207-485 8976

Delamere Holiday Bungalows

Situated on the outskirts of **Delabole**, near glorious sandy beaches and the spectacular scenery of the **North Cornish Coast**. 16 traditionally built bungalows (sleep up to 5/6), all with panoramic views. Set in private lawned grounds. Ideal position near **Tintagel** and **Polzeath** for holiday exploring, surfing etc. Approx. 30 minutes from **Eden Project**. Sorry, no pets.

Mrs J. Snowden • Tel: 01895 234144 • www.delamerebungalows.com

'Shasta Annex'

A short walk from Mawnan Smith, with thatched pub, Italian restaurant, shops. Maenporth's sandy beach, the beautiful Helford river, tropical gardens are a short drive away. Ideal for coastal walking, Falmouth approx. four miles.

Well equipped comfortable ground floor flat, sleeps 2, with patio overlooking lovely mature garden. Cooker, fridge, washing machine, microwave etc. Digital TV with DVD and video player. Bathroom with shower. Double bed. Garden furniture. Night storage heaters. Towels and linen provided. Electricity incl. in price. Off-road parking.

Welcome pack on arrival. Terms from £200–£350 Brochure available.

Mrs Kathleen Terry, 'Shasta', Carwinion Road, Mawnan Smith, Falmouth TR11 5JD Tel: 01326 250775 e-mail: katerry@btopenworld.com

Penquite Farm, Golant, Fowey PL23 1LB

e-mail: varco@farmersweekly.net • website: www.penquitefarm.co.uk

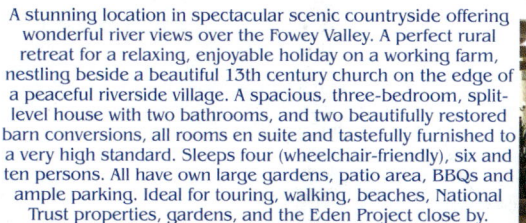

A stunning location in spectacular scenic countryside offering wonderful river views over the Fowey Valley. A perfect rural retreat for a relaxing, enjoyable holiday on a working farm, nestling beside a beautiful 13th century church on the edge of a peaceful riverside village. A spacious, three-bedroom, split-level house with two bathrooms, and two beautifully restored barn conversions, all rooms en suite and tastefully furnished to a very high standard. Sleeps four (wheelchair-friendly), six and ten persons. All have own large gardens, patio area, BBQs and ample parking. Ideal for touring, walking, beaches, National Trust properties, gardens, and the Eden Project close by.

Ruth Varco • Tel & Fax: 01726 833319

Fowey Harbour Cottages

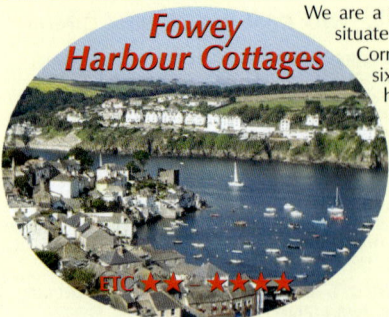

We are a small Agency offering a selection of cottages and flats situated around the beautiful Fowey Harbour on the South Cornish Coast. Different properties accommodate from two to six persons and vary in their decor and facilities so that hopefully there will be something we can offer to suit anyone. All properties are registered with the English Tourism Council and are personally vetted by us.

Short Breaks and weekend bookings accepted subject to availability (mainly out of peak season but sometimes available at "last minute" in season).

**Brochure and details from W. J. B. Hill & Son,
3 Fore Street, Fowey PL23 1AH
Tel: 01726 832211 • Fax: 01726 832901
e-mail: hillandson@talk21.com
www.foweyharbourcottages.co.uk**

ETC ★★ ★★★★

Forget-Me-Not Farm Holidays • Tel: 01566 86284

Situated on Trefranck, our 340-acre family-run beef and sheep farm, in North Cornwall, on the edge of enchanting Bodmin Moor and six miles from the spectacular North Cornwall Heritage Coast.

We offer all year round luxury, 4-star, self-catering acccommodation.
• **Forget-Me-Not Cottage** can comfortably sleep 6 and is tastefully decorated and superbly equipped, with a real log fire and central heating.
• **The Old Wagon House** is a stylish barn conversion and sleeps 2-4, with a 4-poster bed – ideal for romantic breaks. • **The Stable** is an en suite twin annexe to the Old Wagon House. Trefranck is within easy reach of the Eden Project, the Lost Gardens of Heligan, Padstow and the Camel Trail.

Trefranck Farm, St Clether, Launceston PL15 8QN • mobile: 07790 453129
e-mail: holidays@trefranck.co.uk • www.forget-me-not-farm-holidays.co.uk

---

Swallows & Meadow Cottage

**Lower Dutson Farm, Launceston PL15 9SP
Tel & Fax: 01566 776456**

Well-equipped cottages with two/three bedrooms, two bathrooms, TV lounge and kitchen. Situated two miles from historic Launceston with its Norman Castle. Centrally located for visiting National Trust houses and gardens, Dartmoor, Bodmin Moor and the beaches and harbours of Devon and Cornwall. Play fetch with Fly our sheepdog or watch out for the Kingfisher as you relax or fish down by the lake or riverside. Pets welcome by arrangement.
Terms from £185 to £575.

e-mail: holidays@farm-cottage.co.uk
www.farm-cottage.co.uk

Trenannick Cottages

Five delightful cottages converted from 18th century farm buildings, standing at the end of a private, tree-lined drive, in a quiet rural setting. All cottages have small private gardens, and access to barbecue area, children's playing field, and small copse. Ideal touring base for North Cornish coast, two miles from A39, with Crackington Haven, Bude, and Boscastle all nearby. Accommodation varies from two to six persons per cottage, with wheelchair access in the Roundhouse. Open throughout the year, with log fires for those colder evenings. Short Breaks available. Pets welcome in certain cottages. Rates from £145 per week.

Details from **Mrs L. Harrison, Trenannick Farmhouse, Warbstow, Launceston PL15 8RP**
Tel: 01566 781443 • e-mail: trenannick-1@tiscali.co.uk • www.trenannickcottages.co.uk

SELF-CATERING Liskeard, Looe   CORNWALL **131**

CUTKIVE WOOD HOLIDAY LODGES

Nestling in the heart of a peaceful and lovely family-owned country estate, there are six well-equipped cedar-clad lodges. Set on the edge of bluebell woods with wonderful rural views, you can relax and enjoy yourself in this tranquil and idyllic setting. Ideally situated to enjoy year-round holidays. You can help to feed the animals, milk the goats, explore the woods and fields. Big play area. So much to see and do - including memorable beaches, wonderful coasts, walk the moors, theme attractions, historic gems and the Eden Project. Dogs welcome. Short breaks. Open all year.

St Ive, Liskeard, Cornwall PL14 3ND • Tel: 01579 362216
www.cutkivewood.co.uk • holidays@cutkivewood.co.uk

TREMAINE GREEN
for MEMORABLE HOLIDAYS

"A beautiful private hamlet" of 11 traditional cosy Cornish craftsmen's cottages between **Looe** and **Polperro**. Clean, comfortable and well equipped, with a warm friendly atmosphere, for pets with 2 to 8 people. Set in award-winning grounds, only 12 miles from the **Eden Project** with country and coastal walks nearby. Pets £18 pw; owners from £118.

• Towels, Linen, Electric & Hot Water included • Dishwashers in larger cottages • Launderette • Kid's Play Area
• Games Room • Tennis Court • TV/DVD's • Cots & Highchairs • Pubs & Restaurants in 1 mile walking distance

Mr & Mrs J Spreckley, Tremaine Green Country Cottages, Pelynt, Near Looe, Cornwall PL13 2LT
Web: www.tremainegreen.co.uk • e-mail: stay@tremainegreen.co.uk • Tel: (01503) 220333

Talehay Holiday Cottages
Pelynt, Near Looe PL13 2LT
A Quiet Haven in the Countryside near the sea

Cosy, traditional cottages with many original features retained provide superb holiday accommodation on 17C non-working farmstead. Set in 4 acres of unspoilt countryside offering peace and tranquillity with breathtaking coastal and country walks on your doorstep. This is an ideal location for exploring the many delights of Cornwall. C.T.B. approved. Close to the Eden Project.

Let our brochure convince you – Tel: Neil & Theressa Dennett 01503 220252
E-mail: infobooking@talehay.co.uk Website: www.talehay.co.uk

Looking for holiday accommodation?
for details of hundreds of properties throughout the UK visit:

www.holidayguides.com

132　CORNWALL　Looe, Looe Valley, Mawgan Porth, Padstow　**SELF-CATERING**

Raven Rock and Spindrift
Contact: Mrs S. Gill, Bodrigy, Plaidy, Looe PL13 1LF
Tel: 01503 263122

- *Two bungalows adjacent to Plaidy Beach. Spindrift has en suite bedroom, sleeps two; Raven Rock has two bedrooms and sleeps four. Own parking spaces, central heating, wheelchair accessible. Semi-detached bungalows are fully furnished, well equipped and have sea views. Set in peaceful surroundings at Plaidy. Open plan lounge-diner-kitchen. Colour TV. Patio garden. Electricity and gas included in rent. Pet by arrangement. Personally supervised.*
- *Looe is a fishing port with a variety of shops and restaurants and is only a few minutes by car or a 15 to 20 minute walk.*
- *Weekly terms: Spindrift from £200 to £310; Raven Rock from £265 to £420. Short breaks (three days minimum) before Easter and after middle of October.*
- *Apartment in centre of town also available (sleeps 6/8).*

Once part of a Duchy of Cornwall working farm, now farmhouse and farm buildings converted to a high standard to form a nine cottage complex around former farmyard. Sleeping from two to ten. All cottages are well furnished and equipped and prices include electricity, bed linen and towels. Most cottages have a garden. Five acre grounds, set in delightful wooded valley, with tennis, putting, children's play area, fishing lake, animal paddock, games room with pool and table tennis. Separate bar. Laundry. Barbecue. Railcar from Liskeard to Looe stops at end of picnic area. Have a 'car free' day out. Children and well behaved dogs welcome (no dogs in high season, please). Prices from £120 per week.

Badham Farm, St Keyne, Liskeard PL14 4RW
Tel: 01579 343572
e-mail: badhamfarm@yahoo.co.uk • www.badhamfarm.co.uk

Blue Bay Lodge
Serviced Self-Catering Lodges
between Newquay & Padstow at Mawgan Porth, Cornwall
200 yards from the beach
Fully Equipped • Dishwashers • Daily Maid Service • Linen Provided
Contact: J. MCLUSKIE - 01637 860324
www.bluebaycornwall.co.uk • Email: hotel@bluebaycornwall.co.uk

---

❖ Carnevas Farm Holiday Park ❖
Carnevas Farm, St Merryn, Padstow PL28 8PN • **01841 520230**

Situated only half a mile from golden sandy beach, fishing, golf, sailing etc. Quaint harbour village of Padstow only four miles. Bungalows/chalets sleep four/five, have two bedrooms, bathroom, kitchen/diner, airing cupboard, colour TV. Caravans four-berth or six-berth, all have showers, toilets, fridge, colour TV (also separate camping and caravan facilities). Converted barns available, sleep four/six persons, furnished to a high standard. Brochure on request.

www.carnevasholidaypark.co.uk

SELF-CATERING Penzance, Polperro   CORNWALL 133

Barlowenath • St Hilary, Penzance TR20 9DQ

Two cottages on a working farm, in quiet surroundings six miles from Penzance. Good road approach. Ideal for touring Cornish coast – beaches 2 miles, Marazion 2½, St Ives 8 and Land's End 16. Well equipped, with lounge/diner. TV/video. One cottage sleeps 5 in 3 bedrooms, the second sleeps 4 in 2 twin rooms. Linen for hire by arrangement. Electricity by £1 meter, storage heaters extra.

Terms: £195 to £420 weekly, VAT exempt. Available all year.

Mrs Curnow • Telephone & Fax: 01736 710409
e-mail: marian.curnow@tesco.net

POLPERRO Peak House, Talland Hill, Polperro
300-year old holiday cottages, nicely furnished and equipped, in definitely the best position, overlooking the harbour, spectacularly situated, enjoying 15 miles of panoramic sea views stretching to Eddystone Lighthouse. Private sun trap gardens, giving a Mediterranean feel, with private parking. Only 100 yards from the village centre and three to four minutes from the harbourside, beach and National Trust cliff walks. Wake up to this view and enjoy the sights and sounds of the historic fishing port, see this quaint village with narrow streets, old houses and harbour, dating from the 16th century.
Rates: from £175-£575 per week for a cottage.
• Sleep 2 to 8 persons. • Children and pets welcome.
Contact Graham Wright (01579 344080).

Other specialised holiday guides from FHG

Recommended **INNS & PUBS** OF BRITAIN

Recommended **COUNTRY HOTELS** OF BRITAIN

Recommended **SHORT BREAK HOLIDAYS** IN BRITAIN

The bestselling and original **PETS WELCOME!**

The GOLF GUIDE, Where to Play, Where to Stay IN BRITAIN & IRELAND

COAST & COUNTRY HOLIDAYS

SELF-CATERING HOLIDAYS IN BRITAIN

BED & BREAKFAST STOPS

CARAVAN & CAMPING HOLIDAYS

CHILDREN WELCOME! Family Holiday & Days Out Guide

BRITAIN'S BEST LEISURE & RELAXATION GUIDE

Published annually: available in all good bookshops or direct from the publisher:
FHG Guides, Abbey Mill Business Centre, Seedhill, Paisley PA1 1TJ
Tel: 0141 887 0428 • Fax: 0141 889 7204
• E-mail: admin@fhguides.co.uk • Web: www.holidayguides.com

134 CORNWALL   Redruth, St Tudy, Truro   **SELF-CATERING**

HIGHER LAITY FARM
ETC ★★★★★ Self-catering

Portreath Road, Redruth TR16 4HY

3 delightful cottages: The Loft • Byre Cott • Trotters
Full gas heating - Double glazing - Country-style kitchen
Full size gas cooker - Dishwasher - Washer/dryer - Fridge/freezer
Microwave - Colour TV - DVD - Video - Bed linen and towels
High chair & cot available - Gas and electricity inclusive

it's time to relax....

Take advantage of the spectacular North Coast and surrounding countryside. Explore coastal walks, woodland, lakes and cycle trails. Locally, Portreath offers a selection of shops, restaurants and pubs, and The Tate Gallery and Lost Gardens of Heligan, horse riding and golf are within easy reach.

TEL: 01209 842317   E-MAIL: info@higherlaityfarm.co.uk   WEBSITE: www.higherlaityfarm.co.uk

CHAPEL COTTAGES   ST TUDY

Four traditional cottages, sleeping 2 to 5, in a quiet farming area. Ideal for the spectacular north coast, Bodmin Moor, and the Eden Project. Comfortable and well-equipped. Garden and private parking. Rental £150 to £430 per week. Also two smaller cottages for couples at Hockadays, near Blisland - converted from a 17th century barn in a quiet farming hamlet. Rental £140 to £325 per week. Shop and pub/restaurant within walking distance. Regretfully, no pets. Brochure available.

Mrs M. Pestell, 'Hockadays', Tregenna, Blisland PL30 4QJ • Tel: 01208 850146 • www.hockadays.co.uk

---

TRENONA FARM   Ruan High Lanes, Truro, Cornwall TR2 5JS

Two renovated barns near the main farmhouse on working beef and sheep farm. Peaceful location three miles from the South Coast and close to the Eden Project and Lost Gardens of Heligan. **CHY TYAK** sleeps six (plus cot) in a double master bedroom with en suite bathroom; two twin-bedded rooms upstairs. Open-plan kitchen/diner/lounge with high quality furnishings, wide-screen TV, video, CD player, payphone downstairs. **CHY WHEL** is a bungalow sleeping six in one double and two twin-bedded rooms, all with en suite bathrooms. Open-plan kitchen/diner/lounge has all new appliances. Both properties have ample parking with room for boats, trailers and under cover storage for bicycles. Wheelchair access and pets welcome by arrangement.

Tel: 01872 501339 • e-mail: info@trenonafarmholidays.co.uk • www.trenonafarmholidays.co.uk

---

Please note

All the information in this book is given in good faith in the belief that it is correct. However, the publishers cannot guarantee the facts given in these pages, neither are they responsible for changes in policy, ownership or terms that may take place after the date of going to press. Readers should always satisfy themselves that the facilities they require are available and that the terms, if quoted, still apply.

SELF-CATERING   **CUMBRIA 135**

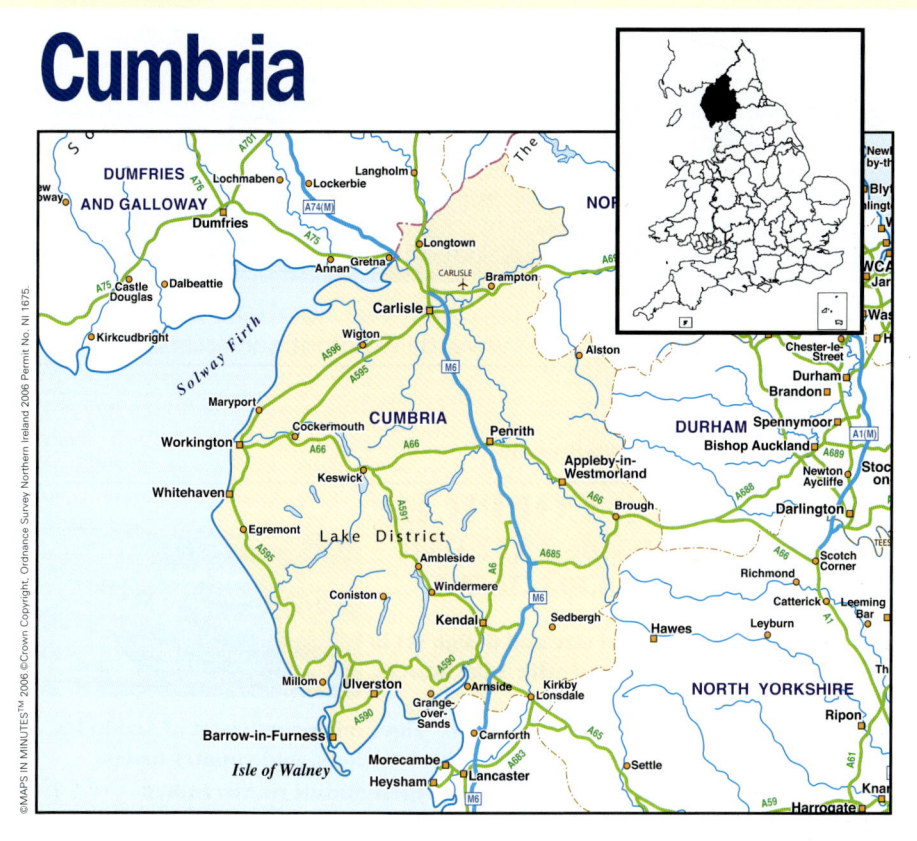

Cumbria

Cumbria - the Lake District has strong literary connections. Visitors can see the sweeping landscapes that inspired the Lake poets, William Wordsworth and Samuel Taylor Coleridge, and the works of writers such as Arthur Ransome and Beatrix Potter. It is an area rich in heritage, with the beautiful ruins of Furness Abbey in the Lake District Peninsula, England's smallest cathedral in Carlisle, Birdoswald Roman Fort and Hadrian's Wall, where the Scots were kept out, and Carlisle Castle where Mary Queen of Scots was imprisoned. South from Carlisle runs the Eden Valley – an area of rolling green landscapes contrasting with the hump-backed open moors of the North Pennines. In the Western Lakes there are the lush and peaceful Ennerdale and Eskdale valleys and the sandstone cliffs of St Bees Head, part of a designated Heritage Coast.

Cumbria has many delightful market towns, such as Alston, the highest market town in England, and Keswick, the jewel of the Northern Lakes. In the south, the cobbled streets of Ulverston have many claims to fame – the birthplace of Quakerism, Stan Laurel and pole vaulting. The Georgian town of Whitehaven was once Britain's third largest port, and further south, Barrow-in-Furness combines a Dock Museum with a modern centre. There are historic houses and beautiful gardens such as Holker Hall with its 25 acres of award-winning gardens and food hall selling succulent produce.

When making enquiries please mention FHG GUIDES

CUMBRIA — **SELF-CATERING**

The Lake District, Cumbria and Eden Valley

There is beauty in every direction as you walk around the peaks and lakes that make this region both unique and adored. They are all within view of outstanding cottages, barns & houses that are personally inspected and cater for everyone from couples and families to pet lovers and groups of friends.

Dales Holiday Cottages

For your choice of over 500 cottages
call **0870 909 9505** or visit **www.dalesholcot.com/cumbria**   A62

Ambleside, Bowness-on-Windermere

RAMSTEADS COPPICE,
Outgate, Ambleside LA22 0NH
Mr Evans - 015394 36583

Six timber lodges of varied size and design set in 15 acres of mixed woodland with wild flowers, birds and native wild animals.
There are also 11 acres of rough hill pasture. Three miles south west of Ambleside, it is an ideal centre for walkers, artists, birdwatchers, and country lovers.
No pets • Children welcome • Open March to November

43A Quarry Rigg, Bowness-on-Windermere

Ideally situated in the centre of the village close to the Lake and all amenities, the flat is in a new development, fully self-contained, and furnished and equipped to a high standard for owner's own comfort and use. Lake views, ideal relaxation and touring centre. Accommodation is for two/three people. Bedroom with twin beds, lounge with TV, video and DVD; convertible settee; separate kitchen with electric cooker, microwave and fridge/freezer; bathroom with bath/shower and WC. Electric heating. Parking for residents.
Rates: Low Season £175 to £220; High Season £220-£300 Weekends/Short Breaks also available • Sleeps 2/3 • Sorry, no pets.
SAE, please, for details to E. Jones, 45 West Oakhill Park, Liverpool, Merseyside L13 4BN

Tel & Fax: 0151-228 5739
e-mail:
eejay@btinternet.com

FHG Guides

publish a large range of well-known accommodation guides.
We will be happy to send you details or you can use the order form at the back of this book.

FHG
K·U·P·E·R·A·R·D

SELF-CATERING Bowness-on-Windermere — CUMBRIA 137

Lakelovers

lakeland's self catering specialists

VisitBritain ★★★ to ★★★★★

Quality Holiday Homes
in the beautiful Lake District

Quality Holiday Homes in England's Beautiful Lake District

Hundreds of VisitBritain inspected and graded properties throughout the southern and central Lake District. Lakelovers are sure to have a property to meet your needs. Free Leisure Club membership with every booking

Tel: 015394 88855 • Fax: 015394 88857
e-mail: bookings@lakelovers.co.uk • www.lakelovers.co.uk

Lakelovers, Belmont House, Lake Road,
Bowness-on-Windermere, Cumbria LA23 3BJ

See also Inside Front Cover

Swallows Nest

Hidden away in the delightful Lickle Valley, some six miles to the south of Coniston and close to lakes and coast.

Hobkinground Farm, Broughton Mills, Broughton-in-Furness LA20 6AU

Swallows Nest is a three-bedroomed cottage sleeping 6-8. Two family bedrooms and third bedroom on the ground floor with en suite and walk-in shower. Spacious lounge with open fire, exposed beams, TV, video and DVD player; dining area; bathroom; well equipped fitted kitchen. Utility room with washer. Oil-fired central heating, ample parking. Sorry no pets. Ten minute walk from our local hostelry which serves good food. From £195 - £895 per week.

Contact: Janet 01229 716338
e-mail: enquiries@hobkinground.co.uk   www.hobkinground.co.uk

Jenkin Cottage

Come and enjoy a peaceful away from it all holiday at our family-run working hill farm three miles from Cockermouth. Jenkin Cottage has a spectacular outlook over open countryside with views extending to the Solway Firth and the Scottish Lowlands. We are in an ideal situation for fell walking on the Buttermere fells or for touring the Lakes by car. The cottage is personally supervised and has a homely atmosphere. We are open all year with long weekends and mid week breaks in the winter months.

◆ All linen provided ◆ Lounge with open log fire ◆ Fully equipped modern kitchen ◆ Full central heating ◆ Sorry, no pets ◆ Children welcome ◆ We also extend a welcome to business people ◆ Terms from £250 to £450 per week ◆ Brochure available.

Mrs M.E. Teasdale, Jenkin Farm and Cottage, Embleton, Cockermouth CA13 9TH
Tel: 017687 76387 • e-mail: janet@sheepsnest.demon.co.uk • www.jenkinfarm.co.uk

Looking for Holiday Accommodation?

FHG
K·U·P·E·R·A·R·D

for details of hundreds of properties throughout the UK visit our website

www.holidayguides.com

SELF-CATERING Grange-over-Sands, Kendal, Keswick   CUMBRIA **139**

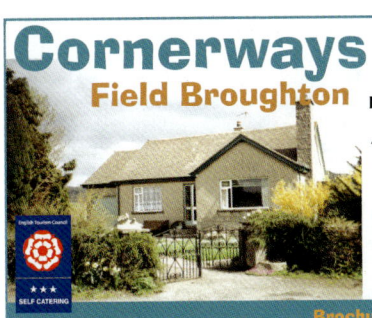

Cornerways
Field Broughton

Detached bungalow, own private garden with parking. Quiet situation with all round Lakeland views. Three miles from historic village of Cartmel, three miles from Newby Bridge, southern end of Lake Windermere. Ideal base for enjoying Lakeland holiday pursuits and countryside. The bungalow has entrance hall, living/dining room with colour TV, fitted breakfast kitchen, fridge/freezer, microwave and full electric cooker. Bathroom/WC. Double and twin-bedded bedrooms sleeping four. Duvets, linen provided. Well equipped. Electric and oil heating by meter reading. Incoming telephone. No pets or children under four years. Personal supervision.
£300 to £450 per week.

Brochure and details from:
Mrs Rigg, Prospect House, Barber Green, Grange-over-Sands LA11 6HU Tel: 015395 36329

The cottage adjoins the 17th century farmhouse in a sunny position with wonderful views. Ideal spot for touring the Lake District and Yorkshire Dales. Two bedrooms (one with double bed, the other with two singles). Bathroom with bath, shower, toilet and washbasin. Large livingroom/kitchen with colour TV, DVD, fridge and cooker. Fitted carpets throughout. Own entrance porch. Shops at Burneside two miles away, Kendal four miles, Windermere eight miles. Linen provided. Car essential – parking.

Working farm • Sleeps 4
Children welcome • No pets
Terms from £210 to £270 weekly.
Burneside, Kendal LA8 9AY

High Underbrow Farm
Tel: 01539 738630

LAKELAND
Cottage Holidays

Self-catering cottages in and around Keswick and beautiful Borrowdale

Tel: 017687 76065
info@lakelandcottages.co.uk
www.lakelandcottages.co.uk

Keswick, Kirkby Lonsdale SELF-CATERING

Courtyard Cottages - Self-Catering at Springs Farm in Keswick

Set in a charming courtyard on a working dairy farm at the foot of the Walla Crag in the heart of the Lake District, this former dairy and byre have been recently converted to create three self-contained cottages offering quality accommodation. All cottages are on one level and are centrally heated. Idyllic location ideal for cyclists, walkers and families alike, with plenty of walks and cycle routes from the doorstep - take a 10 minute stroll into Keswick. Ample parking. Cycle hire available. Small farm shop with general provisions. All cottages are centrally heated and well equipped and are on one level. Non-smoking. Sleep 2-6.

Springs Farm, Springs Road, Keswick CA12 4AN
Tel: 017687 72144 • mobile: 07816 824253 • Fax: 017687 72546
e-mail: info@springs-farm.co.uk • www.springs-farm.co.uk

Irton House Farm
Isel, Cockermouth, Near Keswick CA13 9ST
017687 76380
almond@farmersweekly.net
www.irtonhousefarm.com

Farm location with superb views of lake and mountains. Family accommodation (wheelchair accessible). Sleeps 2/6. Children welcome. Interesting walking area and comfortable motoring. Facilities for fishing, swimming and golf nearby. Ample parking. Also 6-berth static caravan for hire.
Please telephone for colour brochure.

Cragside

Harrison Farm, Whittington, Kirkby Lonsdale, Carnforth, Lancashire LA6 2NX
Tel: 015242 71415

Near Hutton Roof, three miles from Kirkby Lonsdale and central for touring Lake District and Yorkshire Dales. Coast walks on Hutton Roof Crag, famous limestone pavings. Property sleeps 8; one room with double and single bed, one with double and cot, third bedroom with three single beds. Bathroom. Sittingroom, diningroom and kitchen. Everything supplied but linen. Parking space. Pets permitted. Other cottages available, sleeping 2-8. Electric cooker, microwave, fridge, kettle, iron, immersion heater and TV. Electricity and coal extra. Terms from £200 per week. SAE brings quick reply.

Visit the FHG website
www.holidayguides.com
for details of the wide choice of accommodation featured in the full range of FHG titles

FHG
K·U·P·E·R·A·R·D

SELF-CATERING Kirkby Stephen, Kirkoswald, Lamplugh

HARTLEY CASTLE BARN
Hartley, Kirkby Stephen, Cumbria CA17 4JJ

Hartley Castle is a luxury barn conversion built on the ruins of a medieval castle. The spacious accommodation sleeps 6-8, plus cot, and has magnificent views and a private garden. Perfectly located in the charming, unspoilt village of Hartley, only 10 minutes' walk from Kirkby Stephen with its antique shops, restaurants, tearooms and pubs, and an ideal base for walking and exploring the Lakes and Dales. Fishing on the River Eden. Sorry, non-smoking, and no pets. Secure garage and ample parking. Open all year.

Short Breaks from £180 per week • Contact: Mrs Sally Dixon
Tel: 017683 71331 • Mobile: 07837 879061 • e-mail: DJS@hartleycastle.freeserve.co.uk

KIRKOSWALD Crossfield Cottages with Leisure Fishing. Tranquil quality cottages overlooking fishing lake amidst Lakeland's beautiful Eden Valley countryside. Only 30 minutes' drive from Ullswater, North Pennines, Hadrian's Wall and the Scottish Borders. You will find freshly made beds for your arrival, tranquillity and freedom to roam. Good coarse fishing for residents only; fly fishing nearby on River Eden. Cottages are clean, well-equipped and maintained. Laundry area. Exceptional wildlife and walking area. Escape and relax to your home in the country.
- Pets very welcome.

ETC ★★★.
SAE to Crossfield Cottages, Kirkoswald, Penrith CA10 1EU (Tel & Fax: 01768 898711 6pm-10pm for bookings, 24hr Brochure Line).

e-mail: info@crossfieldcottages.co.uk
www.crossfieldcottages.co.uk

HODYOAD COTTAGE

Hodyoad stands in its own private grounds, with extensive views of the surrounding fells in peaceful rural countryside. Mid-way between the beautiful Lakes of Loweswater and Ennerdale, six miles from Cockermouth and 17 from Keswick. Fell walking, boating, pony trekking and trout fishing can all be enjoyed within a three-and-a-half mile radius.

The cottage is fully centrally heated and has two bedrooms to sleep five plus cot. All linen provided. Lounge with colour TV. Kitchen with fitted units, cooker and fridge. Bathroom with shower, washbasin, toilet, shaver point. Laundry room with washing machine and tumble dryer. Car essential, ample parking. Sea eight miles. Open all year. From £230 to £395 per week. For further details please contact:

Mrs J. A. Cook, Hodyoad House, Lamplugh, Cumbria CA14 4TT • Tel: 01946 861338
e-mail: hodyoad@tiscali.co.uk • www.hodyoad.com

Publisher's note

While every effort is made to ensure accuracy, we regret that FHG Guides cannot accept responsibility for errors, misrepresentations or omissions in our entries or any consequences thereof. Prices in particular should be checked.

We will follow up complaints but cannot act as arbiters or agents for either party.

Derbyshire

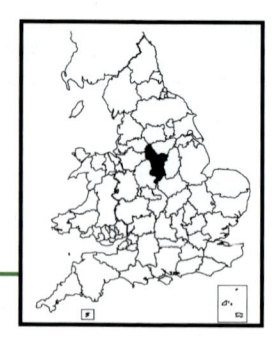

Dairyhouse Farm, Alkmonton, Longford, Near Ashbourne DE6 3DG
Tel & Fax: 01335 330359 • e-mail: michael@dairyhousefarm.org.uk
www.dairyhousefarm.org.uk

Welcome to Dairyhouse Farm, where you will find great accommodation at a price to suit everyone.

THE PIGSTY has been tastefully converted and sleeps four + cot. Fully equipped kitchen/breakfast room, lounge/dining room, ground floor twin bedroom, toilet; upstairs double bedroom with bathroom.

THE LOOSEBOXES sleeps two adults. Four-poster bed, fully equipped kitchen (**ETC ★★★★★**).

All linen and electricity incl. in both properties. No smoking and no pets. The farm is situated in the tranquil Derbyshire Dales, just a short drive from the Peak District. Also convenient for Alton Towers and many National Trust properties.

Wolfscote Grange Farm Cottages
Hartington, Near Buxton, Derbyshire SK17 0AX
Tel & Fax: 01298 84342

Charming cottages nestling beside the beautiful Dove Valley in stunning scenery.

Cruck Cottage is peaceful 'with no neighbours, only sheep' and a cosy 'country living' feel.

Swallows Cottage offers comfort for the traveller and time to relax in beautiful surroundings. It sparkles with olde worlde features, yet has all modern amenities including en suite facilities and spa bathroom.

The farm trail provides walks from your doorstep to the Dales. Open all year.

Weekly terms from £180 to £460 (sleeps 4) & £180 to £570 (sleeps 6).

e-mail: wolfscote@btinternet.com
www.wolfscotegrangecottages.co.uk

SELF-CATERING Hartington, Matlock

DERBYSHIRE 143

Cotterill Farm
Biggin by Hartington, Buxton SK17 0DJ

Five stone cottages, three sleep four persons, one, all on ground floor, sleeps three and one sleeps two. High and tasteful specification, with exposed beams. Patio, substantial garden area and wild flower meadows. The land on which the cottages stand is surrounded by a nature reserve through which a footpath leads to the River Dove.

- Less than half-a-mile from village and pub.
- Surrounded by footpaths/bridleways and cycle trails.
- Housekeeping standards are of the highest.
- Terms from £210 to £500 inclusive.

Telephone: 01298 84447
e-mail: enquiries@cotterillfarm.co.uk
www.cotterillfarm.co.uk

MATLOCK Honeysuckle, Jasmine and Clematis Cottages, Middlehills Farm, Grange Mill, Matlock DE4 4HY (01629 650368).

Relax, unwind, enjoy the peace and tranquillity in one of our warm, welcoming cottages or static caravan. JASMINE - two bedroomed, and HONEYSUCKLE - three bedroomed, are full of character – stone mullions, enclosed south-facing patios. CLEMATIS - two bedroomed, Accessible Category 2, is on one level and especially converted for less-able and wheelchair users. Large bathroom with support rails, wheel-in shower with shower seat. Also fully equipped static caravan for bargain breaks. Meet our friendly pot-bellied pig, and Bess and Ruby are ideal playmates for children of all ages.

- Suitable for disabled guests.

Looking for Holiday Accommodation?

FHG
KUPERARD

for details of hundreds of properties throughout the UK visit our website

www.holidayguides.com

Devon

Devon

Discover the real taste of Devon – freshly caught fish, scrumptious farmhouse cheeses, local ales, award-winning wines and traditional cream teas. From a bar meal in a local inn to a gourmet meal in a country house hotel, Devon is home to some superb, award-winning chefs who are more than a match for the competition, either at home or abroad. With so much to offer why not try one the South Hams or Tamar Valley Food Trails to discover the county's finest restaurants, as well as a few hidden gems!

Discover a vibrant Devon, with sailing regattas, walking, sporting, folk, food and garden festivals, not to mention surfing, rock climbing, hot air ballooning and fishing. Tavistock's Goose Fair, Flaming Tar Barrels, Widecombe Fair and the Blackawton Worm Charming Festival give just a flavour of the more traditional events that take place all year round. The county really is a mecca for golfers, and whether you are a scratch player or a beginner you will be sure to enjoy every minute! Play on a course amidst sand dunes, tread the heathery moorland or be side-tracked by stunning countryside or spectacular seascapes.

Free or reduced rate entry to Holiday Visits and Attractions – see our READERS' OFFER VOUCHERS on pages 7-40

SELF-CATERING DEVON 145

'Easily the best choice of cottages in Devon...'

...and comfortably the best value

Contact us now for a free colour guide
and unbiased recommendation service to the
best value pet friendly cottages around Exmoor
and Devon's unspoilt National Trust Coast.

Bargain breaks from only £35 per person to luxury
manor house for 16 from only £995 per week.

North Devon Holiday Homes

Barnstaple, Devon EX31 1BD

Tel: 01271 376322 ❖ Fax: 01271 346544

e mail: info@northdevonholidays.co.uk   www.northdevonholidays.co.uk

Toad Hall Cottages

250 fabulous and unusual properties situated in truly beautiful waterside rural and village locations throughout Devon, Cornwall & Exmoor.

For our full colour glossy brochure please telephone: (local rate - 24 hours)
0845 612 7978
www.toadhallcottages.com

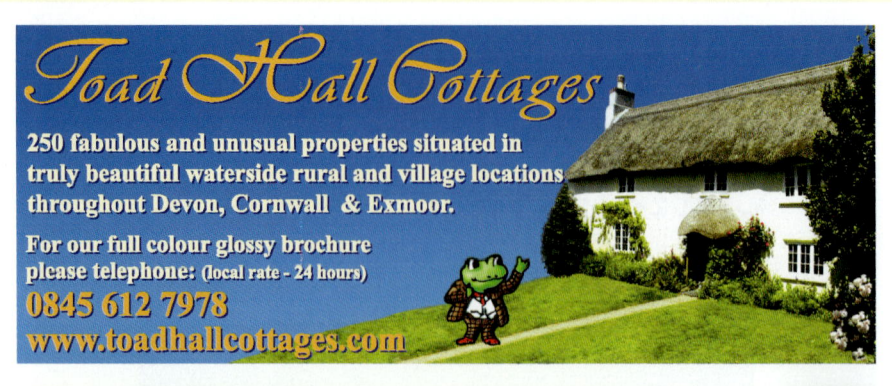

Farm & Cottage Holidays

freedom of choice

Enjoy the freedom and the beauty of this delightful corner of South West England with over 750 of the finest holiday cottages throughout Cornwall, Devon, Somerset and Dorset. All situated in superb coastal & rural locations. View our full collection, search availability and book securely online. The perfect holiday is yours to choose!

holidaycottages.co.uk
01237 479698

- Log Cabins
- Fisherman's Cottages
- Luxury Riverside Apartments
- Barn Conversions

Ashburton

Wooder Manor
Widecombe-in-the-Moor Near Ashburton TQ13 7TR

Cottages and converted coach house, on 170-acre working family farm nestled in the picturesque valley of Widecombe, surrounded by unspoilt woodland, moors and granite tors. Half-a-mile from village with post office, general stores, inn with dining room, church and National Trust Information Centre. Excellent centre for touring Devon with a variety of places to visit and exploring Dartmoor by foot or on horseback. Accommodation is clean and well equipped with colour TV, central heating, laundry room. Children welcome. Large gardens and courtyard for easy parking. Open all year, so take advantage of off-season reduced rates. Short Breaks also available. Two properties suitable for disabled visitors. Colour brochure.

Tel & Fax: 01364 621391
e-mail: angela@woodermanor.com
website: www.woodermanor.com

SELF-CATERING Bideford, Brixham, Colyton, Cullompton   **DEVON 147**

BIDEFORD Waterside Cottage.
Pretty cottage right on the tidal River Torridge with glorious unrestricted views over the river and with moorings for a boat. Back garden wall is on the riverside, and from garden and cottage you can watch boats coming or going, or fish. Enclosed garden with garden furniture. Beach nearby. Two bedrooms. Private parking. On the Coastal Path - ideal for walking. Other sea front cottages available. Ring for prices and vacancies only or send SAE for brochure.
• Dogs welcome.
Mrs F. W. Barnes, 140 Bay View Road, Northam, Bideford, Devon EX39 1BJ (01237 473801)
www.seabirdcottages.co.uk

DEVONCOAST HOLIDAYS

We are an experienced Holiday Letting Agency, with properties ranging from one bedroom flats to three bedroomed houses, all in **Sunny South Devon.** Some have sea views. All are fully equipped with CTV and car parking. Children and pets are welcome. Mini Breaks.
We are open all year. Free brochure and map.

85 BERRYHEAD ROAD, BRIXHAM, DEVON TQ5 9AB
Tel: 07050 33 8889   www.devoncoast.info

BONEHAYNE FARM   COTTAGE: CARAVAN: BOARD
COLYTON, DEVON EX24 6SG

• Family 250 acre working farm • Competitive prices
• Spectacular views • South facing luxury caravan
• Cottage with four-poster and central heating
• Four miles to the beach • Five minutes from Colyton
• Spacious lawns/gardens • Laundry room, BBQ, picnic tables
• Good trout fishing, woods to roam, walks

Mrs Gould
Tel: 01404 871396/871416

www.bonehayne.co.uk   •   e-mail: gould@bonehayne.co.uk

Essentially Fishing Holidays

Luxury holiday lodges, accommodating from 1 to 5 people, fully equipped, with linen, towels, heating and electricity included in the price. The secluded setting, amidst 32 acres of idyllic countryside, includes probably the best coarse/carp fishing in the south west. Situated one mile from Kentisbeare with its well-stocked shop and good pubs, and central for both Exeter and Taunton.
Limited touring caravan pitches available.
Non-smoking. Terms from £305 to £680 per week.

David & Anne Wheeler, Goodiford Mill Fishery, Kentisbeare, Near Cullompton, Devon EX15 2AS
01884 266533 • www.goodifordmillleisure.co.uk

INSTOW Beach Haven Cottage.
Two seafront cottages overlooking the sandy beach. Instow is a quiet yachting village with soft yellow sands and a pretty promenade of shops, old houses, pubs and cafés serving drinks and meals. Beach Haven has extensive beach and sea views from the house and garden (picture shows view from balcony), own parking, gas fired central heating, colour TV, washing machine. Lawned garden overlooking sea with terrace and garden furniture. Coastal walks and cycle trails, boat to Lundy Island. Other sea front cottages available. Ring for prices and vacancies only or send SAE for brochure.
• Sleeps 5/6.   • Dog welcome.
Mrs F. I. Barnes, 140 Bay View Road, Northam, Bideford, Devon EX39 1BJ (01237 473801)
www.seabirdcottages.co.uk

OLDAPORT FARM COTTAGES
All furnished to a high standard • Fully equipped fitted kitchens • Heating in all rooms • Colour TV • Full bed linen provided • Adjacent laundry room • Pay telephone
Orchard Cottage (sleeps 2) • Points Park Cottage (sleeps 2)
Well Park Cottage (sleeps 6) • Pitty Park Cottage (sleeps 6)

Oldaport Farm Cottages, Modbury, Ivybridge PL21 0TG
Tel: 01548 830842 • www.oldaport.com • cathy@oldaport.com

Oldaport is a small grass farm with pedigree sheep and miniature Shetland ponies. It lies in a secluded valley beside the Erme estuary, of great interest to birdwatchers and nature lovers. Convenient for Dartmoor, the South Coast Footpath and the many attractions of South West Devon.

West Millbrook

ADJOINING EXMOOR. Two fully-equipped bungalows and one farmhouse annexe (properties sleep 2/8) in lovely surroundings bordering Exmoor National Park. Ideal for touring North Devon and West Somerset including moor and coast with beautiful walks, lovely scenery and many other attractions. North Molton village is only one mile away. All units have electric cooker, fridge/freezer, microwave and digital TV; two bungalows also have washing machines/dryers. Children's play area; cots and high chairs available free. Linen hire available. Games room. Car parking. Central heating if required. Electricity metered. Out of season short breaks. Weekly prices from £90 to £420. Colour brochure available.
Mike and Rose Courtney, West Millbrook, Twitchen, South Molton EX36 3LP
Tel: 01598 740382 • e-mail: wmbselfcatering@aol.com
www.westcountrynow.com • www.westmillbrook.co.uk

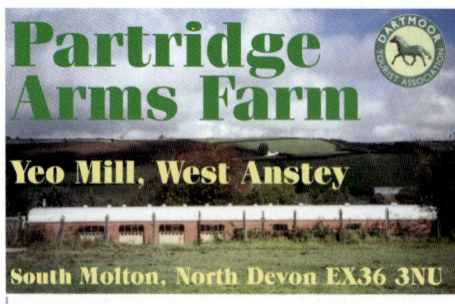

Partridge Arms Farm
Yeo Mill, West Anstey
South Molton, North Devon EX36 3NU
Tel: 01398 341217 • Fax: 01398 341569

Times gone by...
For those who want to enjoy a break in more unusual circumstances, Partridge Arms Farm has a converted, self-catering railway carriage. The carriage is situated on the old Taunton to Barnstaple railway line and, as well as being fully equipped, it sleeps up to 6 people. Children are welcome to stay in the carriage, as are dogs. The railway line offers a delightful and fascinating walk. Visitors can also explore at their leisure the 200 acres of surrounding farmland, which is situated in the Southern foothills of Exmoor. Prices start from £400 per week (no hidden extras).

SELF-CATERING King's Nympton — **DEVON 149**

COLLACOTT FARM COTTAGES

Collacott Farm is set in the heart of beautiful North Devon, in a quiet, rural location. Just four miles from South Molton, it makes an ideal base for exploring all that Devon has to offer – Exmoor, Dartmoor, the Tarka Trail, the dramatic North Coast and the long sandy beaches on the West Coast.

Eight delightful cottages converted from the old farm stone barns, sleeping 2-12 persons, set around the original cobbled courtyard, each with good-sized living space. Each well equipped cottage has its own private garden with patio and barbecue, table and chairs and sun umbrella.

We also have a games room, an all-weather tennis court and a trampoline room. Outdoors, there is a play area and the heated swimming pool.

Collacott Stables, a BHS Approved Riding Centre, offers well schooled, quality horses to suit all ages and abilities. You can learn to ride or brush up your existing skills.

Collacott Farm
King's Nympton, Umberleigh, North Devon EX37 9TP
Tel: 01769 572491 • E-mail: info@collacott.co.uk
www.collacott.co.uk

BRITISH HORSE SOCIETY
APPROVED RIDING ESTABLISHMENT

150 DEVON

South Molton, Totnes, Woolacombe   SELF-CATERING

A most attractive, well equipped, south-facing cottage with large garden, on edge of the village of Bishop's Nympton, three miles from South Molton.

Ideal holiday centre, easy reach of Exmoor, the coast, sporting activities and places of interest.

- Three bedrooms: one double, one twin-bedded with washbasin and one single.
- Two bathrooms with toilets.

- Sitting and dining rooms, large kitchen. Central heating, electric wood/coal effect fires, TV.

One mile sea trout/trout fishing on River Mole. Well behaved pets welcome. Terms April to October from £230.

Mrs J. Greenwell,
Tregeiriog,
Near Llangollen
LL20 7HU
Tel: 01691 600672

Court Green, Bishop's Nympton, Near South Molton • Sleeps 5

TOTNES J. and E. Ball, Higher Well Farm and Holiday Park, Stoke Gabriel, Totnes TQ9 6RN (01803 782289).

A quiet secluded farm park welcoming tents, motor caravans and touring caravans. It is less than one mile from the riverside village of Stoke Gabriel and within four miles of Torbay beaches. Central for touring South Devon. Facilities include modern toilet/shower block with dishwashing and family rooms. Electric hook-ups and hard standings. Launderette, shop and payphone.

- Also static caravans to let from £140 per week or £20 per night.

ETC ★★★★

Resthaven
Holiday Flats

The Esplanade, Woolacombe, Devon EX34 7DJ

On the sea front overlooking the beautiful Combesgate beach. Fantastic views of Morte Point and the coastline.

★ Two self contained flats, sleeping 5 & 9.
★ Family, double and bunk bedrooms all with washbasins.
★ All-electric kitchens. Electricity on £1 meter.
★ Bathrooms with bath & shower.
★ Colour TVs with video and DVD players.
★ Free parking, lighting, hot water and laundry.
★ Terms £160 to £900 per week.

Contact Brian Watts for details and brochure.

Tel: 01271 870248
e-mail: rhflats@orange.net

FHG

Visit the FHG website
www.holidayguides.com
for details of the wide choice of accommodation featured in the full range of FHG titles

K·U·P·E·R·A·R·D

The FHG Directory of Website Addresses

on pages 277-310 is a useful quick reference guide for holiday accommodation with e-mail and/or website details

FHG
K·U·P·E·R·A·R·D

SELF-CATERING

DORSET 151

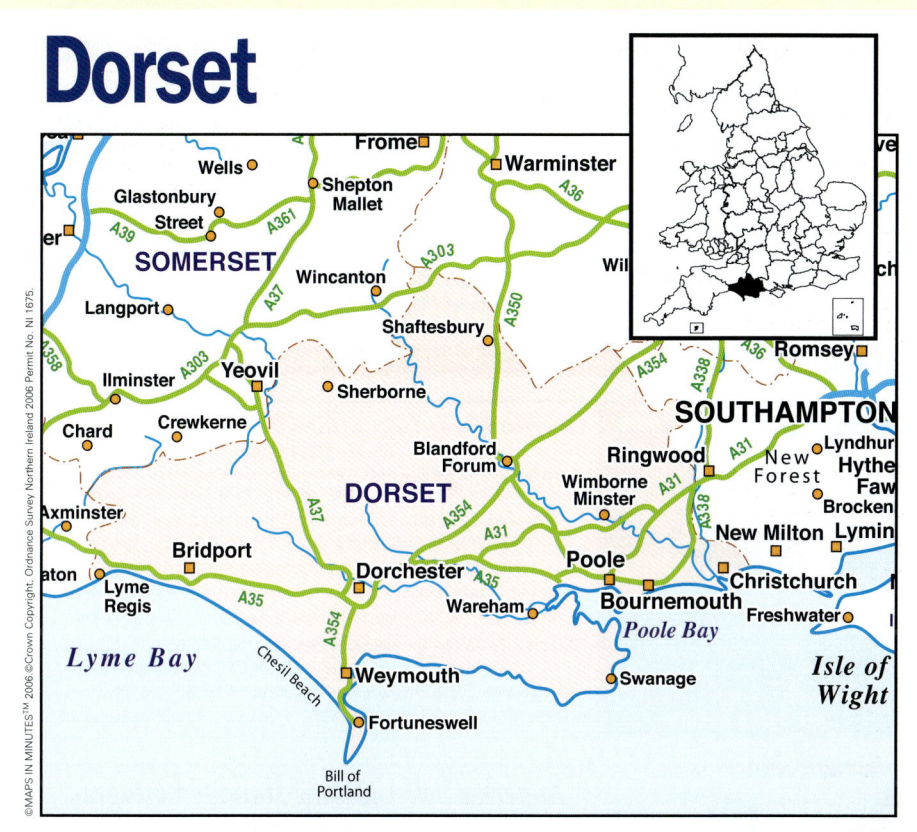

Dorset

Sandbanks, Dorset. Picture courtesy of Poole Tourism

152 DORSET — Abbotsbury, Beaminster, Blandford Forum **SELF-CATERING**

Character Farm Cottages ❖ Langton Herring

SEVEN CHARACTER FARM COTTAGES situated in the villages of Langton Herring and Rodden, nestling on the coastline between picturesque Abbotsbury and Weymouth. This unique part of Dorset's Heritage Coast is ideal for walking, touring, bird-watching and fishing with the added attractions of Abbotsbury's world famous Swannery, The Fleet and Weymouth's safe sandy beaches. The cottages are all comfortably furnished with features such as open fires, beams, inglenooks, walled gardens and ample parking. Pets and children welcome. Logs and linen available.

Enquiries: Mrs J. Elwood, Lower Farmhouse,
Langton Herring, Weymouth DT3 4JB
Tel: 01305 871187 • Fax: 01305 871347

Sleep 2-9
Prices from £185

e-mail: jane@mayo.fsbusiness.co.uk • website: www.characterfarmcottages.co.uk

Orchard End & The Old Coach House
Hooke, Beaminster.

Hooke is a quiet village nine miles from the coast. Good walking country and near Hooke Working Woodland with lovely woodland walks. Coarse fishing nearby.

Orchard End is a stone-built bungalow, with electric central heating and double glazing. Four bedrooms, two bathrooms; sleeps 8. It is on a working dairy farm and is well-equipped and comfortable. Enclosed garden and off-road parking.

The Old Coach House, a cottage sleeping 9, is also finished to a high standard. Four bedrooms, two bathrooms; central heating. Large garden; off-road parking.

Both properties are equipped with washing machine, dryer, dishwasher, fridge/freezers, microwaves and payphones. Both properties **ETC ★★★★**
Terms from £300 to £700 inclusive of VAT, electricity, bed linen and towels.

Contact **Mrs P.M. Wallbridge,
Watermeadow House,
Bridge Farm, Hooke,
Beaminster, Dorset DT8 3PD
Tel: 01308 862619**

enquiries@watermeadowhouse.com • www.watermeadowhouse.co.uk

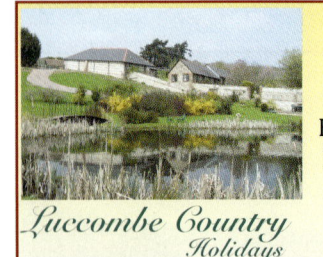

Superior Self-Catering Holiday Cottages

Six attractive and well equipped cottages on private estate
in the centre of Dorset within easy reach of the coast.
Heated indoor pool, gym, games room, tennis court, riding school.
BBQ area, grounds, gardens, fenced ponds. Fishing, farm walks.
Good central base for Heritage Coast and country.
Dogs by arrangement. Wheelchair friendly.

Luccombe Country Holidays

"Something for everyone at Luccombe"

Luccombe, Milton Abbas, Blandford Forum, Dorset DT11 0BE • Tel: 01258 880558
Fax: 01258 881384 • E-mail: mkayll@aol.com • www.luccombeholidays.co.uk

ETC ★★★★ SELF-CATERING

Looking for holiday accommodation?
for details of hundreds of properties
throughout the UK visit:

www.holidayguides.com

SELF-CATERING Bridport, Nettlecombe, Dorchester   DEVON 153

Frogmore Farm   Chideock, Bridport DT6 6HT

Delightful farm cottage on ninety acre grazing farm set in the rolling hills of West Dorset. Superb views over Lyme Bay, ideal base for touring Dorset and Devon or rambling the many coastal and country footpaths of the area. This fully equipped self-catering cottage sleeps five. Three bedrooms. Bed linen supplied. Cosy lounge with woodburner and colour TV, French doors to a splendid columned sun verandah. Children and well behaved dogs welcome. Car essential. Open all year. Short breaks available, also Bed and Breakfast in the 17th century farmhouse. Brochure and terms free on request.

Tel: 01308 456159

La Casita

The Old Station, Nettlecombe, Bridport. Enjoy a peaceful stay in beautiful countryside. Off-road parking, two-and-a-half acres of garden. The 150-year-old stone building, originally the linesmen's hut at Powerstock Station, was later enlarged, forming a fashion designer's studio. Recently double glazed, it has a living/dining room, bedroom, kitchen, shower room, toilet, for one to two non-smoking adult guests (no children or pets). Two single beds; duvets, bed linen and towels provided. Electricity also included (small winter surcharge). Microwave, fridge, TV, heating. Garden furniture, putting. Badger-watching at the adjacent Old Station.

Terms from £170 per week. Low season short stays by arrangement.

SAE please: Mrs D.P. Read, The Old Station, Powerstock, Bridport DT6 3ST • 01308 485301

PUNCKNOWLE MANOR COTTAGES, DORCHESTER

Puncknowle Manor Estate has three holiday lets in the heart of Dorset's lush countryside, only two minutes from the Jurassic Coast.

THE CARRIAGE HOUSE *is a newly renovated three-bedroom cottage, with views from the upstairs living accommodation.*

PUNCKNOWLE MANOR FARMHOUSE *is an ideal location for summer holidays or family gatherings, sleeping 13 in five bedrooms; two bathrooms, large farmhouse kitchen/dining room, private gardens.*

BERWICK MANOR *is our five-star manor sleeping 19, great for summer retreats and special occasions; five doubles, family room, room with three singles. Large gardens. Surrounded by the Bride Valley.*

Contact Rebecca Hutchings,
Puncknowle Manor Estate,
Puncknowle, Dorchester DT2 9BX
Tel: 01308 897706
e-mail: cottages@pknlest.com
www.dorset-selfcatering.co.uk

Note

All the information in this guide is given in good faith in the belief that it is correct. However, the publishers cannot guarantee the facts given in these pages, neither are they responsible for changes in ownership or facilities that may take place after the date of going to press.
Readers should always satisfy themselves that the facilities they require are available and that the terms, if quoted, still apply.

154 DORSET   **Lyme Regis, Wareham, Weymouth**   **SELF-CATERING**

Immerse yourself in rural tranquillity. Set in an Area of Outstanding Natural Beauty, Wootton Fitzpaine nestles amidst rolling Dorset farmland. Within walking distance of the beaches and shops of Charmouth, world famous for its fossils, and three miles from the renowned Cobb at Lyme Regis. Golf, water sports and riding close by. We have four spacious, comfortable, well-furnished three-bedroomed cottages with open fires, inglenooks, heating and all amenities. Also large secluded, secure gardens with furniture, barbecues, parking.

www.westoverfarmcottages.co.uk

• Open all year • Pets and children welcome
• Logs and linen available • Guests are welcome to walk our farm • Terms from £190 to £750 per week, winter breaks available

English Tourism Council — SELF CATERING

Jon Snook and Debby Snook,
Westover Farm Cottages,
Wootton Fitzpaine, Bridport DT6 6NE
01297 560451/561395
e-mail: wfcottages@aol.com

"Dormer Cottage"

"Dormer Cottage", Woodlands, Hyde, Near Wareham

This secluded cottage, cosy and modern, is a converted old barn of Woodlands House. Standing in its own grounds, it is fronted by a small wood with a walled paddock at the back. Pleasant walks in wooded forests nearby. In the midst of "Hardy Country" and ideal for a family holiday and for those who value seclusion. All linen included, beds ready made on guests' arrival and basic shopping arranged on request. Amusements at Bournemouth, Poole and Dorchester within easy reach. Five people and a baby can be accommodated in two double and one single bedrooms; cot and high chair available. Bathroom, two toilets; lounge and diningroom, colour TV. Kitchen with oil fired Aga and electric cooker, fridge, washing machine, small deep freeze, etc. Pets welcome. Open all year. Golf course half-mile; pony trekking, riding nearby. SAE, please, for terms.

Mrs M.J.M. Constantinides, "Woodlands", Hyde, Near Wareham BH20 7NT (01929 471239)

Grade II Cottage with 3 bedrooms, 2 bathrooms, approx. one minute walk to beach, close to harbour.

ETC ★★★★

Other properties available weekly or short breaks.

Weymouth has a lovely sandy beach and picturesque harbour with pavement cafes. There is plenty to do all year round.

**Phone: 01305 834331 • Mobile: 0797 1256160
e-mail: postmaster@buckwells.plus.com
website: www.holidaycottageweymouth.co.uk**

FHG

KUPERARD

Visit the FHG website
www.holidayguides.com
for details of the wide choice of accommodation featured in the full range of FHG titles

SELF-CATERING **Bishop Auckland, Lanchester** DURHAM 155

Durham

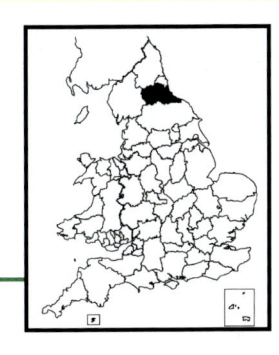

NEW COTTAGE

**New Cottage, 'Law One',
Hollymoor Farm, Cockfield,
Bishop Auckland DL13 5HF
Tel & Fax: 01388 718567/ 718260**

NEW COTTAGE is a delightful little cottage in a very peaceful location.
The accommodation is very cosy and comfortable and all on one level – there are no stairs. Panoramic views from the lounge are a never-ending source of delight – they are stunning, and made even more beautiful in the winter when there is a light dusting of snow. The cottage is also so accessible for country walks and sightseeing, and being able to start walks from the cottage is a real bonus. And the sunsets are something else – truly magnificent.
Rates: £245 per week, all year round.
Details from Mrs Margaret Partridge.

Low Lands Farm
Low Lands, Cockfield, Bishop Auckland, Co. Durham DL13 5AW
Tel 01388 718251 • Mobile: 07745 067754
e-mail: info@farmholidaysuk.com • website: www.farmholidaysuk.com

Two award-winning, beautifully renovated self-catering cottages on a working family farm. If you want peace and quiet in an area full of beautiful unspoilt countryside packed with things to see and do, then come and stay with us. Each cottage sleeps up to four people, plus cot. Beams, log fires, gas BBQ, own gardens and parking. Close to Durham City, the Lake District and Hadrian's Wall. Pets and children most welcome; childminding and equipment available. Terms from £150 to £340, inclusive of linen, towels, electricity and heating.
**Please contact Alison or Keith Tallentire
for a brochure.** Category 3 (one cottage)

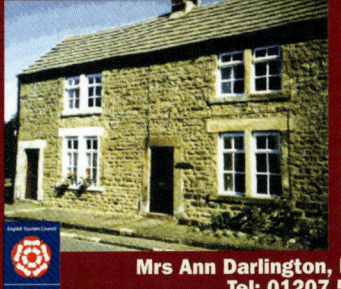

Two country cottages, well equipped and comfortable. Situated in an ideal location for Durham City and Beamish Museum. You will have a free pass for the week to visit our own open farm.

Please write or telephone for brochure.

*Sleep up to four people • Children welcome.
Sorry no pets.*

Rates: from £160 per week.

Mrs Ann Darlington, HALL HILL FARM, Lanchester, Durham DH7 0TA
Tel: 01207 521476 • Tel & Fax: 01388 730300
e-mail: cottages@hallhillfarm.co.uk • www.hallhillfarm.co.uk

Gloucestershire

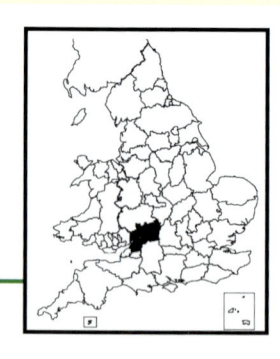

Meadows Home Farm

Home Farm is a family-run working farm set in the small unspoilt village of Bredons Norton, in the heart of the Cotswolds. The farm has been designated an Area of Outstanding Natural Beauty. This is an excellent base for touring the Cotswolds, Worcester, Cheltenham and the Malverns. Superb walking country.

Meadows Home Farm, Bredons Norton, Tewkesbury GL20 7HA • Tel: 01684 772322
www.meadowshomefarm.co.uk

Stable Cottage • sleeps 4/5

A delightful Cotswold stone stable/barn conversion with an open-plan kitchen, dining area and lounge; gas-fired woodburning stove and full gas central heating.
Upstairs are 2 bedrooms and a bathroom. All linen and towels provided. The cottage has its own large garden with tables and chairs.

B&B also available in farmhouse.

Cosy, well equipped, self-contained apartment with open aspects, attached to the farmhouse of a 100 acre livestock farm. Situated on the eastern outskirts of Cheltenham, on the edge of the Cotswold Escarpment. Comfortably furnished, with full central heating and plenty of parking space. Electricity and bed linen included in rental. Ideal position for visiting the lovely Regency town of Cheltenham and the mellow villages of the Cotswolds.

Sorry, no pets allowed. Non-smoking.
Terms from £150 to £220 per week. ETC ★★★

Mr & Mrs J. Close, Coxhorne Farm, London Road, Charlton Kings, Cheltenham GL52 6UY • Tel: 01242 236599

Two Springbank, 37 Hopton Road, Upper Cam GL11 5PD

Fully equipped mid-terraced cottage (sleeps 4 + cot) in pleasant village about one mile from Dursley which has a swimming pool and sports centre.
Superb base for Cotswold Way, touring Severn Vale and Forest of Dean. Few miles from Slimbridge Wildfowl Trust, Berkeley Castle and Westonbirt Arboretum and within easy reach of Gloucester, Bristol, Bath and Cirencester.
Ground floor: sitting room with TV/video and electric fire, dining area, fitted kitchen with fridge/freezer, electric cooker and microwave. Utility room with washing machine; rear lawn and patio. **First floor:** two bedrooms (one double, one twin) and bathroom.
Linen and towels included, also cot and highchair if required.

Sorry no pets or smoking

Rates from £174 to £246 per week (includes electricity) • Off-peak breaks (3 nights) from £114 to £162.
Mrs F.A. Jones, 32 Everlands, Cam, Dursley, Gloucs GL11 5NL • 01453 543047
e-mail: lhandfaj32lg@surefish.co.uk

SELF-CATERING Felton   HEREFORDSHIRE 157

Herefordshire

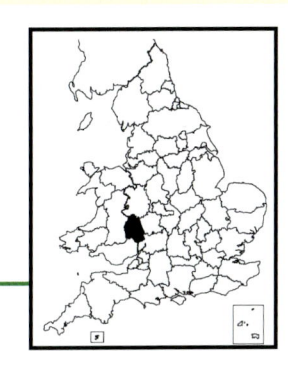

THE LODGE

The Lodge, being the former Verger's cottage, is situated in a tranquil setting just 8 miles north of the historic cathedral town of Hereford, convenient for all of beautiful Herefordshire and the Welsh Borderlands. The Lodge has been completely renovated and restored to its Victorian character, but with new heating, a modern kitchen, a dining room, and a sitting room with video/DVD. The cottage sleeps 5 people in a double and twin room upstairs, with a single room downstairs. Shower rooms on both floors. A cot and high chair are available. Children and pets with responsible owners are most welcome. The cottage is non-smoking. Private parking, patio and garden. Weekly terms from £150 - £300. Short Breaks Sept.- May. Electricity at cost. Linen available at small extra charge. Library of local interest, maps, brochures, route plans and advice available to make your stay enjoyable. The Lodge is cosy and restful.

Marjorie and Brian Roby, Felton House, Felton HR1 3PH • Tel: (01432) 820366
e-mail: bmfelton@tiscali.co.uk • www.SmoothHound.co.uk/hotels/thelodgef.html

Scotland Bank view Picture courtesy of Herefordshire Tourism

Isle of Wight

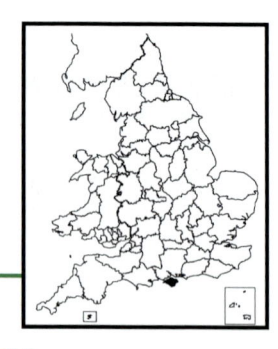

Eating out is a big part of any holiday and **The Isle of Wight** Official Eating Out Guide brings together a wide range of Island eating establishments, offering everything from freshly caught seafood and tasty, organic vegetables to luxury ice creams and locally brewed beers and fine wines.

Many attractions are out of doors to take advantage of the Island's milder than average temperatures. However, if it should rain, there's plenty to choose from. Try The Brading Experience, the Island's Wax Works with its very own Chamber of Horrors, or visit Dinosaur Isle, Britain's first purpose-built dinosaur museum and watch as resident palaeontologists prepare recent finds and uncover the secrets of the past! There are vineyards offering wine tasting, cinemas, theatres and nightclubs as well as sports and leisure centres, a bowling alley and an ice skating rink, home to the Island's very own ice hockey team – the Wight Raiders.

The Island's diverse terrain makes it an ideal landscape for walkers and cyclists of all ages and abilities. During the Isle of Wight Walking Festival in May visitors have the opportunity to take part in over 180 themed walks, ranging from short strolls to challenging full-day hikes, all led by experienced walk leaders.

The Isle of Wight Cycling Season is held at the end of September and whilst some rides need off-road experience, many are ideal for families and recreational cyclists. Pony trekking and beach rides are also popular holiday pursuits and the Island's superb golf courses, beautiful scenery and temperate climate combine to make it the perfect choice for a golfing break.

With up to 350 daily ferry crossings, the Isle of Wight has to be the UK's most accessible Island, and once there, it's easy to get around. There's a comprehensive bus network and a regular train service, which operates between Ryde and Shanklin and connects with the Isle of Wight Steam Railway.

ISLAND COTTAGE HOLIDAYS

ETC ★★★ to ★★★★★

Charming individual cottages in lovely rural surroundings and close to the sea. Over 60 cottages situated throughout the Isle of Wight. Beautiful views, attractive gardens, delightful country walks.

All equipped to a high standard and graded for quality by the Tourist Board.

For a brochure please Tel: **(01929) 480080** • Fax: **(01929) 481070**
e-mail: enq@islandcottageholidays.com • website: www.islandcottageholidays.com
Open all year (Sleep 1 - 12) £171 - £1195 per week. Short breaks available in low season (3 nights) £145 - £395

SELF-CATERING Bonchurch, Totland   **ISLE OF WIGHT/KENT** 159

BONCHURCH Ashcliff Holiday Apartment, Bonchurch PO38 1NT.
Idyllic and secluded position in the picturesque seaside village of Bonchurch. Self-contained ground floor apartment adjoining Victorian house, set in large south-facing gardens with sea views and sheltered by a thickly wooded cliff. Large, private car park.
• Sleeps 2 • Dogs very welcome.
ETC ★★★
For free brochure telephone: 01983 853919.

THE COACH HOUSE is a self-contained apartment in the grounds of Frenchman's Cove Guest House, with delightful views of Tennyson Down and the surrounding countryside.
- Self-catering accommodation for 4.
- Well appointed kitchen area with microwave, fridge/freezer etc.
- Lounge/dining area with TV, DVD.
- En suite master bedroom.
- Ground floor: utility room with washing machine and tumble dryer, WC, sleeping area with bunk beds (suitable for children).
           No smoking • No pets

The Coach House
*Frenchman's Cove,
Alum Bay Old Road, Totland,
Isle of Wight PO39 0HZ*

www.frenchmanscove.co.uk • e-mail: boatfield@frenchmanscove.co.uk
Tel: 01983 752227 • Fax: 01983 755125

Kent

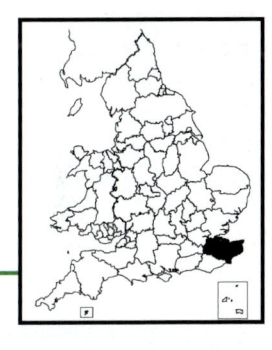

Broadstairs

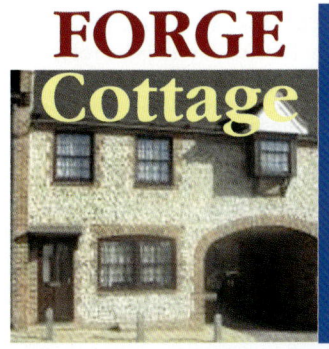

FORGE Cottage

Forge Cottage – Sleeps 5/6
A modern knapped flint fronted cottage built in a traditional period style with a beautiful eye catching wooden floor. Encapsulating the idyllic and enchanting qualities of Broadstairs, Forge Cottage is great for families or for larger groups requiring a fantastic town centre location. Within Broadstairs's conservation area this delightful, spacious and versatile cottage is only a 5-minute stroll from the fabulous sandy Viking Bay and from the heart of the town's wonderful restaurants and shops. Allocated parking for one car.
Weekly Tariff: £410 - £720 (inclusive of services, linen, towels and a welcome pack)

HONEYLANE COTTAGES
PO BOX 286, BROADSTAIRS CT10 3WB
Tel: +44 (0) 1304 619444
E-mail: enquiries@curlewcottages.co.uk
WWW.HONEYLANECOTTAGES.CO.UK

WELCOME TO EXCELLENCE.

Reach Court Farm Cottages, St Margaret's Bay

Situated in the heart of a family-run, working farm, surrounded by open countryside, these five luxury self-contained cottages are very special. They are set around the old farm yard in an attractive setting of lawns and shrubs with open views from the front or rear. The cottages sleep from two to six plus cot and the accommodation is of the highest standard giving them a relaxing country feel with the kitchens equipped with ovens, fridges, microwaves, toasters, coffee makers, etc. There is also a washing machine and tumble dryer in an adjoining laundry room. Reach Court Farm is the nearest farm to France and was known as the "Front Line Farm" during World War II. St Margaret's is a rural village with shops and public houses offering a range of eating facilities. Dover, Folkestone, Canterbury and Sandwich are all within easy reach.

Mrs J. Mitchell, Reach Court Farm,
St Margaret's-at-Cliff, St Margaret's Bay, Dover CT15 6AQ
Tel: 01304 852159
e-mail: jacmitch2002@yahoo.co.uk

Lancashire

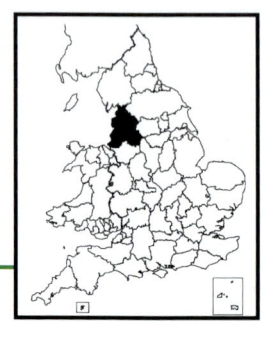

Morecambe, Southport

Gizella
Self-Catering Holiday Accommodation
Mrs G.A. Tamassy, 8 Marine Road West, Morecambe LA3 1BS
Tel: 01524 418269 • mobile: 07901 778260

Mr & Mrs Tamassy welcome you to their luxury holiday flats/flatlets, overlooking gardens, with views over the Bay to the Lakeland Hills. All modern facilities including en suite. Open all year round. Overnight guests welcome. Senior Citizen off-season rates. Send SAE for confirmation. Sorry - no children, no pets. Non-smoking establishment. Sleeps from 1 to 5. Member of Morecambe Bay Warmth of Welcome 3 Keys.

www.morecambeholidayflats.co.uk • www.gizellaholidayflats.co.uk

Sandy Brook Farm,
52 Wyke Cop Road, Scarisbrick, Southport PR8 5LR

Welcome to our small arable farm and 18th century Barn, which has been converted into five superbly equipped holiday apartments. Many of the Barn's original features have been retained and it is furnished in traditional style but also offers all modern amenities. The Barn is situated three-and-a-half miles from the seaside town of Southport and five miles from the historic town of Ormskirk with lots of places to visit in the surrounding area. Families are welcome and cot and high chairs are available. One apartment equipped for wheelchair/disabled guests. Central heating, bed linen and towels are provided free of charge. ETC ★★★

01704 880337 • www.sandybrookfarm.co.uk • e-mail: sandybrookfarm@lycos.co.uk

SELF-CATERING Alford, Louth, Mablethorpe   LINCOLNSHIRE 161

Lincolnshire

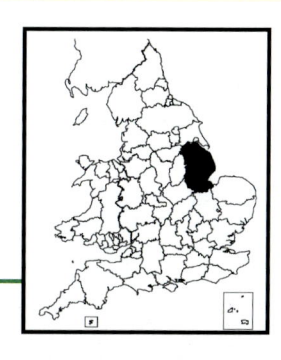

MANOR FARM COTTAGE

Comfortable cottage in rural countryside, midway between the coast and Lincolnshire Wolds. Well equipped including colour TV, video, washing machine, microwave and freezer. Rose garden including picnic table. Suitable area for pets to exercise. Pets and children welcome. Ample parking space.

For further details please contact:
Mrs E. M. Farrow, Manor Farm, Strubby, Alford, Lincolnshire LN13 0LW

Tel: 01507 450228

Shepherd's Cottage, Louth

Fall in love with the experience of staying in our charming 16th century self-catering cottage, situated in the grounds of Grimblethorpe Hall, in the heart of the Lincolnshire Wolds. Restored to a very high standard with original beams and stonework with a very spacious bedroom, lounge and kitchen/ dining area.

Facilities include cooker, microwave, fridge/freezer, washer/dryer, linen and bedding, towels and cloths, full central heating, television, video, DVD, garage and board games. Electricity inclusive. Fabulous walking and cycling routes nearby, including the Viking Way, and visitors may use the private trout lake. An optional evening meal can be waiting for you on your arrival and occasional picnic hampers are available.

Contact: **Annie and Robert Codling**, Grimblethorpe Hall, Grimblethorpe, Near Louth LN11 0RB
Tel: 01507 313671/313440
e-mail: enquiries@ShepherdsHolidayCottage.co.uk • www.ShepherdsHolidayCottage.co.uk

Grange Farmhouse

MALTBY-LE-MARSH, ALFORD LN13 0JP
Tel: 01507 450267

Farmhouse B&B and country cottages set in ten idyllic acres of Lincolnshire countryside. Peaceful base for leisure and sightseeing.

• Private fishing lake • Many farm animals
• Brochure available. Contact Mrs Graves.
• • **Pets welcome** • •

www.grange-farmhouse.co.uk

162 LINCOLNSHIRE   Market Rasen, Skegness   **SELF-CATERING**

Newly converted holiday cottage on site of old Methodist Chapel, in the heart of the Lincolnshire Wolds, adjacent to the Viking Way and the river Bain. Newly equipped to the highest standard and ideally situated on the A157 for travel to Louth or Lincoln.

- Two en suite double bedrooms
- Queen-size (zip and link) beds in both rooms
- Full central heating
- Non-smoking
- Pets by arrangement
- All linen provided

Bainfield Holiday Lodge,
Burgh-on-Bain, Near Louth,
Lincolnshire LN8 6JY
Contact: Marian Walker
Tel: 01507 313540

e-mail: enquiries@BainfieldHolidayLodge.co.uk • www.BainfieldHolidayLodge.co.uk

---

Farm • Fishing • Friendly • Fun
Stay on a real farm on the edge of the village of Burgh le Marsh, only 5 miles from Skegness.

- Children's play area, farm animals.
- Cottages have their own private fishing waters.
- Tennis court, plenty of space, ample parking, gardens.

The Chestnuts
FARM & COUNTRY COTTAGES
WITH PRIVATE FISHING
Wainfleet Road, Burgh Le Marsh,
Lincs PE24 5AH
Tel/Fax: 01754 810904
e-mail: macka@freenetname.co.uk
www.thechestnutsfarm.co.uk

It's great here!

Short Breaks out of season as little as £70. Phone for current price list

For a very quiet rural holiday, visit Chestnuts Country Cottages, only one mile from the farm.

- **Full colour brochure available.**
- **2, 3 and 4 bedroom cottages.**

Other specialised holiday guides from FHG

Recommended **INNS & PUBS** OF BRITAIN

Recommended **COUNTRY HOTELS** OF BRITAIN

Recommended **SHORT BREAK HOLIDAYS** IN BRITAIN

The bestselling and original **PETS WELCOME!**

The **GOLF GUIDE,** *Where to Play, Where to Stay* IN BRITAIN & IRELAND

COAST & COUNTRY HOLIDAYS

SELF-CATERING HOLIDAYS IN BRITAIN

BED & BREAKFAST STOPS

CARAVAN & CAMPING HOLIDAYS

CHILDREN WELCOME! Family Holiday & Days Out Guide

BRITAIN'S BEST LEISURE & RELAXATION GUIDE

Published annually: available in all good bookshops or direct from the publisher:
FHG Guides, Abbey Mill Business Centre, Seedhill, Paisley PA1 1TJ
Tel: 0141 887 0428 • Fax: 0141 889 7204
• E-mail: admin@fhguides.co.uk • Web: www.holidayguides.com

SELF-CATERING Foxley　　　　　　　　　　　　　　　　　　　NORFOLK 163

Norfolk

Located on a working farm, a courtyard of 2/3 bedroomed converted stables, 3 converted barns and 2 cottages, all fully equipped. Ideally situated for the beautiful North Norfolk coast, Sandringham, Norwich, and The Broads. 365 acres of mature woodland adjoining farm – private fishing in owners' lake. Indoor heated swimming pool. Pets welcome at a charge of £10.

**MOOR FARM STABLE COTTAGES,
FOXLEY, NORFOLK NR20 4QP** • Tel or Fax: 01362 688523
e-mail: mail@moorfarmstablecottages.co.uk
www.moorfarmstablecottages.co.uk

When making enquiries please mention FHG GUIDES

Free or reduced rate entry to
Holiday Visits and Attractions – see our
READERS' OFFER VOUCHERS on pages 7-40

Northumberland

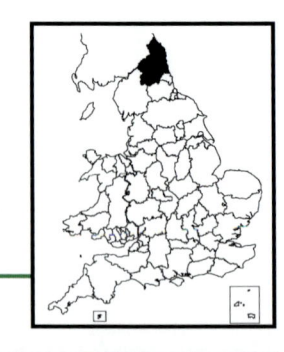

Enjoy a break on the Northumberland Coast

Choose from twelve family-owned and managed cottages along the Northumberland coast.
Three-day short breaks from £70 per cottage during low season.
Beautiful rugged coastline, fishing villages little changed in 100 years, golden beaches, historic castles, wildlife, walks, cycling, fishing, golf, Alnwick Castle & Gardens, National Park, Kielder Water and Forest.

For details and bookings contact: Heritage Coast Holidays,
6G Greensfield Court, Alnwick, Northumberland NE66 2DE
Tel: 01665 604935 (office hours) • Fax: 01670 414739
e-mail: info@heritagecoastholidays.com

Visit our website• www.heritagecoastholidays.com

Alnwick

LINK HOUSE FARM AWARD-WINNING COASTAL ACCOMMODATION

Between the popular fishing villages of Craster and Beadnell, Link House Farm consists of five individual converted holiday cottages and a timber lodge, all equipped to very high standards. Each is completely self-contained, and provides an excellent base for families, walkers and birdwatchers. The farm itself has an impressive collection of peacocks and ornamental pheasants. In the village there is a pub serving meals, and the busy market town of Alnwick is only a short drive away.

All fuel and power incl. • Duvets and pillows provided • Electric cooker, microwave, fridge, auto washer, dishwasher, colour TV, DVD etc • Secure off-road parking • Garden with furniture

Properties sleep 4/10 • www.linkhousefarm.com • ETC ★★★★ Self-catering
Contact: Mrs Hellman, The Granary, Link House Farm, Newton-by-the-Sea, Alnwick NE66 3DF
Tel: 01665 576820 • Fax: 01665 576821 • e-mail: stay@linkhousefarm.com

BUSTON FARM HOLIDAY COTTAGES. Come and enjoy the enchanting coast of Northumberland from one of our luxury four-star self-catering cottages, sleeping 2 to 6. Three cottages on a working farm just outside the historic village of Warkworth, whilst another is nestled within the pretty coastal village of Newton-by-the-Sea, just north of Alnwick. All are truly a home from home, charmingly decorated and extensively equipped, providing you the best possible base for a relaxing break. The Alnwick Garden, Cheviot Hills, Holy Island, Hadrian's Wall and a bounty of castles are but a few local treasures for you to explore. Pets and children welcome.

Buston Farm Holiday Cottages, Low Buston Hall,
Warkworth, Morpeth NE65 0XY
Tel: 01665 714805
e-mail: jopark@farming.co.uk • www.buston.co.uk

SELF-CATERING Alnwick, Bamburgh, Hexham   NORTHUMBERLAND 165

Town Foot Farm, Shilbottle, Alnwick, Northumberland NE66 2HG • Tel/Fax: 01665 575591
e-mail: crissy@villagefarmcottages.co.uk • www.villagefarmcottages.co.uk

Choice of cosy cottages, airy chalets or 17th century farmhouse. Sleep between two and twelve. Perfectly situated; three miles from beaches and historic Alnwick. Fantastic facilities include an indoor forty-foot heated swimming pool, health club, sauna/steam room, tennis court and a games room. Visit our beauty therapist. Also try fishing and riding.

Terms from £145 – £1600

VILLAGE FARM *SELF-CATERING*   Free colour brochure.   ETC ★★★ to ★★★★★

Point Cottages, Bamburgh

A cluster of cottages in a superb location at the end of the Wynding, next to a beautiful golf course on the edge of Bamburgh, only a short drive away from many other attractive Links courses. Bamburgh is an unspoilt coastal village dominated by a magnificent castle and is an ideal base for visiting other parts of historic Northumbria. The cottages overlook the sea with fine views of the Farne Islands and Lindisfarne. Sandy beaches nearby. They share a large garden with lawns and a total of ten car parking spaces are provided (two per cottage). The cottages are in excellent order, have open fire or woodburning stove and are comfortably furnished. Each cottage has its own special atmosphere but all are warm, cosy and well-equipped.

Terms from £205 to £580, weekend breaks from £160. For further information, availability, prices and booking please contact:
John and Elizabeth Sanderson, 30 The Oval, Benton, Newcastle-upon-Tyne NE12 9PP • 0191-266 2800 or 01665 720246 (weekends) • Fax: 0191-215 1290 • e-mail: info@bamburgh-cottages.co.uk • www.bamburgh-cottages.co.uk

Moorgair Cottage

This charming cottage for 4/5 people is attached to the owner's home on a small working farm in rural Northumberland, home of Moorgair Alpacas. The cottage is furnished to a high standard and has every convenience to make your holiday stress free and enjoyable. Cot and high-chair available. Private garden and parking.

From the doorstep there are miles of forest tracks and country lanes for walkers and cyclists, and the cottage is ideally situated to explore Northumberland, Durham and the Scottish Borders. A small shop, post office and two pubs serving food (one with an excellent adventure playground) are within 1½ miles of the cottage.

Vicki Ridley, Moorgair Cottage, Slaley, Hexham NE47 0AN • Tel: 01434 673473
e-mail: g_ridley@lineone.net • www.moorgair.co.uk

Note

All the information in this guide is given in good faith in the belief that it is correct. However, the publishers cannot guarantee the facts given in these pages, neither are they responsible for changes in ownership or facilities that may take place after the date of going to press.

Readers should always satisfy themselves that the facilities they require are available and that the terms, if quoted, still apply.

166 NORTHUMBERLAND — Newcastle-upon Tyne, Thropton **SELF-CATERING**

Burradon Farm Cottages & Houses
Cramlington, Northumberland NE23 7ND
Tel: (0191) 268 3203 • E-mail: judy@burradonfarm.co.uk
www.burradonfarm.co.uk

Luxury self-catering cottages and houses, ideally suited to either holidaymakers or the business person. Conveniently located a few miles from the spectacular Northumbrian coastline and with easy access to Newcastle-upon-Tyne. Spacious, stylish, self-contained properties with fully equipped kitchens, individually designed sitting rooms and fully fitted bathrooms with shower. Double glazing, gas central heating and security system.

A quiet, tranquil setting with good parking facilities and well tended gardens.

Lorbottle Holiday Cottages – Thropton

Situated in the Cheviot Valley, on the edge of the Northumberland National Park, the two cottages share a garden with gas barbecue, and both offer superb views of the surrounding countryside. **MORDUE'S COTTAGE** sleeps five plus cot, **GRANDMA'S COTTAGE** sleeps four plus cot. Both have a well equipped galley kitchen, bathroom with shower, dining room, central heating and gas fire, colour TV/video/CD hi-fi; bed linen supplied. Each has parking for two cars. The farm offers many opportunities for observing wildlife and is an ideal base for exploring the extensive unspoiled coastline, and many places of historic interest.

B&B also available in Victorian farmhouse

Contact: Leslie & Helen Farr, Lorbottle West Steads, Thropton, Near Morpeth NE65 7JT (01665 574672)
e-mail: stay@lorbottle.com • www.lorbottle.com

Looking for Holiday Accommodation?

FHG
K·U·P·E·R·A·R·D

for details of hundreds of properties throughout the UK visit our website

www.holidayguides.com

SELF-CATERING Nottingham

Nottinghamshire

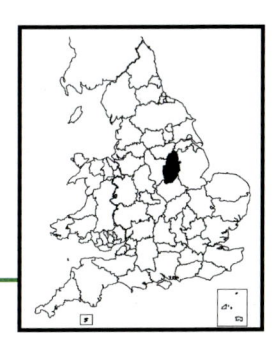

Woodview Cottages, Owthorpe

A warm welcome awaits you at our idyllic cottages located in a beautiful rural setting just 20 minutes from Nottingham/Leicester. Both cottages have been tastefully converted from a traditional barn to provide cosy accommodation with logburning stoves, beamed ceilings and character furniture. Nestling on the edge of the Vale of Belvoir, surrounded by picturesque gardens and beautiful woodland views. Ideal for nature lovers and wildlife enthusiasts. Providing high standards, each self-catering cottage comprises living/dining room and well equipped kitchen. One double, one twin bedroom with linen and towels included. Bathroom and separate shower. Cot/highchair available on request. Ample free parking. Sorry no pets.

Contact: Jane Morley, Newfields Farm, Owthorpe NG12 3GF • Tel & Fax: 01949 81580
e-mail: enquiries@woodviewcottages.co.uk • www.woodviewcottages.co.uk

---

Other specialised holiday guides from **FHG**

Recommended **INNS & PUBS** OF BRITAIN

Recommended **COUNTRY HOTELS** OF BRITAIN

Recommended **SHORT BREAK HOLIDAYS** IN BRITAIN

The bestselling and original **PETS WELCOME!**

The **GOLF GUIDE,** Where to Play, Where to Stay IN BRITAIN & IRELAND

COAST & COUNTRY HOLIDAYS

SELF-CATERING HOLIDAYS IN BRITAIN

BED & BREAKFAST STOPS

CARAVAN & CAMPING HOLIDAYS

CHILDREN WELCOME! Family Holiday & Days Out Guide

BRITAIN'S BEST LEISURE & RELAXATION GUIDE

Published annually: available in all good bookshops or direct from the publisher:
FHG Guides, Abbey Mill Business Centre, Seedhill, Paisley PA1 1TJ
Tel: 0141 887 0428 • Fax: 0141 889 7204
• E-mail: admin@fhguides.co.uk • Web: www.holidayguides.com

Oxfordshire

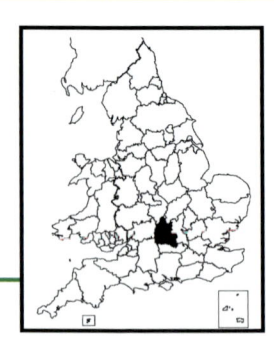

GRANGE FARM COUNTRY COTTAGES

A warm welcome from the Oakey family awaits you at Grange Farm, a working farm set in the small village of Godington.

This lovely location offers all the delights of the English countryside. Converted from Victorian barns, all cottages are equipped to the highest standards. Their style reflects beautiful country charm combined with outstanding levels of comfort. Conveniently located for major airports and motorways. A perfect base for exploring the many delights of North Oxfordshire and the Cotswolds. Broadband access in every cottage, and meeting room facilities. Dogs and horses very welcome.

Private fishing lake • Guests' gardens
Games room • Lovely walks in peaceful, rural surroundings.

Contact: Nigel & Penelope Oakey
Grange Farm Estates, Godington,
Bicester OX27 9AF
Tel: 01869 278778
Mobile: 07919 002132
e-mail: info@grangefarmcottages.co.uk
www.grangefarmcottages.co.uk

Publisher's note

While every effort is made to ensure accuracy, we regret that FHG Guides cannot accept responsibility for errors, misrepresentations or omissions in our entries or any consequences thereof. Prices in particular should be checked.
We will follow up complaints but cannot act as arbiters or agents for either party.

SELF-CATERING Craven Arms

Shropshire

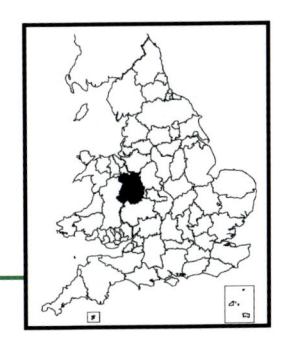

Shropshire is perhaps less well-known than other English counties. This is despite being the birthplace of Charles Darwin, home to the world's first iron bridge (now a World Heritage Site), having not one, but two of the finest medieval towns in England, inspiring the creation of the modern Olympics, and being the kingdom of the real King Arthur. After all, Shropshire is easy enough to find and get to from almost anywhere. (Hint: just north of Birmingham or south of Manchester depending on your direction of travel, and sitting snugly on the Welsh borders).

It may also come as a surprise to find out just how much is on offer. There are plenty of indoor and outdoor attractions, so the weather isn't a problem either. In Ironbridge, you can step into the past at the Ironbridge Gorge Museums where you'll find 10 museums to visit, all following the history of the Industrial Revolution. For retail therapy at its best, small independent shops can be found in all its market towns, full of those special 'somethings' you were looking for and even some things you weren't.

Shrewsbury is the beautiful county town, and home (naturally enough) to the Shrewsbury Summer Season – packed with over 200 events including the Shrewsbury Flower Show and the Cartoon Festival. There is also the Darwin Festival to celebrate the town's most famous son, and the foot-tapping Folk Festival. Ludlow, a medieval town, once the seat of the Welsh parliament, and now famed equally for its events and food, is also full of surprises. The Ludlow Festival is an annual two week gathering of actors, musicians, singers, entertainers, and generally some blooming interesting people to keep you rather amused.

All in all, Shropshire has a surprising amount to offer. So take the Shropshire option – for a great day out, fresh clean air and no jams (except those the W.I. make!)

Strefford Hall
Strefford, Craven Arms SY7 8DE

Set in the lovely South Shropshire countryside surrounded by fields and close to Wenlock Edge. A stable conversion provides two self-catering units. Swallows Nest on the ground floor is ideal for frail or disabled guests. Robins Nest is on the first floor. Each consists of double en suite bedroom, fitted kitchen, large sitting/diningroom with colour TV; central heating and linen included. Fitted carpets. Patio area with seating. Ample parking to the side of the stable. **Terms £180 to £286 per week. Also Bed and Breakfast available in the farmhouse.**

Tel & Fax: 01588 672383 • e-mail: strefford@btconnect.co.uk
website: www.strefford.co.uk or www.streffordhallfarmshop.co.uk

170 SHROPSHIRE   Craven Arms, Ludlow SELF-CATERING

Horseshoe Cottage, Clun Valley

Private self-catering cottage situated in the beautiful gardens of a 17th century Listed house in Clunbury, a village of archaeological interest in a designated Area of Outstanding Natural Beauty – A.E. Housman countryside. Completely furnished and equipped; suitable for elderly and disabled persons.

The Welsh Border countryside is rich in medieval history, unspoilt villages and natural beauty. Enjoy walking on the Long Mynd and Offa's Dyke, or explore Ludlow and Ironbridge.

**Colour TV. Children and pets welcome; cot available.
Ample parking. Terms £150 to £200 per week.
Please write or phone for further details.**

Mrs B. Freeman, Upper House, Clunbury, Craven Arms SY7 0HG • 01588 660629

Mocktree Barns Holiday Cottages

A small group of barns offering comfortable self-catering accommodation around sunny courtyard.• Well-equipped, sleeping between two and six. • Two cottages with no stairs. • Friendly owners. • Open all year. • Short breaks available • Pets and children welcome. • Lovely views, excellent walks • Direct access to footpaths through farmland and woods. • Hereford, Cider Country, Shropshire Hills, Shrewsbury, Ironbridge and the splendid mid-Wales countryside all an easy drive away. • Beautiful Ludlow seven miles. • Golf, fishing, cycling nearby.

**Colour brochure from Clive and Cynthia Prior,
Mocktree Barns, Leintwardine, Ludlow SY7 0LY (01547 540441)
e-mail: mocktreebarns@care4free.net • web: www.mocktreeholidays.co.uk**

VisitBritain

Pets Welcome!

"THE PET WORLD'S VERSION OF THE ULTIMATE HOTEL GUIDE!" (The Times)

Now better than ever and with full colour throughout,

Pets Welcome! is used every year by thousands of discriminating owners who simply refuse to leave their pets "home alone".

Published twice a year in Autumn and Spring.

Only £8.99 from booksellers or direct from the publishers:
**FHG Guides, Abbey Mill Business Centre, Seedhill,
Paisley PA1 1TJ** (postage charged outside UK)

THE ORIGINAL
PETS WELCOME
• GUIDE •

Looking for holiday accommodation?

for details of hundreds of properties throughout the UK including comprehensive coverage of all areas of Scotland try:

www.holidayguides.com

SELF-CATERING Allerford

Somerset

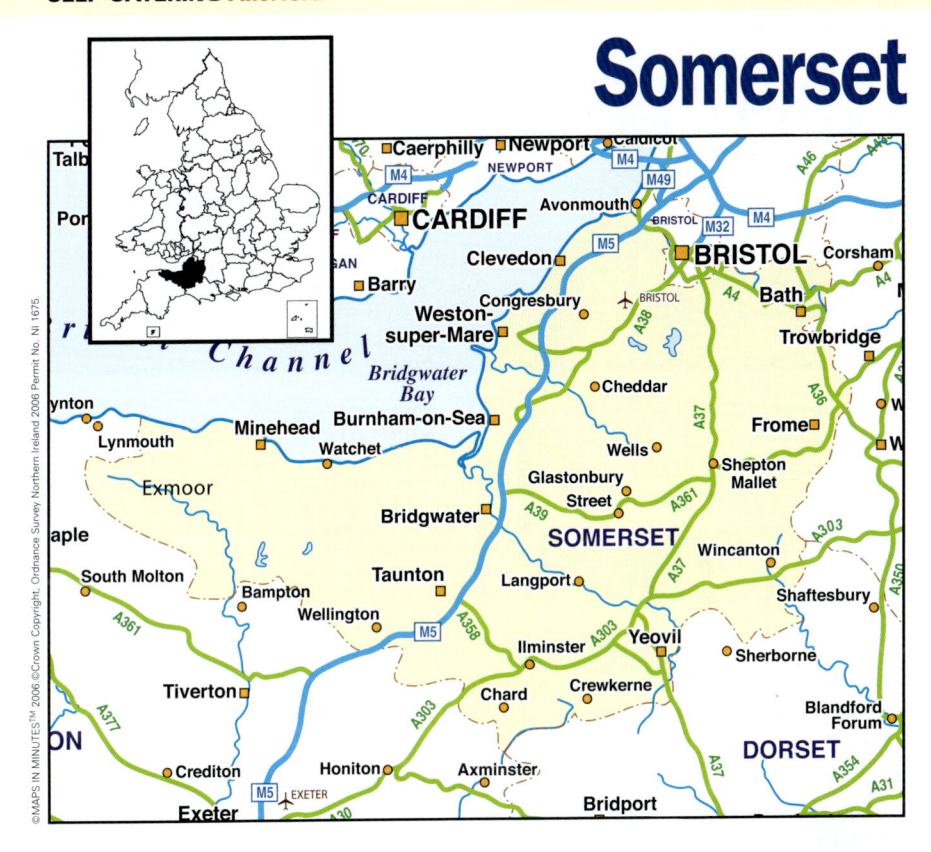

SOMERSET 171

Exmoor •• The Pack Horse
Allerford, Near Porlock, Somerset TA24 8HW
Tel/Fax: 01643 862475
www.thepackhorse.net • e-mail: holidays@thepackhorse.net

Our self-catering apartments and cottage are situated in this unique location within a picturesque National Trust village which has local amenities. The Pack Horse sits alongside the shallow River Aller, overlooking the famous bridge. Enjoy immediate access from our doorstep to the beautiful surrounding countryside, pretty villages, spectacular coast, and Exmoor.

Terms from £230 to £495 per week

OPEN ALL YEAR • PRIVATE PARKING • SHORT BREAKS

Very warm welcome assured

Readers are requested to mention this guidebook when making enquiries about accommodation.

172 SOMERSET   Brean, Burnham-on-Sea, Chard, Langport   SELF-CATERING

Beachside Holiday Park
Coast Rd. Brean. Somerset. TA8 2QZ
Freephone 08000 190322

beachsideholidaypark.co.uk

Caravan holiday homes & chalets available. Full facilities, colour T.V. microwave oven, patio furniture, hire inclusive of bed linen, electricity and gas.
With beachside frontage and situated in the dunes at the edge of Brean village.

Withy Grove Farm

Come and enjoy a relaxing and friendly holiday "Down on the Farm" set in beautiful Somerset countryside. Peaceful rural setting adjoining River Huntspill, famed for its coarse fishing. The farm is ideally situated for visiting the many local attractions including Cheddar Gorge, Glastonbury, Weston-super-Mare and the lovely sandy beach of Burnham-on-Sea. Self-catering cottages are tastefully converted, sleeping 4-5. Fully equipped with colour TV.

★ Heated Swimming Pool ★ Games Room
★ Licensed Bar and Entertainment (in high season)
★ Skittle Alley ★ Laundry

For more information please contact: Mrs Wendy Baker, Withy Grove Farm, East Huntspill, Near Burnham-on-Sea, Somerset TA9 3NP • Telephone: 01278 784471 • www.withygrovefarm.co.uk

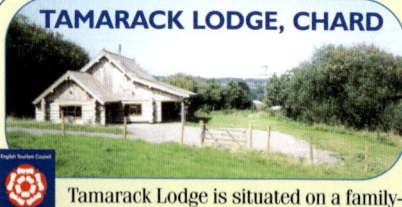

TAMARACK LODGE, CHARD

This luxurious, traditionally styled, ranch house-type log cabin enjoys extensive views of the delightful Yarty Valley. It was purpose-built to provide self-catering holiday accommodation for both able-bodied and disabled people, and sleeps up to eight. It is very wheelchair-friendly, and has two of the three double bedrooms on the ground floor, and a large ground floor wc/shower room. Tamarack Lodge is situated on a family-run beef and sheep farm in the beautiful Blackdown Hills, an Area of Outstanding Natural Beauty near the Somerset/Devon border.
NATIONAL ACCESSIBLE SCHEME LEVEL 1.

Matthew Sparks, Fyfett Farm, Otterford, Chard TA20 3QP • 01823 601270
e-mail: matthew.sparks@tamaracklodge.co.uk • www.tamaracklodge.co.uk

Muchelney Ham Farm, Muchelney Ham, Langport TA10 0DJ

Self-catering cottages built in traditional style adjoining farmhouse.
Double and family bedrooms, en suite.
Large kitchen/diningroom.
One further bathroom downstairs.
Stable cottage has a downstairs bedroom.
Electricity by coin meter. Linen included in price.
Open all year.
Weekly terms from £160 to £420,
or from £125 to £300.

Tel: 01458 250737 • www.muchelneyhamfarm.co.uk

SELF-CATERING Minehead, Shepton Mallet, Taunton, Wells **SOMERSET 173**

MINEHEAD – 16th CENTURY THATCHED COTTAGES

ROSE-ASH – Sleeps 2 ✦ Prettily furnished ✦ All electric.
WILLOW – Sleeps 6 ✦ Inglenook ✦ one double and two twin bedrooms ✦ Oak panelling ✦ Electricity, Gas, CH.
LITTLE THATCH – Sleeps 5 ✦ Inglenook ✦ two double and a single bedroom ✦ Cosy location ✦ Electricity, Gas, CH.

All well equipped and attractively furnished, and situated within ten minutes' walk of shops, sea and moor. All have enclosed patio/garden and private parking. Electricity and gas are metered; bed linen can be provided at extra cost. Pets welcome.

SAE please to: Mr T. Stone, Troytes Farmstead, Tivington, Somerset TA24 8SU
Private car park – Enclosed gardens – Pets Welcome   **Tel: 01643 704531**

KNOWLE FARM

Four cottages converted from stone barns, sleep 2, 4 or 6, with beamed ceilings and log fires, set around a pretty communal garden with a separate play area for children. Two cottages have kitchen/diner, separate lounge; the other two have kitchen, lounge/ diner with ground floor accommodation. They are fully equipped inc. TV/DVD, washing machine, CD player and gas central heating throughout. Bed linen and towels provided; cot/highchair by arrangement. Quiet rural setting. Ideal base for exploring Somerset, close to Wells, Glastonbury, Bath and local family attractions.

Terms: High Season £325 to £575 • Open all year • Short breaks available
• Car essential, ample parking • Sorry, no pets or smoking
• See our website for full details and availability • Brochure available

www.knowle-farm-cottages.co.uk
West Compton, Shepton Mallet BA4 4PD • Tel: 01749 890482 • Fax: 01749 890405

WOODLANDS FARM ~ TAUNTON

Mrs Joan Greenway, Woodlands Farm, Bathealton, Taunton TA4 2AH • Tel: 01984 623271

You can be assured of a warm welcome at our family-run dairy farm situated in the heart of beautiful unspoilt countryside and within easy reach of both the north and south coasts and Exmoor. The wing of the farmhouse sleeps three and is furnished to a high standard. Well equipped kitchen with use of washing machine and dryer. Bathroom with bath and shower. Electricity, central heating and bed linen inclusive. Fishing, golf and horse riding nearby. Terms from £175 to £350 per week.

Please write or phone for colour brochure.

Model Farm, Milton, Wells BA5 3AE

Two single storey barn conversions set in beautiful countryside on a working farm on the edge of the Mendip Hills. Both cottages are one bedroomed - **GARDEN COTTAGE** has a double bed and **COURTYARD COTTAGE** has one double and one single bed. Wookey Hole Caves are nearby and the centre of Wells is just one mile away. Bath, Longleat House and Safari Park, Cheddar Gorge and Clarks Shopping Village are all within easy reach. The area is ideal for walking and the West Mendip Way runs through the farm. Bed linen supplied and cots and highchairs provided.

Mrs Gill Creed • 01749 673363

Wells SELF-CATERING

Honeysuckle Cottage, Worth, Near Wells

A recent barn conversion (sleeps 5) on small working farm in the heart of rural Somerset. Maintains 'olde worlde' charm while offering all modern amenities. The cottage has oil-fired central heating throughout and log-burning stove. One double en suite bedroom, plus one double with adjoining single sharing large bathroom. Spacious kitchen/dining/living room with TV/DVD, and French windows leading to large patio and raised garden looking onto Mendip Hills and surrounding countryside. Kitchen has double oven and hob, dishwasher, washing machine, microwave and large fridge freezer.

Honeysuckle Cottage is a strictly non-smoking cottage.

Details from **Mrs L. Law, Honeycroft Farm, Worth, Wells BA5 1LW**
Tel: 01749 678971 • e-mail: honeycroft2@aol.com

Wrinkle Mead
Contact: Mrs C. Glass,
Islington Farm, Wells BA5 1US
Tel: 01749 673445

Uniquely situated next to the Bishop's Palace, on the edge of the City of Wells (England's smallest city), Wrinkle Mead is a riverside stable conversion of the highest standard, completed in June 2004. In this tranquil setting, the cottage is surrounded by fields and parkland, and is part of Islington Farm, a smallholding of 2.5 acres. There is private parking. Just three minutes away is the ancient Market Place, leading to the High Street where there is a varied selection of shops, restaurants and eating places. Numerous golf courses, walking, riding, cycling and fishing are all available nearby.

Staffordshire

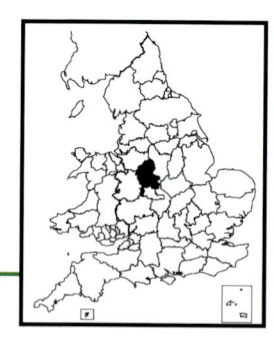

Leek

Situated in Staffordshire Moorlands, one cottage (sleeps 6) and one flat (sleeps 4), overlooking picturesque countryside. Fully equipped, comfortably furnished and carpeted throughout. Cottage, all on ground floor and with three bedrooms (one with four-poster) is suitable for the less able. An ideal base for visits to Alton Towers, the Potteries and Peak District. Patio, play area. Cot and high chair available. Laundry room with auto washer and dryer. Electricity and fresh linen inclusive. Terms from £180 to £350.

EDITH & ALWYN MYCOCK,
'ROSEWOOD COTTAGE and ROSEWOOD FLAT',
LOWER BERKHAMSYTCH FARM, BOTTOM HOUSE,
NEAR LEEK ST13 7QP
Tel & Fax: 01538 308213
www.rosewoodcottage.co.uk

SELF-CATERING Badwell Ash, Bury St Edmunds   SUFFOLK 175

Suffolk

BADWELL ASH HOLIDAY LODGES

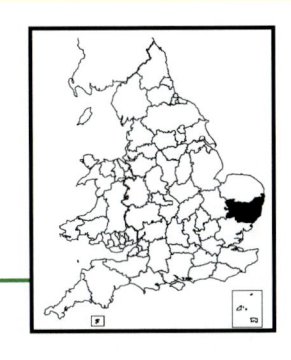

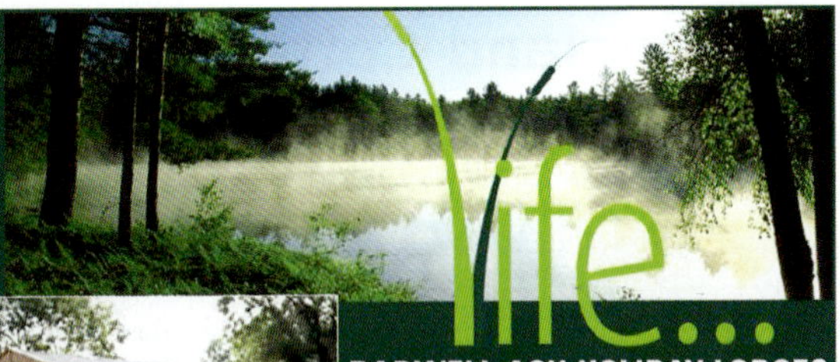

Four hand-crafted Scandinavian Holiday Lodges offering the ultimate luxury retreat in an oasis of calm and tranquillity.
- Exclusively for adults only
- Quality furnishings, fully fitted kitchens, four-poster beds, steam showers and personal outdoor hot tubs
- Electricity, bed linen and towels included in price
- Rural location overlooking private fishing lakes
- Complimentary welcome packs

www.badwellashlodges.co.uk

Badwell Ash, Suffolk IP31 3DJ
Tel: 01359 258444
info@badwellashlodges.co.uk

Rede Hall Farm Park

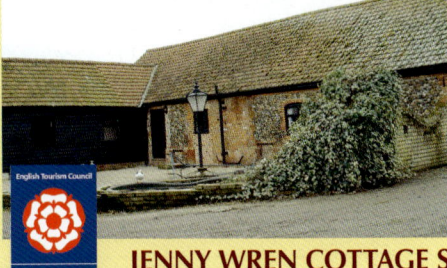

Two well equipped cottages with loads of Suffolk character and charm on moated mixed farm. Ideal for touring East Anglia and the Suffolk coast. Superb local pubs with good food. Open all year. Totally non-smoking.
Hot Tub Spa available for exclusive use (inclusive).

JENNY WREN COTTAGE SLEEPS 6
NUTHATCH COTTAGE SLEEPS 4 (+2)

Oil-fired central heating • Electric cooker, microwave, washer/dryer, dishwasher • TV with DVD/VCR, hi-fi • Children's play area • BBQ with patio furniture • Well behaved dogs welcome
• Livery for horses on request

Rede Hall, Rede, Bury St Edmunds IP29 4UG
Tel: 01284 850695
Fax: 01284 850345
www.redehallfarmpark.co.uk

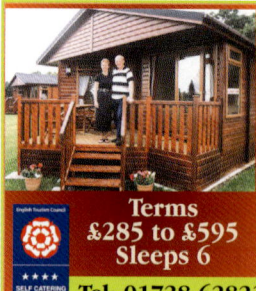

176 SUFFOLK   Eye, Kessingland, Southwold, Woodbridge **SELF-CATERING**

Countryside lodges situated in an idyllic location in North Suffolk. Very well appointed with fitted kitchen including microwave and fridge, en suite master bedroom, family bathroom and a twin bedded room. Open plan lounge with remote control colour TV and a sofa bed that can sleep two adults. Double-glazed, with full central heating. Open all year. Pets and children welcome. Credit cards accepted.

**Terms £285 to £595
Sleeps 6**

Contact: **Peter and Sally Havers, Athelington Hall, Horham, Eye, Suffolk IP21 5EJ**

Tel: 01728 628233 • Fax: 01379 384491 • mobile: 07850 989522
e-mail: peter@logcabinholidays.co.uk • website: www.logcabinholidays.co.uk

---

Kessingland Cottage   Rider Haggard Lane, Kessingland.

- Sleeps 6. • Children and disabled persons welcome. • Available 1st March to 7th January.

An exciting three-bedroomed recently built semi-detached cottage situated on the beach, three miles south of sandy beach at Lowestoft. Fully and attractively furnished with colour TV. Delightful sea and lawn views from floor-to-ceiling windows of lounge. Accommodation for up to six people. Well-equipped kitchen with electric cooker, fridge, hot and cold water; electric immersion heater. Electricity by £1 coin meter. Luxurious bathroom with coloured suite, bath and shower. No linen or towels provided. Only 30 yards to beach and sea fishing. One mile to wildlife country park with mini-train. Buses quarter-of-a-mile and shopping centre half-a-mile. Parking, but car not essential.

Rates: Weekly terms from £95 in early March and late December to £350 in high season.

SAE to Mr S. Mahmood, 156 Bromley Road, Beckenham, Kent BR3 6PG (Tel & Fax: 020 8650 0539).
e-mail: jeeptrek@kjti.freeserve.co.uk • www.k-cottage.co.uk

Southwold • Walberswick

Furnished Holiday Cottages, Houses and Flats, available in this charming unspoilt seaside town. Convenient for beaches, sailing, fishing, golf and tennis. Near to 300 acres of open Common. Attractive country walks and historic churches are to be found in this area, also the fine City of Norwich, the Festival Town of Aldeburgh and the Bird Sanctuary at Minsmere, all within easy driving distance. SAE, please, for brochure with full particulars.

**H.A. Adnams, Estate Agents, 98 High Street, Southwold IP18 6DP
01502 723292 • Fax: 01502 724794
www.haadnams.com**

Anvil Cottage   Woodbridge

Extensively refurbished but retaining its traditional charm, this compact but comfortable, light and airy cottage offers accommodation for up to four adults. Well equipped galley kitchen area and utility room with WC, washing machine, and ironing facilities. Cosy lounge with TV, DVD, video, radio, games, books etc. One double and one twin bedroom, bathroom upstairs. Central heating and secondary double glazing. Secluded courtyard garden with storage shed for bicycles. Off-street parking. Gas, electricity and linen included in hire. No smoking. Pets allowed. Brochure.

**Mr & Mrs R. Blake, 1a Moorfield Road, Woodbridge, Suffolk IP12 4JN
Tel: 01394 382565 • mobile: 07901 773545
e-mail: robert@blake4110.fsbusiness.co.uk**

SELF-CATERING

SUSSEX 177

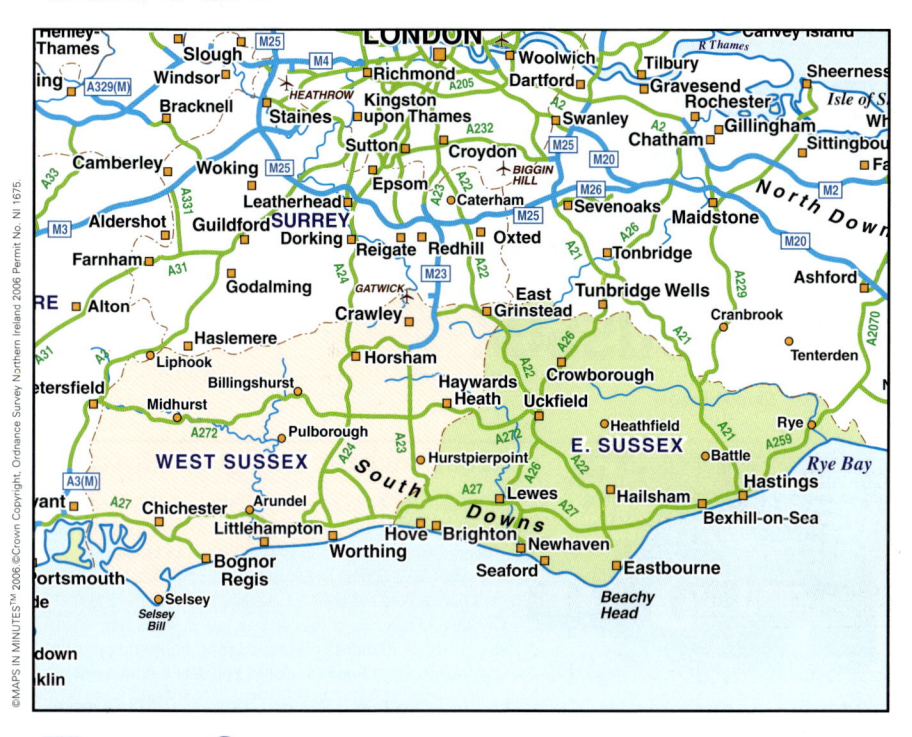

Sussex

East Sussex

Alfriston

Mrs G. Burgess
Polhills
Arlington, Polegate
East Sussex BN26 6SB
01323 870004

Idyllically situated on shore of reservoir and edge of Sussex Downs within easy reach of the sea. Fully furnished period cottage (approached by own drive along the water's edge) available for self-catering holidays from April to October (inclusive). Fly fishing for trout can be arranged during season. Accommodation consists of two double bedrooms; tiled bathroom. Lounge with colour TV; large well-fitted kitchen with fridge freezer, electric cooker, microwave, washing machine; dining room with put-u-up settee; sun lounge. Central heating. Linen supplied. Most rooms contain a wealth of oak beams. Car essential. Ample parking. Shops two miles. Golf, hill climbing locally. Sea eight miles.

Weekly terms from £295 to £340 (electricity included).

Free or reduced rate entry to
Holiday Visits and Attractions – see our
READERS' OFFER VOUCHERS on pages 7-40

178 EAST SUSSEX/WEST SUSSEX   Arlington SELF-CATERING

Lakeside Farm Holiday Bungalows

Situated on the edge of Arlington Reservoir, with views of the South Downs. Eastbourne, Brighton and Lewes within 15 miles; Drusillas Zoo two miles, shopping half a mile. Modern, comfortable accommodation: two double rooms, lounge, dining room, colour TV, bathroom, toilet. Well-equipped kitchen with microwave. Open April to October. Car essential, parking. Suitable for disabled guests. Children welcome; cot and high chair available. Well-controlled pets accepted. Electricity included. Terms from £200 per week.

Mrs P. Boniface, Lakeside Farm Holiday Bungalows, Arlington, Polegate BN26 6SB (01323 870111)
e-mail: pat@lakesidecottages.freeserve.co.uk
www.showpony.com/lakeside

West Sussex

Midhurst, Storrington

Meadowhills Lodge & Cottage

Comfortable one-bedroomed lodge and two-bedroomed cottage situated adjacent to the owner's property, in large gardens which overlook magnificent views over the South Downs. The properties have fishing rights and are in a "Walkers' Paradise". There is golf and polo at Cowdray Park. Fontwell and Goodwood races are within 40 minutes' drive and the south coast is about 20 miles away, pubs ¾ mile. Fully equipped for comfort. Short breaks available. Full details on request.

**Mrs Reeves-Fisher, Meadowhills, Stedham, Midhurst, West Sussex GU29 0PT
Tel: 01730 812609 or Mobile: 07776 262147 • *www.meadowhills.co.uk***

Byre Cottages

Sullington Manor Farm is a 500 acre working beef farm in a tranquil downland location. Byre Cottages are located adjacent to the farmyard and are set around a shared lawn. The five cottages have been attractively converted from Victorian stables and offer cosy and comfortable holiday accommodation with exposed beams and flint walls. The cottages have one, two or three bedrooms and can accommodate two, four and six people. Prices are from £200 to £490 per week, according to season.

**Mr G. Kittle, Sullington Manor Farm, Storrington, West Sussex RH20 4AE
Tel: 01903 745374 • e-mail: kittles@waitrose.com**

Readers are requested to mention this guidebook when making enquiries about accommodation.

SELF-CATERING Stratford-upon-Avon   WARWICKSHIRE

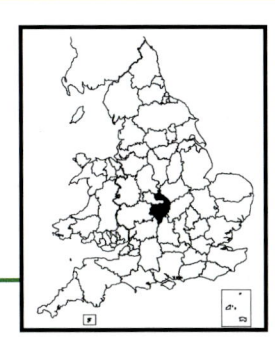

Warwickshire

Crimscote Downs Farm Self-catering Accommodation

PARADISE COTTAGE is a romantic hideaway for two people in a newly converted former shepherd's retreat, with views over the downs. It is full of character, and furnished and equipped to the highest standard.

THE DAIRY is ideal for a family visit, with fully equipped kitchen, sitting room and three en suite bedrooms. It has stunning views and is full of character with beams and wooden floors.

Terms from £195 to £400. Both cottages are fully centrally heated and only 5½ miles from Stratford-upon-Avon. No smoking. Ample parking. Pets by arrangement.

Mrs J. James, The Old Coach House, Whitchurch Farm, Wimpstone, Stratford-upon-Avon CV37 8NS (01789 450275).
e-mail: joan.james@tesco.net • www.stratford-upon-avon.co.uk/crimscote.htm

Useful Guidance for Guests and Hosts

Every year literally thousands of holidays, short breaks and overnight stops are arranged through our guides, the vast majority without any problems at all. In a handful of cases, however, difficulties do arise about bookings, which often could have been prevented from the outset.

It is important to remember that when accommodation has been booked, both parties – guests and hosts – have entered into a form of contract. We hope that the following points will provide helpful guidance.

Guests

- When enquiring about accommodation, be as precise as possible. Give exact dates, numbers in your party and the ages of any children.
- State the number and type of rooms wanted and also what catering you require – bed and breakfast, full board etc. Make sure that the position about evening meals is clear – and about pets, reductions for children or any other special points.
- Read our reviews carefully to ensure that the proprietors you are going to contact can supply what you want. Ask for a letter confirming all arrangements, if possible.
- If you have to cancel, do so as soon as possible. Proprietors do have the right to retain deposits and under certain circumstances to charge for cancelled holidays if adequate notice is not given and they cannot re-let the accommodation.

Hosts

- Give details about your facilities and about any special conditions. Explain your deposit system clearly and arrangements for cancellations, charges etc. and whether or not your terms include VAT.
- If for any reason you are unable to fulfil an agreed booking without adequate notice, you may be under an obligation to arrange suitable alternative accommodation or to make some form of compensation.

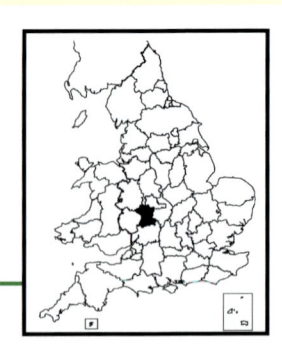

Worcestershire

Netherley Hall Cottages
Mathon, Near Malvern, Worcestershire WR13 5LW

Contact: Vivien Vos
Telephone: 01886-880262
www.netherleyhallcottages.co.uk
enquiries@netherleyhallcottages.co.uk

Netherley Hall Estate is set in over 600 acres of beautiful countryside on the west side of the Malvern Hills, with marvellous woodland walks and wildlife, and only 15 minutes' drive from Malvern town. The self catering accommodation comprises:-

◆ One luxury 4-bedroom farmhouse
5 stars from VisitBritain Quality in Tourism

◆ One 2-bedroom cottage
4 stars from VisitBritain Quality in Tourism

◆ One 1-bedroom cottage
2 stars from VisitBritain Quality in Tourism

Visitors also have the use, by arrangement, of the tennis court and gym at Netherley Hall. Open all the year round. • *Children welcome. Stays are Friday to Friday, but short breaks can be arranged.*
Prices available on the website or on application.

Looking for holiday accommodation?
for details of hundreds of properties throughout the UK visit:

www.holidayguides.com

SELF-CATERING Tenbury Wells   WORCESTERSHIRE 181

Rochford Park Cottages

Tenbury Wells WR15 8SP • Tel & Fax: 01584 781392
e-mail: cottages@rochfordpark.co.uk

Located on one of the Teme valley's working farms,
this former dairy (sleeps 3) and barn (sleeps 8) are now stylish,
comfortable retreats for any holidaymaker.

Explore the farm's footpaths and bridleways, fish in one of its lakes,
play golf on the neighbouring 9-hole links....
Further afield, walk the Malvern Hills, or valleys of the Welsh Marches.

Hereford, Worcester and Ludlow are within 30 miles
as are numerous National Trust and English Heritage
houses and gardens.

Youngsters will enjoy the Severn Valley Railway
and Bewdley Safari Park. Open all year round.
For further details see our website.

www.rochfordpark.co.uk

Looking for Holiday Accommodation?

FHG

K·U·P·E·R·A·R·D

for details of hundreds of
properties throughout the UK
visit our website

www.holidayguides.com

182 YORKSHIRE   **SELF-CATERING**

Yorkshire

Yorkshire Dales, Coast and Wolds

As you set foot into these breathtaking locations, you will be drawn to many diverse sights. Jagged coastlines, expansive moors and ancient castles to name but a few. That is of course should you wish to leave your wonderful, personally inspected cottage. Each with it's own charm whether catering for couples, families or pet lovers.

Dales Holiday Cottages

For your choice of over 500 cottages
call **0870 909 9505** or visit **www.dalesholcot.com**   A66

SELF-CATERING

NORTH YORKSHIRE 183
Askrigg (Wensleydale), Bishop Wilton, Coverdale

North Yorkshire

Situated in Wensleydale, half-a-mile from Bainbridge and one mile from Askrigg, Coleby Hall is a 17th century gabled farmhouse with stone mullioned windows, the west end being to let. A stone spiral staircase leads to two bedrooms; linen provided. The kitchen is equipped with electric cooker, fridge, crockery, etc., and coal fire. The lounge has an inglenook coal fire and TV. Oil-fired central heating throughout.

Coleby has lovely views and is an ideal situation for walking, fishing and driving round the Yorkshire Dales.

Children and pets welcome. Terms from £210 per week.

Mrs E. Scarr, Coleby Hall, Askrigg, Leyburn DL8 3DX
01969 650216 • www.colebyhall.co.uk

THE GRANGE, Bishop Wilton, York YO42 1SA

Comfortably furnished cottages on working stud farm, within easy reach of York, Filey and Scarborough, Castle Howard, Yorkshire Moors National Park and the Steam Railway at Pickering. Accommodation, all ground floor, sleeps 2-4, plus cot, and comprises one double bedroom, open-plan sitting/diningroom with sofa bed, and kitchen. Well behaved pets. Covered parking. One cottage adapted for partially disabled guests. Small lawned area and BBQ. *From £160 to £350 per week,* including heat, power, linen and towels.

Judith Davy
Tel: 01759 369500 • Mobile: 07919 472456
www.thegrangefarm.com

Panoramic views, waterfalls, wild birds and tranquillity

Stone farmhouse with panoramic views, high in the Yorkshire Dales National Park (Herriot family's house in 'All Creatures Great and Small' on TV). Three bedrooms (sleeps 6-8), sitting and dining rooms with wood-burning stoves, kitchen, bathroom, WCs. House has electric storage heating, cooker, microwave, fridge, dishwasher, washing machine, colour TV, telephone. Garden, large barn, stables. Access from lane, private parking, no through traffic. Excellent walking from front door, near Wensleydale. Pets welcome. Self-catering from £400 per week.

Allaker in Coverdale,
West Scrafton, Leyburn, North Yorks DL8 4RM
For bookings telephone 020 8567 4862
e-mail: ac@adriancave.com • www.adriancave.com/allaker

A useful index of towns/counties appears at the back of this book

Free or reduced rate entry to
Holiday Visits and Attractions – see our
READERS' OFFER VOUCHERS on pages 7-40

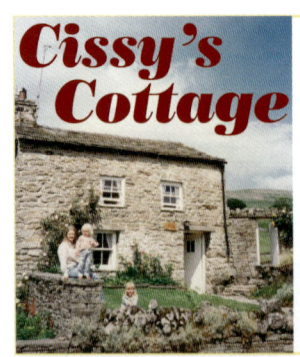

184 NORTH YORKSHIRE Hardraw, Harrogate, Helmsley **SELF-CATERING**

Cissy's Cottage

Hardraw, Hawes, North Yorkshire. Sleeps 4

A delightful 18th century cottage of outstanding character. Situated in the village of Hardraw with its spectacular waterfall and Pennine Way. Market town of Hawes one mile. This traditional stone-built cottage retains many original features including beamed ceilings and an open fire. Sleeping four in comfort, it has been furnished and equipped to a high standard using antique pine and Laura Ashley prints. Equipped with dishwasher, microwave and tumble dryer. Outside, a south-facing garden, sun patio with garden furniture, and a large enclosed paddock make it ideal for children. Cot and high chair if required. Open all year. Terms £125-£325 includes coal, electricity, linen and trout fishing. For brochure, contact:
Mrs Belinda Metcalfe, Southolme Farm, Little Smeaton, Northallerton DL6 2HJ • Tel: 01609 881302/881052

Regent Cottage Harrogate

This early 19th Century Town House, set in a private courtyard, retains many of its original features and has been restored and furnished to a high standard. Comfortably sleeps six, with one double and one twin bedroom on the first floor and an en suite bedroom in the semi-basement. Well equipped kitchen/dining room, formal period sitting room, plus study/sitting room in semi-basement. Colour TV in all main rooms. Full gas-fired central heating, electricity, bed linen and towels included in weekly rental. Parking. No Smoking. Pets by arrangement. Brochure.
Mr & Mrs R. Blake, 1a Moorfield Road, Woodbridge, Suffolk IP12 4JN
Tel: 01394 382565 • mobile: 07901 773545
e-mail: robert@blake4110.fsbusiness.co.uk

VALLEY VIEW FARM
Old Byland, Helmsley, York, North Yorkshire YO62 5LG
Telephone: 01439 798221   ETC ★★★★ SELF-CATERING

Fully re-furbished to high standards for Easter 2006, our six cottages, sleeping 2-10 are situated on a working farm within the scenic countryside of the North Yorkshire Moors National Park, close to Rievaulx Abbey and five miles from the delightful market town of Helmsley. There is good walking with several walks mapped into the surrounding countryside from the farm. Enjoy rural peace and tranquillity in an ideal location for exploring Yorkshire. £257-£610 per week. Dogs welcome by arrangement. Short breaks are offered throughout the year, subject to availability.
e-mail: sally@valleyviewfarm.com
www.valleyviewfarm.com

Looking for holiday accommodation?
for details of hundreds of properties throughout the UK visit:

www.holidayguides.com

SELF-CATERING

NORTH YORKSHIRE 185
Middlesmoor, Northallerton, Pickering, Robin Hood's Bay

ABBEY HOLIDAY COTTAGES

Middlesmoor, commanding unrivalled panoramic views, is situated at the head of picturesque Nidderdale, an Area of Outstanding Natural Beauty. This pretty village offers peace and tranquillity, and is an excellent base for walking and birdwatching, and for exploring Harrogate, Ripon and York. Our traditional stone-built cottages have been modernised and refurbished to a high standard.

Welcome to the heart of Nidderdale
Holmelea Cottage • sleeps 6
Sawmill Cottage • sleeps 5
The Old Joiner's Shop • sleeps 6

All fuel, power, bed linen and towels provided. Cot and high chair available. One well behaved pet welcome (extra pet £10). All cottages non-smoking.

Abbey Holiday Cottages,
12 Panorama Close, Pateley Bridge, Harrogate HG3 5NY
Tel: 01423 712062 • abbeyholiday.cottages@virgin.net
www.abbeyholidaycottages.co.uk

Holmelea Cottage

Hill House Farm Cottages
Julie & Jim Griffith
Hill House Farm
Little Langton, Northallerton DL7 0PZ
e-mail: info@hillhousefarmcottages.com

These former farm buildings sleeping 2/4 have been converted into 4 well-equipped cottages, retaining original beams. Cosily heated for year-round appeal. Peaceful setting with magnificent views. Centrally located between Dales and Moors with York, Whitby and Scarborough all within easy driving distance. Weekly rates from £175 incl. all linen, towels, heating and electricity. Short Breaks available. Pub food 1.5m, Golf 2m, Shops 3m. Pets welcome.

For a free colour brochure please call 01609 770643 or see our website
www.hillhousefarmcottages.com

HUNGATE COTTAGES

Pickering, North Yorkshire YO18 7ET
Telephone: 01751 476382
mobile: 0787 6404152

Luxuriously converted, comfortable and peaceful 18th century limestone farm buildings, centrally heated and beautifully furnished. Well equipped and maintained, most have log fires and are set in mature gardens. All cottages feature fully fitted kitchen, colour TV, video, CD player, radio etc. Prices include heating, electricity and logs, full linen, towels and cancellation insurance. Pets are welcome at some cottages. Enclosed playground for younger children. Ample parking. Disabled facilities in Hungate Garden Cottage. A short walk from the centre of Pickering, and close to the Moors, York and the Heritage Coast.

Rates from £367 to £638 per week.
e-mail: holidays@hungatecottages.co.uk • www.hungatecottages.co.uk

---

Lingers Hill Farm

Semi-detached cosy character cottage, situated on the edge of the village and overlooking the coastline and countryside. Accommodating two to four guests, the cottage has a lounge with beamed ceiling, colour TV, video, fully-equipped kitchen/dining area, two bedrooms, bathroom and toilet. Gas fire and central heating. Electricity by £1 coin meter, gas and linen inclusive. Guests have use of the garden with picnic tables and benches. Shops, Post Office and pub within 250 yards. Excellent base for walking, cycling or touring the magnificent surroundings of the North York Moors National Park.

Terms from £190 to £355, with short breaks available from November to March. SAE, or telephone, for our brochure.

**Mrs F. Harland, Lingers Hill Farm, Thorpe Lane,
Robin Hood's Bay, Whitby YO22 4TQ
Telephone: 01947 880608**

Lingholm Court Holiday Cottages

Situated in open countryside down a peaceful country lane between Scarborough (5 miles) and Filey (3.5 miles). Three barn conversions and the original farmhouse, all set round a spacious enclosed courtyard on a 1200 acre working farm. Fully equipped, and each attractively furnished, providing every comfort. Centrally heated. Farmhouse has enclosed garden and log fires. Ideal for a family seaside holiday or countryside retreat. Short breaks. Discount for two people on weekly lets. Non-smoking/no pets. Brochure.

Mrs Caroline Woodhouse, Lingholm Farm, Lingholm Lane, Lebberston, Scarborough YO11 3PG
Tel: 01723 586365 • e-mail: info@lingholm.co.uk • www.lingholm.co.uk

Honeysuckle Cottage

Lovely, stone-built, self-catering cottage in village of East Ayton on River Derwent. Scarborough 4 miles. Sleeps 2-5 + cot. Patio/garden with gas barbecue. Non-smoking. Pets welcome. Private parking. Open all year. ETC ★★★★
Tel: David & Jane Beeley Tel: 01653 698251
e-mail: enquiries@forgevalleycottages.co.uk
www.forgevalleycottages.co.uk

Scarborough • Whitby • York

The Lodge • Horton Hall Farm
Horton-in-Craven, Skipton BD23 3JT

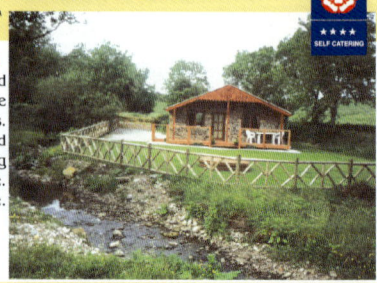

Tel: 01200 445200 • mobile: 07854 754471

Situated in the Ribble valley on the edge of the Forest of Bowland and Yorkshire Dales National Park. This newly built stone lodge stands in its own grounds, beside a stream with countryside views. Tastefully decorated in antique pine with modern kitchen, ramped access and level access shower. Situated 150 metres from working farm with cattle and sheep where visitors are always welcome. Open all year. Terms from £220 to £320. Children welcome. Sorry, no smoking. Sleeps four. Contact: Mrs Edith Thwaite.

e-mail: ediththwaite@hotmail.com
website: www.thelodgehorton.co.uk

New Close Farm

A supa dupa cottage on New Close Farm in the heart of Craven Dales with panoramic views over the Aire Valley. Excellent area for walking, cycling, fishing, golf and touring.

- Two double and one single bedrooms; bathroom.
- Colour TV and video.
- Full central heating and double glazing.
- Bed linen, towels and all amenities included in the price.
- Sorry, no young children, no pets.
- Non-smokers preferred.
- From £300-£350. Winter Short Breaks available.

The weather can't be guaranteed but your comfort can
Kirkby Malham, Skipton BD23 4DP
Tel: 01729 830240 • Fax: 01729 830179
e-mail: brendajones@newclosefarmyorkshire.co.uk
website: www.newclosefarmyorkshire.co.uk

FHG DIPLOMA AWARD WINNER

SELF-CATERING Staithes, Thirsk, Whitby   NORTH YORKSHIRE 187

Garth End Cottage
Staithes

Georgian cottage situated on sea wall in this old fishing village in the North York Moors National Park. Excellent walking centre. Small sandy beach with numerous rock pools. Cottage has feature fireplace, beamed ceilings, pine panelled room, well-equipped kitchen including microwave and dishwasher. Warm, comfortable, well-equipped with heating, electricity and bed linen included in rent. Two lounges, front one with picture window giving uninterrupted panoramic views of sea, harbour and cliffs. Dining kitchen; bathroom with toilet, bath and shower; three bedrooms - one double with king size bed, one twin, one single (two with sea views); colour TV/video. Front terrace overlooking the sea. Sorry, no pets. No smoking.

Terms from £250 • Sleeps 5 • Apply Mrs Hobbs (0113 2665501) • hilaryhobbs@btinternet.com

Rose Cottage Farm Holiday Cottages
Sutton-under-Whitestonecliffe, Thirsk YO7 2QA

Enjoy a stay in our self-catering holiday cottages in the heart of Herriot Country, with superb scenery and wonderful walking. Within easy reach of Thirsk, Helmsley, York, Scarborough, Harrogate, Malton, the North York Moors and the Yorkshire Dales.
BRIAR COTTAGE and **BRAMBLE COTTAGE**
Each sleeps two (twin or king-size bed) • All linen, towels, welcome pack and heating included in price • Laundry facilities available • Shared patio area and secluded lawn • Short breaks available (minimum 3 nights) • Well behaved pets accepted by arrangement.

Tel: 01845 597309 • www.rose-cottage-farm.co.uk

Discover historic Whitby, pretty fishing villages, countryside with way-marked walks. Four cottages, two bedrooms. Private parking. Children and dogs welcome.

Weekly rates from £195 to £500. Please phone or write for brochure.

ETC ★★★★

**MRS JILL McNEIL,
SWALLOW HOLIDAY COTTAGES,
LONG LEAS FARM, HAWSKER,
WHITBY YO22 4LA
01947 603790**

The Old Granary

This 17thC former Old Granary, set on a small farm, overlooks Sandsend Bay and offers one of the finest views in North Yorkshire. The fully equipped two-bedroom cottage has oil central heating and all the comforts of home, plus exposed beams and beautiful oak floors. It is close to Whitby and the steam railway, with excellent walking on the doorstep (Coast to Coast Walk) and is just a five-minute stroll to sandy beaches. An ideal base for exploring North Yorkshire. Sorry, no smoking, no pets.

Mrs Jackie Richardson, Raven Hill Farm, Dunsley, Near Sandsend, Whitby YO21 3TJ
Tel: 01947 893331 • Mobile 0798 9570779 • e-mail: jackie.richardson6@btopenworld.com

188 NORTH YORKSHIRE/WEST YORKSHIRE — Whitby, York SELF-CATERING

Copper Cottage

Set on a small farm with panoramic views over Sandsend Bay, Copper Cottage is a new single storey barn conversion, retaining many features including exposed stone, original beams and solid oak floors throughout. This fully equipped one-bedroom cottage has a super king-size bed (which will unzip and unclip into two singles if preferred). It has all the comforts of home, with the added bonus of a stunning sun lounge with sofa bed and dining area. Enjoy the spectacular views from the patio, or sit in the sunny courtyard. Close to Whitby and only a five-minute stroll to sandy beaches. Sorry, no smoking, no pets.

Mrs Jackie Richardson, Raven Hill Farm, Dunsley, Near Sandsend, Whitby YO21 3TJ
Tel: 01947 893211 • Mobile 0798 9570779 • e-mail: jackie.richardson6@btopenworld.com

YORK Wolds View Holiday Cottages, Yapham, Pocklington. Attractive, well-equipped accommodation situated in unspoilt countryside at the foot of the Yorkshire Wolds. Five units, three of which are suitable for wheelchairs. Themed holidays, with transport provided, exploring the villages and countryside nearby. York only 12 miles. Short Breaks available.
Rates: from £145 to £540 per week.
• Sleep 3-8. • 3 units suitable for wheelchairs. • Pets welcome.
CATEGORY 1,2 AND 3 NATIONAL ACCESSIBLE SCHEME.
For further details contact: Mrs M.S.A. Woodliffe, Mill Farm, Yapham, Pocklington, York YO42 1PH (01759 302172).

West Yorkshire

Keighley

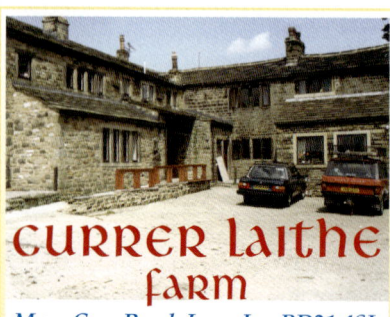

Currer Laithe Farm
Moss Carr Road, Long Lee BD21 4SL

Tel: 01535 604387   www.currerlaithe.co.uk

Pennine hill farm rearing 160 cattle, goats, donkeys. The 16th century house and land, covenanted to the National Trust, have panoramic views of Airedale. Desirable six-bedroomed accommodation all year, bed spaces for 15+ people. En suite or private facilities available. Spacious sittingroom, open fire, beamed and mullioned diningroom, inglenook fireplace, seats 20. Fully furnished kitchen. Holidays for families and groups of friends, weekend anniversaries, reunions, mid-week business, social, educational activities. Potential unlimited. Ten car parking spaces. Terms £90 per day, £500 per week high season. Also twin two-bedroomed cottages sleeping five to seven people with kitchen, sittingroom, toilet/shower from £90 low season, £220 high season. B&B also available at £18.50. Pets and children welcome.

FHG Guides

publish a large range of well-known accommodation guides. We will be happy to send you details or you can use the order form at the back of this book.

FHG
K·U·P·E·R·A·R·D

Caravans & Camping

North Morte Farm, Woolacombe, Devon

Quantock Orchard Caravan Park, Taunton

St Ives Bay Holiday Park, Cornwall

Cambridgeshire

Cambridgeshire

CAMBRIDGE (NEAR) Appleacre Park, Fowlmere, Royston, Herts. SG8 7RU (01763 208354).
Pleasant touring site for camping and caravanning, nine miles south west of Cambridge, three miles from Duxford Air Museum. Directions from Cambridge turn off A10 at "Old English Gentlemen" pub to B1368, site on left, through village; from Royston turn left off A505 to B1368, site on right after Fowlmere sign.
e-mail: appleacrepark@aol.com
www.appleacrepark.co.uk

Cornwall

St Ives Bay Holiday Park

CALL OUR 24hr BROCHURE LINE 0800 317713

The park on the beach

CHALETS • CARAVANS • CAMPING

St Ives Bay Holiday Park is set in sand dunes which run down to its own sandy beach. Many units have superb sea views. There is a large indoor pool and 2 clubs with FREE entertainment on the Park.

www.stivesbay.co.uk

Cumbria

Ambleside, Coniston

Greenhowe Caravan Park
Great Langdale, English Lakeland.

Greenhowe Caravan Park
Great Langdale, Ambleside,
Cumbria LA22 9JU

Greenhowe is a permanent Caravan Park with Self Contained Holiday Accommodation. Subject to availability Holiday Homes may be rented for short or long periods from 1st March until mid-November. The Park is situated in the Lake District half-a-mile from Dungeon Ghyll at the foot of the Langdale Pikes. It is an ideal centre for Climbing, Fell Walking, Riding, Swimming, Water-Skiing. **Please ask about Short Breaks.**

For free colour brochure
Telephone: (015394) 37231 • Fax: (015394) 37464
• Freephone: 0800 0717231 • www.greenhowe.com

Three six-berth, modern, well-equipped caravans situated on a quiet family-run farm site with beautiful views over Coniston Water.

Showers, toilets, gas cookers, fires and water heaters; electric lighting, fridge, TV, kettle, toaster and microwave.

Pets are welcome, and pony trekking can be arranged from the farm. A good base for walking and touring the area. We have a good pub 200 yards down the road. Weekly terms on request.

**Mrs E. Johnson, Spoon Hall, Coniston LA21 8AW
Telephone: 015394 41391**

CARAVANS & CAMPING

CUMBRIA/DEVON 191

Little Asby, Grange-over-Sands

Whygill Head

Two six-berth caravans situated on their own private half acre site, in a quiet farm setting. Situated five miles from Kirkby Stephen, eight miles from Appleby and seven miles from Junction 38 of the M6 at Tebay.
It is an ideal location for walking, relaxing, touring the Yorkshire Dales, Lake District and local market towns. Both caravans are fully equipped with TV, free gas, water and electricity.
One of the caravans is AIA inspected and passed.
Short breaks available. Please ring or write for further information, brochure and tariff.

**Little Asby, Appleby CA16 6QD
Tel: 017683 71531**

GRANGE-OVER-SANDS reaves Farm Caravan Park, Field Broughton, Grange-over-Sands.
Family-run, small quiet grass site with luxury six berth caravans. Fully serviced. Colour TV, fridge. Equipped except for linen. Tourers and tents welcome. Two miles north of Cartmel, two miles south of foot of Lake Windermere. Convenient base for touring Lake District. Personal supervision.
• Open March to October.
ETC ★★★★
SAE for details to Mrs E. Rigg, Prospect House, Barber Green, Grange-over-Sands LA11 6HU (015395 36329 or 36587).

Devon

Woolacombe

North Morte Farm Caravan & Camping, Dept. FHG, Mortehoe, Woolacombe EX34 7EG (01271 870381)

The nearest camping and caravan park to the sea, in perfectly secluded beautiful coastal country. Our family-run park, adjoining National Trust land, is only 500 yards from Rockham Beach, yet only five minutes' walk from the village of Mortehoe with a Post Office, shops, cafes and pubs – one of which has a children's room. Four to six berth holiday caravans for hire and pitches for tents, dormobiles and touring caravans, electric hook-ups available. We have hot showers and flush toilets, laundry room, shop and off-licence; Calor gas and Camping Gaz available; children's play area. Dogs accepted but must be kept on lead. Open Easter to end September. Brochure available.

English Tourism Council ★★★★ HOLIDAY PARK

**Free or reduced rate entry to
Holiday Visits and Attractions – see our
READERS' OFFER VOUCHERS on pages 7-40**

ND/SOMERSET

Northumberland
Hexham

Greencarts is a working farm situated in Roman Wall country, ideally placed for exploring by car, bike or walking. It has magnificent views of the Tyne Valley. Campsite for 30 tents with facilities, and bunk barn with 12 beds, showers and toilet are now open from Easter until the end of October. Prices for campsite are £5 to £10 per tent, plus £1pp. Bunk barn beds from £10. Linen available. Bed and Breakfast also available from £25 to £35.

Mr & Mrs D Maughan, Greencarts Farm, Humshaugh, Hexham NE46 4BW
Tel/Fax: 01434 681320
e-mail: sandra@greencarts.co.uk

GREENCARTS FARM
www.greencarts.co.uk

Somerset
Taunton

Quantock Orchard Caravan Park
The small, clean, friendly park for touring and camping

A small family-run touring park set in the beautiful Quantock Hills close to Exmoor and the coast in a designated Area of Outstanding Natural Beauty. We look forward to welcoming you to our five star park at any time of the year

For colour brochure and tariff call: **01984 618618**
or write to: Michael & Sara Barrett,
Quantock Orchard Caravan Park, Flaxpool,
Crowcombe, Near Taunton, Somerset TA4 4AW
e-mail: qocp@flaxpool.freeserve.co.uk
www.quantockorchard.co.uk

DE LUXE PARK

Publisher's note
While every effort is made to ensure accuracy, we regret that FHG Guides cannot accept responsibility for errors, misrepresentations or omissions in our entries or any consequences thereof. Prices in particular should be checked.
We will follow up complaints but cannot act as arbiters or agents for either party.

Scotland

Brathinch Farm, Brechin, Angus & Dundee — *The Whins, Inverness* — *Riverview House, Callander, in the Trossachs*

Board

The Scottish smoke-free legislation forbids smoking in enclosed places used by the public or where people work.

This means that it is now illegal to smoke inside any building, vehicle or structure like a marquee or caravan apart from your own home or car.

Scotland
Counties

1. Inverclyde
2. West Dunbartonshire
3. Renfrewshire
4. East Renfrewshire
5. City of Glasgow
6. East Dunbartonshire
7. North Lanarkshire
8. Falkirk
9. Clackmannanshire
10. West Lothian
11. City of Edinburgh
12. Midlothian

BOARD   **ABERDEEN, BANFF & MORAY 195**

Aberdeen, Banff & Moray

Aberdeenshire, Banff & Moray Aberdeen and Grampian Highlands is perhaps one of the most culturally distinct in the country. Aberdeen is a vibrant and cultural city with breathtaking architecture, colourful parks and gardens, a variety of shops, bars and restaurants and is full of welcoming charm. Although Grampian encompasses established tourism areas such as Royal Deeside and Speyside there is much more to the area than just Royalty, whisky and castles.

One of the easiest ways to explore Grampian is by following one of the signposted tourist routes and theme trails. Perhaps the most famous of these is the Malt Whisky Trail around magnificent Speyside which links the award winning Speyside Cooperage and eight famous distilleries.

Aberdeenshire is very much Scotland's "Castle Country" and 13 of the region's finest castles and great houses are located along Scotland's only Castle Trail. A lesser known feature of Scotland's North East is the fact that 10% of Scotland's Standing Stones are to be found here. Archaeolink, Scotland's prehistory park, interprets the early history of Grampian and promotes a journey through time for all ages.

Royal Deeside has many attractions associated with Queen Victoria and a succession of British monarchs. There are many well known sites in this part of the region along the Victorian Heritage Trail including Balmoral Castle, home to royalty for 150 years, Crathie Church, Royal Lochnagar Distillery and Loch Muick. Even here there are lesser known corners and it pays to wander off the main roads to explore the rural highways and byways of Deeside and the Mearns. This is a haven for sports and activity enthusiasts with golfers and fishing enthusiasts well catered for, while the more adventurous can try their hands at white water rafting, trekking and riding, gliding and canoeing.

196 ABERDEEN, BANFF & MORAY/ANGUS & DUNDEE   Forres **BOARD**

A warm welcome to our family farm, situated close to Forres, Findhorn and Kinloss. En suite rooms are tastefully furnished to a high standard, with TV and tea/coffee facilities; delicious Scottish cuisine is offered. The farm adjoins the Findhorn Nature Reserve which is popular with birdwatchers. Findhorn village has watersports and a lovely sandy beach. Nearby Findhorn Foundation, with its Eco Village, is world famous, or spend the day touring the coastline dolphin spotting. To the east is Elgin, with Johnston's cashmere outlet.

Mrs Hilda Massie, Milton of Grange Farm, By Forres IV36 2TR
Tel: 01309 676360

This is an excellent base for golf; Coastal, Castle and Malt Whisky Trails; places of historic interest including the Pictish Stone (Sueno) at Forres; to the west Culloden Battlefield and Fort George. Inverness, Gateway to the Highlands, is 30 miles (also airport). No smoking, no pets.
Rates - single from £25 per person to £38 (high season), double from £22.50 per person to £30.00 (high season).

e-mail: hildamassie@aol.com • www.forres-accommodation.co.uk

Sherston House
Hillhead, Forres IV36 2QT
01309 671087 • Fax: 01343 850535

Tastefully restored stone built house one mile from Forres and beside main A96. Large, comfortable, en suite rooms with TV, tea/coffee making facilities, hairdryers and trouser press. Garden area available. Home-cooked dinners available "highly recommended". Wonderful gardens in Forres and Findhorn Village and Foundation also nearby. Excellent location for golf, pony trekking, walking and fishing.

B&B from £25-£30 pppn.

Angus & Dundee

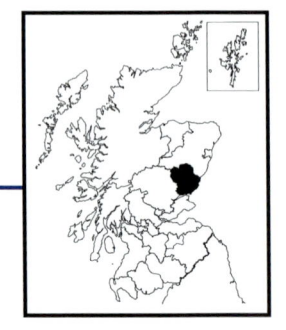

Brechin

Brathinch is an 18th century farmhouse on a family-run working arable farm, with a large garden, situated off the B966 between Brechin and Edzell.
Rooms have private or en suite bathroom, TV and tea/coffee making facilities. Shooting, fishing, golf, castles, stately homes, wildlife, swimming and other attractions are all located nearby.
Easy access to Angus Glens and other country walks. Open all year.
Double £22, twin £23, single £25 - £26.
We look forward to welcoming you.

Brathinch Farm
By Brechin DD9 7QZ
01356 648292 • Fax: 01356 648003
e-mail: adam.brathinch@btinternet.com

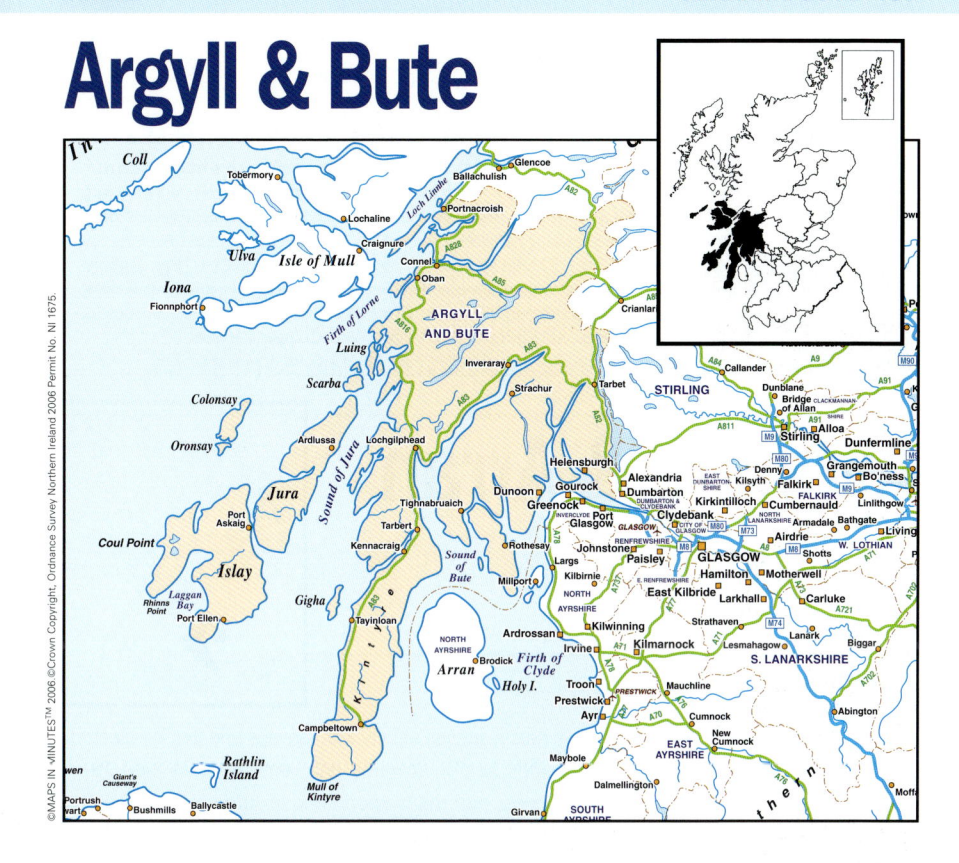

Argyll & Bute

ARGYLL & BUTE is a wonderfully unspoilt area, historically the heartland of Scotland and home to a wealth of fascinating wildlife. Here you may be lucky enough to catch a glimpse of an eagle, a wildcat or an osprey, or even a fine antlered stag. At every step the sea fringed landscape is steeped in history, from prehistoric sculpture at Kilmartin, to the elegant ducal home of the once feared Clan Campbell. There are also reminders of pre-historic times with Bronze Age cup-and-ring engravings, and standing stone circles. On the upper reaches of Loch Caolisport can be found St Columba's Cave, and more recent times are illustrated at the Auchindrain Highland Township south of Inveraray, a friendly little town with plenty to see, including the Jail, Wildlife Park and Maritime Museum.

Bute is the most accessible of the west coast islands, and Rothesay is its main town. Explore the dungeons and grand hall of Rothesay Castle, or visit the fascinating Bute Museum. The town offers a full range of leisure facilities, including a fine swimming pool and superb golf course, and there are vast areas of parkland where youngsters can safely play.

Readers are requested to mention this guidebook when making enquiries about accommodation.

Palace Hotel
GEORGE STREET, OBAN, ARGYLL PA34 5SB
01631 562294 • www.thepalacehotel.activehotels.com

A small family hotel offering personal supervision situated on Oban's sea front with wonderful views over the Bay, to the Mull Hills beyond. All rooms en suite, with colour TV, tea/coffee making facilities, non-smoking. The Palace is an ideal base for a real Highland holiday. By boat you can visit the islands of Kerrera, Coll, Tiree, Lismore, Mull and Iona, and by road Glencoe, Ben Nevis and Inveraray. Fishing, golf, horse riding, sailing, tennis and bowls all nearby. Children and pets welcome. Reductions for children. Please write or telephone for brochure. Competitive rates.

Discounted rates if quoting Farm Holiday Guide at time of booking

Ayrshire & Arran

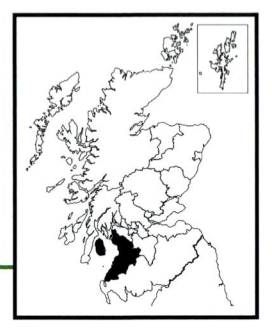

Ayrshire and Arran has always held a special affinity with families and this is reflected in the many fun attractions and activities geared towards children. These include farm parks, theme parks with daring funfair rides, and many sports and leisure centres. There's plenty to see and do with features like the Vikingar Viking Centre at Largs and The Scottish Industrial Railway Centre at Dalmellington adding to established attractions like Culzean Castle and the thriving business built on the life, loves and works of Scotland's best-loved poet, Robert Burns. A visit to the Secret Forest at Kelburn Country Centre is a must – its canopy of trees hides a multitude of surprises, the green man, the spirit of the forest, a Chinese garden with pagoda, and a crocodile swamp. Older visitors may enjoy a visit to Ayr Racecourse, enjoy a shopping spree, or treat themselves to a round on one the area's 44 golf courses. Whether the pace is leisurely or frantic, it's got to be Ayrshire and the Isle of Arran.

Kilmarnock

Mrs Nancy Cuthbertson, West Tannacrieff, Fenwick, Kilmarnock KA3 6AZ
Tel: 01560 600258 • mobile: 07773 226332 • Fax: 01560 600914
e-mail: westtannacrieff@btopenworld.com • www.smoothhound.co.uk/hotels/westtannacrieff.html

A warm welcome awaits all our guests to our dairy farm, situated in the peaceful Ayrshire countryside. Relax in spacious, well-furnished, en suite rooms with all modern amenities, colour TV and tea/coffee making facilities. Large parking area and garden.

Situated off the M/A77 on the B751 road to Kilmaurs, so easily accessible from Glasgow, Prestwick Airport, and the south. An ideal base for exploring Ayrshire's many tourist attractions.

Enjoy a hearty breakfast with home-made breads and preserves, and home baking for supper. Children welcome. Terms from £25 per person. Brochure available.

Borders

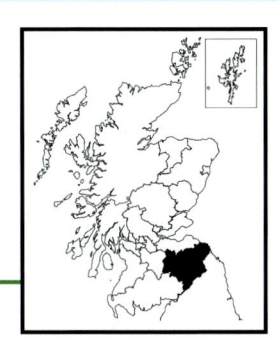

South Mains Farm

South Mains Farm is a working family farm, situated in an elevated position with good views, on the B7016 between Biggar and Broughton. An ideal place to take a break on a North/South journey. Edinburgh 29 miles, Peebles 11 miles. Well situated for touring the Border regions in general.

A comfortable bed and excellent breakfast provided in this centrally heated and well furnished farmhouse. The lounge has a log fire and the bedrooms, two double and one single, have hand-basins, electric blankets and tea/coffee making facilities. Open all year. Car essential, parking.

Terms £20 per night. If you are interested just ring, write or call in. Warm welcome assured.

**Mrs Rosemary Harper,
South Mains Farm, Biggar ML12 6HF
Tel: 01899 860226**

This fine late Victorian farmhouse is situated in the ideal location for visiting the attactions of the "Secret Kingdom" of Northumberland and the wonderful Scottish Borders region. Explore the dramatic coastline with its imposing castles or walk in the rolling hills and valleys - you will find plenty to see and do in this very special area.

Our spacious guest rooms are tastefully decorated and furnished to reflect the Victorian era. Comfy seating, patchwork quilts on period style beds and ample storage. All rooms have colour TV, hairdryer and hospitality tray, en suite or private bathroom. Delicious breakfasts using local prodcuce.

B&B from £30 pppn, Evening meal by arrangement.

**Hay Farm House, Ford and Etal Estate, Cornhill-on-Tweed TD12 4TR
Tel: 01890 820547 • Fax: 01890 820659
e-mail: tinahayfarm@tiscali.co.uk • www.hayfarm.co.uk**

Looking for holiday accommodation?

for details of hundreds of properties throughout the UK including comprehensive coverage of all areas of Scotland try:

www.holidayguides.com

Dumfries & Galloway

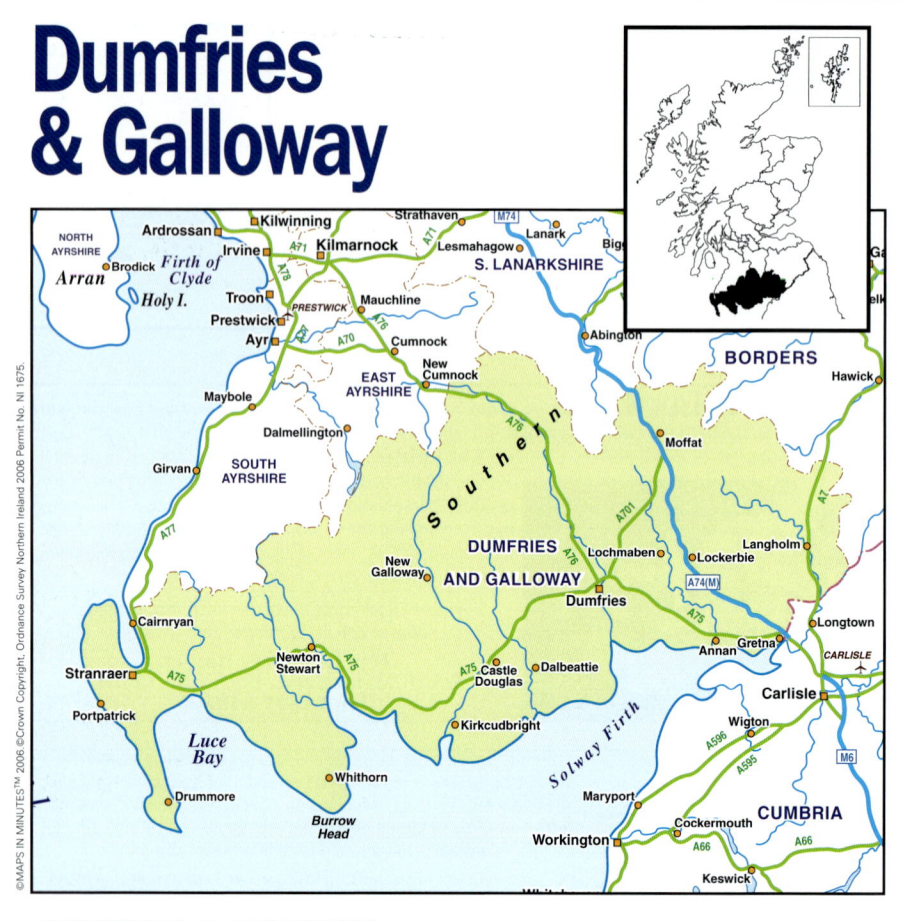

DUMFRIES & GALLOWAY is a mixture of high moorland and sheltered glens, and presents abundant opportunities for hill walking, rambling, fishing for salmon and sea trout, cycling, bird watching and field sports. There are at least 32 golf courses, ranging from the challenging Stranraer course at Creachmore to the scenic, clifftop course at Port Patrick. The Stranraer course has the distinction of being the last course designed by James Braid. The warming influence of the Gulf Stream ensures a mild climate which makes touring a pleasure, and many visitors come here to visit the dozens of interesting castles, gardens, museums and historic sites. In addition, pony trekking and riding plus a never-ending succession of ceilidhs, village fairs, country dances, classical music concerts and children's entertainment guarantee plenty of scope for enjoyment. Discover the many hidden secrets of this lovely and unspoilt landscape such as the pretty little villages along the coast or visit some of the interesting towns in the area including Stranraer, the principal town and ferry port with its busy shopping streets, park and leisure centre. Those who love 'the written word' must surely visit the book town of Wigtown, and the gourmet amongst us will love the new concept of Castle Douglas, the recently designated 'Food Town'.

When making enquiries please mention FHG GUIDES

BOARD Moffat, Portpatrick   DUMFRIES & GALLOWAY/DUNBARTONSHIRE 201

Situated just five minutes' walk from Moffat town centre and one mile off the M74, Annandale House is a haven of peace, surrounded by mature gardens with private parking and storage for cycles. The three well-appointed spacious bedrooms all have central heating, tea/coffee making facilities, hairdryers and colour TVs. There is one en suite double with king-size bed, one twin and one family room. An ideal base for exploring south-west Scotland and the Scottish Borders.

Well behaved pets welcome • Open all year • No smoking in house

Bed and Breakfast from £19.50 ppppn (reduced rates for children). Short Breaks available. Also Self-catering cottage.

Mrs Deakins, Annandale House, Moffat DG10 9SA • Tel: 01683 221460
e-mail: june@annandalehouse.com • www.annandalehouse.com

Julie and Steve Reynolds, owners of the Harbour House Hotel, take pride in offering personal attention and the warmest hospitality.

Choose from the extensive menu of home-cooked Scottish country-style food, either in the bar or in the non-smoking bistro. All bedrooms have en suite or private bathrooms, and most enjoy sea views. The newly refurbished bar is the perfect place for a morning coffee, a lunchtime snack or a cosy evening with a well-conditioned pint or a malt whisky from the extensive selection. Portpatrick is an ideal base for the many leisure opportunities the area has to offer, as well as for visiting Port Logan Botanic Gardens.

Photo by southrhinswebdesign.com

The Harbour House Hotel, 53 Main Street, Portpatrick DG9 8JW
Tel: 01776 810456 • Fax: 01776 810488 • www.harbourhouse.co.uk

Dunbartonshire

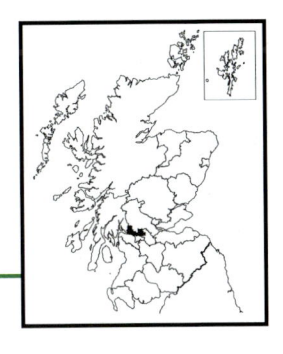

Gartocharn/Loch Lomond

Mardella Farmhouse
Bed & Breakfast
Old School Road, Gartocharn, Dunbartonshire G83 8SD

This peaceful, scenic location on a quiet country lane in magnificent countryside is ideal for you and your pets. Excellent place for walking and touring.

Tel: 01389 830428

Shantron Farm
Luss, Loch Lomond G83 8RH

Guests return often for a relaxing break on our 5000-acre hill sheep farm in quiet and unspoilt countryside with magnificent views over Loch Lomond. At breakfast you can enjoy the sun rising over the Loch while watching the garden birds feed. In the evening guests can sit in the spacious garden and marvel at the clarity of the stars on a clear night. We are 4 miles south of Luss, ideal for touring, hill walking, water sports, golf, and for those attending nearby weddings. Glasgow, Inveraray and Stirling within 1 hour. The National Park Gateway Centre, Aquarium and shops at Lomond Shores are 10 minutes away. **Contact Mrs Anne M.Lennox:** Tel: 01389 850231 • www.farmstay-lochlomond.co.uk • anne@farmstay-lochlomond.co.uk

Fife

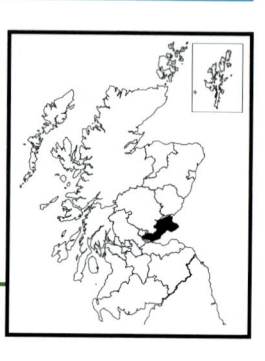

Leven, St Andrews

This quiet Victorian former rectory provides the ideal location for touring. Ideal base for golf enthusiasts, within easy reach of 46 golf courses and only 14 miles from St Andrews. 40 minutes from Edinburgh Airport, Perth and 30-35 minutes from Dundee.

Mrs Pam MacDonald, Dunclutha Guest House, 16 Victoria Road, Leven KY8 4EX
Tel: 01333 425515 • Fax: 01333 422311
e-mail: pam.leven@blueyonder.co.uk
website: www.dunclutha.myby.co.uk

Facilities include three en suite rooms – one double, one twin, one family (sleeps three to four), one family (sleeps three) with private bathroom. Colour TV and tea/coffee facilities in all rooms, cot available. Visitors' lounge with TV. Most credit cards accepted. Open all year. Terms from £28 pppn. Non-smoking.

Only two miles from St Andrews on the picturesque A917 road to Crail, Spinkstown is a uniquely designed farmhouse with views of the sea and surrounding countryside. Bright and spacious, it is furnished to a high standard. Accommodation consists of double and twin rooms, all en suite, with tea/coffee making facilities and colour TV; diningroom and lounge. Substantial farmhouse breakfast to set you up for the day. The famous Old Course, historic St Andrews and several National Trust properties are all within easy reach, as well as swimming, tennis, putting, bowls, horse riding, country parks, nature reserves, beaches and coastal walks. Plenty of parking available. Bed and Breakfast from £27.

e-mail: anne@spinkstown.com
website: www.spinkstown.com
Mrs Anne Duncan, Spinkstown Farmhouse, St Andrews KY16 8PN
Tel & Fax: 01334 473475

BOARD

HIGHLANDS 203

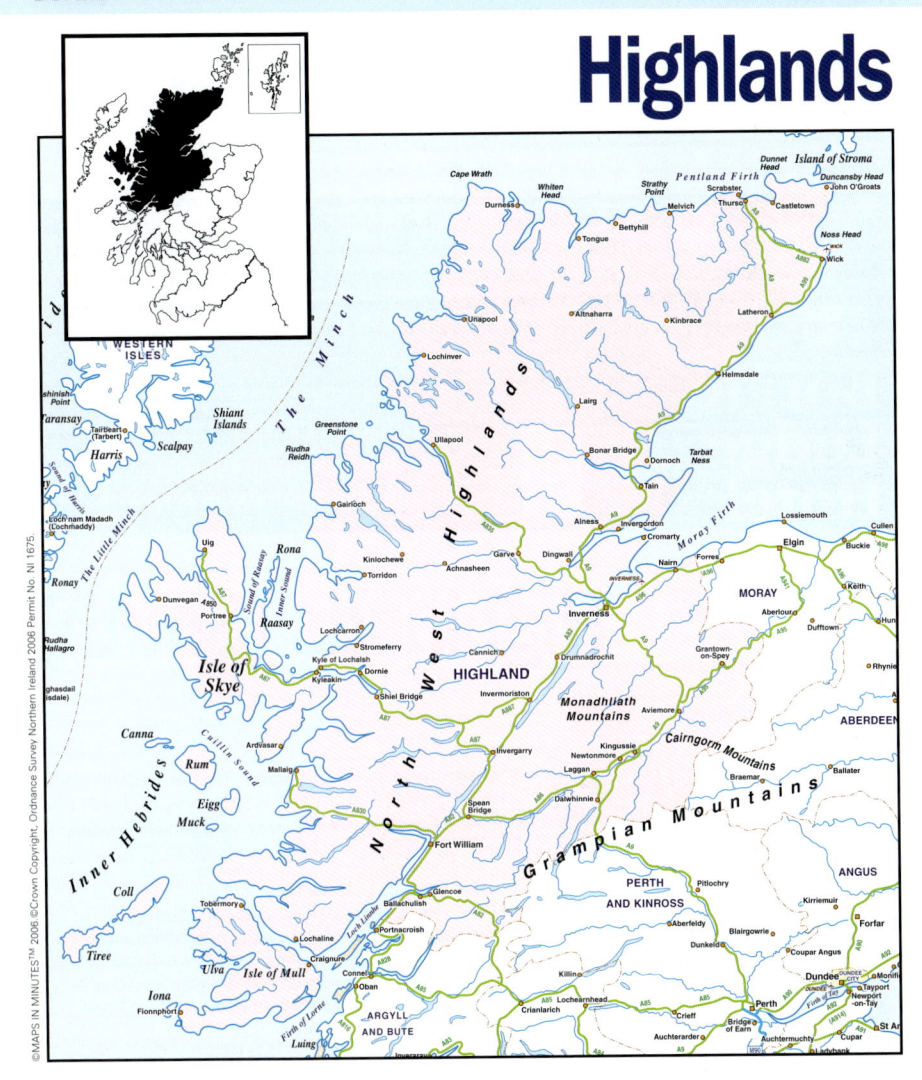

Highlands

Visit the FHG website
www.holidayguides.com
for details of the wide choice of accommodation featured in the full range of FHG titles

FHG

KUPERARD

Highlands (North)

Tongue

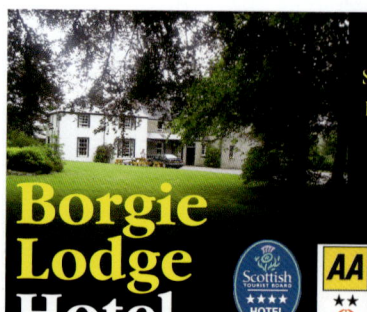

Borgie Lodge Hotel

Skerray, Tongue, Sutherland KW14 7TH

Set in a secluded Highland glen by the stunning River Borgie lies Borgie Lodge, where mouthwatering food, fine wine, roaring log fires and a very warm welcome await after a day's fishing, hill walking, pony trekking or walking on the beach. Relax after dinner with a good malt and tales of salmon, trout and deer.

Tel: 01641 521 332
www.borgielodgehotel.co.uk
e-mail: info@borgielodgehotel.co.uk

Scottish Tourist Board ★★★★
AA ★★

Highlands (South)

Aviemore, Inverness

Eriskay

A family-run Bed and Breakfast, situated in a quiet cul-de-sac in the centre of Aviemore

Ideal base for a holiday, whether it is fishing, skiing, sailing, bird watching, climbing or any other outdoor pursuit – we cater for all.
Purpose-built drying room and secure storage to protect vital outdoor equipment.
Pick-up/drop-off service to and from the Ski Centre or local glens.
Packed lunches and dinners by prior arrangement.
Luxurious guest lounge with blazing log fire. Private off-road parking.
All rooms are en suite or have their own private bathroom, with king and queen-size beds, TV, radio, hairdryers, controllable electric heating, and a host of other extras.
Complete No Smoking policy • Pets accepted by prior arrangement.
We hope that you arrive as a guest and leave as a friend

Craig-na-gower Avenue, Aviemore PH22 1RW • Tel: 01479 810717
E-mail: enquiry@eriskay-aviemore.co.uk • www.eriskay-aviemore.co.uk

The Whins

114 Kenneth Street, Inverness IV3 5QG
Tel: 01463 236215

Comfortable, small, homely, non-smoking accommodation awaits you here. Ten minutes bus and railway stations, with easy access to many golf courses, walking and cycling areas, and a great base for touring North, East and West by car, rail or bus. Two double/twin rooms with TV, tea making, washbasins and heating off season. Bathroom, shared toilet and shower; £17 per person.
Write or phone for full details.

BOARD Tomatin   HIGHLANDS (SOUTH), LANARKSHIRE **205**

TOMATIN Robert Coupar & Lesley Smithers, Glenan Lodge (Licensed), Tomatin IV13 7YT Tel & Fax: 0845 6445793.

The Glenan Lodge is a typical Scottish Lodge situated in the midst of the Monadhliath Mountains in the valley of the Findhorn River, yet only one mile from the A9. It offers typical Scottish hospitality, home cooking, warmth and comfort. The seven bedrooms, including two family rooms, are all en suite, with central heating, tea-making facilities and colour TV. There is a large comfortable lounge and a homely dining room. The licensed bar is well stocked with local malts for the guests. Glenan Lodge caters for the angler, birdwatcher, hillwalker, stalker and tourist alike whether passing through or using as a base. Bed and Breakfast; Dinner optional. Credit cards accepted.
• Non-smoking. • Open all year round.
AA ★★★

e-mail: glenanlodgecouk@hotmail.com   www.glenanlodge.co.uk

Lanarkshire

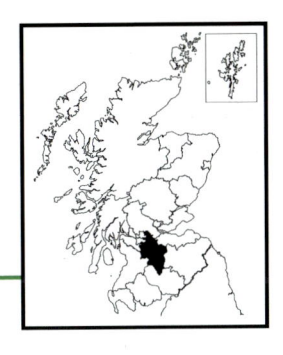

Biggar

WALSTON MANSION FARMHOUSE

We offer a real home from home where guests return year after year to enjoy the friendly atmosphere. Situated in the peaceful village of Walston just five miles from Biggar. We are in an ideal place for touring the Clyde Valley and Scottish Borders. Pets by arrangement. Recommended by *Which? Good Bed and Breakfast Guide*. B&B £19pp, en suite £21pp, evening meal £10pp, 7 nights for the price of 6 nights.

*For details contact: Margaret Kirby, Walston, Carnwath, By Biggar ML11 8NF
Tel & Fax: 01899 810338 • e-mail: kirby-walstonmansion@talk21.com
e-mail: walstonmansions@tiscali.co.uk*

Visit the FHG website
www.holidayguides.com
for details of the wide choice of accommodation featured in the full range of FHG titles

FHG
·K·U·P·E·R·A·R·D·

Perth & Kinross

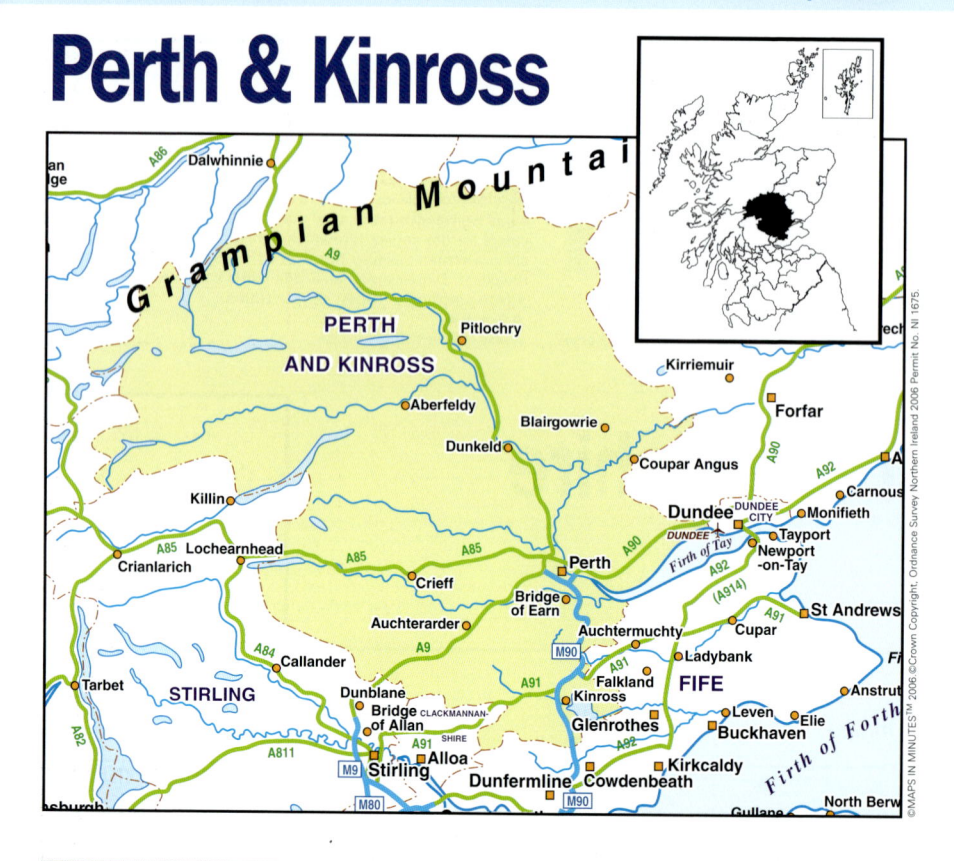

Stanley BOARD

Newmill Farm, Stanley PH1 4PS
Mrs Ann Guthrie • 01738 828281

A family-run farm on the A9, 6 miles north of Perth. Accommodation comprises double and twin en suite rooms and a family room (sleeps 4), with private bathroom. The centrally heated farmhouse has a real coal fire in the lounge. There is a large garden and free secure parking. Situated in the area known as "The Gateway to the Highlands", the farm is ideally placed for those seeking some of the best unspoilt scenery in Western Europe. The numerous castles and historic ruins are testimony to Scotland's turbulent past. There are many famous golf courses and trout rivers in the Perth area, and it is only one hour's drive to both Edinburgh and Glasgow.

e-mail: guthrienewmill@sol.co.uk
www.newmillfarm.co.uk

FHG Guides

publish a large range of well-known accommodation guides. We will be happy to send you details or you can use the order form at the back of this book.

FHG
KUPERARD

BOARD STIRLING & THE TROSSACHS/SCOTTISH ISLANDS **207**

Stirling & The Trossachs

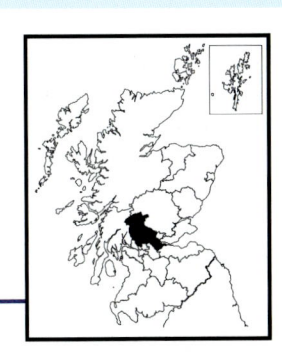

Callander

Riverview House

Leny Road, Callander FK17 8AL
Tel: 01877 330635 • Fax: 01877 339386

Excellent accommodation in the Trossachs area which forms the most beautiful part of Scotland's first National Park. Ideal centre for walking and cycling holidays, with cycle storage available. In the guest house all rooms are en suite, with TV and tea-making. Private parking. Also available self-catering stone cottages, sleep 3 or 4. Sorry, no smoking and no pets. Call Drew or Kathleen Little for details.

e-mail: drew@visitcallander.co.uk
website: www.visitcallander.co.uk

B&B from £25.
Low season and long stay discounts available.
Self-catering cottages from £150 per week
(STB 3 & 4 Stars).

Scottish Islands
Isle of Skye

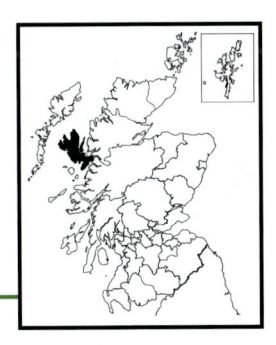

Portree

Set overlooking the picturesque harbour of Portree, The Royal Hotel offers you a quiet, relaxing retreat during your stay on Skye. Accommodation consists of 21 well appointed rooms, most overlooking the harbour and featuring private bathroom facilities and colour TV. Room service is available as well as a fitness centre and sauna for guests to use. The Royal Hotel offers a wide and varied menu serving sea food, lamb, venison and tender Highland beef. Vegetarians are also catered for. There is something for everyone, from walking, climbing and watersports to good food, great local arts & crafts, colourful museums and places of interest.

THE ROYAL HOTEL • Portree, Isle of Skye IV51 9BU
Tel: 01478 612525 • Fax: 01478 613198
e-mail: info@royal-hotel-skye.com • www.royal-hotel-skye.com

Ratings & Awards

For the first time ever the AA, VisitBritain, VisitScotland, and the Wales Tourist Board will use a single method of assessing and rating serviced accommodation. Irrespective of which organisation inspects an establishment the rating awarded will be the same, using a common set of standards, giving a clear guide of what to expect. The RAC is no longer operating an Hotel inspection and accreditation business.

Accommodation Standards: Star Grading Scheme

Using a scale of 1-5 stars the objective quality ratings give a clear indication of accommodation standard, cleanliness, ambience, hospitality, service and food, This shows the full range of standards suitable for every budget and preference, and allows visitors to distinguish between the quality of accommodation and facilities on offer in different establishments. All types of board and self-catering accommodation are covered, including hotels, B&Bs, holiday parks, campus accommodation, hostels, caravans and camping, and boats.

VisitBritain and the regional tourist boards, **enjoyEngland.com, VisitScotland** and **VisitWales,** and **the AA** have full details of the grading system on their websites

The more stars, the higher level of quality

★★★★★
exceptional quality, with a degree of luxury

★★★★
excellent standard throughout

★★★
very good level of quality and comfort

★★
good quality, well presented and well run

★
acceptable quality; simple, practical, no frills

National Accessible Scheme

If you have particular mobility, visual or hearing needs, look out for the National Accessible Scheme. You can be confident of finding accommodation or attractions that meet your needs by looking for the following symbols.

- Typically suitable for a person with sufficient mobility to climb a flight of steps but would benefit from fixtures and fittings to aid balance

- Typically suitable for a person with restricted walking ability and for those that may need to use a wheelchair some of the time and can negotiate a maximum of three steps

- Typically suitable for a person who depends on the use of a wheelchair and transfers unaided to and from the wheelchair in a seated position. This person may be an independent traveller

- Typically suitable for a person who depends on the use of a wheelchair in a seated position. This person also requires personal or mechanical assistance (eg carer, hoist).

Scotland

Roxburgh Newtown Farm. Kelso, Borders — Tulloch Lodges, Forres, Moray — Arisaig House Cottages, Arisaig, Inverness-shire

Self-Catering

Scottish Borders and Highlands

This is no fling, our love affair with Scotland means you will have some of the finest, personally inspected cottages at your fingertips. And when you consider they are located from the Borders to the Highlands – that are just perfect for cycling, fishing and even walking the dog. What more could you need?

Dales Holiday Cottages

For your choice of over 500 cottages
call **0870 909 9500** or visit **www.dalesholcot.com/scotland**   A64

Aberdeen, Banff & Moray

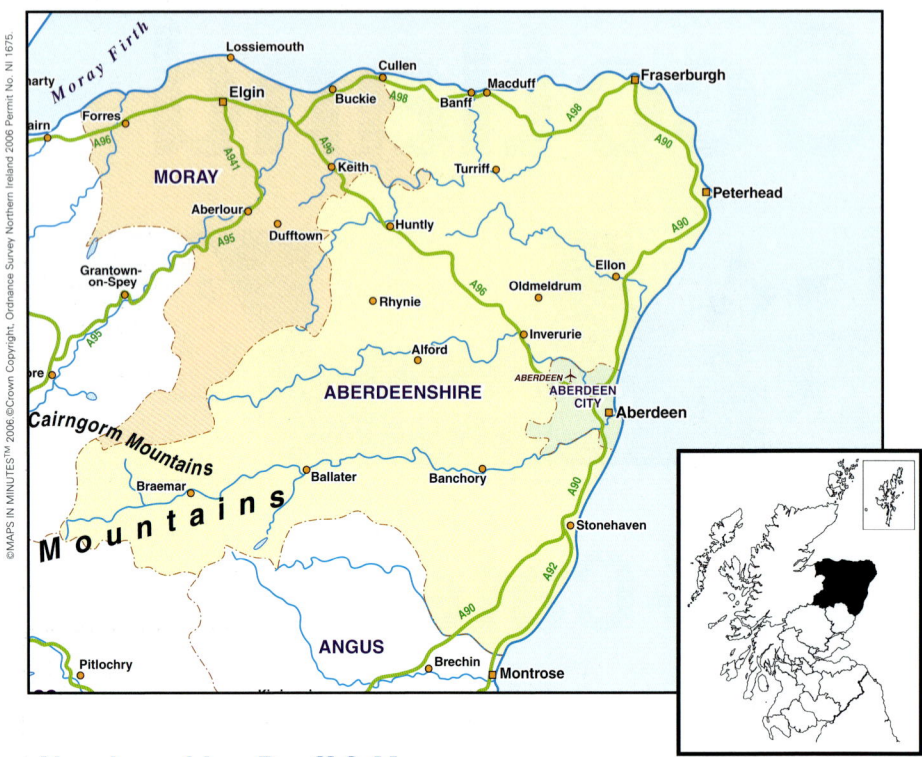

Aberdeenshire, Banff & Moray is perhaps one of the most culturally distinct in the country. Aberdeen is a vibrant and cultural city with breathtaking architecture, colourful parks and gardens, a variety of shops, bars and restaurants and is full of welcoming charm. Although Grampian encompasses established tourism areas such as Royal Deeside and Speyside there is much more to the area than just Royalty, whisky and castles.

As befits the regional capital, Aberdeen is a prosperous city with an international well-travelled population. Aberdeen is a city of many names and it's easy to see how it gets its most popular one – The Granite City. The glory of granite is around you. The impressive turreted Town House in Union Street, the castellated Citadel at The Castlegate and the striking Marischal College – the worlds second largest granite structure. You'll find a cosmopolitan metropolis here – home to five star visitor attractions, such as the Gordon Highlanders Museum and the Maritime Museum, which tells the story of Aberdeen's relationship with the sea from fishing to ship building and then the oil industry. Awarded 'Scottish Museum of the Year' in 1997 this thoughtfully designed steel and glass building links Provost Ross's House – the second oldest dwelling house in Aberdeen – with the former Trinity Church, the resulting imaginative construction winning it two major architectural awards.

Art enthusiasts will love Aberdeen. The city's Art Gallery, which houses a wonderful collection of exhibits from centuries gone by as well as more modern works, is a city centre haven. His Majesty's Theatre has long attracted the 'big names' of ballet, opera, TV and West End fame, while the giants of rock and pop vie with the country's top national orchestras to appear at the Music Hall, the Lemon Tree and Aberdeen Exhibition and Conference Centre. A range of festivals and events throughout the year add to a lively mix of entertainment catering for all tastes.

SELF-CATERING — ABERDEEN, BANFF & MORAY/ANGUS & DUNDEE

Forres, Inverurie

Tulloch Lodges

Peace, Relaxation and Comfort in Beautiful Natural Surroundings

One of the loveliest self-catering sites in Scotland. Modern, spacious, attractive and beautifully equipped Scandinavian lodges for up to 6 in glorious woodland/water setting. Perfect for the Highlands and Historic Grampian, especially the Golden Moray Coast and the Golf, Castle and Malt Whisky Trails. £325-£750 per week. Brochure:

Tulloch Lodges, Rafford, Forres, Moray IV36 2RU
Tel: 01309 673511 • Fax: 01309 671515
e-mail: enquiries@tullochlodges.com
www.tullochlodges.com

STB ★★★/★★★★ Self-Catering

ASSC

This spacious, comfortably furnished, south-facing cottage has one double bedroom with bathroom, and two twin-bedded en suite bedrooms (sleeps 6 + cot). Sitting room, dining room and well equipped kitchen. Barbecue and garden furniture. Private parking.
Ideally situated for visiting the Castle, Stone Circle and Whisky Trails. Members of the ASSC, Green Tourism Scheme (Bronze). VisitScotland's Welcome Schemes for Ancestral Tourism, Bikers, Cyclists, Golfers, Walkers... and not forgetting Children!
Terms £400 - £625 per week
Short Breaks available £400 for 3-day break - Feb, March and Nov. All inclusive of linen and electricity.

Mrs J. Lumsden, Kingsfield House, Kingsfield Road, Kintore, Inverurie AB51 0UD
Tel: 01467 632366 • Fax: 01467 632399

The Greenknowe • Kintore
e-mail: HolidayhomesabzS@aol.com
www.holidayhomesaberdeen.com

Angus & Dundee

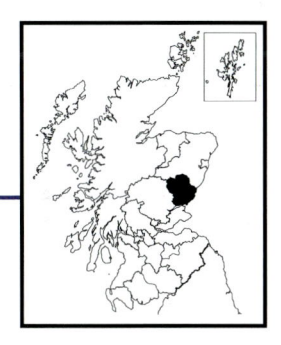

Johnshaven

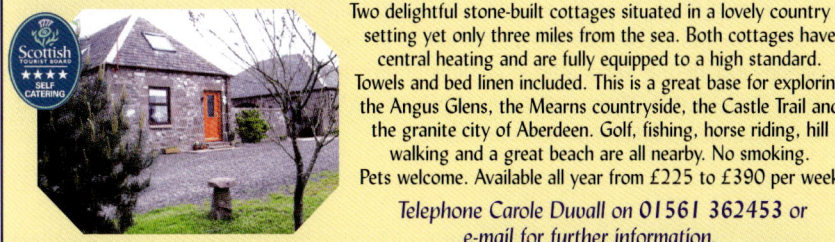

Two delightful stone-built cottages situated in a lovely country setting yet only three miles from the sea. Both cottages have central heating and are fully equipped to a high standard. Towels and bed linen included. This is a great base for exploring the Angus Glens, the Mearns countryside, the Castle Trail and the granite city of Aberdeen. Golf, fishing, horse riding, hill walking and a great beach are all nearby. No smoking. Pets welcome. Available all year from £225 to £390 per week.

Telephone Carole Duvall on 01561 362453 or e-mail for further information.

Brawliemuir Holiday Cottages
Kincardineshire

e-mail: carole@the-duvalls.com
www.brawliemuircottages.co.uk

Argyll & Bute

SELF-CATERING

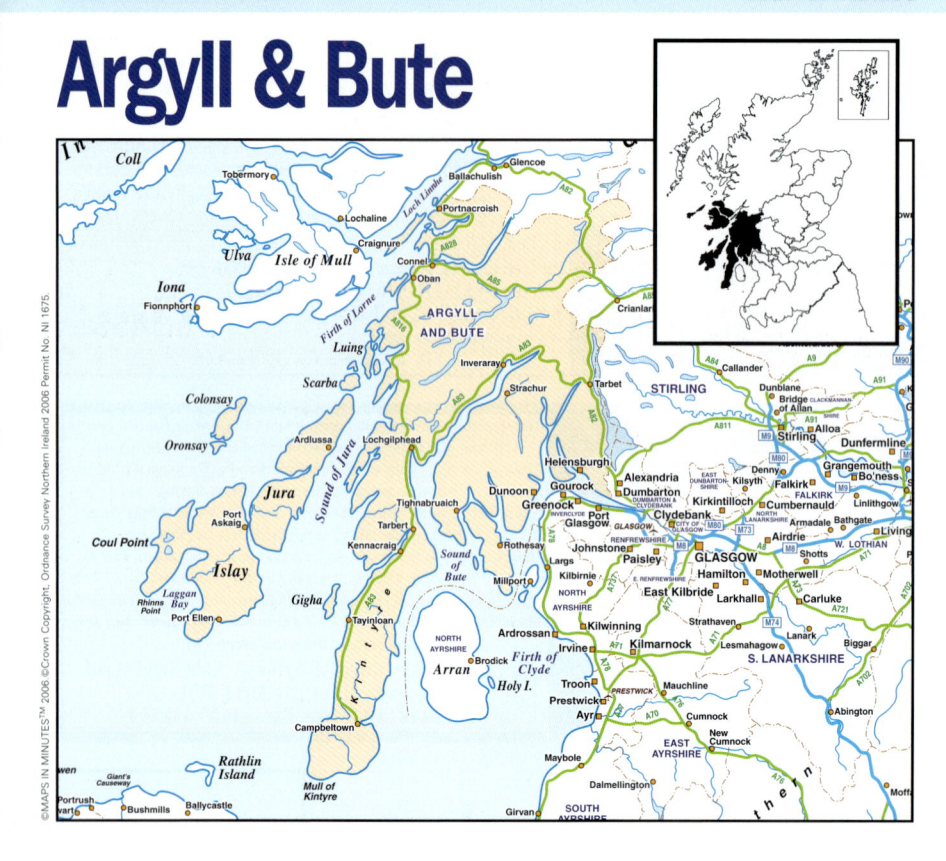

ARGYLL & BUTE, "the coast of the Gaels", one of Scotland's most scenic and historic counties, stretches from the Firth of Clyde resorts of Dunoon to Fort William and Loch Linnhe. The long and often spectacular coastline is broken by sea lochs and peninsulas down to Campbeltown and the Mull of Kintyre, round Loch Fyne to Cowal, the Kyles of Bute, Holy Loch and Loch Long. Ferries are an important part of everyday life as well as tourism in many parts of Argyll – across the Clyde to Dunoon and Rothesay and around Bute to the many off-shore islands, from Cowal to Kintyre, in summer from Arran to Kintyre near Skipness Castle. Argyll is full of interest, by road, rail or sea, from the peaceful Crinan Canal to the busy holiday centre and ferryport of Oban, from the ancient stones and burial cairns of Dunadd and Kilmartin, from the memories of Glen Coe and Glenfinnan, to the hydro power of Cruachan. Other visitor attractions include the National Trust gardens at Arduaine, north of Lochgilphead, the iron works at Bonawe, the island of Bute and Rothesay Castle, and the impressive castle and ruined chapel at Dunstaffnage, north of Oban..

Free or reduced rate entry to
Holiday Visits and Attractions – see our
READERS' OFFER VOUCHERS on pages 7-40

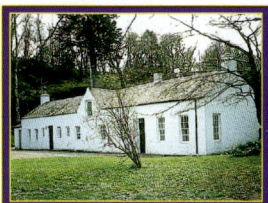

SELF-CATERING Appin, Dalmally, Isle of Seil ARGYLL & BUTE 213

ARDTUR COTTAGES

Two adjacent cottages in secluded surroundings on promontory between Port Appin and Castle Stalker. Ideal for hill walking, climbing, pony trekking, boating and fly-fishing. (Glencoe and Ben Nevis half-hour drive). Tennis court by arrangement. Direct access across the field to sea (Loch Linnhe). First cottage is suitable for up to 8 people in one double and three twin-bedded rooms, large dining/sittingroom/kitchenette and two bathrooms. Second cottage is suitable for 6 people in one double and two twin-bedded rooms, dining/sittingroom/kitchenette and bathroom. Everything provided except linen. Shops one mile; sea 200 yards. Pets allowed. Car essential, parking. Open March/October. Terms from £225 to £385 weekly.

SAE, please for details to Mrs J. Pery, Ardtur, Appin PA38 4DD (01631 730223 or 01626 834172)
e-mail: pery@btinternet.com   web: www.selfcatering-appin-scotland.com

Blarghour Farm
Mrs I. Crawford

Loch Awe-side, by Dalmally, Argyll PA33 1BW
Tel: 01866 833246 • Fax: 01866 833338
e-mail: blarghour@btconnect.com
www.self-catering-argyll.co.uk

At Blarghour Farm, by the shores of lovely Loch Awe, one may choose from four centrally heated and double glazed holiday cottages sleeping from two to six people. Kitchens are well appointed, lounges tastefully decorated and furnished with payphone, TV and gas fire, beds are made up and towels supplied while the two larger houses have shower rooms in addition to bathrooms, all with shaver point. The two larger houses are suitable for children and have cots and high chairs. No pets are allowed. Open all year with Short Breaks welcomed 4th November to 31st March 2007. Centrally situated for touring. Wheelchair access. Illustrated brochure on request.

Scottish Tourist Board **** SELF CATERING   ASSC

Situated on beautiful Seil Island with wonderful views of surrounding countryside. These lovingly restored cottages (one detached and one attached to the main croft house) retain their traditional character while incorporating all modern facilities. The cottages are near to each other and ideal for two families on holiday together. Seil is one of the most peaceful and tranquil spots in the West Highlands, with easy access to neighbouring Isles of Luing and Easdale. Oban, the hub for trips to Mull and Iona, is half an hour's drive away over the famous 18th century "Bridge Over The Atlantic". Wonderful area for hillwalking, cycling, fishing and bird watching. Short breaks from £40 per day.

Kilbride Cottage

KILBRIDE CROFT
Balvicar, Isle of Seil, Argyll PA34 4RD
Contact: Mary & Brian Phillips
tel: 01852 300475
e-mail: kilbridecroft@aol.com
website: www.kilbridecroft.co.uk

Croft Cottage

214 ARGYLL & BUTE — Loch Crinan, Taynuilt **SELF-CATERING**

Duntrune Castle Holiday Cottages

Six traditional self-catering cottages set in the spacious grounds of 12th century Duntrune Castle, which guards the entrance to Loch Crinan. All have been attractively modernised and accommodate two to five persons. The estate comprises 5000 acres and five miles of coastline. Without leaving our land, you can enjoy easy or testing walks, sea or river fishing, and watching the abundant wildlife. Nearby are several riding establishments, a bicycle-hire firm, and a number of excellent restaurants. Prices from £270 to £470 per week. Pets are welcome.

For further details please contact:
Robin Malcolm, Duntrune Castle, Kilmartin, Argyll PA31 8QQ
01546 510283 • website: www.duntrune.com

Three delightful cottages, accommodating 2-6 people. The cottages are fully equipped with laundry facilities, freezers, open fires and gardens to enjoy. Set amidst the most breathtaking of scenery, overlooking the River Awe, Inverawe is ideally situated for holidays. With walking, fishing, golf on the door step, it is a paradise for all country lovers. It is brilliant for touring Argyll, with Glencoe in the north or Crinan Canal and the standing stones in Kilmartin in the south. Oban, our local coastal town, is 17 miles. It is the gateway to the islands and offers many day excursions - a visit to Mull and Duart Castle is a must. Ideal for the family and pets are very welcome.

Inverawe lets you completely relax and get away from it all

Inverawe House, Taynuilt PA35 IHU • 01866 822777 • Fax: 01866 822274
e-mail: holidays@inverawe.co.uk • www.inverawe-fisheries.co.uk

---

Other specialised holiday guides from FHG

Recommended **INNS & PUBS** OF BRITAIN

Recommended **COUNTRY HOTELS** OF BRITAIN

Recommended **SHORT BREAK HOLIDAYS** IN BRITAIN

The bestselling and original **PETS WELCOME!**

The **GOLF GUIDE,** *Where to Play, Where to Stay* IN BRITAIN & IRELAND

COAST & COUNTRY HOLIDAYS

SELF-CATERING HOLIDAYS IN BRITAIN

BED & BREAKFAST STOPS

CARAVAN & CAMPING HOLIDAYS

CHILDREN WELCOME! Family Holiday & Days Out Guide

BRITAIN'S BEST LEISURE & RELAXATION GUIDE

Published annually: available in all good bookshops or direct from the publisher:
FHG Guides, Abbey Mill Business Centre, Seedhill, Paisley PA1 1TJ
Tel: 0141 887 0428 • Fax: 0141 889 7204
• E-mail: admin@fhguides.co.uk • Web: www.holidayguides.com

SELF-CATERING Lochgilphead

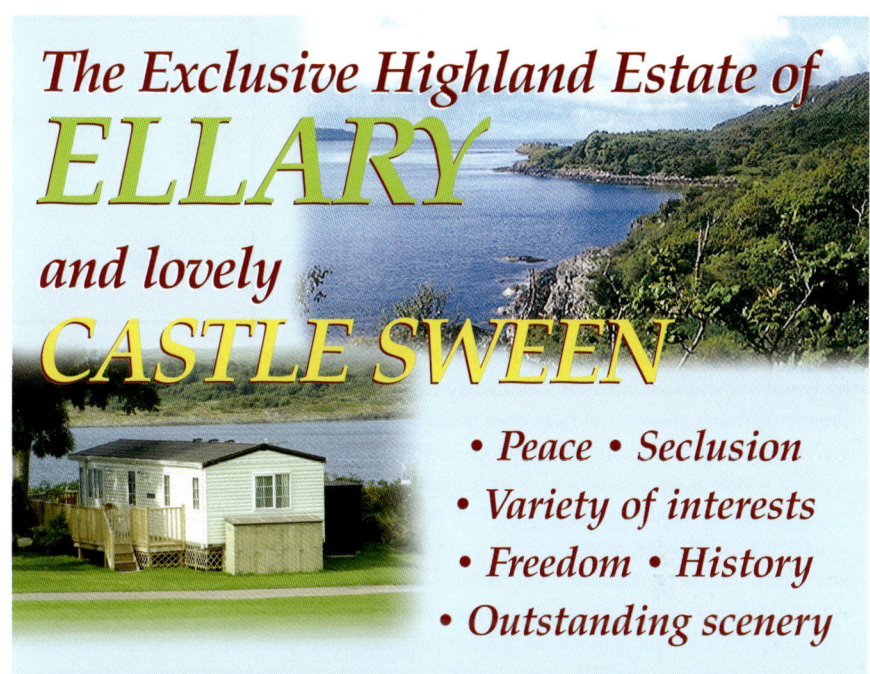

The Exclusive Highland Estate of
ELLARY
and lovely
CASTLE SWEEN

- Peace • Seclusion
- Variety of interests
- Freedom • History
- Outstanding scenery

This 15,000 acre Highland Estate lies in one of the most beautiful and unspoilt areas of Scotland and has a wealth of ancient historical associations within its bounds.

There is St Columba's Cave, one of the first places of Christian Worship in Britain, also Castle Sween, the oldest ruined castle in Scotland, and Kilmory Chapel where there is a fascinating collection of Celtic slabs. There is a wide range of accommodation, from small groups of cottages, many of the traditional stone-built estate type, to modern holiday chalets and super luxury caravans at Castle Sween.

Most of the cottages accommodate up to six, but one will take six/eight.

All units fully equipped except linen. Television reception is included.

Ellary is beautiful at all times of the year and is suitable for windsurfing, fishing, swimming, sailing and the observation of a wide variety of wildlife; there are paths and tracks throughout the estate for the visitor who prefers to explore on foot, and guests will find farmers and estate workers most helpful in their approach.

For further details, brochure and booking forms, please apply to:

ELLARY ESTATE OFFICE, by LOCHGILPHEAD, ARGYLL PA31 8PA

Tel: 01880 770232/770209
or 01546 850223
info@ellary.com
www.ellary.com

Ayrshire & Arran

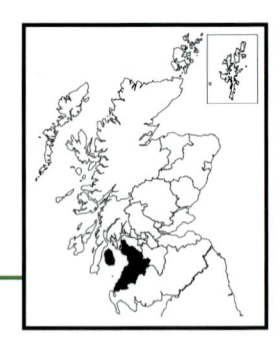

Ayrshire and The Isle of Arran is situated in the South of Scotland, flanked by the Borders to the south and the Central Belt to the north. Here the warm waters of the Gulf Stream meet with miles of sandy beaches and a dramatic coastline littered with rocky outcrops and caves, once a favourite with smugglers. The Island of Arran, as well as being one of Scotland's most accessible islands, is also arguably one of its most truly representative. From the mountainous north, including Goat Fell, highest peak in the south of Scotland, to the undulating south it is easy to see how the island became known as "Scotland in miniature". Few places can boast a heritage like Ayrshire and Arran. Culzean Castle, designed by the famous architect Robert Adam, sits proudly on the edge of a steep cliff. Dundonald Castle, a little further north, was the ancestral home of the Stewart Kings over 600 years ago, and a stunning array of medieval arms and armoury displayed at Dean Castle in Kilmarnock betray a lively and rebellious past, as do the scattering of ruins that punctuate the landscape.

AYR. Self-catering cottages/apartments.
Seven cottages conveniently placed for exploring Burns Country, golfing on world famous links courses, or simply enjoying the stunning coastline. Five properties are centrally located in Ayr, one in Prestwick and one in Edinburgh - all in quiet residential locations, a short walk from the town centre, beach and railway. All have gas central heating, teletext TV, radio alarm clock, hairdryer, shaving point, gardens (except Riverside and Harbour View Apartment, Ayr) and parking. All have modern fitted kitchen with washing machine, microwave, fridge/ freezer etc and bathroom with bath and/or electric shower. Bed linen hire available.
Rates: from £150 to £500 per week.
• Sleep 2-5.
Contact: Mrs Anne Hardie, Woodcroft, 23 Midton Road, Ayr KA7 2SF (01292 264383; Fax: 01292 270245).
e-mail: robin.hardie@virgin.net
www.woodcroftcottages.co.uk

1 Guildford Street, Millport, Isle of Cumbrae
e-mail: b@1-guildford-street.co.uk • www.1-guildford-street.co.uk

Five flats and one house to cater for 2-10 persons. Two large luxury four-star flats to suit extended family. Superb sea views. Heating included in rates. Small garden. Sorry, no pets. Close to shops, pubs, restaurants.

Only a 15 minute ferry crossing from Largs, the Isle of Cumbrae is a small, friendly, unspoilt island, with cycling, golf, walking, bowling, sailing and birdwatching. Open all year.

Terms from £150 to £610 per week.
Mrs Barbara McLuckie, Muirhall Farm, Larbert, Stirlingshire FK5 4EW • Tel: 01324 551570 • Fax: 01324 551223

SELF-CATERING Ashkirk, Cockburnspath, Galashiels   BORDERS 217

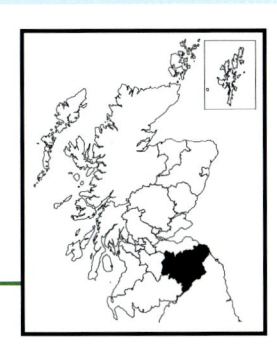

Borders

Headshaw is an 850 acre working farm overlooking the valley of the River Ale, a tributary of the River Teviot which flows into the River Tweed, famous for its trout and salmon fishing. The main work of the farm is rearing sheep and cattle. The four self-catering cottages are situated away from the main farmsteading buildings and originally provided accommodation for farm workers. They have been refurbished to provide fully equipped holiday cottages sleeping between five and seven persons, all with oil-fired central heating, well equipped kitchens, and linen can be provided on request. Ashkirk is situated in the heart of the Scottish Borders and is an ideal base for touring and sightseeing. Self-catering apartment in Edinburgh also available.

Mrs Nancy Hunter, Headshaw Farm Holidays, Headshaw Farm, Ashkirk, By Selkirk TD7 4NT

HEADSHAW FARM HOLIDAYS

Tel: 01750 32233
Fax: 01750 32269
e-mail: headshaw@aol.com
www.headshaw.co.uk

COCKBURNSPATH. Neuk Farm Holiday Cottages, The Neuk, Cockburnspath, Berwickshire TD13 5YH (01368 830459; Fax: 01368 830394).
Cottages to let on a busy working farm. Situated one mile off the A1, two miles from the beach, 10 miles south of Dunbar and 15 miles north of Eyemouth. An ideal base to explore the Scottish Borders, Edinburgh and Lothians, East Coast and Northumberland. Gas central heating, microwave, washing machine, fridge, gas hob, electric oven, digital freeview and music system. Bedding, towels, gas and electricity provided at no extra cost. Local amenities include fishing, golf, nature trails, historic houses, castles, museums and beautiful beaches.
Rates: from £175 to £300 per week.
• Sorry no pets. • Open all year.
VisitScotland ★★★★

e-mail: info@chesterfieldcaravanpark.co.uk   www.chesterfieldcaravanpark.co.uk

---

The "Henhoose" at Over Langshaw Farm is especially nice and has two delightful bedrooms. A basket of food welcomes guests and there is a lovely kitchen with Rayburn cooker. The farm is organic, with dairy cows, sheep, lots of wildlife and rehoused hens.

Walk the Southern Upland Way then enjoy the views from the sunroom, or snuggle by the Squirrel woodstove. Melrose and Galashiels four miles; Edinburgh 30 miles. Sleeps 4.

**Mrs Sheila Bergius, Over Langshaw Farm, Langshaw, Galashiels TD1 2PE
Tel & Fax: 01896 860244**

e-mail: bergius@overlangshaw.fsnet.co.uk • www.organicholidays.com

Kelso, Newcastleton SELF-CATERING

PLUM BRAES BARN Three lovely cottages, standing in an elevated position with wonderful views, on an organic farm in a peaceful setting two miles from the beautiful market town of Kelso. River walk perfect for picnics, birdwatching and fishing.
* PLUM TREE (sleeps 2) - romantic cottage with spiral stairs and a balcony bedroom.
* GARDEN BANK (sleeps 4) - ground level, with two en suite rooms.
* COCKLE KITTY (sleeps 4) - ground level with original hemmel arch and beamed ceiling.

Each has a log-burning stove, central heating, dishwasher, king-size Austrian sleigh bed and French windows. New all-weather tennis court and tennis coaching. Sky TV

EDMONSTON HOUSE (sleeps 4-10) is a chalet style farmhouse nearby, with commanding views. Four/five bedrooms, one at ground level; large private garden. **Also available - flat in Edinburgh**

For further details please contact: Maggie Stewart, Cliftonhill Farm, Kelso TD5 7QE (01573 225028) e-mail: maggie@plumbraesbarn.com • www.plumbraesbarn.co.uk • www.plumbraesbarn.com

01573 450250

Kelso Borders
Roxburgh Newtown Farm, Kelso, TD5 8NN

Two cottages in a lovely picturesque rural location surrounded by open countryside with views of the Eildon Hills in the distance. **Jimmy's** sleeps 6 and has 2 bathrooms and **Swallow** sleeps 2 people. Both are modernised, comfortably furnished stone cottages on our farm in the Tweed valley, 5 miles from the charming Scottish Borders town of Kelso. **Barnhill** in nearby St Boswells is a modern detached bungalow which sleeps up to 7 in four spacious bedrooms with two bathrooms.

All properties have central heating and the price includes all heating, electricity and beds made ready for your arrival.

e-mail: fhg@twemlow.net • www.twemlow.net

NEWCASTLETON. Pamela Copeland, Bailey Mill Courtyard Apartments and Trekking Centre, Bailey Mill, Newcastleton TD9 0TR (016977 48617; Fax: 016977 48074).
A warm welcome awaits you from Pam and Ian on this small farm holiday complex, nestling on the Roxburghshire/Cumbrian border. The rural self-contained apartments create a courtyard setting or enjoy Bed and Breakfast or Full Board riding holidays in the farmhouse. Forest trekking and lessons in outdoor school. Colour TV, heating (oil), electricity and linen included in the rent. On site sauna, jacuzzi, toning table, games room, laundry, babysitting, fully licensed bar and meals. Enjoy walking or trekking through surrounding forests. Central touring area for Lake District, Hadrian's Wall and Scotland. Colour brochure available.
Rates: Self-catering £98-£598, Bed and Breakfast from £28 per person.
ETC ★★/★★★
e-mail: pam@baileymill.fsnet.co.uk   www.holidaycottagescumbria.co.uk

Free or reduced rate entry to
Holiday Visits and Attractions – see our
READERS' OFFER VOUCHERS on pages 7-40

FHG Guides

publish a large range of well-known accommodation guides.
We will be happy to send you details or you can use the order form at the back of this book.

SELF-CATERING

Dumfries & Galloway

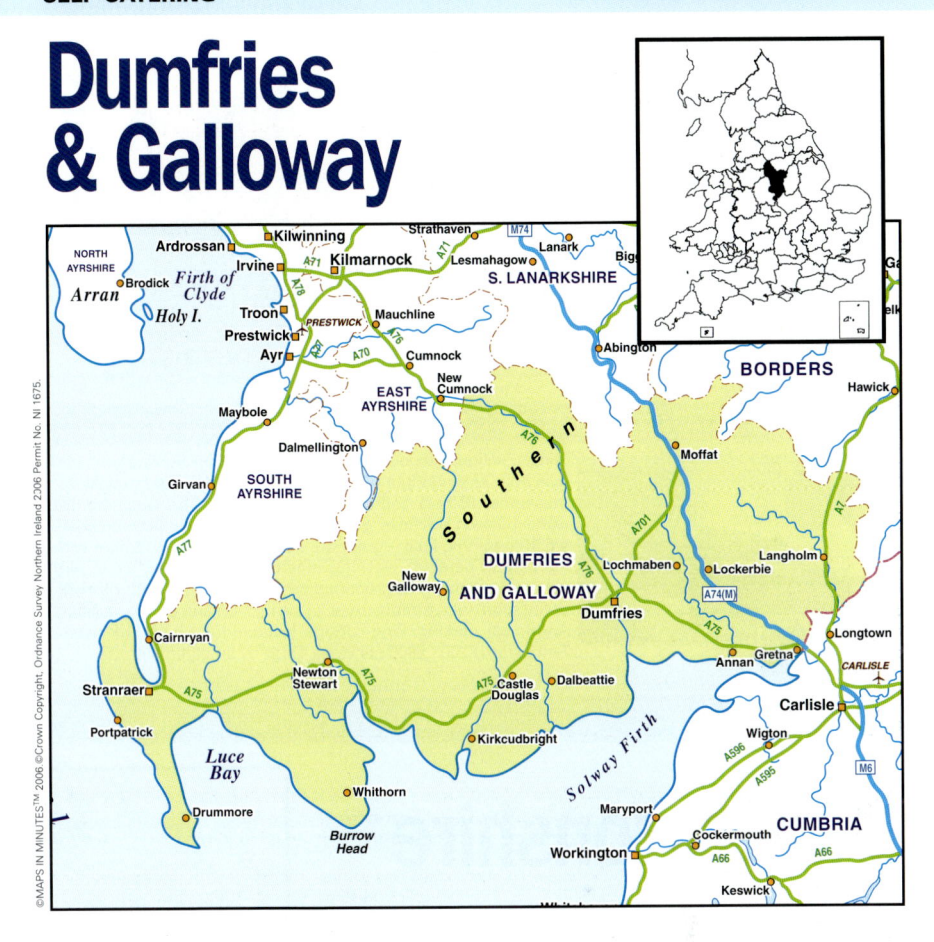

DUMFRIES & GALLOWAY If you arrive from the south on the M6 motorway and turn off eastwards the first region you will come to after the Welcome to Scotland sign is Dumfries & Galloway. The countryside here is a mixture of high moorland and sheltered glens and presents abundant opportunities for hill walking, rambling, fishing for salmon and sea trout, cycling, bird watching and field sports. There are at least 32 golf courses, ranging from the challenging Stranraer course at Creachmore to the scenic, clifftop course at Port Patrick. The Stranraer course has the distinction of being the last course designed by James Braid. The warming influence of the Gulf Stream ensures a mild climate which makes touring a pleasure, and many visitors come here to visit the dozens of interesting castles, gardens, museums and historic sites. In addition, pony trekking and riding plus a never ending succession of ceilidhs, village fairs, country dances, classical music concerts and children's entertainment guarantee plenty of scope for enjoyment.

When making enquiries please mention FHG GUIDES

Castle Douglas, Kirkcudbright

Spacious detached house on the edge of the village, in a largely unspoilt area in the heart of bonnie Galloway. Very well equipped and comfortable, tastefully decorated with a mix of traditional and modern features the accommodation is especially suited to families or groups. Splendid for walking, cycling, touring, fishing, sailing, golf, horse-riding, gardens and beaches, etc. Village amenities include hotels, cafe and shops within easy walking distance.
- Sleeps 8/9 + cot • Bed linen provided
- Pets by arrangement • Large garden with parking or touring space • Terms from £270 to £400 per week

For brochure apply to: **Mrs G. Carolyn Veitch, Low Creoch, Gatehouse of Fleet, Castle Douglas DG7 2BH (01557 814224)**

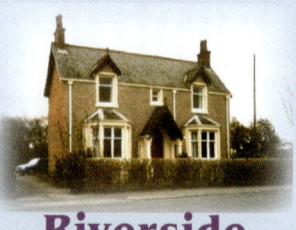

Riverside
Gatehouse of Fleet, Castle Douglas DG7 2EG

HIGH KIRKLAND HOLIDAY COTTAGES - KIRKCUDBRIGHT

Three traditional stone-built Galloway cottages on working farm, one mile from Kirkcudbright with its interesting harbour, art exhibitions, museums, 18 hole golf course, wildlife park, bird watching, hill walking, fishing, river trips, gardens and historical sites. Accommodate 4/6/10 persons. Fully equipped, spacious accommodation with full central heating; washing machine, microwave. Linen hire service available and groceries can be ordered for your arrival. Utility room with tumble dryer, cycle lock-up and drying facilities. Ample car parking. One cottage suitable for wheelchair users. Terms from £200 - £800 per week. Dogs by arrangement.

Contact: Mr & Mrs R.G. Dunlop, Cannee Farm, Kirkcudbright DG6 4XD

01557 330684 • holidaycottages@cannee.co.uk • www.highkirkland.co.uk

Dunbartonshire

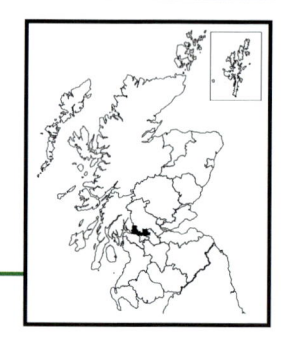

Luss

Shemore Farm Holiday Cottage
Luss, Loch Lomond

Regulars enjoy returning to this traditional stone cottage attractively situated on our 5000 acre hill sheep farm, 300 ft above Loch Lomond, over which the Cottage has magnificent views. We are 4 miles south of the picturesque village of Luss, ideal for touring, hill walking, bird watching, water sports, golf, and for those attending nearby weddings. Glasgow, Inveraray and Stirling within 1 hour; Oban, Fort William and Perth a slightly longer drive. The National Park Gateway Centre, Aquarium and shops at Lomond Shores are 10 minutes away. There is something for all the family during your stay at Shemore. **Contact Mrs Anne M.Lennox:**
Tel: 01389 850231 • www.farmstay-lochlomond.co.uk • anne@farmstay-lochlomond.co.uk

SELF-CATERING EDINBURGH & LOTHIANS/FIFE **221**

Edinburgh & Lothians

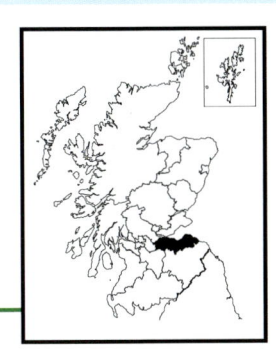

Rosewell

Hunter Holiday Cottages

Thornton Farm, Rosewell, Edinburgh EH24 9EF
Tel: 0131-448 0888 • Fax: 0131-440 2082

HUNTER HOLIDAY COTTAGES offer a range of cottages in beautiful countryside only eight miles from Edinburgh City Centre. These superior cottages are recently renovated, have all modern facilities and sleep four to ten plus. They provide the ideal base for the perfect Scottish holiday from their location in Midlothian's historic countryside. There is easy access to Scotland's capital and the major routes to the rest of Scotland. For more information visit our website...

e-mail: info@edinburghcottages.com
www.edinburghcottages.com

Contact Margot Crichton.
Telephone for availability for Short Breaks

Fife

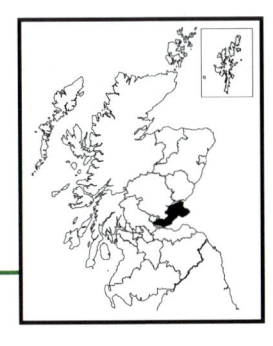

Auchtermuchty

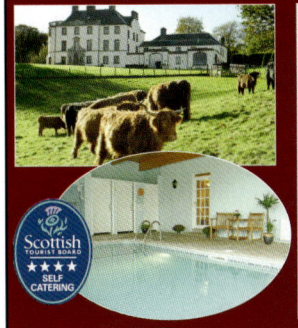

Pitcairlie House

Pitcairlie presents a rare opportunity to stay in a 16th century mansion within a 120-acre estate, home to a variety of wildlife, Highland cattle, sheep, horses and magnificent trees and flowers. Just 4 miles away is the historic village of Falkland. The Victorian wing of the house has been converted to provide 4 impressive guest apartments, and The Lodge House provides a fifth.

• Open all year • Use of indoor heated pool and sauna • Furnished and equipped to highest standards, most bedrooms with bathroom en suite • Fully fitted kitchen • Gas central heating • All linen and towels provided • Laundry room • High chair etc on request.

Pitcairlie House, Auchtermuchty, Fife KY14 6BX
Tel: 01337 827411 • Mobile: 07831 646157
e-mail: rosemary@pitcairlie-leisure.co.uk • www.pitcairlie-leisure.co.uk

Highlands

SELF-CATERING

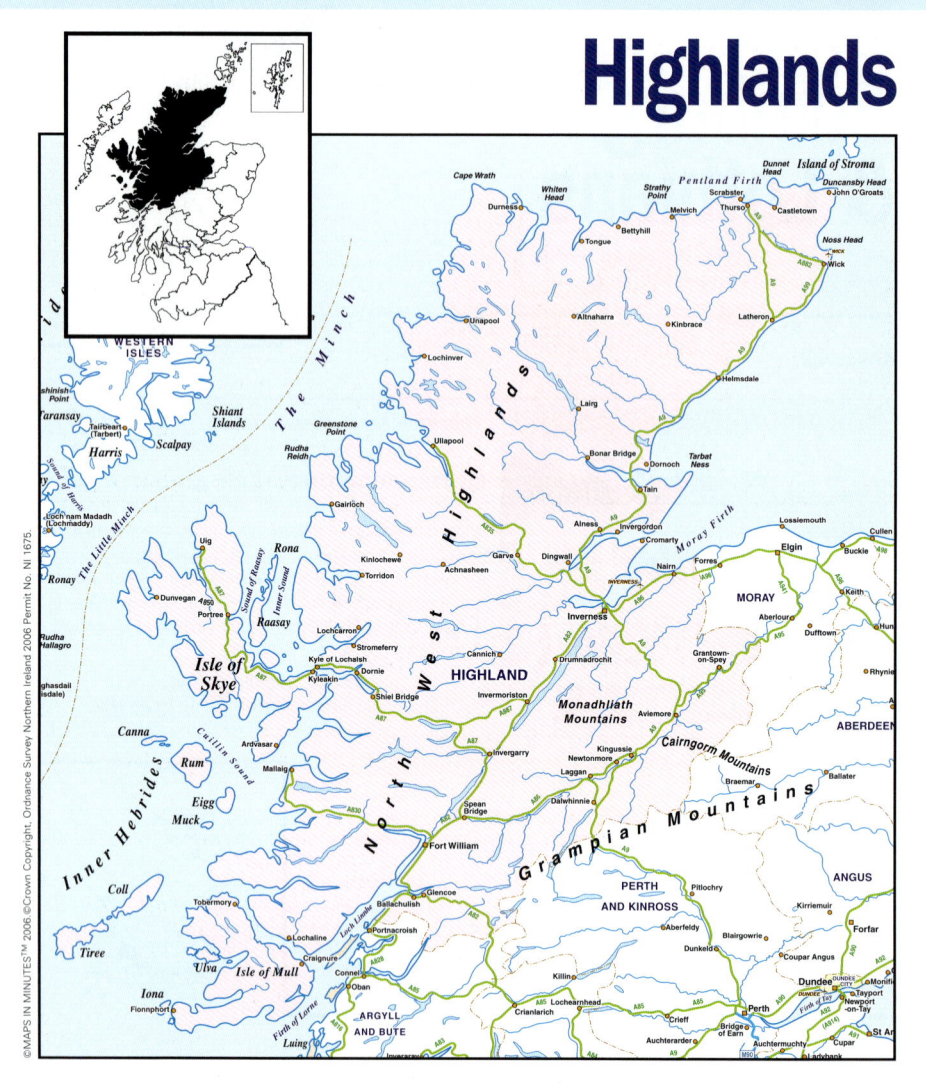

Visit the FHG website
www.holidayguides.com
for details of the wide choice of
accommodation featured in
the full range of FHG titles

FHG KUPERARD

SELF-CATERING   HIGHLANDS (NORTH) /HIGHLANDS (SOUTH)   223

Highlands (North)

Ardgay

Detached cottage, sleeping 6, standing in its own grounds with private parking. Dornoch Cathedral (where Madonna and Guy Ritchie were married), Royal Dornoch Golf Course and beautiful safe sandy beaches only 14 miles away. Skibo Castle, Tain, Brora and Golspie golf courses all within easy reach. Angling, mountain biking, hill walking, wildlife and forest walks all available locally.

Tariff £150 to £220 per week.

The cottage is clean, comfortable and well equipped. Immersion heater for hot water; electric fires in all rooms.

Mrs M.C. MacLaren, The Poplars, Ardgay, Sutherland IV24 3BG • 01863 766302

Highlands (South)

Arisaig, Boat of Garten

Arisaig House Cottages – *luxurious secluded accommodation in mature woodland*

- ACHNAHANAT in the grounds of Arisaig House, sleeps up to 8
- THE BOTHY set at the end of the walled gardens, sleeps up to 8
- THE COURTYARD self-contained apartment on first floor, sleeps 2
- FAGUS LODGE set in mature gardens, sleeps up to 6
- GARDENER'S COTTAGE set in gardens off small courtyard, sleeps up to 3
- ROSHVEN overlooks walled gardens of Arisaig House, sleeps up to 4

ASSC

Set in an area of breathtaking coastal and hill scenery, and wonderful sandy beaches. Mountain bike hire, and fishing on Loch Morar can be arranged. Golf 7 miles, swimming pool 13 miles. Hard tennis court. Day trips to the Small Isles and to Skye. ON-LINE BOOKING.

Achnahanat

Details from: Andrew Smither, Arisaig House Cottages, Beasdale, Arisaig, Inverness-shire PH39 4NR
Tel/Fax: 01687 462 686
e-mail: enquiries@arisaighouse-cottages.co.uk • www.arisaighouse-cottages.co.uk

Tyndrum • Boat of Garten

Completely renovated, well furnished self-catering accommodation retaining the original pine panelling in the lounge.

Set in a rural village, Boat of Garten in beautiful Strathspey, six miles from Aviemore, an ideal base for touring. Fishing is available locally on the River Spey, just two minutes away, with attractive riverside picnic spots. The famous Osprey nest is nearby, at Loch Garten RSPB Reserve. Local steam train journeys, good golf and water sports; skiing at Cairngorm in season. Shop and pub half a mile.

Large lounge, attractive dining/sitting room, spacious fully fitted dining kitchen, shower room. First floor: bathroom, one double and one twin room, both with washbasin, and one single bedroom. Colour TV with Sky digital; dishwasher, microwave, washer/dryer and deep freeze. Electricity, bed linen and towels inclusive. Parking. Large garden.

Contact: Mrs N.C. Clark, Dochlaggie, Boat of Garten PH24 3BU   Tel: 01479 831342

SPEYSIDE LEISURE PARK

Self-Catering Holidays in the Heart of the Highlands

The park is situated in a quiet riverside setting with mountain views, only a short walk from Aviemore centre and shops. We offer a range of warm, well equipped chalets, cabins and caravans, including a caravan for the disabled. Prices include electricity, gas, linen, towels and use of our heated indoor pool and sauna. There are swings, a climbing frame and low level balance beams for the children. Permit fishing is available on the river. Discounts are given on some local attractions.

Families, couples or groups will find this an ideal location for a wide range of activities including:

- Horse riding • Golf • Fishing • Hillwalking
- RSPB Reserves • Mountain and Watersports • Reindeer herd
- Steam railway and the Whisky Trail

Only slightly further afield there are many places of interest such as Culloden Moor, Fort George and of course, the not to be missed, Loch Ness. Accommodation sleeps from 4-8, but we offer a reduced rate for a couple. Short Breaks are available. Sorry, no pets, except guide and hearing dogs.

Speyside Leisure Park
Dalfaber Road, Aviemore, Inverness-shire PH22 1PX
Tel: 01479 810236 • Fax: 01479 811688
E-mail: fhg@speysideleisure.com • www.speysideleisure.com

SELF-CATERING HIGHLANDS (SOUTH) 225
Cullodon (by Inverness), Fort William, Invergarry

BLACKPARK FARM
Westhill, Inverness IV2 5BP

This newly built holiday home is located one mile from Culloden Battlefield with panoramic views over Inverness and beyond. Fully equipped with many extras to make your holiday special, including oil fired central heating to ensure warmth on the coldest of winter days. Ideally based for touring the Highlands including Loch Ness, Skye etc. Extensive information is available on our website.
A Highland welcome awaits you.

Tel: 01463 790620 • Fax: 01463 794262
e-mail: i.alexander@blackpark.co.uk • website: www.blackpark.co.uk

FORT WILLIAM. Ben View Self Catering.
A fully-equipped detached house with garage and small garden. It is ideally situated on the A82 Glasgow - Inverness road, only three minutes' walk from Fort William town centre, bus and rail stations and the Leisure Centre. The accommodation comprises one double room with en suite facilities, two twin-bedded rooms and a shower room with WC. The house has a well equipped fitted kitchen and a spacious, luxurious dining/lounge area with log fire. Bedding is provided and a travel cot is available on request. Starter pack is also available if desired.
• Sleeps 6.
Contact Mrs E. Smith, Ben View Guest House, Belford Road, Fort William PH33 6ER (01397 772017).
www.benviewguesthouse.co.uk
e-mail: BenView@gowanbrae.co.uk

Great Glen Holidays
Torlundy, Fort William PH33 6SW
Tel: 01397 703015 • Fax 01397 703304

Eight timber chalets situated in woodland with spectacular mountain scenery. These spacious two bedroom lodges are attractively furnished with linen provided. On working Highland farm. Riding, fishing and walking on farm. Ideal for family holidays and an excellent base for touring; four miles from town.
Sleep 4-6. Prices from £250 to £510 per week

e-mail:info@fortwilliam-chalets.co.uk
www.fortwilliam-chalets.co.uk

INVERGARRY. Miss J. Ellice, Taigh-an-Lianach, Aberchalder Estate, Invergarry PH35 4HN (01809 501287).
Three self-catering properties, all ideal for hill walkers and country lovers. Salmon and trout fishing available. ABERCHALDER LODGE: traditional Highland shooting lodge extensively modernised to give a high standard of comfort, sleeps 12. TAIGH AN LIANACH: modern self contained bed-sit, secluded and peaceful, sleeps two. LEAC COTTAGE: a secluded cottage which combines old world charm with a high standard of comfort, sleeps three. Heated kennels available.
• Sleep 2-12 persons. • Children welcome. • Well behaved dogs welcome.
Please phone or fax 01809 501287.

The FHG Directory of Website Addresses
on pages 277-310 is a useful quick reference guide for holiday accommodation with e-mail and/or website details

INVERMORISTON
Holiday Chalets

Spectacular location by Loch Ness at the heart of the Highlands of Scotland. Comfortable, well equipped self-catering chalets in spacious grounds, or alongside enchanting River Moriston Falls and bridges. Only a few minutes' walk to the village and amenities. Excellent base to explore, hill walk, fish, cycle and much more. Pets welcome in some chalets. Launderette and children's games areas on site.

Glenmoriston, Highlands IV63 7YF
Tel: 01320 351254 • Fax: 01320 351343
www.invermoriston-holidays.com
e-mail: ihc@ipw.com

WILDERNESS COTTAGES, LOCH NESS, WEST COAST & PERTHSHIRE

Open all year • Sleep 2-12 • Pets welcome   ASSC

Escape to the country with Wilderness Cottages and leave behind the hectic lifestyle you lead today. Visit any time of the year, enjoy a romantic winter break, snuggled up by the log fire, or during the summer and experience the natural beauty of Scotland. We have a small selection of quality self catering cottages from rustic appeal to 5-star luxury. Log fires, sea views, countryside to seashore we can provide a cottage to suit you. Walking, Munro bagging, cyclings, golfing, birdwatching, fishing or just chilling, whatever your pastime visit a Wilderness Cottage for your perfect retreat. Pets with responsible owners are very welcome..

CONTACT: Gordon & Corinne Roberts, Roebuck Cottage, Errogie, Stratherrick, Inverness-shire IV2 6UH • TEL 01456 486358
e-mail: corinne@wildernesscottages.co.uk • www.wildernesscottages.co.uk

Lanarkshire

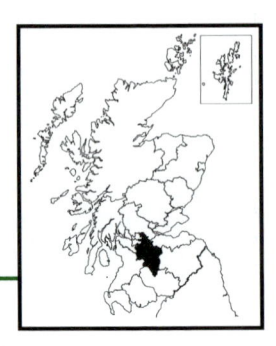

Biggar (Clyde Valley)

CARMICHAEL COUNTRY COTTAGES
Westmains, Carmichael, Biggar ML12 6PG • Tel: 01899 308336 • Fax: 01899 308481
200 year old stone cottages in this 700 year old family estate. We guarantee comfort, warmth and a friendly welcome in an accessible, unique, rural and historic time capsule. We farm deer, cattle and sheep and sell meats and tartan - Carmichael of course. Open all year. Terms from £225 to £595.
ASSC   15 cottages with a total of 32 bedrooms. Private tennis court and fishing loch, cafe, farm shop and visitor centre
e-mail: chiefcarm@aol.com • website: www.carmichael.co.uk/cottages

SELF-CATERING MORAYSHIRE/PERTH & KINROSS 227

Morayshire

Fochabers

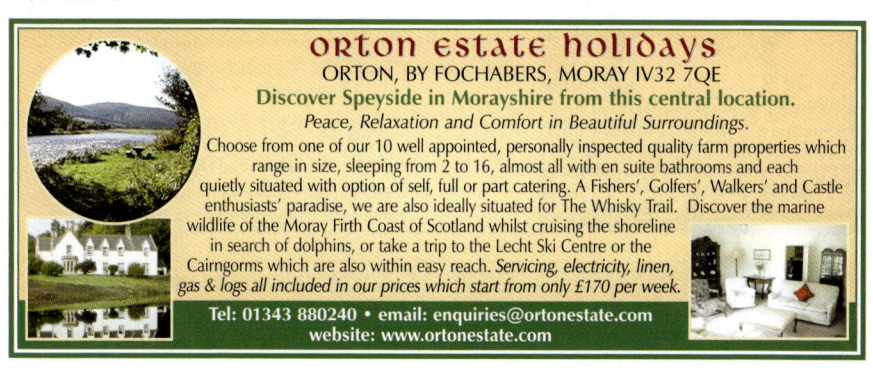

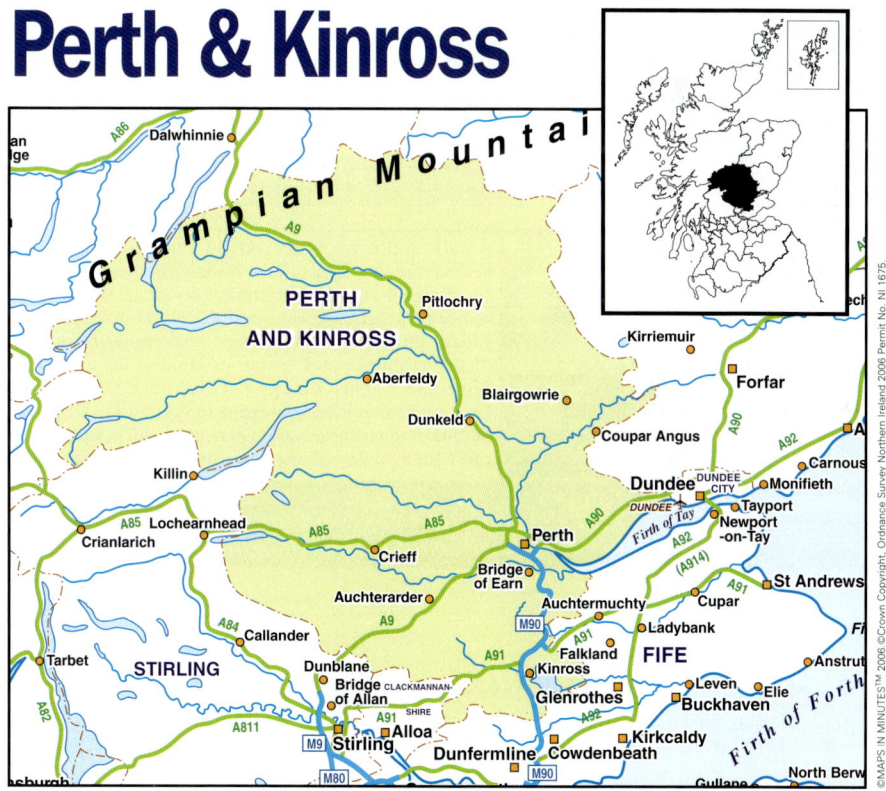

orton estate holidays
ORTON, BY FOCHABERS, MORAY IV32 7QE
Discover Speyside in Morayshire from this central location.
Peace, Relaxation and Comfort in Beautiful Surroundings.
Choose from one of our 10 well appointed, personally inspected quality farm properties which range in size, sleeping from 2 to 16, almost all with en suite bathrooms and each quietly situated with option of self, full or part catering. A Fishers', Golfers', Walkers' and Castle enthusiasts' paradise, we are also ideally situated for The Whisky Trail. Discover the marine wildlife of the Moray Firth Coast of Scotland whilst cruising the shoreline in search of dolphins, or take a trip to the Lecht Ski Centre or the Cairngorms which are also within easy reach. *Servicing, electricity, linen, gas & logs all included in our prices which start from only £170 per week.*

Tel: 01343 880240 • email: enquiries@ortonestate.com
website: www.ortonestate.com

Perth & Kinross

Readers are requested to mention this guidebook when making enquiries about accommodation.

228 PERTH & KINROSS Aberfeldy, Dunkeld, Methven SELF-CATERING

LOCH TAY LODGES

Acharn, By Aberfeldy PH15 2HR

Escape the rat race. Enjoy the tranquillity, the grandeur, the beauty and the comfort of Highland Perthshire. Walk around the farm in the woods or up the mountains, play golf, fish, tour or sail. Fully modernised stone building Listed for its architectural interest. Self-catering. Log Fires. Well behaved dogs welcome. Linen provided.

Tel: 01887 830209
Fax: 01887 830802
e-mail: remony@btinternet.com
www.lochtaylodges.co.uk

LAIGHWOOD HOLIDAYS
NEAR DUNKELD
For your comfort and enjoyment

We can provide properties from a large de luxe house for eight to well-equipped cottages and apartments for two to six, some open all year. All are accessible by tarmac farm roads. Laighwood is centrally located for sightseeing and for all country pursuits, including golf, fishing and squash. Sorry, no pets. Brochure on request from:

Laighwood Holidays, Laighwood, Dunkeld PH8 0HB.
Telephone: 01350 724241 • Fax: 01350 724212
e-mail: holidays@laighwood.co.uk • website: www.laighwood.co.uk

A warm welcome awaits you at Cloag Farm where our self-catering cottages offer you the opportunity to enjoy the peace and quiet of the countryside. Each sleeps up to 4, but there are discounts available for couples all year. Cloag Farm is seven miles west of Perth, just north of Methven village, and ideally positioned for exploring Perthshire, with its rich legacy of castles and historic sites. Looking further afield, day trips to Edinburgh, Glasgow, St Andrews, Loch Ness and Glencoe are all popular with our visitors, many of whom return to visit us again.

Contact: David and Moyra Smythe, Cloag Farm, Methven, Perth PH1 3RR
Phone: +44 (0) 1738 840239 • Fax: +44 (0) 1738 840156
e-mail: info@cloagfarm.co.uk • www.cloagfarm.co.uk

Looking for holiday accommodation?

for details of hundreds of properties throughout the UK including comprehensive coverage of all areas of Scotland try:

www.holidayguides.com

CARAVANS & CAMPING　　　　　　　　　　　　　ARGYLL & BUTE 229

SCOTLAND
Caravans & Camping
Argyll & Bute

Kinlochleven, Lochgilphead

CAOLASNACON
Caravan & Camping Park, Kinlochleven PA40 4RS

There are 20 static six-berth caravans for holiday hire on this lovely site with breathtaking mountain scenery on the edge of Loch Leven — an ideal touring centre.

Caravans have electric lighting, Calor gas cookers and heaters, toilet, shower, fridge and colour TV. There are two toilet blocks with hot water and showers and laundry facilities. Children are welcome and pets allowed. Open from April to October. Milk, gas, soft drinks available on site; shops three miles. Sea loch fishing, hill walking and boating; boats and rods for hire, fishing tackle for sale.

For details contact Mrs Patsy Cameron — 01855 831279

CASTLE SWEEN

Around picturesque Castle Sween, the oldest ruined castle in Scotland, and ingeniously placed to take advantage of the natural contours of the ground, is a selection of super luxury caravans on excellent sites affording magnificent views and first-class amenities. The area is one of the most superb in the West of Scotland, quiet, peaceful and relaxing, and the great attraction of Castle Sween is the freedom to follow your own inclination in the way of holiday pastimes. Walkers will find their paradise. Naturalists will be fascinated by the plentiful wild life, there is sea and loch fishing, boats and dinghies can be launched and sailed in the waters of the loch.

The accommodation is in super luxury caravans. The manager's house, office and a well-stocked shop are situated in the middle of the complex, as well as a restaurant and bar.

Brochure, full details of accommodation, booking forms etc., can be obtained on application to:
CASTLE SWEEN BAY (HOLIDAYS) LTD, ELLARY, LOCHGILPHEAD, ARGYLL PA31 8PA

Tel: 01880 770232　　　　e-mail: info@ellary.com
　　　　　　　　　　　　　　website: www.ellary.com

See also Self-catering Section

Ayrshire & Arran

Ballantrae

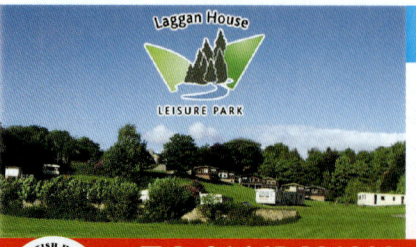

Relax in Ayrshire

Laggan House Leisure Park has beautiful grounds to relax in. Bar, heated swimming pool, sauna, children's playground. Lovely views to coast. Beaches three miles. Short breaks and weekly rentals available in luxury caravans. Dogs welcome.

New and previously owned caravans for sale

Tel: 01465 831229 • Fax: 01465 831511
email: lhlp@lagganhouse.co.uk
See us on our website www.lagganhouse.co.uk

Borders

Cockburnspath

COCKBURNSPATH Chesterfield Caravan Park, The Neuk, Cockburnspath, Berwickshire TD13 5YH (01368 830459; Fax: 01368 830394).
A quiet, secluded family-run park lying between gently sloping hills. Situated one mile off the A1, two miles from the beach, 10 miles south of Dunbar and 15 miles north of Eyemouth. An ideal base to explore the Scottish Borders, Edinburgh and Lothians, the East Coast and Northumberland. Facilities include toilets, showers, electric hook-ups, dishwashing area, laundry room, large play area. Local amenities include fishing, golf, nature trails, historic houses, castles, museums and beautiful beaches.
Rates: from £9.50 per night.
• Facilities for disabled available. • Open from the end of March until the end of October.
VisitScotland ★★★★

e-mail: info@chesterfieldcaravanpark.co.uk   www.chesterfieldcaravanpark.co.uk

Note

All the information in this guide is given in good faith in the belief that it is correct. However, the publishers cannot guarantee the facts given in these pages, neither are they responsible for changes in ownership or facilities that may take place after the date of going to press.
Readers should always satisfy themselves that the facilities they require are available and that the terms, if quoted, still apply.

Dumfries & Galloway

Newton Stewart

NEWTON STEWART Whitecairn Farm Caravan Park, Glenluce, Newton Stewart DG8 0NZ (01581 300267).
Peacefully set by a quiet country road, one-and-a-half-miles from the village of Glenluce with panoramic views over the rolling Galloway countryside to Luce Bay. This family-run park offers a choice of three different caravan types sleeping up to six, all of a high standard and fully equipped. Amenities include children's play area, launderette, telephone, toilet blocks and shower rooms. Electric hook-ups on touring pitches. The six-acre site offers freedom for children of all ages. Colour brochure available.
* Sleep up to 6. • Dogs are welcome under strict control.
* Open all year.
STB ★★★★ *HOLIDAY PARK.*
www.whitecairncaravans.co.uk

Perthshire

Comrie

COMRIE West Lodge Caravan Park, Comrie PH6 2LS (01764 670354).
Two to six berth caravans for hire fully equipped with gas cooker, running water, toilet, electric fridge, lighting, colour TV and gas fire. Crockery, cutlery, cooking utensils, blankets and pillows are provided. Sheets and towels can be hired. All caravans have toilets and showers. Pitches available for tents, tourers, motor homes. One modern shower block on site, with showers and hot and cold running water; electric hook-ups; modern launderette and dish washing area, shop. Fishing, golf, tennis, bowling, hill-walking and canoeing all within easy reach. Watersports available on nearby Loch Earn. Ideal for touring, 23 miles north of Stirling and 23 miles west of Perth.
Rates: from £30 to £45 nightly, £200 to £260 weekly; VAT, electricity and gas incl. Tents and tourers £8-£16 nightly.
* Open 1st April to 31st October.
STB ★★★★ *SELF-CATERING.*
www.westlodge.bravehost.com

Looking for holiday accommodation?
for details of hundreds of properties
throughout the UK including
comprehensive coverage of all areas of Scotland try:

www.holidayguides.com

Your guides to Good Holidays 2007

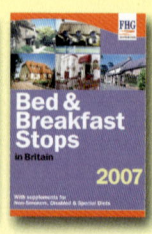

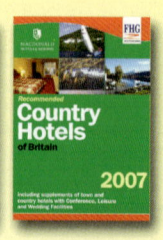

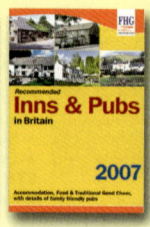

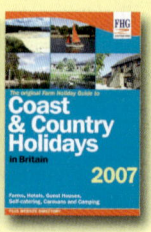

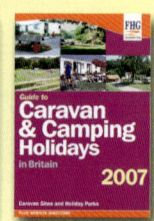

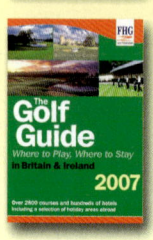

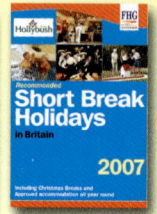

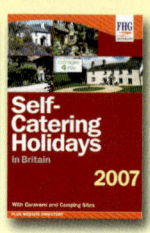

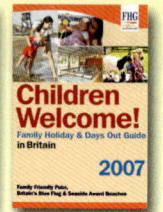

BRITAIN'S BEST LEISURE & RELAXATION GUIDE user-friendly guide to all kinds of holidays **ONLY £4.99**

BED & BREAKFAST STOPS ever more popular independent guide with over 1000 entries **£7.99**

Recommended COUNTRY HOTELS a quality selection of Britain's best Country Houses and Hotels **£7.99**

Recommended INNS & PUBS accommodation, food and traditional good cheer **£7.99**

COAST & COUNTRY HOLIDAYS holidays for all the family, from traditional farm houses to inns, guesthouses and small hotels **£7.99**

CARAVAN & CAMPING HOLIDAYS covers every type of caravan and camping facility **£7.99**

THE GOLF GUIDE Where to Play / Where to Stay a detailed list covering virtually every club and course in the UK with hotels and other accommodation nearby – recommended by golfers, to golfers **£9.99**

PETS WELCOME! the pet world's version of the ultimate hotel guide, over 1000 properties where pets and their owners are made welcome **£8.99**

Recommended SHORT BREAK HOLIDAYS approved accommodation all year round for short breaks **£7.99**

SELF CATERING HOLIDAYS perhaps the widest selection of self-catering accommodation **£7.99**

CHILDREN WELCOME! Family Holiday and Days Out guide **£7.99**

Available from bookshops or larger newsagents

FHG GUIDES LTD Abbey Mill Business Centre, Seedhill, Paisley, Renfrewshire PA1 1TJ

www.holidayguides.com

The best-selling series of UK Holiday Guides

Wales

Photos: Lawrenny Lodge, Barmouth, Gwynedd    East Hook Farm, Haverfordwest, Pembrokeshire    Gwernstablau, Machynlleth, Powys

Board

Ratings & Awards

For the first time ever the AA, VisitBritain, VisitScotland, and the Wales Tourist Board will use a single method of assessing and rating serviced accommodation. Irrespective of which organisation inspects an establishment the rating awarded will be the same, using a common set of standards, giving a clear guide of what to expect. The RAC is no longer operating an Hotel inspection and accreditation business.

Accommodation Standards: Star Grading Scheme

Using a scale of 1-5 stars the objective quality ratings give a clear indication of accommodation standard, cleanliness, ambience, hospitality, service and food, This shows the full range of standards suitable for every budget and preference, and allows visitors to distinguish between the quality of accommodation and facilities on offer in different establishments. All types of board and self-catering accommodation are covered, including hotels, B&Bs, holiday parks, campus accommodation, hostels, caravans and camping, and boats.

VisitBritain and the regional tourist boards, **enjoyEngland.com, VisitScotland** and **VisitWales,** and **the AA** have full details of the grading system on their websites

The more stars, the higher level of quality

★★★★★
exceptional quality, with a degree of luxury

★★★★
excellent standard throughout

★★★
very good level of quality and comfort

★★
good quality, well presented and well run

★
acceptable quality; simple, practical, no frills

National Accessible Scheme

If you have particular mobility, visual or hearing needs, look out for the National Accessible Scheme. You can be confident of finding accommodation or attractions that meet your needs by looking for the following symbols.

Typically suitable for a person with sufficient mobility to climb a flight of steps but would benefit from fixtures and fittings to aid balance

Typically suitable for a person with restricted walking ability and for those that may need to use a wheelchair some of the time and can negotiate a maximum of three steps

Typically suitable for a person who depends on the use of a wheelchair and transfers unaided to and from the wheelchair in a seated position. This person may be an independent traveller

Typically suitable for a person who depends on the use of a wheelchair in a seated position. This person also requires personal or mechanical assistance (eg carer, hoist).

Anglesey & Gwynedd

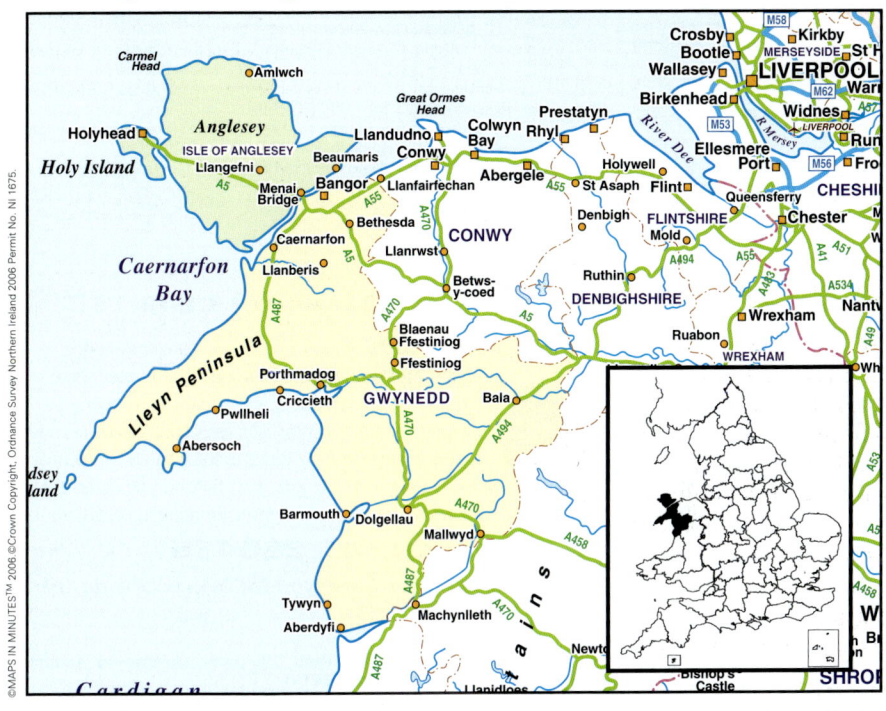

ANGLESEY & GWYNEDD, the northernmost area of Wales, bordered by the Irish sea, has something for everyone. Its beautiful coastline has glorious sandy beaches which offer safe bathing, and there are quaint coastal resorts with attractive harbours and maritime activities, The stunning Snowdonia National Park, right at its centre, covers 823 miles of beautiful, unspoilt countryside and a wide range of leisure activities can be enjoyed. Natural attractions abound throughout the area - mountains, forests, lakes, rivers and waterfalls all wait to be explored, and man-made attractions include castles, railways and industrial archaeology.

Looking for holiday accommodation?

for details of hundreds of properties throughout the UK including comprehensive coverage of all areas of Scotland try:

www.holidayguides.com

236 ANGLESEY & GWYNEDD   Bala, Barmouth, Harlech **BOARD**

BALA Mrs C. A. Morris, Tai'r Felin Farm, Frongoch, Bala LL23 7NS (01678 520763).
Tai'r Felin Farm is a working farm, situated three miles north of Bala (A4212 and B4501). Double and twin bedrooms available with beverage tray and clock radio. Dining room; beamed lounge with colour TV, central heating. Excellent base for touring Snowdonia National Park, watersports, walking, fishing and sailing Bala Lake. National White Water Centre one mile. Hearty breakfast. Recommended for excellent cooking and friendly atmosphere. Relax and enjoy a homely welcome. Walkers and cyclists welcome. Car essential.
Rates: Bed and Breakfast from £24
WTB ★★ *FARM.*

LAWRENNY LODGE   BARMOUTH LL42 1SU

Toby and Chantal welcome you to the Lawrenny Lodge, Barmouth. We have eight bedrooms (7 en suite), some overlooking the harbour and estuary, and are only 5 minutes from town centre. All rooms have TV and tea and coffee making facilities. Varied evening menu, residential licence and private car park. Now fully non-smoking. Pets welcome. Check out our website for more information.

01341 280466

E-MAIL: ENQUIRIES@LAWRENNYLODGE.CO.UK • WWW.LAWRENNYLODGE.CO.UK

HARLECH Mrs G.M. Evans, Glanygors, Llandanwg, Harlech LL46 2SD (01341 241410).
This three-star guest house with two acres of land is situated 400 yards from a sandy beach, and has beautiful views of the mountains. It is one-and-a-half miles from Harlech Castle, golf club and swimming pool, and within a quarter-mile of train station. Ideal place for bird-watching. Presenting good home-cooking in a homely and relaxed atmosphere and run by a Welsh-speaking family. Accommodation comprises one double, one twin and one family bedrooms, all with washbasin, TV and tea-making facilities; bathroom, toilet; TV lounge and diningroom. Central heating and electric blankets for winter months.
Rates: Bed and Breakfast from £20 per night. Reduced rates for children.
• Open all year.

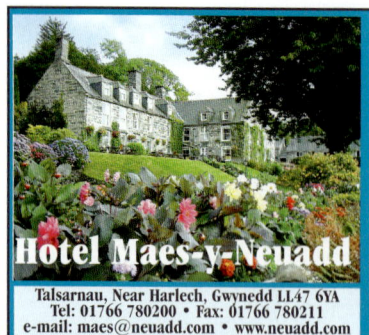

Hotel Maes-y-Neuadd

Nestling on a wooded mountainside, amidst some of the most beautiful scenery in Britain, this gracious and historic manor has won numerous awards for its all-round excellence. Comfort and luxury walk hand in hand in its delightfully furnished rooms and the views on all sides are spectacular. After a day's exploration of the Snowdonia National Park, seaside or the many visitor attractions, guests may enjoy an aperitif in the oak-beamed bar or on the terrace, followed by a delicious four-course meal prepared by chef patron Peter Jackson and his team, featuring fresh local produce. Children under seven can be served between 6 and 7pm from their own menu. Surrounded by 80 acres of parkland and walled kitchen gardens, Maes-y-Neuadd has all the ingredients for a memorable and relaxing holiday. Bedrooms and suites, both in the main house and Coach House annexe, are sumptuously appointed, ensuring sound and restful repose.

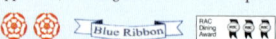

Talsarnau, Near Harlech, Gwynedd LL47 6YA
Tel: 01766 780200 • Fax: 01766 780211
E-mail: maes@neuadd.com • www.neuadd.com

BOARD Betws-y-Coed, Ruthin NORTH WALES 237

North Wales

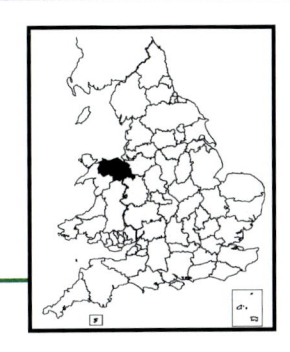

Hill farm in Wales. TV, teamaking, en suite. Set in National Park/ Snowdonia. Very quiet and well off the beaten track. A great welcome and good food. Many return visits. £20 B&B.

MISS MORRIS, TY COCH FARM-TREKKING CENTRE, PENMACHNO, BETWS-Y-COED LL25 0HJ
01690 760248
e-mail: cindymorris@tiscali.co.uk

Mrs Gaenor Jones welcomes you to Bryn Coch Farm Bed & Breakfast. We are a working farm situated near the historic town of Ruthin on the edge of Clocaenog Forest. Peaceful and comfortable location with plenty of walks and cycle routes nearby.

Two bedrooms - one twin, one triple, both en suite - plus a cosy guest lounge/dining room with original beams and log fire. Evening meal available using local produce.

Prices from £25 pppn, evening meal £12.

For further information contact me at
Bryn Coch, Clawddnwydd, Ruthin LL15 2NA
or on **01824 750603**
or e-mail: gaenorjones@hotmail.com

Please note

All the information in this book is given in good faith in the belief that it is correct. However, the publishers cannot guarantee the facts given in these pages, neither are they responsible for changes in policy, ownership or terms that may take place after the date of going to press. Readers should always satisfy themselves that the facilities they require are available and that the terms, if quoted, still apply.

Pembrokeshire

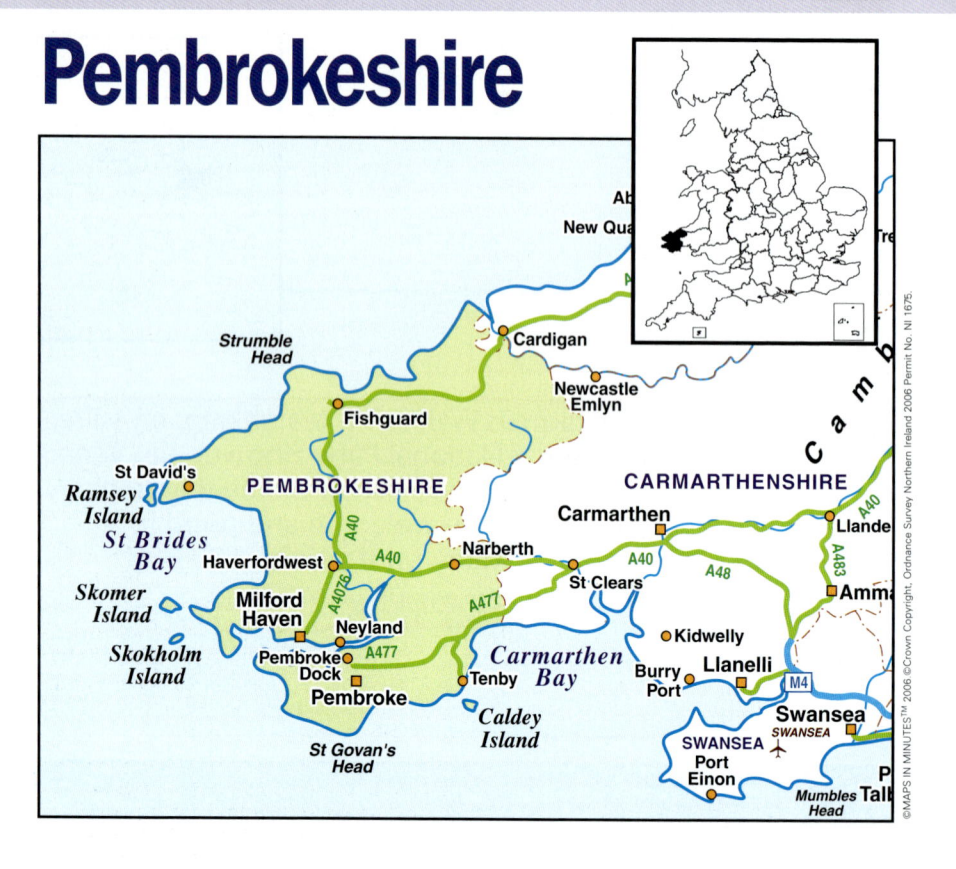

PEMBROKESHIRE'S entire coastline is a designated National Park, with its sheltered coves and wooded estuaries, fine sandy beaches and some of the most dramatic cliffs in Britain. The islands of Skomer, Stokholm and Grasholm are home to thousands of seabirds, and Ramsey Island, as well as being an RSPB Reserve boasts the second largest grey seal colony in Britain. Pembrokeshire's mild climate and the many delightful towns and villages, family attractions and outdoor facilities such as surfing, water skiing, diving, pony trekking and fishing make this a favourite holiday destination.

Please note

All the information in this book is given in good faith in the belief that it is correct. However, the publishers cannot guarantee the facts given in these pages, neither are they responsible for changes in policy, ownership or terms that may take place after the date of going to press. Readers should always satisfy themselves that the facilities they require are available and that the terms, if quoted, still apply.

BOARD Broad Haven, Haverfordwest, PEMBROKESHIRE 239

Albany Guest House

Albany is a friendly, family-run Bed & Breakfast. Three en suite rooms, double, single or twin, all with tea/coffee making facilities, TV, central heating, and access at all times (some rooms have sea views). Parking.

Two minutes from sandy beach of Broad Haven and leading to Little Haven. Within walking distance are shop/Post Office, cafe, pub/ restaurant and Coastal Path. Windsurfing, swimming, diving and boat trips to Skomer and Grassholm bird islands (puffins, razorbills etc); seal pups in bays September/October. Coastal bus May to September. Nearby are St Davids, Tenby, Oakwood etc and sandy beaches.

**Mrs F. Morgan, Albany Guest House,
27 Millmoor Way, Broad Haven,
Haverfordwest SA62 3JJ
Tel: 01437 781051
info@albanyguesthouse.tiscali.co.uk
www.albanyguesthouse.co.uk**

Norchard Farmhouse
**Boulston, Near Uzmaston,
Haverfordwest SA62 4AH
Tel: 01437 765596**

Ideally placed for enjoying the beauty, history and sporting opportunities available in Pembrokeshire, Norchard is a tastefully furnished Georgian farmhouse set on country estate lands, 3 miles from Haverfordwest, close to the Western Cleddau. Relax in the guests' sitting room which has colour TV, and French doors opening out onto a traditional cottage garden. Full breakfast is served in the stone-floored kitchen, or outside on the terrace, Welsh weather permitting!

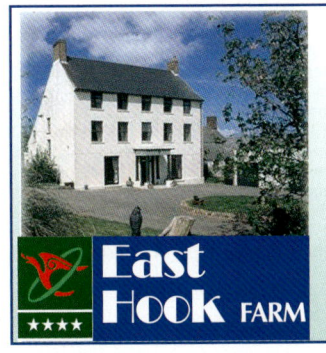

East Hook Farm

Howard and Jen welcome you to their Georgian Farmhouse surrounded by beautiful countryside, four miles from the coastline and three miles from Haverfordwest. Double, twin and family suite available, all en suite. Ground floor rooms available. Pembrokeshire produce used for and breakfast.

Bed and Breakfast from £28 to £32 pp.

Self-Catering cottage available.

**Mr and Mrs Patrick, East Hook Farm,
Portfield Gate, Haverfordwest, Pembroke SA62 3LN
01437 762211 • www.easthookfarmhouse.co.uk**

Visit the FHG website
www.holidayguides.com
for details of the wide choice of accommodation featured in the full range of FHG titles

·K·U·P·E·R·A·R·D·

Powys

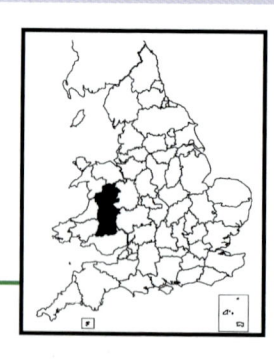

Caebetran Farm

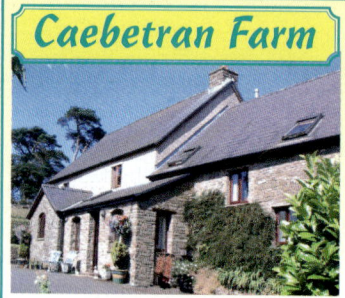

A warm welcome, a cup of tea and home-made cakes await you when you arrive at Caebetran. Well off the beaten track, where there are breathtaking views of the Brecon Beacons and the Black Mountains, and just across a field is a 400 acre common, ideal for walking, bird-watching or just relaxing. The rooms are all en suite and have colour TV and tea making facilities. The dining room has separate tables, there is also a comfortable lounge with colour TV and video. Caebetran is an ideal base for exploring this beautiful, unspoilt part of the country with pony trekking, walking, birdwatching, wildlife, hang-gliding and so much more. For a brochure and terms please write, telephone or fax.

"Arrive as visitors and leave as our friends".
Winners of the 'FHG Diploma' for Wales 1998/99. Welcome Host.
Gwyn and Hazel Davies Caebetran Farm, Felinfach, Brecon, Powys LD3 0UL • Tel: 01874 754460
e-mail: hazelcaebetran@aol.com • www.caebetranfarmhousebedandbreakfastwales.com

BRECON Mrs A. Harpur, Llanbrynean Farm, Llanfrynach, Brecon LD3 7BQ (01874 665222).
Llanbrynean is a fine, traditional, Victorian farmhouse peacefully situated on the edge of the picturesque village of Llanfrynach, three miles south-east of Brecon. We are in an ideal spot for exploring the area - the Brecon Beacons rise behind the farm and the Brecon/Monmouth canal flows through the fields below. We are a working family sheep farm with wonderful pastoral views and a large garden. The house is spacious and comfortable with a friendly, relaxed atmosphere. We have two double en suite bedrooms and one twin with private bathroom. All have tea/coffee facilities. There is a sitting room with TV. Excellent pub food within easy walking distance.
Rates: Bed and Breakfast from £24 per person.
• Working farm.
e-mail: simon.harpur@tiscali.co.uk

---

e-mail: carol@blaencar.co.uk • www.blaencar.co.uk
Enjoy the warmth and quality of a true Welsh welcome on a working family farm in the heart of the Brecon Beacons National Park. Eight miles west of Brecon, this lovingly refurbished farmhouse with a wealth of charm and character offers superior accommodation and comfort for discerning guests looking for something special. Three luxurious en suite bedrooms have all facilities. The peace and tranquility of this quiet, accessible location provides an ideal base for relaxation, touring and exploring in unspoilt countryside. Friendly country pub a pleasant 15 minute walk.

Mrs Carol Morgan, Blaencar Farm, Sennybridge, Brecon, Powys LD3 8HA
01874 636610

GOLD

BOARD Llandrindod Wells, Machynlleth, Newtown, Welshpool   POWYS 241

Holly Farm

Tastefully restored Tudor farmhouse on working farm in peaceful location. En suite bedrooms with breathtaking views over fields and woods, colour TV, beverage trays. Two lounges with log fires. Renowned for excellent food. Wonderful area for wildlife, walking, cycling, near Red Kite feeding station. Safe parking. Brochure on request.

Bed, Breakfast and Evening Meal weekly from £245 to £260. Bed and Breakfast from £24 to £30 per day.

Mrs Ruth Jones, Holly Farm, Howey, Llandrindod Wells LD1 5PP
Tel & Fax: 01597 822402 • Taste of Wales Tourism Award • Farm Stay UK Member

Gwernstablau
Llanwrin, Machynlleth SY20 8QH
Tel: 01650 511688

Gwernstablau is a tranquil 17th century farmhouse set in its own five acre grounds. It tastefully combines the old world charm of a wealth of beamed ceilings and open log fires with the convenience of modern central heating and en suite accommodation.

Dinner can be enjoyed in the distinctive dining room with its galleried landing, crystal chandelier and antique furniture.

Bed and Breakfast £26. Enjoy a short break or longer stay. Individual attention assured.

www.gwern-stablau.com

Highgate House

Near Newtown SY16 3LF
Tel: 01686 623763
Fax: 01686 629194

Chris & Sarah Smith welcome you to this lovely black-and-white farmhouse set in the rolling mid Wales hills. There are three large double rooms and a single, all with en suite shower room, TV and hospitality tray. A traditional breakfast is served in the oak-beamed dining room, with home-made preserves and locally produced meat and eggs; special diets catered for on request. There is also a comfortable drawing room, with a log fire for cooler days. Highgate is an ideal base for visiting Offa's Dyke and Powis Castle, and for walking, birdwatching, and touring the lakes and mountains.

Luxury holiday cottages also available for self-catering.
e-mail: highgatehouse@hotmail.com
www.highgate-accommodation.co.uk

Lane Farm

A ***warm welcome awaits*** on our working organic beef and sheep farm situated between Welshpool and Shrewsbury. Nestling beneath the tranquil Breidden Hills in the picturesque Severn Valley, ideally situated to explore The Marches, Shropshire Hills and Mid Wales. Accommodation consists of four spacious, modern, en suite bedrooms, two the ground floor. All rooms have central heating, TV, beverage tray and radio alarm clock. Hearty farmhouse breakfasts. Local pubs offering excellent evening meals just a short drive or walk away.

Ample safe parking • Free fishing by arrangement • Non smoking throughout

Tel: 01743 884288 • Lane Farm, Criggion, Near Shrewsbury, Powys SY5 9BG
e-mail: lane.farm@ukgateway.net • www.lanefarmbedandbreakfast.co.uk

Looking for Holiday Accommodation?

for details of hundreds of properties throughout the UK visit our website

www.holidayguides.com

Wales

Self-Catering

Trowley Farmhouse, Builth Wells, Powys

Tyddyn Heilyn, Criccieth, Anglesey & Gwynedd

Cottage Retreats, Abermawr

Anglesey & Gwynedd

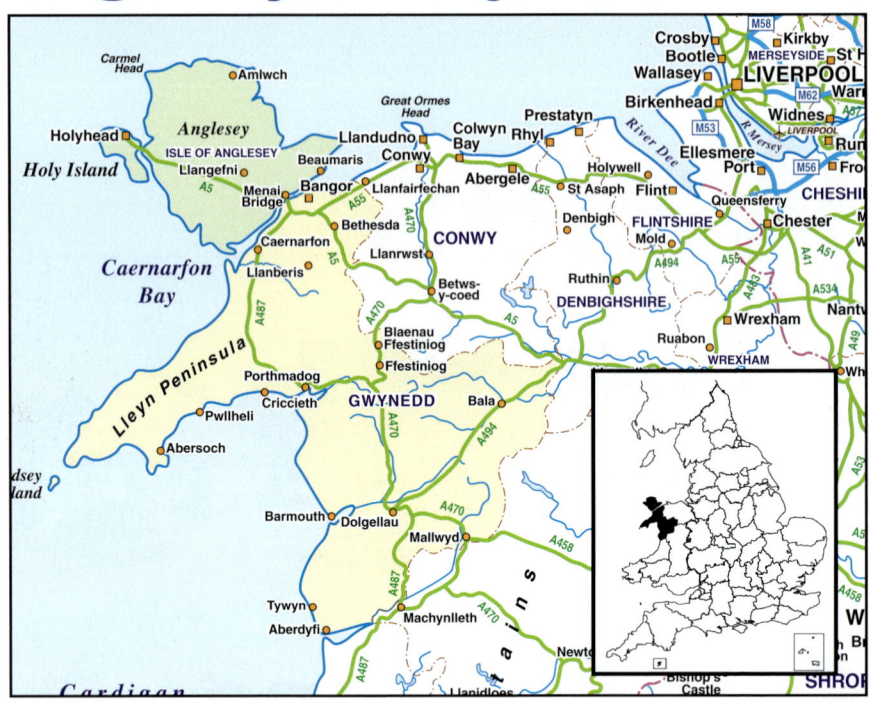

QUALITY COTTAGES
AROUND THE MAGNIFICENT WELSH COAST
Away from the Madding Crowd • Near safe sandy beaches

A small specialist agency with over 44 years experience of providing quality self-catering, offers privacy, peace and unashamed luxury. The first Wales Tourist Board Self-Catering Award Winner. Highest residential standards.
Dishwashers, Microwaves, Washing Machines, Central Heating. No Slot meters.
LOG FIRES • LINEN PROVIDED • PETS WELCOME FREE!

All in coastal areas famed for scenery, walks, wild-flowers, birds, badgers and foxes.

Free colour brochure from F.G. Rees "Quality Cottages", Cerbid, Solva, Haverfordwest, Pembrokeshire SA62 6YE
Telephone: (01348) 837871 • Website: www.qualitycottages.co.uk

FHG Guides
publish a large range of well-known accommodation guides. We will be happy to send you details or you can use the order form at the back of this book.

SELF CATERING

ANGLESEY & GWYNEDD 245
Abersoch, Bala, Bodorgan, Caernarfon

ABERSOCH. Quality Cottages.
Around the magnificent Welsh Coast. Away from the madding crowd. Near safe sandy beaches. A small specialist agency offering privacy, peace and unashamed luxury. First Wales Tourist Board Self Catering Gold Award Winner. Residential standards - Dishwashers, Microwaves, Washing Machines, Central Heating, Log Fires, No Slot Meters. Linen provided. Pets welcome free. All in coastal areas famed for scenery, walks, wild flowers, birds, badgers and foxes. Free colour brochure **S.C. Rees, "Quality Cottages", Cerbid, Solva, Haverfordwest, Pembrokeshire SA62 6YE (01348 837791).**
website: www.qualitycottages.co.uk

BALA Megan W. Pugh, Glanllyn, Llanuwchllyn, Bala, LL23 7ST (01678 540227).
17th century gatehouse lodge lovingly restored with all new furnishings and fittings, comprising one en suite double bedroom, one twin and one single bedroom, luxury bathroom with spa bath, large oak kitchen/diner and a lounge with Sky TV and DVD player. All rooms are on ground floor level with level entry at front door suitable for wheelchairs. Occupants have access to 16 acres of parkland bordering on Wales' largest natural lake. This parkland is also a touring caravan and camping park from April to September. There is access to the lake and river for fishing, sailing and canoeing.
- Working farm. • Sleeps 5 adults and 1 child.
- Children welcome. • Disabled guests welcome.

WTB ★★★★★ *SELF-CATERING.*
e-mail: info@glanllyn.com   www.glanllyn.com

WTB ★★★★   *Croeso*

- Comfortable three-bedroomed dormer bungalow with enclosed garden • Safe for children and dogs (welcome!)
- Near excellent beaches, forest, coastal footpath
- Birdwatching area • Snowdonia approximately 30 minutes drive. • Fully equipped; bedding and electricity inclusive
- Colour TV/video, microwave • Off-road parking

MRS J. GUNDRY, FARMYARD LODGE, BODORGAN, ANGLESEY LL62 5LW   • Tel: 01407 840977

BRYN BRAS CASTLE

Delightful castle apartments within unique romantic turreted Regency Castle, set in the gentle foothills of Snowdonia. Centrally situated amidst breathtaking scenery, ideal for exploring North Wales' magnificent mountains, beaches, resorts, heritage and history. Near local country inns/restaurants, shops. Each spacious apartment is fully self-contained, gracious, peaceful and clean, with distinctive individual character, comfortable furnishings, and generously and conveniently appointed from antiques to dishwasher etc. Thirty-two acres of tranquil landscaped gardens with sweeping lawns, woodland walks of natural beauty and panoramic hill-walking overlooking the sea, Anglesey and Mount Snowdon. Enjoy the comfort, warmth, privacy and relaxation of this castle of timeless charm in truly tranquil surroundings. Mild climate. Open all year, including for Short Breaks. Sleeps 2-4 persons. Regret no children. Fully inclusive rents, including breakfast cereals etc. e.g from £195 for 2 nights for 2 persons. Weekly £450-£850. **Brochure sent with pleasure.**

Llanrug, Near Caernarfon, North Wales LL55 4RE • Tel & Fax: Llanberis (01286) 870210
e-mail: holidays@brynbrascastle.co.uk • www.brynbrascastle.co.uk   ★★★★★

Listed Building Grade II★

246 ANGLESEY & GWYNEDD

SELF-CATERING
Caernarfon, Criccieth, Pentraeth

CAERNARFON Plas-Y-Bryn Chalet Park, Bontnewydd, Near Caernarfon LL54 7YE (01286 672811).
Our small park is situated two miles from the historic town of Caernarfon. Set into a walled garden it offers safety, seclusion and beautiful views of Snowdonia. It is ideally positioned for touring the area. Shop and village pub nearby. A selection of chalets and caravans is available.
Rates: from £120 to £430 per week for the caravans and £120 to £550 per week for the chalets.
• Well-behaved pets always welcome.
WTB ★★★★ *SELF-CATERING.*
e-mail: philplasybryn@aol.com
www.plasybrynholidayscaernarfon.co.uk

TYDDYN HEILYN
CHWILOG, CRICCIETH LL53 6SW
Tel: 01766 810441

Comfortably renovated Welsh stone cottage with character. Cosy, double-glazed, centrally heated and enjoying mild Gulf Stream climate, with holiday letting anytime. Two bedrooms with sea views. Ramped entrance from outside to an en suite bedroom. Ample parking area and enclosed garden with doggy walk. Positioned on Llyn Peninsula, 3 miles Criccieth, on edge of Snowdonia with a one mile tree-lined walk to beach.

CRICCIETH. Quality Cottages.
Around the magnificent Welsh Coast. Away from the madding crowd. Near safe sandy beaches. A small specialist agency offering privacy, peace and unashamed luxury. First Wales Tourist Board Self Catering Gold Award Winner. Residential standards - Dishwashers, Microwaves, Washing Machines, Central Heating, Log Fires, No Slot Meters. Linen provided. Pets welcome free. All in coastal areas famed for scenery, walks, wild flowers, birds, badgers and foxes. Free colour brochure **S.C. Rees, "Quality Cottages", Cerbid, Solva, Haverfordwest, Pembrokeshire SA62 6YE (01348 837781).**
website: www.qualitycottages.co.uk

Pen-y-Garnedd Holiday Cottage
Near Pentraeth, Isle of Anglesey LL75 8YW

WTB ★★★ • Open all year
Fully refurbished detached cottage on a working smallholding with goats, chickens, ducks, turkeys, lambs and calves.
Electric heating and logburner in lounge • TV/DVD, stereo
• One double bedroom; second bedroom with bunk beds and single bed. Cot available • Fully equipped kitchen • Bathroom with power shower • Enclosed garden • Private parking.
Caravan Club Approved Site (CCL5)
Well behaved children and pets welcome.
Tel: 01248 450580

Readers are requested to mention this guidebook when making enquiries about accommodation.

North Wales

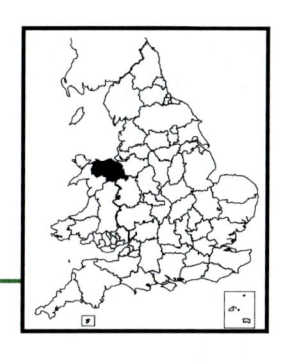

BETWS-Y-COED Mrs E. Thomas, Bryn Farm, Nebo, Llanrwst LL26 0TE (01690 710315).
Self-contained fully equipped farmhouse flat on a beef and sheep farm. Situated in the Snowdonia National Park and approximately five miles from Betws-y-Coed with beautiful rural views. The accommodation comprises small double bedroom and large bathroom upstairs. Ground floor has a kitchen/diner/lounge including microwave, fridge/freezer, TV and video. Central heating in winter. Small patio with garden furniture at front of property. Ideally situated for peace and quiet. Excellent base for country walks. Short Breaks available out of season.
* Sleeps 2. • Sorry no pets.
* Open all year except Christmas and New Year.

Tyn-y-Groes, Near Conwy

Homely Victorian stone cottage in picturesque Conwy valley. Mountain views. Enjoy walking, mountains, beaches, bird watching. Bodnant Gardens, RSPB reserve and Conwy castle, harbour and marina close by. Victorian Llandudno, Betws-y-Coed, Anglesey, Caernarfon and Snowdon easy distance. Good local food and pubs. Enclosed garden, patio, furniture. Roadside parking. Gas fired central heating. Lounge with gas fire, dining room, kitchen, utility. Two double bedded rooms, one small single; blankets/duvet provided. Bathroom with bath, shower, toilet and basin. Colour TV, electric cooker, fridge, microwave, washing machine and tumbler dryer. Terms £195-£315; heating, electricity included. Linen extra. Pets welcome. Open all year. No children under five years.

Mrs G. Simpole, 105 Hay Green Road, Terrington-St-Clement, King's Lynn, Norfolk PE34 4PU
Tel: 01553 828897
Mobile: 0798 9080665

Brongain

Looking for holiday accommodation?
for details of hundreds of properties throughout the UK visit:

www.holidayguides.com

Ceredigion

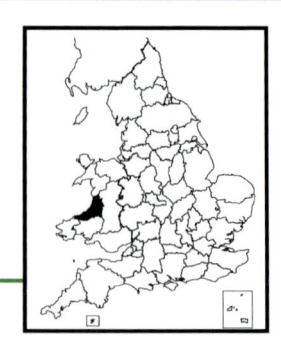

Aberporth, Cardigan, Llamgrannog SELF-CATERING

ABERPORTH. Quality Cottages.
Around the magnificent Welsh Coast. Away from the madding crowd. Near safe sandy beaches. A small specialist agency offering privacy, peace and unashamed luxury. First Wales Tourist Board Self Catering Gold Award Winner. Residential standards - Dishwashers, Microwaves, Washing Machines, Central Heating, Log Fires, No Slot Meters. Linen provided. Pets welcome free. All in coastal areas famed for scenery, walks, wild flowers, birds, badgers and foxes. Free colour brochure **S.C. Rees, "Quality Cottages", Cerbid, Solva, Haverfordwest, Pembrokeshire SA62 6YE (01348 837871).**
website: www.qualitycottages.co.uk

Parc Farm Holiday Cottages, Oakford, Near Llanarth SA47 0RX

Cardigan Bay and the harbour town of Aberaeron are just three and a half miles away from these comfortable stone cottages situated amidst beautiful farmland and quiet wooded valleys close to the sea.

With lovely gardens to enjoy and relax in, overlooking trout ponds and set in picturesque village in 14 acres of land.

New Quay five and a half miles away boasts a sandy beach with slipway water sports, tennis and boat trips for fishing or watching the dolphins offshore. Also many beautiful spots and sandy coves to explore and enjoy. Whilst inland, less than an hour's drive away, lies spectacular mountain scenery. Ideal for walking, cycling, birdwatching and horse riding.

Mr and Mrs Dunn • 01545 580390

CARDIGAN. Quality Cottages.
Around the magnificent Welsh Coast. Away from the madding crowd. Near safe sandy beaches. A small specialist agency offering privacy, peace and unashamed luxury. First Wales Tourist Board Self Catering Gold Award Winner. Residential standards - Dishwashers, Microwaves, Washing Machines, Central Heating, Log Fires, No Slot Meters. Linen provided. Pets welcome free. All in coastal areas famed for scenery, walks, wild flowers, birds, badgers and foxes. Free colour brochure **S.C. Rees, "Quality Cottages", Cerbid, Solva, Haverfordwest, Pembrokeshire SA62 6YE (01348 837871).**
website: www.qualitycottages.co.uk

LLANGRANNOG.Quality Cottages.
Around the magnificent Welsh Coast. Away from the madding crowd. Near safe sandy beaches. A small specialist agency offering privacy, peace and unashamed luxury. First Wales Tourist Board Self Catering Gold Award Winner. Residential standards - Dishwashers, Microwaves, Washing Machines, Central Heating, Log Fires, No Slot Meters. Linen provided. Pets welcome free. All in coastal areas famed for scenery, walks, wild flowers, birds, badgers and foxes. Free colour brochure **S.C. Rees, "Quality Cottages", Cerbid, Solva, Haverfordwest, Pembrokeshire SA62 6YE (01348 837871).**
website: www.qualitycottages.co.uk

Pembrokeshire

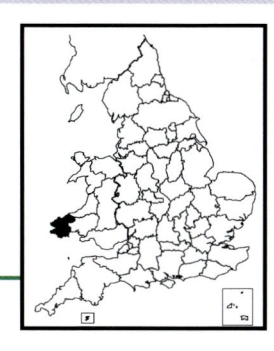

QUALITY COTTAGES

AROUND THE MAGNIFICENT WELSH COAST

Away from the Madding Crowd • Near safe sandy beaches

A small specialist agency with over 44 years experience of providing quality self-catering, offers privacy, peace and unashamed luxury. The first Wales Tourist Board Self-Catering Award Winner. Highest residential standards.
Dishwashers, Microwaves, Washing Machines, Central Heating. No Slot meters.
LOG FIRES • LINEN PROVIDED • PETS WELCOME FREE!

All in coastal areas famed for scenery, walks, wild-flowers, birds, badgers and foxes.
Free colour brochure from F.G. Rees "Quality Cottages", Cerbid, Solva, Haverfordwest, Pembrokeshire SA62 6YE
Telephone: (01348) 837871 • Website: www.qualitycottages.co.uk

Abermawr

Pembrokeshire Coast Newport to St Davids

Charming, individual cottages situated near sandy beaches, rocky bays and spectacular cliff walks. Traditional stone-built cottages or modern properties, many with central heating and wood-burning stoves. All furnished to high residential standards, fully equipped and personally supervised. Watersports, golf, birdwatching and wild flowers. Boat trips to the islands. Explore the Preseli Mountains, castles, cromlechs and Iron Age forts. Visit art galleries and craft workshops, relax in country pubs and quality restaurants. Pets and children welcome. Sleep 2-10.

Jane Stiles, Cil-y-Cwm, Nant-y-Ffynnon, Letterston, Haverfordwest SA62 5SX (01348 840879).
www.cottageretreats.net

e-mail: jane.stiles@virgin.net

BOSHERTON. Quality Cottages.
Around the magnificent Welsh Coast. Away from the madding crowd. Near safe sandy beaches. A small specialist agency offering privacy, peace and unashamed luxury. First Wales Tourist Board Self Catering Gold Award Winner. Residential standards - Dishwashers, Microwaves, Washing Machines, Central Heating, Log Fires, No Slot Meters. Linen provided. Pets welcome free. All in coastal areas famed for scenery, walks, wild flowers, birds, badgers and foxes. Free colour brochure **S.C. Rees, "Quality Cottages", Cerbid, Solva, Haverfordwest, Pembrokeshire SA62 6YE (01348 837871).**
website: www.qualitycottages.co.uk

PEMBROKESHIRE
Goodwick, Newgale, St Davids, Solva, Tenby

SELF-CATERING

Carne Farm

Stone cottage adjoining farmhouse, sleeps six in three bedrooms, also a spacious residential caravan for six with two bedrooms, each with its own garden where children can play safely. In peaceful countryside on 350 acre dairy and sheep farm between Fishguard and Strumble Head, three miles from the sea. Within easy reach of many beaches by car, ideal for walking and bird-watching. No linen supplied. Children welcome. TV, microwave, cots, high chairs. Baby sitting available. You can be sure of a warm welcome and visitors can feed calves and watch the milking.
Contact: Mrs Rosemary Johns

Goodwick, Pembrokeshire SA64 0LB
Tel: 01348 891665

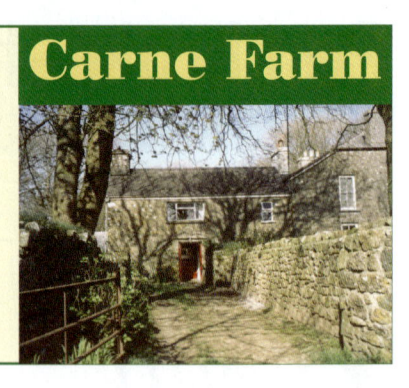

NEWGALE. Quality Cottages.
Around the magnificent Welsh Coast. Away from the madding crowd. Near safe sandy beaches. A small specialist agency offering privacy, peace and unashamed luxury. First Wales Tourist Board Self Catering Gold Award Winner. Residential standards - Dishwashers, Microwaves, Washing Machines, Central Heating, Log Fires, No Slot Meters. Linen provided. Pets welcome free. All in coastal areas famed for scenery, walks, wild flowers, birds, badgers and foxes. Free colour brochure **S.C. Rees, "Quality Cottages", Cerbid, Solva, Haverfordwest, Pembrokeshire SA62 6YE (01348 837871).**
website: www.qualitycottages.co.uk

ST DAVIDS. Quality Cottages.
Around the magnificent Welsh Coast. Away from the madding crowd. Near safe sandy beaches. A small specialist agency offering privacy, peace and unashamed luxury. First Wales Tourist Board Self Catering Gold Award Winner. Residential standards - Dishwashers, Microwaves, Washing Machines, Central Heating, Log Fires, No Slot Meters. Linen provided. Pets welcome free. All in coastal areas famed for scenery, walks, wild flowers, birds, badgers and foxes. Free colour brochure **S.C. Rees, "Quality Cottages", Cerbid, Solva, Haverfordwest, Pembrokeshire SA62 6YE (01348 837871).**
website: www.qualitycottages.co.uk

SOLVA. Quality Cottages.
Around the magnificent Welsh Coast. Away from the madding crowd. Near safe sandy beaches. A small specialist agency offering privacy, peace and unashamed luxury. First Wales Tourist Board Self Catering Gold Award Winner. Residential standards - Dishwashers, Microwaves, Washing Machines, Central Heating, Log Fires, No Slot Meters. Linen provided. Pets welcome free. All in coastal areas famed for scenery, walks, wild flowers, birds, badgers and foxes. Free colour brochure **S.C. Rees, "Quality Cottages", Cerbid, Solva, Haverfordwest, Pembrokeshire SA62 6YE (01348 837871).**
website: www.qualitycottages.co.uk

TENBY. Quality Cottages.
Around the magnificent Welsh Coast. Away from the madding crowd. Near safe sandy beaches. A small specialist agency offering privacy, peace and unashamed luxury. First Wales Tourist Board Self Catering Gold Award Winner. Residential standards - Dishwashers, Microwaves, Washing Machines, Central Heating, Log Fires, No Slot Meters. Linen provided. Pets welcome free. All in coastal areas famed for scenery, walks, wild flowers, birds, badgers and foxes. Free colour brochure **S.C. Rees, "Quality Cottages", Cerbid, Solva, Haverfordwest, Pembrokeshire SA62 6YE (01348 837871).**
website: www.qualitycottages.co.uk

When making enquiries please mention FHG GUIDES

Free or reduced rate entry to Holiday Visits and Attractions – see our READERS' OFFER VOUCHERS on pages 7-40

SELF CATERING Whitland   PEMBROKESHIRE/POWYS **251**

A country estate of over 450 acres, including 2 miles of riverbank. See a real farm in action, the hustle and bustle of harvest, newborn calves and lambs. Choose from 6 character stone cottages, lovingly converted traditional farm buildings, some over 200 years old.

Farm holidays at Gwarmacwydd

Each cottage is fully furnished and equipped, electricity and linen included, with all year round heating. Children welcome. Brochure available. Contact: **Mrs Angela Colledge, Llanfallteg, Whitland, Pembrokeshire SA34 0XH. SELF CATERING ★★★★ COTTAGES**
t 01437 563 260 f 01437 563 839 w www.gwarmacwydd.co.uk

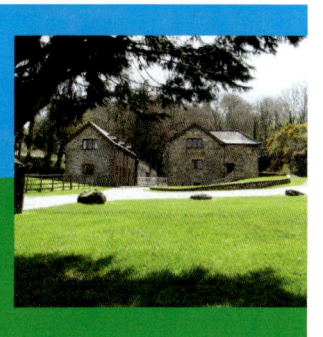

Powys

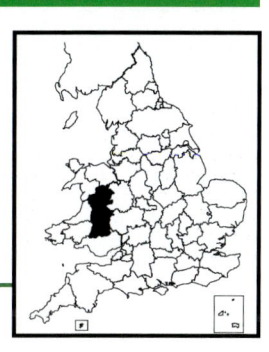

Hay-on-Wye, Newtown

TROWLEY FARMHOUSE. Detached farmhouse in unspoilt location on 400-acre working farm. Views of Black Mountains and Brecon Beacons. Oak beams, stone walls and large farmhouse kitchen retain much of the 16th century character, with every modern convenience to make your stay comfortable.
- Sleeps up to 14 - three twin and two family rooms.
- All fuel and linen (except towels) incl. Home-cooked meal service.
- Ample parking, garden with barbecue.
- A warm welcome for you and your pets.

www.trowleyfarmhouse.co.uk
WTB ★★★★

Mrs R. Lewis, LLanbedr Hall, Painscastle, Builth Wells, Powys LD2 3JH
01497 851665 • e-mail: ruth@trowleyfarmhouse.co.uk

Highgate Holiday Cottages are situated 3 miles from Newtown, a charming market town on the Welsh Borders. There are six beautifully appointed, newly converted, luxury self-catering barn cottages, three sleeping 8 and three sleeping 6. Set in a traditional old farmyard setting with trout pool and beautiful gardens.
• All have underfloor heating throughout and are decorated, furnished and equipped to a very high standard • Bed linen and towels provided • Barbecue and furniture • Ample parking
• 20 acres of private pastureland with woodland and wildlife pool.
Contact: Chris & Sarah Smith, Highgate, Near Newtown SY16 3LF
Tel: 01686 623763 • Fax: 01686 629194
e-mail: highgatehouse@hotmail.com
www.highgate-accommodation.co.uk

Short Breaks available

WALES
Caravans & Camping
Anglesey & Gwynedd

Porthmadog

Modern, comfortable 2-bedroom caravan, with own enclosure and garden on farm. Spacious lounge; microwave, fridge etc. Stay amid the finest coastal and wildlife countryside of North Wales - set in the Snowdonia National Park yet near the sea. Magnificent views of Criccieth Castle and Cardigan Bay. Ideal for walking, cycling or just relaxing. Near village. SAE or telephone for details.

Tyddyn Deucwm Isaf
Penmorfa
Porthmadog LL49 9SD

Mrs E. A. J. Williams
Tel: 01766 513683

Ireland
Co. Clare

Ballyvaughan

Ballyvaughan **Village and Country Holiday Homes** offer a range of quality self-catering holiday accommodation in the unspoilt and charming village of Ballyvaughan on the southern shores of Galway Bay in the heartland of the world famous Burren district of County Clare. You can choose from our four-star cottages, which sleep up to six, or one of our apartments, which sleep up to three. All our village accommodation is located in the centre of the village with a good choice of restaurants and pubs. Our location is an ideal base to explore the unique Burren landscape or tour the west coast of Ireland. All our accommodation is available all year and is very suitable for off-season bookings.
Visit our comprehensive website for more details. Terms from €299 to €799.
Mr George Quinn, Frances Street, Kilrush, Co.Clare • 00353 659 051977
e-mail: vchh@iol.ie • www.ballyvaughan-cottages.com

COUNTRY INNS   BEDFORDSHIRE/CHESHIRE 253

Country Inns

Bedfordshire

Leighton Buzzard

THE Globe INN

Globe Lane, Stoke Road, Old Linslade,
Leighton Buzzard, Bedfordshire LU7 7TA

★ Canal-side location with access over own bridge.
★ Beer garden with outdoor eating facilities
★ Bar/Lounge open all day, every day
★ Children welcome ★ Children's play area
★ Dining area with non-smoking section
★ Excellent choice of food served 12 noon to 9pm daily
★ Cask Marque Accredited 2005
★ Booking Highly Recommended

Tel: 01525 373338 • Fax: 01525 850551

Cheshire

Congleton

The Plough at Eaton

Macclesfield Road, Eaton,
Near Congleton, Cheshire CW12 2NH
Tel: 01260 280207 • Fax: 01260 298377
e-mail: theploughinn@hotmail.co.uk • www.plough-eaton.co.uk

RAC
Guest
Accommodation
◆◆◆◆

*T*raditional oak beams and blazing log fires in winter reflect the warm and friendly atmosphere of this half-timbered former coaching inn which dates from the 17th century. The heart of the 'Plough' is the kitchen where food skilfully prepared is calculated to satisfy the most discerning palate. Luncheons and dinners are served seven days a week with traditional roasts on Sundays. In peaceful, rolling countryside near the Cheshire/Staffordshire border, this is a tranquil place in which to stay and the hostelry has elegantly colour-co-ordinated guest rooms, all with spacious bathrooms, LCD colour television, direct-dial telephone and tea and coffee-making facilities amongst their impressive appointments. Wireless internet access available.

Cornwall

Liskeard

COLLIFORD TAVERN
Colliford Lake, Near St Neot, Liskeard, Cornwall PL14 6PZ • Tel: 01208 821335
e-mail: info@colliford.com • www.colliford.com

Set in attractive grounds which include a children's play area, ponds and a working waterwheel, this delightfully furnished free house offers good food and bar snacks. Sprucely-appointed guest rooms are spacious and have en suite shower, colour television, radio alarm, beverage maker and numerous thoughtful extras. An unusual feature of the tavern is a 37' deep granite well. In the midst of the scenic splendour of Bodmin Moor, this is a relaxing country retreat only a few minutes' walk from Colliford Lake, so popular with fly fishermen. Both north and south coasts are within easy driving distance and terms are most reasonable.

Cumbria

Brampton, Carlisle

The Blacksmiths Arms
Talkin Village, Brampton, Cumbria CA8 1LE
Tel: 016977 3452 • Fax: 016977 3396
e-mail: blacksmithsarmstalkin@yahoo.co.uk
www.blacksmithstalkin.co.uk

The Blacksmith's Arms offers all the hospitality and comforts of a traditional country inn. Enjoy tasty meals served in the bar lounges, or linger over dinner in the well-appointed restaurant. The inn is personally managed by the proprietors, Anne and Donald Jackson, who guarantee the hospitality one would expect from a family concern. Guests are assured of a pleasant and comfortable stay. There are eight lovely bedrooms, all en suite. Peacefully situated in the beautiful village of Talkin, the inn is convenient for the Borders, Hadrian's Wall and the Lake District. There is a good golf course, walking and other country pursuits nearby.

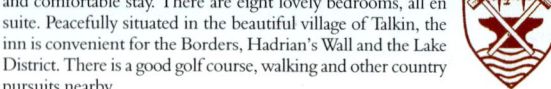

GRAHAM ARMS HOTEL
Longtown, Near Carlisle, Cumbria CA6 5SE

A warm welcome awaits at this 180-year-old former Coaching Inn. Situated six miles from the M6 (J44) and Gretna Green, The Graham Arms makes an ideal overnight stop or perfect touring base for the Scottish Borders, English Lakes, Hadrian's Wall and much more. 16 comfortable en suite bedrooms, including four-poster and family rooms with TV, radio etc. Meals and snacks served throughout the day. Friendly 'local's bar' and new 'Sports bar' serving real ale, extra cold lagers, cocktails and a fine selection of malt whiskies. Secure courtyard parking for cars, cycles and motorcycles. Beautiful woodland and riverside walks!
Visit our website on www.grahamarms.com • Tel: 01228 791213 • Fax: 01228 794110
Email: office@grahamarms.com • Website: www.grahamarms.com
Bed and full traditional breakfast £32–£36. Special rates for weekend and midweek breaks. RAC ★★

COUNTRY INNS   CUMBRIA/GLOUCESTERSHIRE/SHROPSHIRE 255

Ennerdale Bridge

With an informal and relaxed atmosphere on one of the most attractive stretches of Wainwright's Coast to Coast footpath, this splendid small hotel presents first-rate food and accommodation. Several real ales are served and there is an extensive bar menu including daily 'specials'. Traditional comforts are very much in evidence and bedrooms have central heating, digital colour television, direct-dial telephone and tea and coffee-makers. Although one of the smaller lakes, Ennerdale can fairly claim to be the most beautiful. From here, valley paths, forest tracks and lake shores offer a variety of rewarding walks suitable for all ages and capabilities. Other activities available include fishing, canoeing, bird watching and pony trekking.

Shepherd's Arms Hotel
Ennerdale Bridge, Lake District National Park CA23 3AR
Tel: 01946 861249
e-mail: shepherdsarms@btconnect.com
website: www.shepherdsarmshotel.co.uk

Gloucestershire

Lydney

THE FOUNTAIN INN & LODGE
Parkend, Royal Forest of Dean, Gloucestershire GL15 4JD.

Traditional village inn, well known locally for its excellent meals and real ales. A Forest Fayre menu offers such delicious main courses as Lamb Steak In Woodland Berry Sauce and Gloucester Sausage in Onion Gravy, together with a large selection of curries, vegetarian dishes, and other daily specials. Centrally situated in one of England's foremost wooded areas, the inn makes an ideal base for sightseeing, or for exploring some of the many peaceful forest walks nearby.
All bedrooms (including one specially adapted for the less able) are en suite, decorated and furnished to an excellent standard, and have television and tea/coffee making facilities. Various half-board breaks are available throughout the year.

Tel: 01594 562189 • Fax: 01594 564438 • e-mail: thefountaininn@aol.com • www.thefountaininnandlodge.com

Shropshire

Ludlow

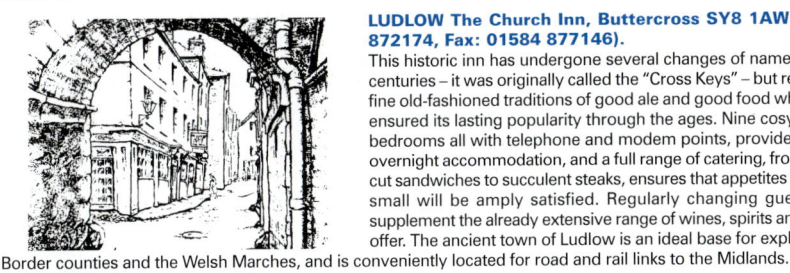

LUDLOW The Church Inn, Buttercross SY8 1AW (01584 872174, Fax: 01584 877146).
This historic inn has undergone several changes of name over the centuries – it was originally called the "Cross Keys" – but retains the fine old-fashioned traditions of good ale and good food which have ensured its lasting popularity through the ages. Nine cosy en suite bedrooms all with telephone and modem points, provide first-rate overnight accommodation, and a full range of catering, from freshly cut sandwiches to succulent steaks, ensures that appetites large and small will be amply satisfied. Regularly changing guest beers supplement the already extensive range of wines, spirits and ales on offer. The ancient town of Ludlow is an ideal base for exploring the Border counties and the Welsh Marches, and is conveniently located for road and rail links to the Midlands.
• Children welcome.
ETC/AA/RAC ◆◆◆◆, *CAMRA*.
www.thechurchinn.com

Surrey

Haslemere

The Wheatsheaf Inn
Freehouse • Accommodation • Restaurant
Grayswood Road, Grayswood, Haslemere GU27 2DE
Tel: 01428 644440 • Fax: 01428 641285
e-mail: ken@thewheatsheafgrayswood.co.uk
www.thewheatsheafgrayswood.co.uk

- Situated in the village of Grayswood, one mile north of Haslemere on the A286.
- Close to Goodwood, Guildford, Midhurst and Petworth; fast train services to Portsmouth and London.
- Dine in the newly refurbished conservatory or in the large bar area.
- Comfortable bedrooms, all en suite, with colour TV, telephone and hospitality tray.

AA ★★★ HOTEL

Readers are requested to mention this guidebook when making enquiries about accommodation.

Useful Guidance for Guests and Hosts

Every year literally thousands of holidays, short breaks and overnight stops are arranged through our guides, the vast majority without any problems at all. In a handful of cases, however, difficulties do arise about bookings, which often could have been prevented from the outset.

It is important to remember that when accommodation has been booked, both parties – guests and hosts – have entered into a form of contract. We hope that the following points will provide helpful guidance.

Guests

- When enquiring about accommodation, be as precise as possible. Give exact dates, numbers in your party and the ages of any children.
- State the number and type of rooms wanted and also what catering you require – bed and breakfast, full board etc. Make sure that the position about evening meals is clear – and about pets, reductions for children or any other special points.
- Read our reviews carefully to ensure that the proprietors you are going to contact can supply what you want. Ask for a letter confirming all arrangements, if possible.
- If you have to cancel, do so as soon as possible. Proprietors do have the right to retain deposits and under certain circumstances to charge for cancelled holidays if adequate notice is not given and they cannot re-let the accommodation.

Hosts

- Give details about your facilities and about any special conditions. Explain your deposit system clearly and arrangements for cancellations, charges etc. and whether or not your terms include VAT.
- If for any reason you are unable to fulfil an agreed booking without adequate notice, you may be under an obligation to arrange suitable alternative accommodation or to make some form of compensation.

Family-Friendly Pubs and Inns

Family-Friendly Pubs and Inns

This is a selection of establishments which make an extra effort to cater for parents and children. The majority provide a separate children's menu or they may be willing to serve small portions of main course dishes on request; there are often separate outdoor or indoor play areas where the junior members of the family can let off steam while Mum and Dad unwind over a drink.

For more details, please see individual entries under county headings.

NB: Many other inns, pubs and hotels listed in the main section of the book but not included in this Supplement also welcome children – please see individual entries.

Key

- half portions
- children's menu
- garden or play area
- baby-changing facilities
- high chairs
- family room

THE CROWN HOTEL
16 High Street, Amersham,
Buckinghamshire HP7 0DH
01494 721541
www.dhillonhotels.co.uk

CROWN & PUNCHBOWL
High Street, Horningsea,
Cambridgeshire CB5 9JG
Tel: 01223 860643
www.cambscuisine.com

COACH HOUSE HOTEL
Flint Cross, Newmarket Road, Near
Melbourn Cambridgeshire SG8 7PN
Tel: 01763 208272
www.coachhousehotel.co.uk

THE DOG INN
Wellbank Lane, Over Peover, Near
Knutsford, Cheshire WA16 8UP
Tel: 01625 861421
www.doginn-overpeover.co.uk

COLEDALE INN
Braithwaite, Near Keswick,
Cumbria CA12 5TN
Tel: 017687 78272
www.coledale-inn.co.uk

Family-Friendly Pubs and Inns

- half portions
- children's menu
- garden or play area
- baby-changing facilities
- high chairs
- family room

BROTHERSWATER INN
Patterdale, Penrith,
Cumbria CA11 0NZ
Tel: 017684 82239
www.sykeside.co.uk

NEW INN HOTEL
High Street, Clovelly, Near
Bideford, Devon EX39 5TQ
Tel: 01237 431303
www.clovelly.co.uk

THE HOOPS INN
Horns Cross, Near Clovelly,
Bideford, Devon EX39 5DL
Tel: 01237 451222
www.hoopsinn.co.uk

WHITE HART HOTEL
Fore Street, Okehampton,
Devon EX20 1HD
Tel: 01837 52730/54514
www.thewhitehart-hotel.com

THE BELL HOTEL
The Quay, Sandwich,
Kent CT13 9EF
Tel: 01304 613388
www.bellhotelsandwich.co.uk

ANGEL & ROYAL HOTEL
4-5 High Street, Grantham,
Lincolnshire NG31 6PN
Tel: 01476 565816
www.angelandroyal.co.uk

THE TALLY HO INN
Aswarby, Near Sleaford,
Lincolnshire NG34 8SA
Tel: 01529 455205
www.tally-ho-aswarby.co.uk

Family-Friendly Pubs and Inns

THE OLD RAM INN
Ipswich Road (A140),
Tivetshall St Mary, Norfolk NR15 2DE
Tel: 01379 676794
www.theoldram.com

THE TOM MOGG INN
Station Road, Burtle,
Near Bridgwater, Somerset TA7 8NU
Tel: 01278 722399
www.tommogg.co.uk

THE CROWN HOTEL
Exford, Exmoor National Park,
Somerset TA24 7PP
Tel: 01643 831554/5
www.crownhotelexmoor.co.uk

LORD POULETT ARMS
High Street, Hinton St George,
Somerset TA17 8SE
Tel: 01460 73149
www.lordpoulettarms.com

THE FOUNTAIN INN
1 St Thomas Street, Wells,
Somerset BA5 2UU
Tel: 01749 672317
www.fountaininn.co.uk

THE CROWN AT WELLS
Market Place, Wells,
Somerset BA5 2RP
Tel: 01749 673457
www.crownatwells.co.uk

THE SIX BELLS
The Green, Bardwell, Bury St
Edmunds, Suffolk IP13 1AW
Tel: 01359 250820
www.sixbellsbardwell.co.uk

WORSLEY ARMS HOTEL
Hovingham, North Yorkshire YO62 4LA
Tel: 01653 628234
www.worsleyarms.com

Family-Friendly Pubs and Inns

- half portions
- children's menu
- garden or play area
- baby-changing facilities
- high chairs
- family room

WHITE ROSE HOTEL
Leeming Bar, Northallerton,
North Yorkshire DL7 9AY
Tel: 01677 422707/424941
www.whiterosehotel.co.uk

WHITE SWAN INN
Market Place, Pickering, North
Yorkshire YO18 7AA
Tel: 01751 472288
www.white-swan.co.uk

MURRAY ARMS HOTEL
Gatehouse of Fleet, Castle Douglas,
Kirkcudbrightshire DG7 2HY
Tel: 01557 814207
www.murrayarmshotel.co.uk

LAIRD & DOG HOTEL
5 High Street, Lasswade, Near
Edinburgh, Midlothian EH18 1NA
Tel: 0131 663 9219
www.lairdanddog.btinternet.co.uk

OAK TREE INN
Balmaha, Loch Lomond, G63 0JQ
Tel: 01360 870357
www.oak-tree-inn.co.uk

WATERHOUSE INN
The Square, Balloch Road,
Balloch G83 8LE
Tel: 01389 752120
www.waterhouseinn.co.uk

THE BELLACHROY
Dervaig, Isle of Mull PA75 6QW
Tel: 01688 400314
www.thebellachroy.co.uk

Family-Friendly Pubs and Inns 261

HUNTER'S MOON INN
Llangattock Lingoed, Near
Abergavenny, NP7 8RR
Tel: 01873 821499
www.hunters-moon-inn.co.uk

KING ARTHUR HOTEL
Higher Green, Reynoldston,
Swansea, South Wales SA31 1AD
Tel: 01792 390775
www.kingarthurhotel.co.uk

Readers are requested to mention this guidebook when making enquiries about accommodation.

Looking for Holiday Accommodation?

FHG
K·U·P·E·R·A·R·D

for details of hundreds of properties throughout the UK visit our website on

www.holidayguides.com

Pet-Friendly Pubs and Inns

Please note that these establishments may not feature in the man section of this book

ENGLAND

BERKSHIRE

The Greyhound Eton Wick, Berkshire SL4 6JE
A picturesque pub with plenty of walks close by. Food served daily.
Tully the Shepherd and Harvey the Retriever are the resident pets.
Sunday lunch only £5.95 between 12 noon - 3pm
Tel: 01753 863925 • www.thegreyhoundetonwick.co.uk

UNCLE TOM'S CABIN
Hills Lane, Cookham Dean, Berkshire (01628 483339).
Dogs allowed throughout.
Pet Regulars: Flossie and Ollie (Old English Sheepdog). Free dog biscuit pub.

THE GREYHOUND (known locally as 'The Dog')
The Walk, Eton Wick, Berkshire (01753 863925).
Dogs allowed throughout the pub.
Pet Regulars: Harvey (Retriever), retrieves anything, including Beer mats. Tully - German Shepherd.

THE OLD BOOT
Stanford Bingley, Berkshire (01189 744292).
Pets welcome in bar area.
Pet Regulars: Resident dog Skip - Black Labrador.

THE TWO BREWERS
Park Street, Windsor, Berkshire (01753 855426).
Dogs allowed, public and saloon bars.
Pet Regulars: Molly (Newfoundland), Bear (Black Labrador), Rufus (Springer Spaniel), Mr Darcy (Poodle), Rosie (Chocolate Labrador), Lilly (English Bulldog), Molly (Fox Terrier), McIntosh (Highland Terrier) and Lulu & Paddy (Cocker Spaniels).

Publisher's note

While every effort is made to ensure accuracy, we regret that FHG Guides cannot accept responsibility for errors, misrepresentations or omissions in our entries or any consequences thereof. Prices in particular should be checked.
We will follow up complaints but cannot act as arbiters
or agents for either party.

Pet-Friendly Pubs and Inns

BUCKINGHAMSHIRE

WHITE HORSE
Village Lane, Hedgerley, Buckinghamshire SL2 3UY (01753 643225).
Dogs allowed at tables on pub frontage, beer garden (on leads), public bar.

FROG AT SKIRMETT
Skirmett, Henley-on-Thames, Buckinghamshire RG9 6TG (01491 638996)
Dogs welcome, pet friendly.

GEORGE AND DRAGON
High Street, West Wycombe, Buckinghamshire HP14 3AB (01494 464414)
Pet friendly.

CAMBRIDGESHIRE

YE OLD WHITE HART
Main Street, Ufford, Peterborough, Cambridgeshire (01780 740250).
Dogs allowed in non-food areas.

CHESHIRE

THE GROSVENOR ARMS
Chester Road, Aldford, Cheshire CH3 6HJ (01244 620228)
Pet friendly.
Pet Regulars: resident dog "Sadie" (Labrador).

CORNWALL

DRIFTWOOD SPARS HOTEL
Trevaunance Cove, St Agnes, Cornwall (01872 552428).
Dogs allowed everywhere except the restaurant.
Pet Regulars: Buster (Cornish Labrador cross with a Seal) - devours anything.

JUBILEE INN
Pelynt, Near Looe, Cornwall PL13 2JZ (01503 220312).
Dogs allowed in all areas except restaurant; accommodation for guests with dogs.

THE MILL HOUSE INN
Trebarwith Strand, Tintagel, Cornwall PL34 0HD (01840 770200).
Pet friendly.

THE MOLESWORTH ARMS HOTEL
Molesworth Street, Wadebridge, Cornwall PL27 7DP (01208 812055).
Dogs allowed in all public areas and in hotel rooms.
Pet Regulars: Thomson Cassidy (Black Lab), Ruby Cassidy and Lola (Black Lab).

Visit the FHG website
www.holidayguides.com
for details of the wide choice of accommodation
featured in the full range of FHG titles

Pet-Friendly Pubs and Inns

The Snooty Fox Kirkby Lonsdale
The Snooty Fox is a newly refurbished Jacobean Inn, offering 9 en suite rooms, award-winning restaurant and lounge bar. Situated in the heart of the market town of Kirkby Lonsdale and boasting fine cask ales and log fires, The Snooty Fox is the perfect base from which to explore both the Lake District and Yorkshire Dales.
Tel: 01524 271308 • www.thesnootyfoxhotel.co.uk
AA/RAC/ETC ★★

CUMBRIA

THE BRITANNIA INN
Elterwater, Ambleside, Cumbria LA22 9HP (015394 37210).
Dogs allowed in all areas except dining room and residents' lounge.
Pet Friendly.

THE MORTAL MAN HOTEL
Troutbeck, Windermere, Cumbria LA23 IPL (015394 33193).
Pets allowed everywhere except restaurant.

STAG INN
Dufton, Appleby, Cumbria (017683 51608).
Dogs allowed in non-food bar, beer garden, village green plus cottage.
Pet Regulars: Sofie (Labrador) and Jeanie (Terrier).

WATERMILL INN
School Lane, Ings, Near Staveley, Kendal, Cumbria (01539 821309).
Dogs allowed in beer garden, Wrynose bottom bar.
Pet Regulars: Blot (sheepdog), Finn (mongrel) and Pub dog Shelley (German Shepherd). Owners cannot walk dogs past pub, without being dragged in! Biscuits and water provided.

DERBYSHIRE

THE GEORGE HOTEL
Commercial Road, Tideswell, Near Buxton, Derbyshire SK17 8NU (01298 871382).
Dogs allowed in snug and around the bar, water bowls provided.

DOG AND PARTRIDGE COUNTRY INN & MOTEL
Swinscoe, Ashbourne, Derbyshire (01335 343183).
Dogs allowed throughout, except restaurant.
Pet Regulars: Include Mitsy (57); Rusty (Cairn); Spider (Collie/GSD) and Rex (GSD).

DEVONSHIRE ARMS
Peak Forest, Near Buxton, Derbyshire SK17 8EJ (01298 23875)
Pet friendly.

FHG Guides
publish a large range of well-known accommodation guides. We will be happy to send you details or you can use the order form at the back of this book.

FHG
K·U·P·E·R·A·R·D

Pet-Friendly Pubs and Inns

DEVON

THE SHIP INN
Axmouth, Devon EX12 4AF (01297 21838).
A predominantly catering pub, so dogs on a lead please.
Pet Regulars: Kym (Boxer), Soxy (cat). Also 2 Japanese Quail, 2 Cockatiels and 2 Kaki Riki (New Zealand Lovebirds).

BRENDON HOUSE
Brendon, Lynton, North Devon EX35 6PS (01598 741206).
Dogs very welcome and allowed in tea gardens, guest bedrooms by arrangement.
Owner's dogs - Drummer, Piper and Angus (Labradors).

THE BULLERS ARMS
Chagford, Newton Abbot, Devon (01647 432348).
Dogs allowed throughout pub, except dining room/kitchen. "More than welcome".

CROWN AND SCEPTRE
2 Petitor Road, Torquay, Devon TQ1 4QA (01803 328290).
Dogs allowed in non-food bar, family room, lounge. All dogs welcome.
Pet Regulars: Two Jack Russells - Scrappy Doo and Minnie Mouse.

THE JOURNEY'S END INN
Ringmore, Near Kingsbridge, South Devon TQ7 4HL (01548 810205).
Dogs allowed throughout the pub.

PALK ARMS INN
Hennock, Bovey Tracey, Devon TQ13 9QS (01626 836584).
Pets welcome.

THE ROYAL OAK INN
Dunsford, Near Exeter, Devon EX6 7DA (01647 252256).
Dogs allowed in bars, beer garden, accommodation for guests with dogs.
Pet Regulars: Kizi. Resident Dogs - Connie and Posie.

THE POLSHAM ARMS
Lower Polsham Road, Paignton, Devon (01803 558360).
Dogs allowed throughout the pub.
Pet Regulars: Patch, owner brings his supply of dog biscuits, and Bracken (German Shepherd).

THE SEA TROUT INN
Staverton, Near Totnes, Devon TQ9 6PA (01803 762274).
Dogs welcome in lounge and public bar, beer garden, owners' rooms (but not on beds).
Pet Regulars: Buster (resident dog) partial to Guiness.

Julie and Shaun invite you to **The Trout & Tipple**
Dogs welcome, bowls of water and treats available on request. Children welcome.
Non-smoking dining room and games room. Real Ales include locally brewed Jail Ale and Dartmoor Best. Lunch on Sunday.
Parkwood Road, Tavistock, Devon PL19 0JS
Tel: 01822 618886   www.troutandtipple.co.uk

Pet-Friendly Pubs and Inns

THE DEVONSHIRE INN
Sticklepath, Okehampton, Devon EX20 2NW (01837 840626).
Dogs allowed in non-food bar, car park, beer garden, family room and guest rooms.
Pet Regulars: Clarrie and Rosie (Terriers).

THE TROUT & TIPPLE
(A386 - Tavistock to Okehampton Road), Parkwood Road, Tavistock, Devon PL10 0JS (01822 618886)
Dogs welcome at all times in bar, games room and patio.
Pet regulars include: Connor and Fenrhys (Black Labradors) - sometimes misbehave. Casey (Bronze Springer) - always after food. Border, Chaos and Mischief (Border Collies), Snoopy (Rhodesian Ridgeback) likes his beef dinners. Also, our own dog - Dave (Lurcher).

DORSET

THE ANVIL HOTEL
Sailsbury Road, Pimperne, Blandford, Dorset DT11 8UQ (01258 453431).
Pets allowed in bar, lounge and bedrooms.

THE SQUARE AND COMPASS
Swanage, Dorset BH19 3LF (01929 439229).
Well-behaved dogs allowed - but beware of the chickens!

DRUSILLA'S INN
Wigbeth, Horton, Dorset (01258 840297).
Well-behaved dogs welcome.

DURHAM

MOORCOCK INN
Hill Top, Eggleston, Teesdale, County Durham DL12 9AU (01833 650395).
Pet Regulars: Thor, the in-house hound dog, and Raymond, the resident hack, welcome all equine travellers; Gem (Jack Russell); Arnie (Ginger Tom); Poppy (Jack Russell); Haflinger - the horse.

TAP AND SPILE
27 Front Street, Framwellgate Moor, Durham DH1 5EE (0191 386 5451).
Dogs allowed throughout the pub.

THE ROSE TREE
Low Road West, Shincliff, Durham DH1 2LY (0191-386 8512).
Pets allowed in bar area and garden.
Pet Regulars: "Benson" (Boxer), "Ben" (Miniature White Poodle) and "Oliver" (King Charles).

THE SEVEN STARS
High Street North, Shincliff, Durham (0191-384 8454).
Dogs welcome in bar area only.

Readers are requested to mention this FHG publication when seeking accommodation

Pet-Friendly Pubs and Inns

ESSEX

WHITE HARTE
The Quay, Burnham-on-Crouch, Essex CM0 8AS (01621 782106).
Pets welcome.
Pet Regulars: Resident dog "Tilly" (Collie).

THE OLD SHIP
Heybridge Basin, Heybridge, Maldon, Essex (01621 854150).
Dogs allowed downstairs only, on lead.

GLOUCESTERSHIRE

THE OLD STOCKS HOTEL
The Square, Stow on the Wold, Gloucestershire GL54 1AF (01451 830666).
Dogs allowed in the beer garden, accommodation for dogs and their owners also available.
Pet Regulars: Ben (Labrador) enjoys bitter from the drip trays and Casey (Doberman) often gets carried out as he refuses to leave.

GREATER LONDON

THE PHOENIX
28 Thames Street, Sunbury on Thames, Middlesex (01932 785358).
Dogs allowed on lead in beer garden, family room. Capability 2 Grading.
Pet Regulars: Sammy (Black Labrador).

THE TIDE END COTTAGE
Ferry Road, Teddington, Middlesex (0208 977 7762).
Dogs allowed throughout the pub, except dining area.
Pet Regulars: Mimi (Labrador), Toffee (Terrier), Gracie (Guide Dog) and Fiona.

Other specialised holiday guides from FHG

Recommended **INNS & PUBS** OF BRITAIN

Recommended **COUNTRY HOTELS** OF BRITAIN

Recommended **SHORT BREAK HOLIDAYS** IN BRITAIN

The bestselling and original **PETS WELCOME!**

The **GOLF GUIDE,** Where to Play, Where to Stay IN BRITAIN & IRELAND

COAST & COUNTRY HOLIDAYS

SELF-CATERING HOLIDAYS IN BRITAIN

BED & BREAKFAST STOPS

CARAVAN & CAMPING HOLIDAYS

CHILDREN WELCOME! Family Holiday & Days Out Guide

BRITAIN'S BEST LEISURE & RELAXATION GUIDE

Published annually: available in all good bookshops or direct from the publisher:
FHG Guides, Abbey Mill Business Centre, Seedhill, Paisley PA1 1TJ
Tel: 0141 887 0428 • Fax: 0141 889 7204
• E-mail: admin@fhguides.co.uk • Web: www.holidayguides.com

Pet-Friendly Pubs and Inns

HAMPSHIRE

The Victory Inn, High Street, Hamble SO31 4HA
Tel: 02380 453105

Grade II Listed family pub. Enjoy a fine and inexpensive meal or simply enjoy a drink. All food is home-made - à la carte menu and chef's specials. There are no strangers at The Victory, just friends you have yet to meet. Budgie, Viv and Debs all the staff welcome you to Hampshire's Finest. Pet Regular - Chester (Boxer)

THE SUN
Sun Hill, Bentworth, Alton, Hampshire GU34 5JT (01420 562338)
Pets welcome throughout the pub.
Pet Regulars: Willow (Collie), Hazel and Purdey (Jack Russells) and "Dilweed" the cat.

HIGH CORNER INN
Linwood, Near Ringwood, Hampshire BH24 3QY (01425 473973).
Dogs, and even horses, are catered for here.

THE CHEQUERS
Ridgeway Lane, Lower Pennington, Lymington, Hants (01590 673415).
Dogs allowed in non-food bar, outdoor barbecue area (away from food).
Pet Regulars: Rusty Boyd - parties held for him. Resident pet - D'for (Labrador).

THE VICTORY
High Street, Hamble-le-Rice, Southampton, Hampshire (023 80 453105).
Dogs allowed.
Pet Regulars: Chester (Boxer).

HERTFORDSHIRE

THE BLACK HORSE
Chorley Wood Common, Dog Kennel Lane, Rickmansworth, Herts (01923 282252).
Dogs very welcome and allowed throughout the pub, on a lead.

THE RED LION
Chenies Village, Rickmansworth, Hertfordshire WD3 6ED (01923 282722).
Pets welcome in bar area only.
Pet Regulars: Resident dog Bobby (Collie mixture), Paddy and Mollie (Boxers).

THE ROBIN HOOD AND LITTLE JOHN
Rabley Heath, near Codicote, Hertfordshire (01438 812361).
Dogs allowed in non-food bar, car park tables, beer garden.
Pet Regulars: Pongo (Dalmation) and Eailey (Labrador). The locals of the pub have close to 50 dogs between them, most of which visit from time to time. The team includes a two Labrador search squad dispatched by one regular's wife to indicate time's up. When they arrive he has five minutes' drinking up time before all three leave together.

**FREE or REDUCED RATE entry to Holiday Visits and Attractions –
see our READERS' OFFER VOUCHERS on pages 37-52**

Pet-Friendly Pubs and Inns

KENT

KENTISH HORSE
Cow Lane, Mark Beech, Edenbridge, Kent (01342 850493).
Dogs allowed in reserved area on lead, outside included.

THE SWANN INN
Little Chart, Kent TN27 0QB (01233 840702).
Dogs allowed - everywhere except restaurant.

LANCASHIRE

Assheton Arms
Downham, Clitheroe
BB7 4BJ
01200 441227
e-mail: asshetonarms@aol.com
www.assheton-arms.co.uk

Popular but unspoilt pub in traditional village with stone cottages. Good walks. Food served Mon-Sat 12pm-2pm, Sun 12pm-2.30pm and 7pm-10pm. *Children and dogs welcome. Disabled access.*

MALT'N HOPS
50 Friday Street, Chorley, Lancashire PR6 0AH (01257 260967).
Dogs allowed throughout pub if kept under control.

LINCOLNSHIRE

THE BLUE DOG INN
Main Street, Sewstern, Grantham, Lincs NG33 5QR (01476 860097).
Dogs allowed.
Pet Regulars: Cassie (Scottie) shares biscuits with Beth (pub cat); Nelson (Terrier), Diesel (Springer Spaniel) and Ted (Spaniel).

Note

All the information in this guide is given in good faith in the belief that it is correct. However, the publishers cannot guarantee the facts given in these pages, neither are they responsible for changes in ownership or facilities that may take place after the date of going to press.
Readers should always satisfy themselves that the facilities they require are available and that the terms, if quoted, still apply.

Pet-Friendly Pubs and Inns

MERSEYSIDE

THE SCOTCH PIPER
Southport Road, Lydiate, Merseyside (0151 526 0503).
Dogs allowed throughout the pub.

NORFOLK

THE OLD RAILWAY TAVERN
Eccles Road, Quidenham, Norwich, Norfolk NR16 2JG (01953 888223).
Dogs allowed, must be on lead.
Pet Regulars: Pub dogs Flo (German Shepherd) and Benji (Jack Russell).

THE HOSTE ARMS
The Green, Burnham Market, King's Lynn, Norfolk PE31 8HD (01328 738777).
Dogs allowed throughout the pub, except restaurant.
Pet Regulars: "Augustus" and "Sweep" (Black Labradors).

THE ROSE AND CROWN
Nethergate Street, Harpley, King's Lynn, Norfolk (01485 520577).
Well behaved dogs welcome.

OXFORDSHIRE

THE BELL
Shenington, Banbury, Oxfordshire OX15 6NQ (01295 670274).
Pets allowed throughout.
Pet Regulars: Resident pub dogs "Oliver" (Great Dane) and "Daisy" (Labrador).

THE PLOUGH INN
High Street, Finstock, Chipping Norton, Oxfordshire (01993 868333).
Dogs more than welcome.
Pet Regulars: Zac (Sheepdog), Strumpet and Trollop (Labradors).

THE BELL INN
High Street, Adderbury, Oxon (01295 810338).
Dogs allowed throughout the pub.
Owner's dogs: Murphy and Dizzy (Lancashire Heelers) and Rika (Rottweiler).

SHROPSHIRE

THE TRAVELLERS REST INN
Church Stretton, Shropshire (01694 781275).
Well-mannered pets welcome - but beware of the cats!

LONGMYND HOTEL
Cunnery Road, Church Stretton, Shropshire SY6 6AG (01694 722244).
Dogs allowed in owners' hotel bedrooms but not in public areas.
Pet Regulars: Bruno and Frenzie; and owner's dogs, Sam and Sailor.

FHG Guides

publish a large range of well-known accommodation guides.
We will be happy to send you details or you can use the order form at the back of this book.

Pet-Friendly Pubs and Inns

SOMERSET

CASTLE OF COMFORT HOTEL
Dodington, Nether Stowey, Bridgwater, Somerset TA5 1LE (01278 741264).
Pet friendly.

THE SPARKFORD INN
High Street, Sparkford, Somerset BA22 7JN (01963 440218).
Dogs allowed in bar areas but not in restaurant; safe garden and car park.

THE BUTCHERS ARMS
Carhampton, Somerset (01643 821333).
Dogs allowed in bar. B&B accommodation available.

HOOD ARMS
Kilve, Somerset TA5 1EA (01278 741210)
Pets welcome.

THE SHIP INN
High Street, Porlock, Somerset (01643 862507).
Dogs allowed throughout and in guests' rooms.
Pet Regulars: Include Silver (Jack Russell); Sam (Black Lab) and Max (Staffordshire). Resident Pets include Brit (Spaniel) and Holly (Belgian Shepherd).

STAFFORDSHIRE

The Hollybush Inn
Denford Road, Denford, Leek, Staffordshire ST13 7JT

Dating back to the 17th century, this former corn mill is a favourite with people cruising the Caldon Canal. Features include quarry-tiled floors, open fires, copper and brass ornaments, and old oak beams. Open all day, the Inn has a good selection of beers, wines, ales and other refreshments. Food is also available seven days a week, all dishes prepared in the inn's own kitchens, using fresh, locally sourced produce whenever possible.

The Inn works hard to make sure that all its customers feel welcome, including its four-legged friends.

Tel: 01538 371819

Looking for holiday accommodation?
for details of hundreds of properties throughout the UK visit:

www.holidayguides.com

Pet-Friendly Pubs and Inns

SUFFOLK

The Ickworth Hotel, Horringer, Bury St Edmunds IP29 5QE
Tel: 01284 735350 • Fax: 01284 736300
e-mail: ickworth@ickworthhotel.com • www.luxuryfamilyhotels.com

"Overall Winner of Winalot Approved Dog Friendly Award"

Warm and welcoming hotel with more than a dash of style and much comfort situated in the rolling green acres of Ickworth parkland. Elegant, individually styled bedrooms and stunning apartments. Delicious food in Frederick's Restaurant or the less formal Cafe Inferno. Dogs welcome - specific dietary requirements catered for; doggy massage available.

THE KINGS HEAD
High Street, Southwold, Suffolk IP18 6AD (01502 724517).
Well-behaved dogs welcome.

SIX BELLS AT BARDWELL
The Green, Bardwell, Bury St Edmunds, Suffolk IP31 1AW (01359 250820).
Dogs allowed in guest bedrooms by arrnagement but not allowed in bar and restaurant.

SURREY

THE PLOUGH
South Road, Woking, Surrey GU21 4JL (01483 714105).
Pets welcome in restricted areas.

THE SPORTSMAN
Mogador Road, Mogador, Surrey (01737 246655).
Adopted dogs congregate at this pub.
Pet Regulars: Meesha (Border Collie) and Max (German Shepherd).

THE CRICKETERS
12 Oxenden Road, Tongham, Farnham, Surrey (01252 333262).
Dogs allowed in beer garden on lead.

SUSSEX

THE FORESTERS ARMS
High Street, Fairwarp, Near Uckfield, East Sussex TN22 3BP (01825 712808).
Dogs allowed in the beer garden and at car park tables, also inside.
Dog biscuits always available.

THE PLOUGH
Crowhurst, Near Battle, East Sussex TN33 9AY (01424 830310).
Dogs allowed in non-food bar, car park tables, beer garden.

QUEENS HEAD
Village Green, Sedlescombe, East Sussex (01424 870228).
Dogs allowed throughout the pub.

Pet-Friendly Pubs and Inns

THE SLOOP INN
Freshfield Lock, Haywards Heath, West Sussex RH17 7NP (01444 831219).

Dogs allowed in public bar and garden.
THE SPORTSMAN'S ARMS
Rackham Road, Amberley, Near Arundel, West Sussex BN18 9NR (01798 831787).
Dogs allowed in the bar area.

WILTSHIRE

THE HORSE AND GROOM
The Street, Charlton, Near Malmesbury, Wiltshire (01666 823904).
Dogs welcome in bar.
Pet Regulars: Troy and Gio (Labradors).

THE PETERBOROUGH ARMS
Dauntsey Lock, Near Chippenham, Wiltshire SN15 4HD (01249 890409).
All pets welcome in bar.
Resident pets - Poppy, Holly, Lilly and Dotty (4 generations of Jack Russell).

THE THREE HORSESHOES
High Street, Chapmanslade, Near Westbury, Wiltshire (01373 832280).
Dogs allowed in non-food bar and beer garden.
Three horses overlooking the beer garden.

YORKSHIRE

BARNES WALLIS INN
North Howden, Howden, East Yorkshire (01430 430639).
Guide dogs only

KINGS HEAD INN
Barmby on the Marsh, East Yorkshire DN14 7HL (01757 630705).
Dogs allowed in non-food bar.
Pet Regulars: Many and varied!

THE FORESTERS ARMS
Kilburn, North Yorkshire YO6 4AH (01347 868386).
Dogs allowed throughout, except restaurant.
Pet Regulars: Ainsley (Black Labrador).

NEW INN HOTEL
Clapham, Near Settle, North Yorkshire LA2 8HH (015242 51203).
Dogs allowed in bar, beer garden, bedrooms.

SIMONSTONE HALL
Hawes, North Yorkshire DL8 3LY (01969 667255).
Dogs allowed except dining area.
Dogs of all shapes, sizes and breeds welcome.
-*
THE SPINNEY
Forest Rise, Balby, Doncaster, South Yorkshire DN4 9HQ (01302 852033).
Dogs allowed throughout the pub.
Pet Regulars: Wyn (Labrador) a guide dog and Buster (Staff). Resident dog Paddy (Irish Setter).

Pet-Friendly Pubs and Inns

THE ROCKINGHAM ARMS
8 Main Street, Wentworth, Rotherham, South Yorkshire S62 7LO (01226 742075).
Pets welcome.
Pet Regulars: Sheeba (Springer Spaniel), Charlie and Gypsy (Black Labradors), Sally (Alsatian) and Rosie (Jack Russell).

THE GOLDEN FLEECE
Lindley Road, Blackley, near Huddersfield, West Yorkshire (01422 372704).
Guide Dogs only.

WALES

ANGLESEY & GWYNEDD

THE GRAPES HOTEL
Maentwrog, Blaenau Ffestiniog, Gwynedd LL41 4HN (01766 590365).
Pets allowed in bar area only.

THE BUCKLEY HOTEL
Castle Street, Beaumaris, Isle of Anglesey LL58 8AW (01248 810415).
Dogs allowed throughout the pub, except in the dining room and bistro.
Pet Regulars: Cassie (Springer Spaniel) and Rex (mongrel), dedicated 'companion' dogs, also Charlie (Spaniel).

NORTH WALES

THE WEST ARMS HOTEL
Llanarmon Dyffryn Ceiriog, Llangollen, North Wales LL20 7LD (01691 600665).
Welcome pets.

PEMBROKESHIRE

THE FARMERS
14-16 Goat Street, St David's, Pembrokeshire (01437 721666).
Pets welcome in the pub area.

POWYS

SEVERN ARMS HOTEL
Penybont, Llandrindod Wells, Powys LD1 5UA (01597 851224).
Dogs allowed in the bar, but not the restaurant, and in the rooms - but not on the beds.

Please note
All the information in this book is given in good faith in the belief that it is correct. However, the publishers cannot guarantee the facts given in these pages, neither are they responsible for changes in policy, ownership or terms that may take place after the date of going to press. Readers should always satisfy themselves that the facilities they require are available and that the terms, if quoted, still apply.

Pet-Friendly Pubs and Inns

SCOTLAND

ABERDEEN, BANFF & MORAY

THE CLIFTON BAR
Clifton Road, Lossiemouth, Moray (01343 812100).
Dogs allowed in beer garden only.

ROYAL OAK
Station Road, Urquhart, Elgin, Moray (01343 842607).
Dogs allowed throughout pub.
Pet Regulars: Jack (Collie).

ARGYLL & BUTE

CAIRNDOW STAGECOACH INN
Cairndow, Argyll PA26 8BN (01499 600286).
Pets welcome.

THE BALLACHULISH HOTEL
Ballachulish, Argyll PA39 4JY (01855 811606).
Dogs allowed in the lounge and guests' bedrooms, excluding food areas.

EDINBURGH & LOTHIANS

JOHNSBURN HOUSE
Johnsburn Road, Balerno, Lothians EH14 7BB (0131-449 3847).
Pets welcome in bar area only.
Pet Regulars: Resident dog "Topaz" (Great Dane).

LAIRD & DOG
Lasswade, Midlothian (0131-663 9219).
Dogs allowed in bar.
Pet Regulars: Fleetwood (cat). Many pet regulars. Drinking bowls.

PERTH & KINROSS

FOUR SEASONS HOTEL
St Fillans, Perthshire (01764 685333).
Dogs allowed in all non-food areas.

THE MUNRO INN
Main Street, Strathyre, Perthshire FK18 8NA (01877 384333).
Dogs allowed throughout pub, lounge, games room, beer garden and bedrooms (except restaurant).
Pet Regulars: Residents Jess (black mongrel with brown eyes) and Jules (white lurcher with blue eyes). Bring your dog to visit! Water and dog biscuits always available.

Readers are requested to mention this FHG guidebook when seeking accommodation

Looking for Holiday Accommodation?

for details of hundreds of properties throughout the UK visit our website

www.holidayguides.com

DIRECTORY OF WEBSITE AND E-MAIL ADDRESSES

A quick-reference guide to holiday accommodation with an e-mail address and/or website, conveniently arranged by country and county, with full contact details.

Holiday Parks/Touring & Camping
Cinque Ports Leisure
- website: www.cplholidays.com

•LONDON

B & B
Sohel & Anne Armanios, 67 Rannoch Road, Hammersmith, LONDON W6 9SS
Tel: 020 7385 4904
- website: www.thewaytostay.co.uk

Hotel
Athena Hotel, 110-114 Sussex Gardens, Hyde Park, LONDON W2 1UA
Tel: 020 7706 3866
- e-mail: athena@stavrouhotels.co.uk
- website: www.stavrouhotels.co.uk

Hotel
Barry House Hotel, 12 Sussex Place, Hyde Park, LONDON W2 2TP Tel: 0207 723 7340
- e-mail: hotel@barryhouse.co.uk
- website: www.barryhouse.co.uk

Hotel
Elizabeth Hotel, 37 Eccleston Square, LONDON SW1V 1PB Tel: 020 7828 6812
- e-mail: info@elizabethhotel.com
- website: www.elizabethhotel.com

Hotel
The Elysee Hotel, 25-26 Craven Terrace, LONDON W2 3EL Tel: 020 7402 7633
- e-mail: information@hotelelysee.co.uk
- website: www.hotelelysee.co.uk

Hotel
Gower Hotel, 129 Sussex Gardens, Hyde Park, LONDON W2 2RX
Tel: 020 7262 2262
- e-mail: gower@stavrouhotels.co.uk
- website: www.stavrouhotels.co.uk

www.holidayguides.com

Hotel
Lincoln House Hotel, 33 Gloucester Place, Marble Arch, LONDON W1V 8HY
Tel: 0207 486 7630
- e-mail: reservations@lincoln-house-hotel.co.uk
- website: www.lincoln-house-hotel.co.uk

B & B
Manor Court Hotel, 7 Clanricarde Gardens, LONDON W2 4JJ Tel: 020 7792 3361 or 020 7727 5407
- e-mail: enquiries@manorcourthotel.com
- website: www.abc-london.com
          www.123europe-londonhotels.com

Hotel
Queens Hotel, 33 Anson Road, Tufnell Park, LONDON N7 Tel: 020 7607 4725
- e-mail: queens@stavrouhotels.co.uk
- website: www.stavrouhotels.co.uk

•BEDFORDSHIRE

Self-Catering
Bluegate Farm Holiday Cottages
Bluegate Farm, Stanbridge, LEIGHTON BUZZARD, Beds LU7 9JD
Tel: 01525 210621
- e-mail: enquiries@bluegatecottages.co.uk
- website: www.bluegatecottages.co.uk

Farmhouse / B & B / Self-Catering Cottages
Mrs M. Codd, Highfield Farm, Tempsford Road, SANDY, Beds SG19 2AQ
Tel: 01767 682332
- e-mail: margaret@highfield-farm.co.uk
- website: www.highfield-farm.co.uk

•BERKSHIRE

Inn
Julie Plastow, The Greyhound, 16 Common Road, ETON WICK, Berkshire SL4 6JE
Tel: 01753 863 925
- e-mail: thegreyhoundpub@hotmail.com
- website: thegreyhoundetonwick.co.uk

WEBSITE DIRECTORY

Hotel
Clarence Hotel, 9 Clarence Road, WINDSOR, Berkshire SL4 5AE
Tel: 01753 864436
- e-mail: enquiries@clarence-hotel.co.uk
- website: www.clarence-hotel.co.uk

•BUCKINGHAMSHIRE

B & B / Self-Catering Cottages
Poletrees Farm, Ludgershall Road, Brill, AYLESBURY, Buckinghamshire HP18 9TZ
Tel: 01844 238276
- e-mail: poletrees.farm@virgin.net
- web: www.countryaccom.co.uk/poletrees-farm

•CAMBRIDGESHIRE

B & B
Hilary & Brian Marsh, The Meadow House
2A High Street, BURWELL, Cambridgeshir CB5 0HB Tel: 01638 741 926
- e-mail: hilary@themeadowhouse.co.uk
- website: www.themeadowhouse.co.uk

Guest House
Dykelands Guest House, 157 Mowbray Road, CAMBRIDGE, Cambridgeshire CB1 7SP
Tel: 01223 244300
- website: www.dykelands.com

Self-Catering
Mrs J. Farndale, Cathedral House, 17 St Mary's Street, ELY, Cambridgeshire CB7 4ER
Tel: 01352 662124
- e-mail: farndale@cathedralhouse.co.uk
- website: www.cathedralhouse.co.uk

B & B
Chequer Cottage, 43 Streetly End, HORSEHEATH, Cambridgeshire CB1 6RP
Tel: 01223 891 522
- e-mail: stay@chequercottage.com
- website: www.chequercottage.com

•CHESHIRE

Guest House / Self-Catering
Mrs Joanne Hollins, Balterley Green Farm, Deans Lane, BALTERLEY, near Crewe Cheshire CW2 5QJ Tel: 01270 820 214
- e-mail: greenfarm@balterley.fsnet.co.uk
- website: www.greenfarm.freeserve.co.uk

Guest House
Mitchell's of Chester, 28 Hough Green, CHESTER, Cheshire CH4 8JQ
Tel: 01244 679 004
- e-mail: mitoches@dialstart.net
- website: www.mitchellsofchester.com

Guest House / Self-Catering
Mrs Angela Smith, Mill House and Granary, Higher Wych, MALPAS, Cheshire SY14 7JR
Tel: 01948 780362
- e-mail: angela@videoactive.co.uk
- website: www.millhouseandgranary.co.uk

Farm House / B & B
Jean Callwood, Lea Farm, Wrinehill Road, Wybunbury, NANTWICH, Cheshire CW5 7NS. Tel: 01270 841429
- e-mail: contactus@leafarm.freeserve.co.uk
- website: www.leafarm.co.uk

•CORNWALL

Self-catering
Graham Wright, Guardian House, Barras Street, Liskeard, Cornwall PL14 6AD
Tel: 01579 344080

Self-Catering
Cornish Traditional Cottages, Blisland, BODMIN, Cornwall PL30 4HS
Tel: 01208 821666
- e-mail: info@corncott.com
- website: www.corncott.com

Self-Catering
Mrs Angela Clark, Darrynane Cottages, Darrynane, St Breward, BODMIN, Cornwall PL30 4LZ. Tel: 01208 850885
- e-mail: enquiries@darrynane.co.uk
- website: www.darrynane.com

Self-Catering
Penrose Burden Holiday Cottages, St Breward, BODMIN, Cornwall PL30 4LZ
Tel: 01208 850277 or 01208 850617
- website: www.penroseburden.co.uk

Self-Catering
Trevella, Treveighan, St Teath, BODMIN, Cornwall PL30 3JN
Tel: 01208 850 529
- e-mail: david.trevella@btconnect.com
- website: www.trevellacornwall.co.uk

Readers are requested to mention this FHG guidebook when seeking accommodation

WEBSITE DIRECTORY 279

Touring Caravan & Camping Park
Budemeadows Touring Park, BUDE,
Cornwall EX23 0NA Tel: 01288 361646
- e-mail: holiday@budemeadows.com
- website: www.budemeadows.com

Self-Catering
Langfield Manor, Broadclose, BUDE,
Cornwall EX23 8DP Tel: 01288 352 415
- e-mail: info@langfieldmanor.co.uk
- website: www.langfieldmanor.co.uk

Guest House
Stratton Gardens, Cot Hill, Stratton, BUDE,
Cornwall EX23 9DN Tel: 01288 352500
- e-mail: moira@stratton-gardens.co.uk
- website: www.stratton-gardens.co.uk

Farm
Mrs Margaret Short, Langaton Farm,
Whitstone, Holsworthy, BUDE, Cornwall
EX22 6TS Tel: 01288 341 215
- e-mail: langatonfarm@hotmail.com
- website: www.langaton-farm-holidays.co.uk

Self-Catering Cottage
Lower Kitleigh Cottage, Week St Mary, near
BUDE, Cornwall
Contact: Mr & Mrs T. Bruce-Dick, 114 Albert
Street, London NW1 7NE
Tel: 0207 485 8976
- e-mail: timbrucedick@yahoo.co.uk
- website: www.tbdarchitects.co.uk

Hotel
Wringford Down Hotel, Hat Lane,
CAWSAND, Cornwall PL10 1LE
Tel: 01752 822287
- e-mail: a.molloy@virgin.net
- website: www.cornwallholidays.co.uk

Self-Catering
Mineshop Holiday Cottages,
CRACKINGTON HAVEN, Bude,
Cornwall EX23 0NR Tel: 01840 230338
- e-mail: info@mineshop.co.uk
- website: www.mineshop.co.uk

Self-Catering
Delamere Holiday Bungalows, DELABOLE,
Cornwall
Contact: Mrs J. Snowden Tel: 01895 234144
- website: www.delamerebungalows.com

Self-Catering
Cornish Holiday Cottages, Killibrae, West
Bay, Maenporth, FALMOUTH, Cornwall
TR11 5HP Tel: 01326 250 339
- e-mail: info@cornishholidaycottages.net
- website: www.cornishholidaycottages.net

Self-Catering
Mr M. Watson, Creekside Holiday Cottages,
Strangwith House, Restronguet,
FALMOUTH, Cornwall TR11 5ST
Tel: 01326 375972
- e-mail: martin@creeksidecottages.co.uk
- website: www.creeksidecottages.co.uk

Self-Catering
Colin Kemp, Pantiles,
6 Stracey Road, FALMOUTH,
Cornwall TR11 4DW Tel: 01326 211838
- e-mail: colinkemp@lineone.net
- website: www.falmouthapartments.co.uk

Hotel
Rosemullion Hotel, Gyllyngvase Hill,
FALMOUTH, Cornwall TR11 4DF
Tel: 01326 314 690
- e-mail: gail@rosemullionhotel.demon.co.uk
- www.SmoothHound.co.uk/hotels/rosemullion.

Self-Catering
Mrs K Terry, "Shasta", Carwinion Road,
Mawnan Smith, FALMOUTH, Cornwall
TR11 5JD Tel: 01326 250775
- e-mail: katerry@btopenworld.com
- website: www.cornwallonline.com

Guest House
Jenny Lake, Wickham Guest House,
21 Gyllyngvase Terrace, FALMOUTH,
Cornwall TR11 4DL Tel: 01326 311140
- e-mail: enquiries@wickhamhotel.freeserve.co.uk
- website: www.wickham-hotel.co.uk

Self-Catering
Mrs Furniss, Lancrow Farm, near FOWEY,
Cornwall PL24 2SA Tel: 01726 814 263
- e-mail: sarahfurniss@aol.com
- website: www.foweyvacations.com

Self-Catering
Mrs S. Trewhella, Mudgeon Vean Farm,
St Martin, HELSTON Cornwall TR12 6DB
Tel: 01326 231341
- e-mail: mudgeonvean@aol.com
- website: www.cornwall-online.co.uk/mudgeon-vean/ctb.html

Self-Catering
Mrs W.J. Morris, Bossava Cottage,
LAMORNA, Penzance, Cornwall TR19 6XG
Tel: 01736 732 420
- e-mail: junekernow@aol.com
- website: www.lamornaholidays.com

Hotel / Lodges
Trethorne Golf Club, Kennards House,
LAUNCESTON, Cornwall PL15 8QE
Tel: 01566 86903
- e-mail: jon@trethornegolfclub.com
- website: www.trethornegolfclub.com

WEBSITE DIRECTORY

Self-Catering Cottages
Swallows & Meadow Cottage, Lower Dutson Farm, LAUNCESTON, Cornwall PL15 9SP Tel: 01566 776456
- e-mail: francis.broad@farm-cottage.co.uk
- website: www.farm-cottage.co.uk

Self-Catering
Celia Hutchinson,
Caradon Country Cottages, East Taphouse, LISKEARD, Cornwall PL14 4NH
Tel: 01579 320255
- e-mail: celia@caradoncottages.co.uk
- website: www.caradoncottages.co.uk

Self-Catering
Mr Lowman, Cutkive Wood Holiday Lodges, St Ive, LISKEARD, Cornwall PL14 3ND
Tel: 01579 362216
- e-mail: holidays@cutkivewood.co.uk
- website: www.cutkivewood.co.uk

Holiday Home Caravans / Tents & Touring
Mullion Holiday Park, Near Helston, LIZARD, Cornwall TR12 7LT Tel: 0870 444 0080
- e-mail: bookings@weststarholidays.co.uk
- website: www.weststarholidays.co.uk

Caravan Park
Looe Bay Holiday Park, LOOE, Cornwall PL13 1NX Tel: 0870 444 0080
- e-mail: bookings@weststarholidays.co.uk
- website: www.weststarholidays.co.uk

Self-Catering
Mr P. Brumpton, Talehay Holiday Cottages, Pelynt, Near LOOE, Cornwall PL13 2LT
Tel: 01503 220252
- e-mail: paul@talehay.co.uk
- website: www.talehay.co.uk

Self-Catering
Tremaine Green Country Cottages, Tremaine Green, Pelynt, Near LOOE, Cornwall PL13 2LT. Tel: 01503 220333
- e-mail: stay@tremainegreen.co.uk
- website: www.tremainegreen.co.uk

Self-Catering
Mr & Mrs Holder, Valleybrook Holidays, Peakswater, Lansallos, LOOE, Cornwall PL13 2QE Tel: 01503 220493
- e-mail: admin@valleybrookholidays.co.uk
- website: www.valleybrookholidays.co.uk

Self-Catering Cottages
Wringworthy Cottages, LOOE, Cornwall PL13 1PR Tel: 01503 240 685
- e-mail: pets@wringworthy.co.uk
- website: www.wringworthy.co.uk

Self-Catering
St Anthony Holidays, St Anthony, MANACCAN, Helston, Cornwall TR12 6JW
Tel: 01326 231357
- e-mail: info@stanthony.co.uk
- website: www.stanthony.co.uk

Hotel
Blue Bay Hotel, Trenance, MAWGAN PORTH, Cornwall TR8 4DA
Tel: 01637 860324
- e-mail: hotel@bluebaycornwall.co.uk
- website: www.bluebaycornwall.co.uk

B & B
Mrs Dawn Rundle, Lancallan Farm, MEVAGISSEY, St Austell, Cornwall PL26 6EW Tel: 01726 842 284
- e-mail: dawn@lancallan.fsnet.co.uk
- website: www.lancallanfarm.co.uk

B & B
Mr & Mrs M. Limer, Alicia, 136 Henver Road, NEWQUAY, Cornwall TR7 3EQ
Tel: 01637 874328
- e-mail: aliciaguesthouse@mlimer.fsnet.co.uk
- website: www.alicia-guesthouse.co.uk

Guest House
Pensalda Guest House, 98 Henver Road, NEWQUAY, Cornwall TR7 3BL
Tel: 01637 874 601
- e-mail: karen_pensalda@yahoo.co.uk±
- website: www.pensalda-guesthouse.co.uk

Hotel
St George's Hotel, 71 Mount Wise, NEWQUAY, Cornwall TR7 2BP
Tel: 01637 873010
- e-mail: enquiries@stgeorgeshotel.free-online.co.uk
- website: www.st-georges-newquay.co.uk

Caravan & Camping / Self-Catering
Quarryfield Caravan & Camping Park, Crantock, NEWQUAY, Cornwall
Contact: Mrs A. Winn, Tretherras, Newquay, Cornwall TR7 2RE
Tel: 01637 872 792
- website: www.quarryfield.co.uk

Hotel
Tregea Hotel, 16-18 High Street, PADSTOW, Cornwall PL28 8BB Tel: 01841 532 455
- e-mail: info@tregea.co.uk
- website: www.tregea.co.uk

B & B
Mrs Owen, Penalva Private Hotel, Alexandra Road, PENZANCE, Cornwall TR18 4LZ
Tel: 01736 369 060
- website: www.penalva.co.uk

WEBSITE DIRECTORY   281

Holiday Park
Perran Sands Holiday Park, PERRANPORTH, Cornwall TR6 0AQ Tel: 01872 573742
- website: www.touringholidays.co.uk

Hotel / Inn
Cornish Arms, Pendoggett, PORT ISAAC, Cornwall PL30 3HH Tel: 01208 880263
- e-mail: info@cornisharms.com
- website: www.cornisharms.com

Guest House
Mrs E. Neal, Tamarind, 12 Shrubberies Hill, PORTHLEVEN, Cornwall TR13 9EA Tel: 01326 574303
- e-mail: lizzybenzimra@hotmail.com
- www.web-direct.co.uk/porthleven/tamarind.html

Hotel
Rosevine Hotel, Porthcurnick Beach, PORTSCATHO, Near St Mawes, Cornwall TR2 5EW Tel: 01872 580206
- e-mail: info@rosevine.co.uk
- website: www.rosevine.co.uk

Caravan & Camping
Globe Vale Holiday Park, Radnor, REDRUTH, Cornwall TR16 4BH Tel: 01209 891183
- e-mail: info@globevale.co.uk
- website: www.globevale.co.uk

Hotel
Penventon Park Hotel, West End, REDRUTH, Cornwall TR15 1TE Tel: 01209 20 3000
- e-mail: enquiries@penventon.com
- website: www.penventon.com

Caravan & Camping
Wheal Rose Caravan & Camping Park, Scorrier, REDRUTH, Cornwall TR16 5DD Tel: 01209 891496
- e-mail: whealrose@aol.com
- website: www.whealrosecaravanpark.co.uk

Guest House
Mrs Merchant, Woodpeckers, RILLA MILL, Callington, Cornwall PL17 7NT Tel: 01579 363717
- e-mail: alison.merchant@virgin.net
- website: www.woodpeckersguesthouse.co.uk

Hotel
The Beacon Country House Hotel, Goonvrea Road, ST AGNES, Cornwall TR5 0NW Tel:01872 552 318
- e-mail: info@beaconhotel.co.uk
- website: www.beaconhotel.co.uk

Caravan & Camping / Holiday Park
Chiverton Park, Blackwater, ST AGNES, Cornwall TR4 8HS Tel: 01872 560667
- e-mail: info@chivertonpark.co.uk
- website: www.chivertonpark.co.uk

Hotel / Inn
Driftwood Spars Hotel, Trevaunance Cove, ST AGNES, Cornwall TR5 0RT Tel: 01872 552428/553323
- website: www.driftwoodspars.com

Hotel / B & B
Penkerris, Penwinnick Road, ST AGNES, Cornwall TR5 0PA Tel: 01872 552262
- e-mail: info@penkerris.co.uk
- website: www.penkerris.co.uk

Guest House
Mr Gardener, The Elms, 14 Penwinnick Road, ST AUSTELL, Cornwall PL25 5DW Tel: 01726 74981
- website: www.edenbb.co.uk

Farmhouse
Mrs Diana Clemes, Tregilgas Farm, Gorran, ST AUSTELL, Cornwall PL26 6ND Tel: 01726 842342
- e-mail: dclemes88@aol.com

Self-Catering
Big-Picture Holiday Apartments, ST IVES, Cornwall Tel: 07803 129918
- e-mail: sarah@bigpictureholidays.co.uk
- website: www.bigpictureholidays.co.uk

Self-Catering
R.G. Pontefract, The Links Holiday Flats, Church Lane, Lelant, ST IVES, Cornwall TR26 3HY Tel: 01736 753326
- e-mail: jackpontefract@aol.com

Guest House
Angela & Barrie Walker, Rivendell, 7 Porthminster Terrace, ST IVES, Cornwall TR26 2DQ Tel: 01736 794923
- e-mail: rivendellstives@aol.com
- website: www.rivendell-stives.co.uk

Self-Catering
Sandbank Holidays, ST IVES BAY, Hayle, St Ives, Cornwall TR27 5BL Tel: 01736 752594
- website: www.sandbank-holidays.co.uk

Self-Catering
Mr & Mrs C.W. Pestell, Hockadays, Tregenna, Near Blisland, ST TUDY, Cornwall PL30 4QJ Tel: 01208 850146
- e-mail: holidays@hockadaysholidaycottages.co.uk
- website: www.hockadaysholidaycottages.co.uk

Self-Catering
Mrs R. Reeves, Polstraul, Trewalder, Delabole, ST TUDY, Cornwall PL33 9ET Tel: 01840 213 120
- e-mail: aandr.reeves@virgin.net
- website: www.maymear.co.uk

Self-Catering
Mrs Susan Tanzer, Trewithian Farm,
ST WENN, Bodmin, Cornwall PL30 5PH
Tel: 01208 895 181
- e-mail: trewithian@hotmail.co.uk
- www.cornwall-online.co.uk/trewithianfarm

Self-Catering
Mrs Sandy Wilson, Salutations, Atlantic
Road, TINTAGEL, Cornwall PL34 0DE
Tel: 01840 770287
- e-mail: sandyanddave@tinyworld.co.uk
- website: www.salutationstintagel.co.uk

Touring Caravan Park
Summer Valley Touring Park, Shortlanesend,
TRURO, Cornwall TR4 9DW
Tel: 01872 277878
- e-mail: res@summervalley.co.uk
- website: www.summervalley.co.uk

Farm / B & B / Self-Catering Cottages
Mrs P. Carbis. Trenona Farm Holidays, Ruan
High Lanes, TRURO, Cornwall TR2 5JS
Tel: 01872 501339
- e-mail: info@trenonafarmholidays.co.uk
- website: www.trenonafarmholidays.co.uk

Farm
Pengelly Farmhouse, Pengelly Farm,
Burlawn, WADEBRIDGE, Cornwall PL27 7LA
Tel: 01208 814 217
- e-mail: hodgepete@hotmail.com
- website: www.pengellyfarm.co.uk

•CUMBRIA

Inn
The Britannia Inn, Elterwater, AMBLESIDE,
Cumbria LA22 9HP Tel: 015394 37210
- e-mail: info@britinn.co.uk
- website: www.britinn.co.uk

Hotel
Crow How Country House, Rydal Road,
AMBLESIDE, Cumbria LA22 9PN
Tel: 015394 32193
- e-mail: stay@crowhowcountryhouse.co.uk
- website: www.crowhowcountryhouse.co.uk

Caravan Park
Greenhowe Caravan Park, Great Langdale,
AMBLESIDE, Cumbria LA22 9JU
Tel: 015394 37231
- e-mail: enquiries@greenhowe.com
- website: www.greenhowe.com

Hotel / Guest House
Ian & Helen Burt, The Old Vicarage,
Vicarage Road, AMBLESIDE, Cumbria
LA22 9DH. Tel: 015394 33364
- e-mail: info@oldvicarageambleside.co.uk
- website: www.oldvicarageambleside.co.uk

B & B
Broom House, Long Martin, APPLEBY-IN-
WESTMORLAND, Cumbria CA16 6JP
Tel: 01768 361 318
- website: www.broomhouseappleby.co.uk

Guest House
Barbara & Derick Cotton, Glebe House,
Bolton, APPLEBY-IN-WESTMORLAND,
Cumbria CA16 6AW Tel: 01768 361125
- e-mail: derick.cotton@btinternet.com
- website: www.glebeholidays.co.uk

B & B
Sharon Moore, Annisgarth B & B, 48 Craig
Walk, BOWNESS-ON-WINDERMERE,
Cumbria LA23 2JT Tel: 015394 43866
- website: www.annisgarth.co.uk

Self-Catering
Lakelovers, Belmont House, Lake Road,
BOWNESS-ON-WINDERMERE,
Cumbria LA23 3BJ Tel: 015294 88855
- e-mail: bookings@lakelovers.co.uk
- website: www.lakelovers.co.uk

Self-Catering / Farm
Mrs J. M. Almond, Irton House Farm,
Isel, COCKERMOUTH, Cumbria CA13 9ST
Tel: 017687 76380
- e-mail: almond@farmersweekly.net
- website: www.irtonhousefarm.com

B & B
Mosser Heights, Mosser, COCKERMOUTH,
Cumbria CA13 0SS Tel: 01900 822644
- e-mail: AmandaVickers@aol.com

Guest House
Rose Cottage Guest House, Lorton Road,
COCKERMOUTH, Cumbria CA13 9DX
Tel: 01900 822189
- website: www.rosecottageguest.co.uk

B & B
Birkhow Cottage, ESKDALE, Cumbria
Contact: Sally Tel: 017687 76836
- e-mail: sally@hollinhead.co.uk

Guest House
Mr & Mrs J. D. Bromage, Forest How Guest
House, ESKDALE GREEN, Cumbria CA19 1TR
Tel: 019467 23201
- website: www.foresthow.co.uk

www.holidayguides.com

WEBSITE DIRECTORY *283*

Holiday Park
Lakeland Leisure Park, Moor Lane,
Flookburgh, Near GRANGE-OVER-SANDS,
Cumbria LA11 7LT Tel: 01539 558556
- website: www.touringholidays.co.uk

Farm / Self-Catering
Mr P. Brown, High Dale Park Farm, High Dale
Park, Salterthwaite, Ulverston, GRIZEDALE
FOREST, Cumbria LA12 8LJ
Tel: 01229 860226
- e-mail: peter@lakesweddingmusic.com
- www.lakesweddingmusic.com/accomm

Self-Catering Cottages
Hideaways, The Square, HAWKSHEAD,
Cumbria LA22 0NZ Tel: 015394 42435
- e-mail: bookings@lakeland-hideaways.co.uk
- website: www.lakeland-hideaways.co.uk

Hotel
Ivy House Hotel, Main Street, HAWKSHEAD,
Cumbria LA22 0NS Tel: 015394 36204
- e-mail: ivyhousehotel@btinternet.com
- website: www.ivyhousehotel.com

Self-Catering
Keswick Cottages, 8 Beechcroft,
Braithwaite, KESWICK, Cumbria CA12 5RS
Tel: 017687 78555
- e-mail: info@keswickcottages.co.uk
- website: www.keswickcottages.co.uk

Guest House
Rickerby Grange Guest House, Portinscale,
KESWICK, Cumbria CA12 5RH
Tel: 017687 72344
- e-mail: stay@rickerbygrange.co.uk
- website: www.rickerbygrange.co.uk

Self-Catering
Mrs S.J. Bottom, Crossfield Cottages,
KIRKOSWALD, Penrith, Cumbria CA10 1EU
Tel: 01768 898711
- e-mail: info@crossfieldcottages.co.uk
- website: www.crossfieldcottages.co.uk

Self-Catering
Routen House & Little Paddock,
LAKE DISTRICT, Cumbria
Contact: Mrs J. Green Tel: 01604 626383
- e-mail: joanne@routenhouse.co.uk
- website: www.routenhouse.co.uk

Farm
Esthwaite How Farmhouse, NEAR SAWREY,
Ambleside, Cumbria LA22 0LB
Tel: 01539 436 450
- e-mail: elizabeth@esthwaitehow.co.uk
- website: www.esthwaitehow.co.uk

B & B
Mr Bell, Albany House, 5 Portland Place,
PENRITH, Cumbria CA11 7QN
Tel: 01768 863072
- e-mail: info@albany-house.org.uk
- website: www.albany-house.org.uk

Guest House
Blue Swallow Guest House,
11 Victoria Road, PENRITH, Cumbria
CA11 8HR Tel: 01768 866335
- e-mail: blueswallow@tiscali.co.uk
- website: www.blueswallow.co.uk

Self-Catering
Mr & Mrs Iredale, Carrock Cottages,
Carrock House, Hutton Roof, PENRITH,
Cumbria CA11 0XY Tel: 01768 484111
- e-mail: info@carrockcottages.co.uk
- website: www.carrockcottages.co.uk

Self-Catering
Mark Cowell, Church Court Cottages,
Gamblesby, PENRITH, Cumbria CA10 1HR
Tel: 01768 881682
- e-mail: markcowell@tiscali.co.uk
- website: www.gogamblesby.co.uk

B & B
Greenah Crag, Troutbeck, PENRITH,
Cumbria CA11 0SQ Tel: 017684 83233
- e-mail: greenahcrag@lineone.net
- website: www.greenahcrag.co.uk

Golf Club
Seascale Golf Club, The Banks, SEASCALE,
Cumbria CA20 1QL Tel: 01946 728202
- e-mail: seascalegolfclub@btconnect.com
- website: www.seascalegolfclub.co.uk

Self-Catering / Caravan & Camping
Tanglewood Caravan Park, Causeway Head,
SILLOTH-ON-SOLWAY, Cumbria CA7 4PE
Tel: 016973 31253
- e-mail: tanglewoodcaravanpark@hotmail.com
- website: www.tanglewoodcaravanpark.co.uk

Hotel
Golf Hotel, SILLOTH-ON-SOLWAY,
Cumbria CA7 4AB Tel: 016973 31438
- e-mail: golf.hotel@virgin.net
- website: www.golfhotelsilloth.co.uk

Self-Catering / Caravan
Fell View Holidays, Glenridding,
Penrith, ULLSWATER, Cumbria CA11 0PJ
Tel: 01768 482342; Evening: 01768 867420
- e-mail: enquiries@fellviewholidays.com
- website: www.fellviewholidays.com

WEBSITE DIRECTORY

B & B / Self-Catering
Barbara Murphy, Land Ends Country Lodge, Watermillock, Near Penrith, ULLSWATER, Cumbria CA11 0NB Tel: 01768 486438
• e-mail: infolandends@btinternet.com
• website: www.landends.co.uk

Guest House
Fir Trees Guest House, Lake Road, WINDERMERE, Cumbria LA23 2EQ
Tel: 015394 42272
• e-mail: enquiries@fir-trees.com
• website: www.fir-trees.com

Guest House
Green Gables, 37 Broad Street, WINDERMERE LA23 2AB Tel: 015394 43886
• e-mail: greengables@fsbdial.co.uk
  info@greengablesguesthouse.co.uk

Guest House
Josette & Mark Bayley,
Holly-Wood Guest House, Holly Road, WINDERMERE, Cumbria LA23 2AF
Tel: 015394 42219
• e-mail: info@hollywoodguesthouse.co.uk
• website: www.hollywoodguesthouse.co.uk

Guest House
Meadfoot Guest House, New Road, WINDERMERE, Cumbria LA23 2LA
Tel: 015394 42610
• website: www.meadfoot-guesthouse.co.uk

• DERBYSHIRE

B & B
Compton House, 27- 31 Compton, ASHBOURNE, Derbyshire DE6 1BX
Tel: 01335 343100
• e-mail: enquiries@comptonhouse.co.uk
• website: www.comptonhouse.co.uk

B & B
Mrs M Harris, The Courtyard,
Dairy House Farm, Alkmonton, Longford, ASHBOURNE, Derbyshire DE6 3DG
Tel: 01335 330187
• e-mail: michael@dairyhousefarm.org.uk
• website: www.dairyhousefarm.org.uk

Inn
The Dog & Partridge Country Inn, Swinscoe, ASHBOURNE, Derbyshire DE6 2HS Tel: 01335 343183
• e-mail: info@dogandpartridge.co.uk
• website: www.dogandpartridge.co.uk

B & B
Mrs A.M. Whittle, Stone Cottage,
Green Lane, Clifton, ASHBOURNE, Derbyshire DE6 2BL Tel: 01335 343377
• e-mail: info@stone-cottage.fsnet.co.uk
• website: www.stone-cottage.fsnet.co.uk

B&B
Mrs J. Salisbury, Turlow Bank, Hognaston, ASHBOURNE, Derbyshire DE6 1PW
Tel: 01335 370299
• e-mail: turlowbank@w3z.co.uk
• website: www.turlowbank.co.uk

Self-Catering
P. Skemp, Cotterill Farm,
BIGGIN-BY-HARTINGTON, Buxton, Derbyshire SK17 0DJ Tel: 01298 84447
• e-mail: enquiries@cotterillfarm.co.uk
• website: www.cotterillfarm.co.uk

Hotel
Biggin Hall Hotel, Biggin-by-Hartington, BUXTON, Derbyshire SK17 0DH
Tel: 01298 84451
• e-mail: enquiries@bigginhall.co.uk
• website: www.bigginhall.co.uk

Guest House
Mr & Mrs Hyde, Braemar Guest House,
10 Compton Road, BUXTON,
Derbyshire SK17 9DN Tel: 01298 78050
• e-mail: buxtonbraemar@supanet.com
• website:
www.cressbrook.co.uk/buxton/braemar

Self-Catering
Mrs Gillian Taylor, Priory Lea Holiday Flats, 50 White Knowle Road, BUXTON, Derbyshire SK17 9NH Tel: 01298 23737
• e-mail: priorylea@tiscali.co.uk
• website:
www.cressbrook.co.uk/buxton/priorylea

FHG
K·U·P·E·R·A·R·D

Readers are requested to mention this FHG guidebook when seeking accommodation

WEBSITE DIRECTORY 285

Self-Catering
Mr R. D. Hollands, Wheeldon Trees Farm, Earl Sterndale, BUXTON, Derbyshire SK17 0AA Tel: 01298 83219
- e-mail: hollands@easterndale.fsnet.co.uk
- website: www.wheeldontreesfarm.co.uk

Hotel
Charles Cotton Hotel, Hartington, Near BUXTON, Derbyshire SK17 0AL
Tel: 01298 84229
- e-mail: info@charlescotton.co.uk
- website: www.charlescotton.co.uk

Caravan & Camping Park
Newhaven Caravan & Camping Park, Newhaven, NEAR BUXTON, Derbyshire SK17 0DT Tel: 01298 84300
- website: www.newhavencaravanpark.com

Farm / B & B
Mrs Catherine Dicken, Bonehill Farm, Etwall Road, Mickleover, DERBY, Derbyshire DE3 0DN Tel: 01332 513553
- website: www.bonehillfarm.co.uk

Farm / Self-Catering
J. Gibbs, Wolfscote Grange, HARTINGTON, Near Buxton, Derbyshire SK17 0AX
Tel: 01298 84342
- e-mail: wolfscote@btinternet.com
- website: www.wolfscotegrangecottages.co.uk

Guest House
Ivy House Farm, Stanton-by-Bridge, NEAR MELBOURNE, Derby, Derbyshire DE73 7HT
Tel: 01332 863152
- e-mail: mary@guesthouse.fsbusiness.co.uk
- website: www.ivy-house-farm.com

Self-Catering
Angela Kellie, Shatton Hall Farm, Bamford, Hope Valley, PEAK DISTRICT, Derbyshire S33 0BG Tel: 01433 620635
- e-mail: ahk@peakfarmholidays.co.uk
- website: www.peakfarmholidays.co.uk

• DEVON

Self-Catering
Farm & Cottage Holidays, DEVON
Tel: 01237 479698
- e-mail: enquiries@farmcott.co.uk
- website: www.holidaycottages.co.uk

Self-Catering
Helpful Holidays, Mill Street, Chagford, DEVON TQ13 8AW Tel: 01647 433593
- e-mail: help@helpfulholidays.com
- website: www.helpfulholidays.com

Self-Catering
Toad Hall Cottages, DEVON
Tel: 01548 853089 (24 Hours)
- e-mail: thc@toadhallcottages.com
- website: www.toadhallcottages.com

Self-Catering
Robin & Wren Cottages, ASHBURTON, Devon
Contact: Mrs M. Phipps, Newcott Farm, Poundsgate, Newton Abbot TQ13 7PD
Tel: 01364 631421
- e-mail: enquiries@newcott-farm.co.uk
- website: www.newcott-farm.co.uk

B & B
The Durant Arms, ASHPRINGTON, Totnes, Devon TQ9 7UP Tel: 01803 732240
- e-mail: info@thedurantarms.com
- website: www.thedurantarms.com

Self-Catering
Braddon Cottages, ASHWATER, Beaworthy, Holsworthy, Devon Tel: 01409 211350
- e-mail: holidays@braddoncottages.co.uk
- website: www.braddoncottages.co.uk

B & B / Self-Catering
Mrs S.J. Avis, Lea Hill, Membury, AXMINSTER, Devon EX13 7AQ
Tel: 01404 881881
- e-mail: reception@leahill.co.uk
- website: www.leahill.co.uk

Self-Catering
North Devon Holiday Homes, 19 Cross Street, BARNSTAPLE, Devon EX31 1BD Tel: 01271 376322
- e-mail: info@northdevonholidays.co.uk
- website: www.northdevonholidays.co.uk

Farm / B & B
Jenny Cope, North Down Farm B & B, Pyncombe Lane, Wiveliscombe, BARNSTAPLE, Devon TA4 2BL
Tel: 01984 623730
- e-mail: jennycope@tiscali.co.uk
- website: www.north-down-farm.co.uk

Hotel
Sandy Cove Hotel, Combe Martin Bay, BERRYNARBOR, Devon EX34 9SR
Tel: 01271 882243/882888
- website: www.sandycove-hotel.co.uk

B & B / Self-Catering
Mr & Mrs Lewin, Lake House Cottages and B&B, Lake Villa, BRADWORTHY, Devon EX22 7SQ Tel: 01409 241962
- e-mail: info@lakevilla.co.uk
- website: www.lakevilla.co.uk

WEBSITE DIRECTORY

Caravan & Camping
Berry Barton Caravan Park, BRANSCOMBE, Seaton, Devon EX12 3BD Tel: 01297 680208
• email: berrybarton@amserve.com
• website: www.berrybarton.co.uk

Self-Catering / Organic Farm
Little Comfort Farm Cottages, Little Comfort Farm, BRAUNTON, North Devon EX33 2NJ Tel: 01271 812414
• e-mail: info@littlecomfortfarm.co.uk
• website: www.littlecomfortfarm.co.uk

Self-Catering
Marsdens Cottage Holidays, 2 The Square, BRAUNTON, Devon EX33 2JB Tel: 01271 813777
• e-mail: holidays@marsdens.co.uk
• website: www.marsdens.co.uk

Self-Catering
Devoncourt Holiday Flats, Berryhead Road, BRIXHAM, Devon TQ5 9AB Tel: 01803 853748
• website: www.devoncourt.info

Guest House
Woodlands Guest House, Parkham Road, BRIXHAM, South Devon TQ5 9BU Tel: 01803 852040
• e-mail: woodlandsbrixham@btinternet.com
• website: www.dogfriendlyguesthouse.co.uk
   www.woodlandsdevon.co.uk

Self-Catering / B & B / Caravans
Mrs Gould, Bonehayne Farm, COLYTON, Devon EX24 6SG Tel: 01404 871416/871396
• e-mail: gould@bonehayne.co.uk
• website: www.bonehayne.co.uk

Self-Catering
Watermouth Cove Cottages, Watermouth, Near COMBE MARTIN, Devon EX34 9SJ Tel: 0870 2413168
• e-mail: stay@coastalvalleyhideaways.co.uk
• website: www.coastalvalleyhideaways.co.uk

Holiday Park
Manleigh Holiday Park, Rectory Road, COMBE MARTIN, Devon EX34 0NS Tel: 01271 883353
• e-mail: info@manleighpark.co.uk
• website: www.manleighpark.co.uk

www.holidayguides.com

B & B
Miss Audrey Isaac, Crowborough, Georgeham, Braunton, CROYDE, Devon EX33 1JZ Tel: 01271 891005
• website: www.crowboroughfarm.co.uk

Self-Catering
Mrs S.R. Ridalls, The Old Bakehouse, 7 Broadstone, DARTMOUTH, Devon TQ6 9NR Tel: 01803 834585
• e-mail: ridallsleisure@aol.com
• website: www.oldbakehousedartmouth.co.uk

Self-Catering
Watermill Cottages, Higher North Mill, Hansel, DARTMOUTH, Devon TQ6 0LN Tel: 01803 770219
• e-mail: graham@hanselpg.freeserve.co.uk
• website: www.watermillcottages.co.uk

Farm B & B
Mrs Karen Williams, Stile Farm, Starcross, EXETER, Devon EX6 8PD Tel: 01626 890268
• e-mail: info@stile-farm.co.uk
• website: www.stile-farm.co.uk

Self-Catering
The Independent Traveller, The Bury, Thorverton, EXETER, Devon EX5 5NT Tel: 01392 860 807
• e-mail: help@gowithit.co.uk
• website: www.gowithit.co.uk

Holiday Park
Devon Cliffs Holiday Park, Sandy Bay, EXMOUTH, Devon EX8 5BT Tel: 01395 226226
• website: www.touringholidays.co.uk

Hotel
Devoncourt Hotel, Douglas Avenue, EXMOUTH, Devon EX8 2EX Tel: 01395 272277
• website: www.devoncourt.com

Caravan & Camping
Mrs Megan Daglish, Tamarstone Farm, Bude Road, Pancrasweek, HOLSWORTHY, Devon EX22 7JT Tel: 01288 381734
• e-mail: pets@tamarstone.co.uk
• website: www.tamarstone.co.uk

Hotel / Guest House
St Brannocks House, St Brannocks Road, ILFRACOMBE, Devon EX34 8EQ Tel: 01271 863873
• e-mail: barbara@stbrannockshotel.co.uk
• website: www.stbrannockshotel.co.uk

WEBSITE DIRECTORY

Farm / B & B
Venn Farm, Ugborough, IVYBRIDGE, Devon PL21 0PE Tel: 01364 73240
• e-mail: info@vennfarm.co.uk
• website: www.vennfarm.co.uk

Self-Catering
Beachdown Holiday Bungalows, Beachdown House, Challaborough Bay, KINGSBRIDGE, South Devon
Tel: 01548 810089
• e-mail: enquiries@beachdown.co.uk   or
                petswelcome@beachdown.co.uk
• website: www.beachdown.co.uk

Hotel
Alford House Hotel, Alford Terrace, LYNTON, Devon EX35 6AT
Tel: 01598 752359
• e-mail: enquiries@alfordhouse.co.uk
• website: www.alfordhouse.co.uk

Caravan Park
Pennymoor Caravan Park, MODBURY, Near Ivybridge, Devon PL21 0SB
Tel: 01548 830542 or 01548 830020
• e-mail: enquiries@pennymoor-camping.co.uk
• website: www.pennymoor-camping.co.uk

Guest House
The Smugglers Rest Inn, North Morte Road, MORTEHOE, North Devon EX34 7DR
Tel: 01271 870891
• e-mail: info@smugglersmortehoe.co.uk
• website: www.smugglersmortehoe.co.uk

Farm B & B
Mrs T.M. Merchant, Great Sloncombe Farm, MORETONHAMPSTEAD, Newton Abbot, Devon TQ13 8QF Tel: 01647 440595
• e-mail: hmerchant@sloncombe.freeserve.co.uk
• website: www.greatsloncombefarm.co.uk

Hotel
Riversford Hotel, Limers Lane, NORTHAM, Bideford, Devon EX39 2RG
Tel: 01237 474239
• e-mail: riversford@aol.com
• website: www.riversford.co.uk

Self-Catering
Crab Cottage, NOSS MAYO, South Devon
Tel: 01425 471 372
• website: www.crab-cottage.co.uk

Farm Guest House
Mrs Ann Forth, Fluxton Farm, OTTERY ST MARY, Devon EX11 1RJ
Tel: 01404 812218
• website: www.fluxtonfarm.co.uk

Self-Catering
Mr & Mrs Dillon, Boswell Farm Cottages, Sidford, Near SIDMOUTH, Devon EX10 0PP
Tel: 01395 514162
• e-mail: dillon@boswell-farm.co.uk
• website: www.boswell-farm.co.uk

Caravan & Camping
Harford Bridge Holiday Park, Peter Tavy, TAVISTOCK, Devon PL19 9LS
Tel: 01822 810349
• e-mail: enquiry@harfordbridge.co.uk
• website: www.harfordbridge.co.uk

Farm / B & B
Mary & Roger Steer, Rubbytown Farm, Gulworthy, TAVISTOCK, Devon PL19 8PA
Tel: 01822 832493
• e-mail: jimmy.steer@virgin.net
• website: www.rubbytown-farm.co.uk

Guest House
Mrs Arnold, The Mill, Lower Washfield, TIVERTON, Devon EX16 9PD
Tel: 01884 255297
• e-mail: arnold5@washfield.freeserve.co.uk
• website: www.washfield.freeserve.co.uk

Hotel
Heathcliff House Hotel, 16 Newton Road, TORQUAY, Devon TQ2 5BZ
Tel: 01803 211580
• e-mail: heathcliffhouse@btconnect.com
• website: www.heathcliffhousehotel.co.uk

Hotel
The Aveland Hotel, Babbacombe, TORQUAY, Devon TQ1 3PT Tel: 01803 326622
• e-mail: avelandhotel@aol.com
• website: www.avelandhotel.co.uk

Hotel
Grosvenor House Hotel, Falkland Road, TORQUAY, Devon TQ2 5JP
Tel: 01803 294110
• e-mail: fhg@grosvenorhousehotel.co.uk
• website: www.grosvenorhousehotel.co.uk

Self-Catering
Mrs H. Carr, Sunningdale Apartments, 11 Babbacombe Downs Road, TORQUAY, Devon TQ1 3LF Tel: 01803 325786
• e-mail: allancarr@yahoo.com
• website: www.sunningdaleapartments.co.uk

Readers are requested to mention FHG guides when seeking accommodation

Self-Catering
West Pusehill Farm Cottages,
West Pusehill Farm, Pusehill,
WESTWARD HO!, Devon EX39 5AH
Tel: 01237 475638 or 01237 474622
• e-mail: info@wpfcottages.co.uk
• website: www.wpfcottages.co.uk

Golf Club
Royal North Devon Golf Club, Golf Links
Road, WESTWARD HO!, Devon EX39 1HD
Tel: 01237 473817
• e-mail: info@royalnorthdevongolfclub.co.uk
• website: www.royalnorthdevongolfclub.co.uk

Caravan & Camping
North Morte Farm Caravan & Camping Park,
Mortehoe, WOOLACOMBE, Devon
EX34 7EG. Tel: 01271 870381
• e-mail: info@northmortefarm.co.uk
• website: www.northmortefarm.co.uk

Self-Catering
David Mallet, Dartmoor Country Holidays,
Bedford Bridge, Horrabridge, YELVERTON,
Devon PL20 7RY Tel: 01822 852651
• website: www.dartmoorcountryholidays.co.uk

•DORSET

Self-catering
Dorset Coastal Cottages, The Manor House,
Winfrith Newburgh, Dorchester,
Dorset DT2 8JR Tel: 0800 980 4070
• e-mail: hols@dorsetcoastalcottages.com
• website: www.dorsetcoastalcottages.com

Self-Catering
Dorset Cottage Holidays
Tel: 01929 553443
• e-mail: enq@dhcottages.co.uk
• website: www.dhcottages.co.uk

Inn
The Anvil Inn, Salisbury Road, Pimperne,
BLANDFORD, Dorset DT11 8UQ
Tel: 01258 453431
• e-mail: theanvil.inn@btconnect.com
• website: www.anvilinn.co.uk

Self-Catering
Iona Holiday Flat, 71 Sea Road,
BOURNEMOUTH, Dorset BH5 1BG
Contact: Andrew Hooper
Tel: 01202 460517 or 07967 027025
• e-mail: hoops2@ntlworld.com
• website: www.ionaholidayflat.co.uk

Guest House
Cransley Hotel, 11 Knyveton Road, East
Cliff, BOURNEMOUTH, Dorset BH1 3QG
Tel: 01202 290067
• e-mail: info@cransley.com
• website: www.cransley.com

Hotel
Southbourne Grove Hotel, 96 Southbourne
Road, BOURNEMOUTH, Dorset BH6 3QQ
Tel: 01202 420 503
• e-mail: neil@pack1462.freeserve.co.uk

Hotel
White Topps, 45 Church Road,
Southbourne, BOURNEMOUTH,
Dorset B46 4BB Tel: 01202 428868
• e-mail: thedoghotel@aol.com
• website: www.whitetopps.co.uk

Guest House
Hazel & Keith Ingram, Woodside Hotel,
29 Southern Road, Southbourne,
BOURNEMOUTH, Dorset BH6 3SR
Tel: 01202 427213
• e-mail: enquiries@woodsidehotel.co.uk
• website: www.woodsidehotel.co.uk

Inn
The Fox & Hounds Inn, Duck Street,
CATTISTOCK, Dorchester, Dorset DT2 0JH
Tel: 01300 320 444
• e-mail: info@foxandhoundsinn.com
• website: www.foxandhoundsinn.com

Hotel
The Queens Armes Hotel, The Street,
CHARMOUTH, Dorset DT6 6QF
Tel: 01297 560339
• e-mail: darkduck@btconnect.com
• website: www.queensarmeshotel.co.uk

Looking for holiday accommodation?
for details of hundreds of properties
throughout the UK including
comprehensive coverage of all areas of Scotland try:

www.holidayguides.com

WEBSITE DIRECTORY 289

Golf Club
Parley Court Golf Course Ltd, Parley Green Lane, Hurn, CHRISTCHURCH, Dorset
Tel: 01202 591600
- e-mail: info@parleygolf.co.uk
- website: www.parleygolf.co.uk

Guest House
Church View Guest House, Winterbourne Abbas, DORCHESTER, Dorset DT2 9LS
Tel: 01305 889 296
- e-mail: stay@churchview.co.uk
- website: www.churchview.co.uk

Caravan Park
Giants Head Caravan & Camping Park, Old Sherborne Road, Cerne Abbas, DORCHESTER, Dorset DT2 7TR
Tel: 01300 341242
- e-mail: holidays@giantshead.co.uk
- website: www.giantshead.co.uk

Farm / Self-Catering
Tamarisk Farm, West Bexington, DORCHESTER, Dorset DT2 9DF
Tel: 01308 897784
- e-mail: holidays@tamariskfarm.com
- website: www.tamariskfarm.com

Hotel
Cromwell House Hotel, LULWORTH COVE, Dorset BH20 5RJ
Tel: 01929 400253
- e-mail: catriona@lulworthcove.co.uk
- website: www.lulworthcove.co.uk

Self-Catering
Westover Farm Cottages, Wootton Fitzpaine, Near LYME REGIS, Dorset DT6 6NE
Tel: 01297 560451/561395
- e-mail: wfcottages@aol.com
- website: www.westoverfarmcottages.co.uk

Holiday Park
Rockley Park Holiday Park, Hamworthy, POOLE, Dorset BH15 4LZ
Tel: 01202 679393
- website: www.touringholidays.co.uk

Holiday Park
Sandford Holiday Park, Holton Heath, POOLE, Dorset BH16 6JZ
Tel: 0870 444 0080
- e-mail: bookings@weststarholidays.co.uk
- website: www.weststarholidays.co.uk

Farm / Self-Catering
White Horse Farm, Middlemarsh, SHERBORNE, Dorset DT9 5QN
Tel: 01963 210212
- e-mail: enquiries@whitehorsefarm.co.uk
- website: www.whitehorsefarm.co.uk

Hotel
The Knoll House, STUDLAND BAY, Dorset BH19 3AW Tel: 01929 450450
- e-mail: info@knollhouse.co.uk
- website: www.knollhouse.co.uk

Hotel
The Limes Hotel, 48 Park Road, SWANAGE, Dorset BH19 2AE Tel: 01929 422664
- e-mail: info@limeshotel.net
- website: www.limeshotel.net

B & B
Fairway Bed and Breakfast, 7A Demoulham Road, SWANAGE, Dorset BH19 1NR
Tel: 01929 423 367
- e-mail: rita@ritawaller.plus.com
- website: www.swanagefairway.co.uk

Farm/ Guest House/ Caravan & Camping
Luckford Wood House, East Stoke, WAREHAM, Dorset BH20 6AW
Tel: 01929 463098/07888 719002
- e-mail: info@luckfordleisure.co.uk
- website: www.luckfordleisure.co.uk

Guest House/ Self-Catering
Glenthorne Castle Cove, 15 Old Castle Road, WEYMOUTH, Dorset DT4 8QB
Tel: 01305 777281
- e-mail: info@glenthorne-holidays.co.uk
- website: www.glenthorne-holidays.co.uk

Holiday Park
Littlesea Holiday Park, Lynch Lane, WEYMOUTH, Dorset DT4 9DT
Tel: 01305 774414
- website: www.touringholidays.co.uk

B & B
Mrs Karina Hill, Pebble Villa, Enkworth Road, Preston, WEYMOUTH, Dorset DT3 6JT Tel: 01305 837 469
- e-mail: stay@pebblevilla.co.uk
- website: www.weymouthbedandbreakfast.net

Holiday Park
Seaview & Weymouth Bay Holiday Parks, Preston, WEYMOUTH, Dorset DT3 6D2
Tel: 01305 833037
- website: www.touringholidays.co.uk

FHG Guides

publish a large range of well-known accommodation guides. We will be happy to send you details or you can use the order form at the back of this book.

•DURHAM

Self-Catering Cottages
Low Lands Farm, Lowlands, Cockfield, BISHOP AUCKLAND, Durham DL13 5AW
Tel: 01388 718251
- e-mail: info@farmholidaysuk.com
- website: www.farmholidays.com

Hotel
The Teesdale Hotel, MIDDLETON-IN-TEESDALE, Durham DL12 0QG
Tel: 01833 640264
- e-mail: john@teesdalehotel.co.uk
- website: www.teesdalehotel.co.uk

Farm / Self-Catering Cottage
Frog Hall Cottage, Herdship Farm, Harwood Inn, TEESDALE, Durham DL12 0YB
Tel: 01833 622215
- e-mail: kath.herdship@btinternet.com
- website: www.herdship.co.uk

Hotel
Ivesley Equestrian Centre, Ivesley, WATERHOUSES, Durham DH7 9HB
Tel: 0191 373 4324
- e-mail: ivesley@msn.com
- website: www.ridingholidays-ivesley.co.uk

•ESSEX

B & B / Self-Catering
Mrs B. Lord, Pond House, Earls Hall Farm, CLACTON-ON-SEA, Essex CO16 8BP
Tel: 01255 820458
- e-mail: brenda_lord@farming.co.uk
- website: www.earlshallfarm.info

Farm
Rye Farm, Rye Lane, COLCHESTER, Essex, CO2 0JL Tel: 01206 734 350
- e-mail: peter@buntingp.fsbusiness.co.uk
- website: www.buntingp.fsbusiness.co.uk

•GLOUCESTERSHIRE

Hotel
Chester House Hotel, Victoria Street, BOURTON-ON-THE-WATER, Gloucs GL54 2BU Tel: 01451 820286
- e-mail: info@chesterhousehotel.com
- website: www.chesterhousehotel.com

Farmhouse B & B
Box Hedge Farm B & B, Box Hedge Farm Lane, Coalpit Heath, BRISTOL, Gloucs BS36 2UW Tel: 01454 250786
- e-mail: marilyn@bed-breakfast-bristol.com
- website: www.bed-breakfast-bristol.com

Lodge
Thornbury Golf Centre, Bristol Road, Thornbury, BRISTOL, Gloucs BS35 3XL
Tel: 01454 281144
- e-mail: info@thornburygc.co.uk
- website: www.thornburygc.co.uk

B & B
Mrs C. Hutsby, Holly House, Ebrington, CHIPPING CAMPDEN, Gloucs GL55 6NL
Tel: 01386 593213
- e-mail: hutsbybandb@aol.com
- website: www.hollyhousebandb.co.uk

B & B
Mrs Z.I. Williamson, Kempsford Manor, Kempsford, Near FAIRFORD, Gloucs GL7 4EQ Tel: 01285 810131
- e-mail: ipek@kempsfordmanor.co.uk
- website: www.kempsfordmanor.co.uk

B & B
Anthea & Bill Rhoton, Hyde Crest, Cirencester Road, MINCHINHAMPTON, Gloucs GL6 8PE.
Tel: 01453 731631
- e-mail: anthea@hydecrest.demon.co.uk
- website: www.hydecrest.co.uk

Self-Catering
Richard Drinkwater, Rose's Cottage, The Green, Broadwell, MORETON-IN-MARSH, Gloucs GL56 0UF
Tel: 01451 830007
- e-mail: richard.drinkwater@ukonline.co.uk

Self-Catering
Orion Holidays, Cotswold Water Park, Gateway Centre, Lake 6, Spine Road, SOUTH CERNEY, Gloucs GL7 5TL
Tel: 01285 861839
- e-mail: bookings@orionholidays.com
- website: www.orionholidays.com

B & B
Mrs Wendy Swait, Inschdene, Atcombe Road, SOUTH WOODCHESTER, Stroud, Gloucs GL5 5EW
Tel: 01453 873254
- e-mail: swait@inschdene.co.uk
- website: www.inschdene.co.uk

Farmhouse B & B
Robert Smith, Corsham Field Farmhouse, Bledington Road, STOW-ON-THE-WOLD, Gloucs GL54 1JH. Tel: 01541 831750
- e-mail: farmhouse@corshamfield.co.uk
- website: www.corshamfield.co.uk

www.holidayguides.com

WEBSITE DIRECTORY *291*

B & B
The Limes, Evesham Road, STOW-ON-THE-WOLD, Gloucs GL54 1EN
Tel: 01451 830034 or 01451 831056
• e-mail: thelimes@zoom.co.uk

Farm / Self-Catering
Mrs Anne Meadows, Home Farm, Bredons Norton, TEWKESBURY, Gloucs GL20 7HA
Tel: 01684 772 332
• e-mail: info@meadowshomefarm.co.uk
• website: www.meadowshomefarm.co.uk

Hotel / Golf Club
Tewkesbury Park Hotel, Golf & Country Club, Lincoln Green lane, TEWKESBURY, Gloucs GL20 7DN Tel: 0870 609 6101
• e-mail: tewkesburypark@corushotels.com
• website: www.tewkesburypark.co.uk

•HAMPSHIRE

B & B
Mrs Arnold-Brown, Hilden B&B, Southampton Road, Boldre, BROCKENHURST, Hampshire SO41 8PT Tel: 01590 623682
• website: www.newforestbandb-hilden.co.uk

Campsite
Lower Tye Campsite, Copse Lane, HAYLING ISLAND, Hampshire
Tel: 02392 462479
• e-mail: lowertye@aol.com
• website: www.haylingcampsites.co.uk

Holiday Park
Hayling Island Holiday Park, Manor Road, HAYLING ISLAND, Hampshire PO11 0QS
Tel: 0870 444 0800
• e-mail: bookings@weststarholidays.co.uk
• website: www.weststarholidays.co.uk

B & B
Mrs P. Ellis, Efford Cottage, Everton, LYMINGTON, Hampshire SO41 0JD
Tel: 01590 642315
• e-mail: effordcottage@aol.com
• website: www.effordcottage.co.uk

B & B
Mr & Mrs Farrell, Honeysuckle House, 24 Clinton Road, LYMINGTON, Hampshire SO41 9EA Tel: 01590 676635
• e-mail: skyblue@beeb.net

Hotel
Bramble Hill Hotel, Bramshaw, Near LYNDHURST, New Forest, Hampshire SO43 7JG Tel: 02380 813165
• website: www.bramblehill.co.uk

Hotel
Crown Hotel, High Street, LYNDHURST, Hampshire SO43 7NF Tel: 023 8028 2922
• e-mail: reception@crownhotel-lyndhurst.co.uk
• website: www.crownhotel-lyndhurst.co.uk

Caravans for Hire
Downton Holiday Park, Shorefield Road, MILFORD-ON-SEA, Hampshire SO41 0LH
Tel: 01425 476131/01590 642515
• e-mail: info@downtonholidaypark.co.uk
• website: www.downtonholidaypark.co.uk

Self Catering
Gorse Cottage, Balmer Lawn Road, Brockenhurst, NEW FOREST, Hampshire
Contact: Mr J. Gilbert Tel: 0870 3210020
• e-mail: info@ gorsecottage.co.uk
• website: www.gorsecottage.co.uk

Hotel
Woodlands Lodge Hotel, Bartley Road, Woodlands, NEW FOREST, Southampton Hampshire SO40 7GN Tel: 023 8029 2257
• e-mail: reception@woodlands-lodge.co.uk
• website: www.woodlands-lodge.co.uk

B & B / Guest House
Michael & Maureen Burt, Fraser House, Salisbury Road, Blashford, RINGWOOD (NEW FOREST), Hampshire BH24 3PB
Tel: 01425 473958
• e-mail: mail@fraserhouse.net
• website: www.fraserhouse.net

Guest House
Mrs Thelma Rowe, Tiverton B & B, 9 Cruse Close, SWAY, Hampshire SO41 6AY
Tel: 01590 683092
• e-mail: ronrowe@talk21.com
• website: www.tivertonnewforest.co.uk

•HEREFORDSHIRE

Hotel
Hedley Lodge, Belmont Abbey, HEREFORD, Herefordshire HR2 9RZ Tel: 01432 374747
• e-mail: hedley@belmontabbey.org.uk
• website: www.hedleylodge.com

Self-catering
Mrs Williams, Radnor's End, Huntington, KINGTON, Herefordshire HR5 3NZ
Tel: 01544 370289
• e-mail: enquiries@the-rock-cottage.co.uk
• website: www.the-rock-cottage.co.uk

•ISLE OF WIGHT

Self-Catering
Island Cottage Holidays, ISLE OF WIGHT
Tel: 01929 480080
• e-mail: enq@islandcottageholidays.com
• website: www.islandcottageholidays.com

Caravan Park
Hillgrove Park, Field Lane, St Helens, RYDE,
Isle of Wight PO33 1UT Tel: 01983 872802
• e-mail: holidays@hillgrove.co.uk
• website: www.hillgrove.co.uk

Guest House
Mrs V. Hudson, Strang Hall, Uplands Road,
TOTLAND, Isle of Wight PO39 0DZ
Tel: 01983 753189
• e-mail: strang_hall@hotmail.com
• website: www.strang-hall.co.uk

•KENT

Self-Catering Cottages
Garden Of England
Contact: The Mews Office, 189a High Street, Tonbridge, KENT TN9 1BX
Tel: 01732 369168
• e-mail: holidays@gardenofenglandcottages.co.uk
• website: www.gardenofenglandcottages.co.uk

Self-Catering Cottages
Fairhaven Holiday Cottages, KENT
Tel: 01208 821255
• website: www.fairhaven-holidays.co.uk

Guest House
S. Twort, Heron Cottage, Biddenden,
ASHFORD, Kent TN27 8HH. Tel: 01580 291358
• e-mail: susantwort@hotmail.com
• website: www.heroncottage.info

Farm B & B
Alison & Jim Taylor, Boldens Wood,
Fiddling Lane, Stowting, FOLKESTONE,
Ashford, Kent TN25 6AP Tel: 01303 812011
• e-mail: StayoverNight@aol.com
• website: www.countrypicnics.com

Hotel
Collina House Hotel, 5 East Hill, TENTERDEN,
Kent TN30 6RL Tel: 01580 764852/764004
• e-mail: enquiries@collinahousehotel.co.uk
• website: www.collinahousehotel.co.uk

www.holidayguides.com

•LANCASHIRE

Hotel
The Chadwick Hotel, South Promenade,
LYTHAM ST ANNES, Lancashire FY8 1NS
Tel: 01253 720061
• e-mail: sales@thechadwickhotel.com
• website: www.thechadwickhotel.com

Self-Catering
Don-Ange Holiday Apartments,
29 Holmfield Road, BLACKPOOL,
Lancashire FY2 9TB Tel: 01253 355051
• e-mail: donange@msn.com
• website: www.donange.cjb.net

Holiday Park
Marton Mere Holiday Village, Mythop Road,
BLACKPOOL, Lancashire FY4 4XN
Tel: 01253 767544
• website: www.touringholidays.co.uk

•LEICESTERSHIRE & RUTLAND

Golf Club
Birstall Golf Club, Station Road, BIRSTALL,
Leicestershire LE4 3BB Tel: 0116 267 4322
• e-mail: sue@birstallgolfclub.co.uk
• website: www.birstallgolfclub.co.uk

Guest House
Richard & Vanessa Peach, The Old Rectory,
4 New Road, Belton In Rutland, OAKHAM,
Rutland LE15 9LE Tel: 01572 717279
• e-mail: bb@iepuk.com
• website: www.theoldrectorybelton.co.uk

•LINCOLNSHIRE

Self-Catering
S. Jenkins, Grange Farm Riding School
Holiday Cottages, Waltham Road,
BARNOLDBY-LE-BECK, Grimsby,
Lincolnshire DN37 0AR Tel: 01472 822216
• e-mail: sueuk4000@netscape.net
• website: www.grangefarmcottages.com

Caravan & Camping
The White Cat Caravan & Camping Park,
Shaw Lane, Old Leake, BOSTON,
Lincolnshire PE22 9LQ Tel: 01205 870121
• e-mail: kevin@klannen.freeserve.co.uk
• website: www.whitecatpark.com

Hotel
Branston Hall Hotel, BRANSTON,
Lincolnshire LN4 1PD Tel: 01522 793305
• e-mail: info@branstonhall.com
• website: www.branstonhall.com

Holiday Park
Thorpe Park Holiday Centre,
CLEETHORPES, North East Lincolnshire
DN35 0PW Tel: 01472 813395
* website: www.touringholidays.co.uk

Self-Catering / Caravans
Woodland Waters, Willoughby Road,
Ancaster, GRANTHAM,
Lincolnshire NG31 3RT Tel: 01400 230888
* e-mail: info@woodlandwaters.co.uk
* website: www.woodlandwaters.co.uk

Farm B & B
Mrs C.E. Harrison, Baumber Park, Baumber,
HORNCASTLE, Lincolnshire LN9 5NE
Tel: 01507 578235
* e-mail: baumberpark@amserve.com
* website: www.baumberpark.com

Holiday Park
Golden Sands Holiday Park, Quebec Road,
MABLETHORPE, Lincolnshire LN12 1QJ
Tel: 01507 477871
* website: www.touringholidays.co.uk

Farmhouse B & B
S Evans, Willow Farm, Thorpe Fendykes,
SKEGNESS, Lincolnshire PE24 4QH
Tel: 01754 830316
* e-mail: willowfarmhols@aol.com
* website: www.willowfarmholidays.co.uk

•MERSEYSIDE

Guest House
Holme Leigh Guest House, 93 Woodcroft
Road, Wavertree, LIVERPOOL,
Merseyside L15 2HG Tel: 0151 734 2216
* e-mail: info@homeleigh.com
* website: www.holmeleigh.com

•NORFOLK

Self-Catering
Sand Dune Cottages, Tan Lane,
CAISTER-ON-SEA, Great Yarmouth,
Norfolk NR30 5DT Tel: 01493 720352
* e-mail: sand.dune.cottages@amserve.net
* website:
www.eastcoastlive.co.uk/sites/sanddunecottages.php

Farmhouse B & B
Mrs M. Ling, The Rookery, Wortham, DISS,
Norfolk IP22 1RB. Tel: 01379 783236
* e-mail: russell.ling@ukgateway.net
* www.avocethosting.co.uk/rookery/home.htm

Self-Catering
Idyllic Cottages at Vere Lodge,
South Raynham, FAKENHAM,
Norfolk NR21 7HE Tel: 01328 838261
* e-mail: major@verelodge.co.uk
* website: www.idylliccottages.co.uk

Holiday Park
Wild Duck Holiday Park, Howards Common,
Belton, GREAT YARMOUTH,
Norfolk NR31 9NE Tel: 01493 780268
* website: www.touringholidays.co.uk

Self-Catering
Blue Riband Holidays, HEMSBY,
Great Yarmouth, Norfolk NR29 4HA
Tel: 01493 730445
* website: www.BlueRibandHolidays.co.uk

Farm
Little Abbey Farm, Low Road, Pentney,
KING'S LYNN, Norfolk PE32 1JF
Tel: 01760 337348
* e-mail: enquiries@littleabbeyfarm.co.uk
* website: www.littleabbeyfarm.co.uk

B & B
Dolphin Lodge, 3 Knapton Road, Trunch,
NORTH WALSHAM, Norfolk NR28 0QE
Tel: 01263 720961
* e-mail: dolphin.lodge@btopenworld.com
* website: www.dolphinlodges.net

Hotel
Elderton Lodge Hotel, THORPE MARKET,
Cromer, Norfolk NR11 8TZ
Tel: 01263 833547
* e-mail: enquiries@eldertonlodge.co.uk
* website: www.eldertonlodge.co.uk

Self-Catering
Mr & Mrs Castleton, Poppyland Holiday
Cottages, The Green, THORPE MARKET,
Norfolk NR11 8AJ Tel: 01263 833219
* e-mail: poppylandjc@netscape.net
* website: www.poppyland.com

Self-Catering
Winterton Valley Holidays, WINTERTON-
ON-SEA/CALIFORNIA, Norfolk
Contact: 15 Kingston Avenue,Caister-on-
Sea NR30 5ET Tel: 01493 377175
* e-mail: info@wintertonvalleyholidays.co.uk
* website: www.wintertonvalleyholidays.co.uk

**Readers are requested to
mention this FHG guide when
seeking accommodation**

• NORTHAMPTONSHIRE

Farmhouse B&B
Mrs B. Hawkins, Pear Tree Farm, Aldwincle,
KETTERING, Northants NN14 3EL
Tel: 01832 720614
- e-mail: beverley@peartreefarm.net
- website: www.peartreefarm.net

• NORTHUMBERLAND

Self-Catering
Mrs M. Thompson, Heritage Coast Holidays,
6G Greensfield Court, ALNWICK,
Northumberland NE66 2DE
Tel: 01665 604935
- e-mail: info@heritagecoastholidays.com
- website: www.heritagecoastholidays.com

Self-Catering Cottages
Buston Farm Holiday Cottages, Low Buston
Hall, Warkworth, ALNWICK, Morpeth,
Northumberland NE65 0XY
Tel: 01665 714805
- e-mail: jopark@farming.co.uk
- website: www.buston.co.uk

Hotel
The Blue Bell Hotel, Market Place,
BELFORD, Northumberland NE70 7NE
Tel: 01668 213543
- e-mail: bluebel@globalnet.co.uk
- website: www.bluebellhotel.com

Self-Catering
Swinhoe Farmhouse, BELFORD,
Northumberland NE70 7LJ
Tel: 016682 13370
- e-mail: valerie@swinhoecottages.co.uk
- website: www.swinhoecottages.co.uk

Hotel / Self-Catering
Riverdale Hall Hotel, BELLINGHAM,
Northumberland NE48 2JT
Tel: 01434 220254
- e-mail: reservations@riverdalehallhotel.co.uk
- website: www.riverdalehallhotel.co.uk

Self-Catering
2, The Courtyard, BERWICK-UPON-TWEED
Contact: J. Morton, 1, The Courtyard, Church
Street, Berwick-upon-Tweed TD15 1EE
Tel: 01289 308737
- e-mail: jvm@patmosphere.uklinux.net
- website: www.berwickselfcatering.co.uk

Hotel
The Cobbled Yard Hotel, 40 Walkergate,
BERWICK-UPON-TWEED, Northumberland
TD15 1DJ Tel: 01289 308407
- e-mail: cobbledyardhotel@berwick35.fsnet.co.uk
- website: www.cobbledyardhotel.com

B & B
Friendly Hound Cottage, Ford Common,
BERWICK-UPON-TWEED, Northumberland
TD15 2QD Tel: 01289 388554
- e-mail: friendlyhound@aol.com
- website: www.friendlyhoundcottage.co.uk

Holiday Park
Haggerston Castle Holiday Park, Beal, Near
BERWICK-UPON-TWEED, Northumberland
TD15 2PA Tel: 01289 381333
- website: www.touringholidays.co.uk

B & B / Farm / Camping
Mrs S. Maughan, Greencarts Farm, Near
Humshaugh, HEXHAM, Northumberland
NE46 4BW Tel: 01434 681320
- e-mail: sandra@greencarts.co.uk
- website: www.greencarts.co.uk

Self-Catering
Burradon Farm Cottages & Houses,
Burradon Farm, Cramlington, NEWCASTLE-
UPON-TYNE, Northumberland NE23 7ND
Tel: 0191 2683203
- e-mail: judy@burradonfarm.co.uk
- website: www.burradonfarm.co.uk

Self-Catering Cottages
Lorbottle Holiday Cottages, THROPTON,
Northumberland
Contact: Leslie & Helen Far, Lorbottle, West
Steads, Thropton, Near Morpeth,
Northumberland NE65 7JT
Tel: 01665 574672
- e-mail: stay@lorbottle.com
- website: www.lorbottle.com

Guest House / B & B
Mrs M. Halliday, Beck'n'Call, Birling West
Cottage, WARKWORTH, Northumberland
NE65 0XS Tel: 01665 711653
- e-mail: beck-n-call@lineone.net
- website: www.beck-n-call.co.uk

Please mention this publication when making enquiries about accommodation featured in these pages

WEBSITE DIRECTORY 295

• NOTTINGHAMSHIRE

Farm / B & B
Mrs D. Hickling, Woodside Farm, Long Lane, BARKESTONE-LE-VALE, Nottinghamshire NG13 0HQ Tel: 01476 870336
• e-mail: hickling-woodside@supanet.com
• website: www.woodsidebandb.co.uk

Visitor Attraction
White Post Farm Centre, FARNSFIELD, Nottinghamshire NG22 8HL
Tel: 01623 882977
• website: www.whitepostfarmcentre.co.uk

•OXFORDSHIRE

Self-Catering
Cottage in the Country Cottage Holidays Tukes Cottage, 66 West Street, Chipping Norton, Oxfordshire OX7 5ER
Tel: 0870 027 5930
• e-mail: enquiries@cottageinthecountry.co.uk
• website: www.cottageinthecountry.co.uk

Self-Catering Cottages
Grange Farm Country Cottages, Grange Farm Estates, Godington, BICESTER, Oxfordshire OX27 9AF Tel: 01869 278 778
• e-mail: info@grangefarmcottages.co.uk
• website: www.grangefarmcottages.co.uk

Leisure Park
Cotswold Wildlife Park, BURFORD, Oxfordshire OX18 4JN Tel: 01993 823006
• website: www.cotswoldwildlifepark.co.uk

B & B
The Old Bakery, Skirmett, Near HENLEY-ON-THAMES, Oxfordshire RG9 6TD
Tel: 01491 410716
• e-mail: lizzroach@aol.com

Guest House
The Bungalow, Cherwell Farm, Mill Lane, Old Marston, OXFORD, Oxfordshire OX3 0QF Tel: 01865 557171
• e-mail: ros.bungalowbb@btinternet.com
• www.cherwellfarm-oxford-accomm.co.uk

Guest House
Nanford Guest House, 137 Iffley Road, OXFORD, Oxfordshire, OX4 1EJ
Tel: 01865 244743
• e-mail: b.cronin@btinternet.com
• website: www.nanfordguesthouse.com

B & B
Fords Farm, Ewelme, WALLINGFORD, Oxfordshire OX10 6HU Tel: 01491 839272
• e-mail: fordsfarm@callnetuk.com
• website: www.country-accom.co.uk/fords-farm/

Guest House
Mrs Elizabeth Simpson, Field View, Wood Green, WITNEY, Oxfordshire OX28 1DE
Tel: 01993 705485
• e-mail: bandb@fieldview-witney.co.uk
• website: www.fieldview-witney.co.uk

B & B
Mr & Mrs N. Hamilton, Gorselands Hall, Boddington Lane, North Leigh, between WOODSTOCK and WITNEY, Oxfordshire OX29 6PU Tel: 01993 882292
• e-mail: hamilton@gorselandshall.com
• website: www.gorselandshall.com

•SHROPSHIRE

Golf Club / Self-Catering Cottages
Cleobury Mortimer Golf Club, Wyre Common, CLEOBURY MORTIMER, Kidderminster, Worcestershire DY14 8HQ
Tel: 01299 271112
• e-mail: enquiries@cleoburygolfclub.com
• website: www.cleoburygolfclub.com

•SHROPSHIRE

Guest House
Ron & Jenny Repath, Meadowlands, Lodge Lane, Frodesley, DORRINGTON, Shropshire SY5 7HD Tel: 01694 731350
• e-mail: meadowlands@talk21.com
• website: www.meadowlands.co.uk

Self-Catering
Clive & Cynthia Prior, Mocktree Barns Holiday Cottages, Leintwardine, LUDLOW, Shropshire SY7 0LY Tel: 01547 540441
• e-mail: mocktreebarns@care4free.net
• website: www.mocktreeholidays.co.uk

B & B / Self-Catering
Mrs E. Purnell, Ravenscourt Manor, Woofferton, LUDLOW, Shropshire SY8 4AL
Tel: 01584 711905
• e-mail: elizabeth@ravenscourtmanor.plus.com
• website: www.internet-tsp.co.uk/ravenscourt
 www.cottagesdirect.com

Inn / Hotel
The Four Alls Inn, Woodseaves, MARKET DRAYTON, Shropshire TF9 2AG
Tel: 01630 652995
• e-mail: inn@thefouralls.com
• website: www.thefouralls.com

Farmhouse / B & B
Sambrook Manor, Sambrook, NEWPORT, Shropshire TF10 8AL Tel: 01952 550356
• website: www.sambrookmanor.com

WEBSITE DIRECTORY

B & B
The Mill House, High Ercall, TELFORD, Shropshire TF6 6BE Tel: 01952 770394
• e-mail: mill-house@talk21.com
• website: www.ercallmill.co.uk

•SOMERSET

Self-Catering
The Pack Horse, ALLERFORD, Near Porlock, Somerset TA24 8HW Tel: 01643 862475
• e-mail: holidays@thepackhorse.net
• website: www.thepackhorse.net

B&B
Mrs C. Bryson, Walton Villa, 3 Newbridge Hill, BATH, Somerset BA1 3PW Tel: 01225 482792
• e-mail: walton.villa@virgin.net
• website: www.walton.izest.com

B & B / Self-Catering
Mrs P. Foster, Pennsylvania Farm, Newton-St-Loe, NEAR BATH, Somerset BA2 9JD Tel: 01225 314912
• website: www.pennsylvaniafarm.co.uk

Inn
The Talbot 15th Century Coaching Inn, Selwood Street, Mells, Near BATH, Somerset BA11 3PN Tel: 01373 812254
• e-mail: roger@talbotinn.com
• website: www.talbotinn.com

Farm Guest House / Self-Catering
Jackie & David Bishop, Toghill House Farm, Freezing Hill, Wick, Near BATH, Somerset BS30 5RT. Tel: 01225 891261
• e-mail: accommodation@toghillhousefarm.co.uk
• website: www.toghillhousefarm.co.uk

Self-Catering / Caravans
Beachside Holiday Park, Coast Road, BREAN, Somerset TA8 2QZ Tel: 01278 751346
• e-mail: enquiries@beachsideholidaypark.co.uk
• website: www.beachsideholidaypark.co.uk

Self-Catering
Westward Rise Holiday Park, South Road, BREAN, Burnham-on-Sea, Somerset TA8 2RD Tel: 01278 751310
• e-mail: westwardrise@breansands.freeserve.co.uk
• website: www.breansands.freeserve.co.uk

Farmhouse / Self-Catering
Josephine Smart, Leigh Farm, Old Road, Pensford, NEAR BRISTOL, Somerset BS39 4BA Tel: 01761 490281
• website: www.leighfarm.co.uk

Holiday Park
Burnham-On-Sea Holiday Village, Marine Drive, BURNHAM-ON-SEA, Somerset TA8 1LA Tel: 01278 783391
• website: www.touringholidays.co.uk

Farm / Self-Catering Cottages
Mrs Wendy Baker, Withy Grove Farm, East Huntspill, NEAR BURNHAM-ON-SEA, Somerset TA9 3NP Tel: 01278 784471
• website: www.withygrovefarm.co.uk

Farm / B & B
Mrs C. Bacon, Honeydown Farm, Seaborough Hill, CREWKERNE, Somerset TA18 8PL Tel: 01460 72665
• e-mail: c.bacon@honeydown.co.uk
• website: www.honeydown.co.uk

Guest House
Mrs M. Rawle, Winsbere House, 64 Battleton, DULVERTON, Somerset TA22 9HU Tel: 01398 323278
• e-mail: info@winsbere.co.uk
• website: www.winsbere.co.uk

Inn
Exmoor White Horse Inn, Exford, EXMOOR, Somerset TA24 7PY Tel: 01643 831229
• e-mail: user@exmoor-whitehouse.co.uk
• website: www.exmoor-whitehorse.co.uk

Farm Self-Catering & Camping
Westermill Farm, Exford, EXMOOR, Somerset TA24 7NJ Tel: 01643 831216 or 01643 831238
• e-mail: fhg@westermill.com
• website: www.westermill.com

Farm Self-Catering
Jane Styles, Wintershead Farm, Simonsbath, EXMOOR, Somerset TA24 7LF Tel: 01643 831222
• e-mail: wintershed@yahoo.co.uk
• website: www.wintershead.co.uk

B & B / Half-Board / Self-Catering / Towing Pitches
St Audries Bay Holiday Club, West Quantoxhead, MINEHEAD, Somerset TA4 4DY Tel: 01984 632515
• e-mail: mrandle@staudriesbay.co.uk
• website: www.staudriesbay.co.uk

Self-Catering
Wood Dairy, Wood Lane, NORTH PERROTT, Somerset TA18 7TA Tel: 01935 891532
• e-mail: liz@acountryretreat.co.uk
• website: www.acountryretreat.co.uk

Self-Catering Cottages
Knowle Farm, West Compton, SHEPTON MALLET, Somerset BA4 4PD Tel: 01749 890482
• website: www.knowle-farm-cottages.co.uk

WEBSITE DIRECTORY *297*

Guest House / B & B
Blorenge House, 57 Staplegrove Road,
TAUNTON, Somerset TA1 1DG
Tel: 01823 283005
• e-mail: enquiries@blorengehouse.co.uk
• website: www.blorengehouse.co.uk

Guest House
The Old Mill, Netherclay, Bishop's Hull,
TAUNTON, Somerset TA1 5AB
Tel: 01823 289732
• website: www.theoldmillbandb.co.uk

Self-Catering
Mrs J Greenway, Woodlands Farm,
Bathealton, TAUNTON, Somerset TA4 2AH
Tel: 01984 623271
• website: www.woodlandsfarm-holidays.co.uk

B & B
G. Clark, Yew Tree Farm, THEALE,
Near Wedmore, Somerset BS28 4SN
Tel: 01934 712475
• e-mail: yewtreefarm@yewtreefarmbandb.co.uk
• website: www.yewtreefarmbandb.co.uk

Self-Catering
Croft Holiday Cottages, 2 The Croft, Anchor
Street, WATCHET, Somerset TA23 0BY
Tel: 01984 631121
• e-mail: croftcottages@talk21.com
• website: www.cottagessomerset.com

B&B
Cricklake Farm, Bartlett Bridge, Cocklake,
WEDMORE, Somerset BS28 4HH
Tel: 01934 712736
• e-mail: info@cricklakefarm.co.uk
• website: www.cricklakefarm.co.uk

Guest House
Infield House, 36 Portway, WELLS,
Somerset BA5 2BN Tel: 01749 670989
• e-mail: infield@talk21.com
• website: www.infieldhouse.co.uk

B & B
Susan Crane, Birdwood House, Bath Road,
WELLS, Somerset BA5 3EW
Tel: 01749 679250
• website: www.birdwood-bandb.co.uk

Farm / B & B
Mrs Sheila Stott, "Lana", Hollow Farm,
Westbury-Sub-Mendip, NEAR WELLS,
Somerset BA5 1HH Tel: 01749 870635
• e-mail: sheila@stott2366.freeserve.co.uk

Mrs H.J. Millard, Double-Gate B&B Ltd,
Godney, WELLS, Somerset BA5 1RX
Tel: 01458 832215
• e-mail: doublegatefarm@aol.com
• website: www.doublegatefarm.com

Hotel / Self-Catering
Francesca Day, Timbertop Aparthotel,
8 Victoria Park, WESTON-SUPER-MARE,
Somerset BS23 2HZ
Tel: 01934 631178 or 01934 424348
• e-mail: stay@aparthoteltimbertop.com
• website: www.aparthoteltimbertop.com

•STAFFORDSHIRE

Caravan & Camping / Holiday Park
The Star Caravan & Camping Park,
Star Road, Cotton, Near ALTON TOWERS
Staffordshire ST10 3DW
Tel: 01538 702219
• website: www.starcaravanpark.co.uk

Farm B & B / Self-Catering
Mrs M. Hiscoe-James, Offley Grove Farm,
Adbaston, ECCLESHALL, Staffordshire
ST20 0QB. Tel: 01785 280205
• e-mail: accom@offleygrovefarm.freeserve.co.uk
• website: www.offleygrovefarm.co.uk

Self-catering
The Raddle Log Cabins, Quarry Bank,
Hollington, Near Tean, STOKE-ON-TRENT,
Staffordshire ST10 4HQ Tel: 01889 507278
•e-mail: peter@logcabin.co.uk
•website: www.logcabin.co.uk

Guest House
Mrs Griffiths, Prospect House Guest House,
334 Cheadle Road, Cheddleton, LEEK,
Staffordshire ST13 7BW Tel: 01782 550639
• e-mail: prospect@talk21.com
• website: www.prospecthouseleek.co.uk

•SUFFOLK

Guest House
Kay Dewsbury, Manorhouse, The Green,
Beyton, BURY ST EDMUNDS, Suffolk IP30 9AF
Tel: 01359 270960
• e-mail: manorhouse@beyton.com
• website: www.beyton.com

Self-catering
Rede Hall Farm Park, Rede,
BURY ST EDMUNDS, Suffolk IP29 4UG
Tel: 01284 850695
• e-mail: oakley@soils.fsnet.co.uk
• website: www.redehallfarmpark.co.uk

Self-Catering
Mr & Mrs D. Cole, The Close, Middlegate
Barn, DUNWICH, Suffolk IP17 3DP
Tel: 01728 648741
• e-mail: middlegate@aol.com

WEBSITE DIRECTORY

Self-Catering
Mr P. Havers, Athelington Hall, Norham, EYE, Suffolk IP21 5EJ Tel: 01728 628233
- e-mail: peter@logcabinholidays.co.uk
- website: www.logcabinholidays.co.uk

Guest House
The Grafton Guest House, 13 Sea Road, FELIXSTOWE, Suffolk IP11 2BB
Tel: 01394 284881
- e-mail: info@grafton-house.com
- website: www.grafton-house.com

B & B / Self-Catering
Mrs Sarah Kindred, High House Farm, Cransford, Woodbridge, FRAMLINGHAM, Suffolk IP13 9PD Tel: 01728 663461
- e-mail: b&b@highhousefarm.co.uk
- website: www.highhousefarm.co.uk

Self-Catering
Kessingland Cottages, Rider Haggard Lane, KESSINGLAND, Suffolk.
Contact: S. Mahmood,
156 Bromley Road, Beckenham,
Kent BR3 6PG Tel: 020 8650 0539
- e-mail: jeeptrek@kjti.freeserve.co.uk
- website: www.k-cottage.co.uk

Farm / Guest House
Sweffling Hall Farm, Sweffling, SAXMUNDHAM, Suffolk IP17 2BT
Tel: 01728 663644
- e-mail: stephenmann@suffolkonline.net
- website: www.sweflinghallfarm.co.uk

Self-Catering
Southwold Self-Catering Properties.
H.A. Adnams, 98 High Street, SOUTHWOLD, Suffolk IP18 6DP
Tel: 01502 723292
- e-mail: haadnams_lets@ic24.net
- website: www.haadnams.com

Self-Catering Cottage
Anvil Cottage, WOODBRIDGE, Suffolk
Contact: Mr & Mrs R. Blake, IA Moorfield Road, Woodbridge, Suffolk IP12 4JN
Tel: 01394 382 565
- e-mail: robert@blake4110.fsbusiness.co.uk

Self-Catering
Windmill Lodges Ltd, Redhouse Farm, Saxtead, WOODBRIDGE, Suffolk IP13 9RD
Tel: 01728 685338
- e-mail: holidays@windmilllodges.co.uk
- website: www.windmilllodges.co.uk

www.holidayguides.com

•SURREY

Guest House
The Lawn Guest House, 30 Massetts Road, Horley, GATWICK, Surrey RH6 7DF
Tel: 01293 775751
- e-mail: info@lawnguesthouse.co.uk
- website: www.lawnguesthouse.co.uk

Hotel
Chase Lodge Hotel, 10 Park Road, Hampton Wick, KINGSTON-UPON-THAMES, Surrey KT1 4AS. Tel: 020 8943 1862
- e-mail: info@chaselodgehotel.com
- website: www.chaselodgehotel.com
   www.surreyhotels.com

•EAST SUSSEX

Self-Catering
"Pekes", CHIDDINGLY, East Sussex
Contact: Eva Morris, 124 Elm Park Mansions, Park Walk, London SW10 0AR
Tel: 020 7352 8088
- e-mail: pekes.afa@virgin.net
- website: www.pekesmanor.com

Guest House
Ebor Lodge, 71 Royal Parade, EASTBOURNE, East Sussex BN22 7AQ
Tel: 01323 640792
- e-mail: info@eborlodge.co.uk
- website: www.eborlodge.co.uk

Self-Catering Cottages
Caburn Cottages, Ranscombe Farm, GLYNDE, Lewes, East Sussex BN8 6AA
Tel: 01273 858062
- e-mail: enquiries@caburncottages.co.uk
- website: www.caburncottages.co.uk

Guest House / Self-Catering
Longleys Farm Cottage, Harebeating Lane, HAILSHAM, East Sussex BN27 1ER
Tel: 01323 841227
- e-mail: longleysfarmcottagebb@dsl.pipex.com
- website: www.longleysfarmcottage.co.uk

Hotel
Grand Hotel, Grand Parade, St. Leonards, HASTINGS, East Sussex TN38 0DD
Tel: 01424 428510
- e-mail: petermann@grandhotelhastings.co.uk
- website: www.grandhotelhastings.co.uk

Bed & Breakfast
Barbara Martin, Little Saltcote, 22 Military Road, RYE, East Sussex TN31 7NY
Tel: 01797 223210
- e-mail: info@littlesaltcote.co.uk
- website: www.littlesaltcote.co.uk

WEBSITE DIRECTORY

Hotel
Rye Lodge Hotel, Hilders Cliff, RYE, East Sussex TN31 7LD Tel: 01797 223838
- e-mail: chris@ryelodge.co.uk
- website: www.ryelodge.co.uk

B & B
Jeake's House, Mermaid Street, RYE, East Sussex TN31 7ET
Tel: 01797 222828
- e-mail: stay@jeakeshouse.com
- website: www.jeakeshouse.com

Hotel
Flackley Ash Hotel & Restaurant, Peasmarsh, Near RYE, East Sussex TN31 6YH. Tel: 01797 230651
- e-mail: enquiries@flackleyashhotel.co.uk
- website: www.flackleyashhotel.co.uk

• WEST SUSSEX

B & B
Mrs Vicki Richards, Woodacre, Arundel Road, Fontwell, ARUNDEL, West Sussex BN18 0QP Tel: 01243 814301
- e-mail: wacrebb@aol.com
- website: www.woodacre.co.uk

B & B
Broxmead Paddock, Broxmead Lane, Bolney, HAYWARDS HEATH, West Sussex RH17 5RG
Tel: 01444 881458
- e-mail: broxmeadpaddock@hotmail.com
- website: www.broxmeadpaddock.eclipse.co.uk

Self-Catering
Mrs M. W. Carreck, New Hall Holiday Flat and Cottage, New Hall Lane, Small Dole, HENFIELD, West Sussex BN5 9YJ
Tel: 01273 492546
- website: www.newhallcottage.co.uk

Touring Park
Warner Touring Park, Warner Lane, SELSEY, West Sussex PO20 9EL Tel: 01243 604499
- website: www.bunnleisure.co.uk

Guest House
Manor Guest House, 100 Broadwater Road, WORTHING, West Sussex BN14 8AN
Tel: 01903 236028
- e-mail: stay@manorworthing.com
- website: www.manorworthing.com

• WARWICKSHIRE

Guest House / B & B
Julia & John Downie, Holly Tree Cottage, Pathlow, STRATFORD-UPON-AVON, Warwickshire CV37 0ES Tel: 01789 204461
- e-mail: john@hollytree-cottage.co.uk
- website: www.hollytree-cottage.co.uk

Guest House
The Croft, Haseley Knob, WARWICK, Warwickshire CV35 7NL Tel: 01926 484447
- e-mail: david@croftguesthouse.co.uk
- website: www.croftguesthouse.co.uk

• WEST MIDLANDS

Hotel
Featherstone Farm Hotel, New Road, Featherstone, WOLVERHAMPTON, West Midlands WV10 7NW Tel: 01902 725371
- e-mail: info@featherstonefarm.co.uk
- website: www.featherstonefarm.co.uk

• WILTSHIRE

Guest House
Alan & Dawn Curnow, Hayburn Wyke Guest House, 72 Castle Road, SALISBURY, Wiltshire SP1 3RL Tel:01722 412627
- e-mail: hayburn.wyke@tinyonline.co.uk
- website: www.hayburnwykeguesthouse.co.uk

• WORCESTERSHIRE

Farmhouse / B & B
The Barn House, BROADWAS ON TEME, Worcestershire WR6 5NS Tel: 01886 888733
- e-mail: info@barnhouseonline.co.uk
- website: www.barnhouseonline.co.uk

Guest House
Ann & Brian Porter, Croft Guest House, Bransford, GREAT MALVERN, Worcester, Worcestershire WR6 5JD Tel: 01886 832227
- e-mail: hols@crofthousewr6.fsnet.co.uk
- website: www.croftguesthouse.com

Self-Catering Cottages
Rochford Park, TENBURY WELLS, Worcestershire WR15 8SP
Tel: 01584 781 372
- e-mail: cottages@rochfordpark.co.uk
- website: www.rochfordpark.co.uk

FHG Readers are requested to mention this FHG guide when seeking accommodation

•NORTH YORKSHIRE

Self-Catering
Recommended Cottage Holidays, Eastgate House, Pickering, NORTH YORKSHIRE
Tel: 01751 475547
• website: www.recommended-cottages.co.uk

Farmhouse B & B
Mrs Julie Clarke, Middle Farm, Woodale, COVERDALE, Leyburn,
North Yorkshire DL8 4TY Tel: 01969 640271
• e-mail: j-a-clarke@amserve.com
• www.yorkshirenet.co.uk/stayat/middlefarm

Holiday Park
Blue Dolphin Holiday Park, Gristhorpe Bay, FILEY, North Yorkshire YO14 9PU
Tel: 01723 515155
• website: www.touringholidays.co.uk

Holiday Park
Primrose Valley Holiday Park, Primrose Valley, NEAR FILEY, North Yorkshire YO14 9RF Tel: 01723 513771
• website: www.touringholidays.co.uk

Holiday Park
Reighton Sands Holiday Park, Reighton Gap, NEAR FILEY, North Yorkshire YO14 9SH • Tel: 01723 890476
• website: www.touringholidays.co.uk

Farmhouse B&B
Mr & Mrs Richardson, Egton Banks Farmhouse, GLAISDALE, Whitby, North Yorkshire YO21 2QP Tel: 01947 897289
e-mail: egtonbanksfarm@agriplus.net
•website: www.egtonbanksfarm.agriplus.net

Country Inn
The Foresters Arms, Main Street, GRASSINGTON, Near Skipton,
North Yorkshire BD23 5AA
Tel: 01756 752349
• e-mail: theforesters@totalise.co.uk
• website: www.forestersarmsgrassington.co.uk

Caravan & Camping
Bainbridge Ings Caravan & Camping Site, HAWES, North Yorkshire DL8 3NU
Tel: 01969 667354
• e-mail: janet@bainbridge-ings.co.uk
• website: www.bainbridge-ings.co.uk

Hotel
Stone House Hotel, Sedbusk, HAWES, Wensleydale, North Yorkshire DL8 3PT
Tel: 01969 667571
• e-mail: daleshotel@aol.com
• website: www.stonehousehotel.com

Guest House
The New Inn Motel, Main Street, HUBY, York, North Yorkshire YO61 1HQ
Tel: 01347 810219
• enquiries@newinnmotel.freeserve.co.uk
• website: www.newinnmotel.co.uk

Guest House
Mr B.L.F. Martin, The Old Star, West Witton, LEYBURN, North Yorkshire DL8 4LU
Tel: 01969 622949
• e-mail: enquiries@theoldstar.com
• website: www.theoldstar.com

Self-Catering
Abbey Holiday Cottages, MIDDLESMOOR. 12 Panorama Close, Pateley Bridge, Harrogate, North Yorkshire HG3 5NY
Tel: 01423 712062
• e-mail: abbeyholiday.cottages@virgin.net
• website: www.abbeyholidaycottages.co.uk

B & B
Banavie, Roxby Road, Thornton-Le-Dale, PICKERING, North Yorkshire YO18 7SX
Tel: 01751 474616
• e-mail: info@banavie.co.uk
• website: www.banavie.uk.com

Guest House / Self-Catering
Sue & Tony Hewitt, Harmony Country Lodge, 80 Limestone Road, Burniston, SCARBOROUGH, North Yorkshire
YO13 0DG Tel: 0800 2985840
• e-mail: mail@harmonylodge.net
• website: www.harmonylodge.net

B & B
Beck Hall, Malham, SKIPTON, North Yorkshire BD23 4DJ Tel: 01729 830332
• e-mail: simon@beckhallmalham.com
• website: www.beckhallmalham.com

Inn
Gamekeepers Inn, Long Ashes Park, Threshfield, NEAR SKIPTON, North Yorkshire BD23 5PN Tel: 01756 752434
• e-mail: info@gamekeeperinn.co.uk
• website: www.gamekeeperinn.co.uk

Self-Catering
Mrs Jones, New Close Farm, Kirkby Malham, SKIPTON, North Yorkshire BD23 4DP
Tel: 01729 830240
• brendajones@newclosefarmyorkshire.co.uk
• website: www.newclosefarmyorkshire.co.uk

Self-Catering
Allaker in Coverdale, WEST SCRAFTON, Near Leyburn, North Yorkshire
Contact Mr A. Cave Tel: 020 8567 4862
• e-mail: ac@adriancave.com
• website: www.adriancave.com/allaker

WEBSITE DIRECTORY *301*

Guest House
Ashford Guest House, 8 Royal Crescent, WHITBY, North Yorkshire YO21 3EJ
Tel: 01947 602138
• e-mail: info@ashfordguesthouse.co.uk
• website: www.ashfordguesthouse.co.uk

Self-Catering
Mrs Jill McNeil, Swallow Holiday Cottages, Long Leas Farm, Hawsker, WHITBY, North Yorkshire YO22 4LA Tel: 01947 603790
• e-mail: jillian@swallowcottages.co.uk
• website: www.swallowcottages.co.uk

Self-Catering
Mr J.N. Eddleston,
Greenhouses Farm Cottages,
Greenhouses Farm, Lealholm,
Near WHITBY, North Yorkshire YO21 2AD
Tel: 01947 897486
• e-mail: n_eddleston@yahoo.com
• www.greenhouses-farm-cottages.co.uk

Self-Catering
The Old Granary & Copper Cottage,
Ravenhill Farm, Dunsley, NEAR WHITBY,
North Yorkshire YO21 3TJ
Tel: 01947 893331
• e-mail: jackie.richardson6@btopenworld.com

Self-Catering
White Rose Holiday Cottages,
NEAR WHITBY, North Yorkshire
Contact: Mrs J. Roberts, 5 Brook Park,
Sleights, Near Whitby, North Yorkshire
YO21 1RT Tel: 01947 810763
• e-mail: enquiries@whiterosecottages.co.uk
• website: www.whiterosecottages.co.uk

Guest House
Mrs J.M. Wood, Ascot House,
80 East Parade, YORK, North Yorkshire
YO31 7YH Tel: 01904 426326
• e-mail: admin@ascothouseyork.com
• website: www.ascothouseyork.com

Self-Catering Cottages
The Grange Farm Holiday Cottages,
Bishop Wilton, York, North Yorkshire
YO42 1SA Tel: 01759 369500
• e-mail: richarddavy@supanet.com
• website: www.thegrangefarm.com

Guest House / Self-Catering
Mr Gary Hudson, Orillia House, 89 The Village, Stockton on Forest, YORK, North Yorkshire YO3 9UP Tel: 01904 400600
• e-mail: info@orilliahouse.co.uk
• website: www.orilliahouse.co.uk

Guest House / Camping
Mrs Jeanne Wilson, Robeanne House, Driffield Lane, Shiptonthorpe, YORK, North Yorkshire YO43 3PW Tel: 01430 873312
• e-mail: robert@robeanne.freeserve.com
• website: www.robeannehouse.co.uk

Guest House
St George's, 6 St George's Place, YORK, North Yorkshire YO24 1DR
Tel: 01904 625056
• e-mail: sixstgeorg@aol.com
• website: http://members.aol.com/sixstgeorg/

Self-Catering
Mr N. Manasir, York Lakeside Lodges, Moor Lane, YORK, North Yorkshire YO24 2QU
Tel: 01904 702346
• e-mail: neil@yorklakesidelodges.co.uk
• website: www.yorklakesidelodges.co.uk

•SOUTH YORKSHIRE

Golf Club
Sandhill Golf Club, Middlecliffe Lane, Little Houghton, BARNSLEY, South Yorkshire S72 0HW Tel: 01226 753444
• e-mail: vwistow@sandhillgolfclub.co.uk
• website: www.sandhillgolfclub.co.uk

B & B
Padley Farm Bed & Breakfast, Dungworth Green, Bradfield, SHEFFIELD,
South Yorkshire S6 6HE Tel: 01142 851427
• e-mail: info@padleyfarm.co.uk
• website: www.padleyfarm.co.uk

•WEST YORKSHIRE

Farm / B & B / Self-Catering Cottages
Currer Laithe Farm, Moss Carr Road, Long Lee, KEIGHLEY, West Yorkshire BD21 4SL
Tel: 01535 604387
• website: www.currerlaithe.co.uk

FHG Guides publish a large range of well-known accommodation guides. We will be happy to send you details or you can use the order form at the back of this book.

•SCOTLAND

Self-Catering Cottages
Islands & Highlands Cottages, Bridge Road, Portree, Isle of Skye, SCOTLAND IV51 9ER
Tel: 01478 612123
• website: www.islands-and-highlands.co.uk

•ABERDEEN, BANFF & MORAY

Hotel
Banchory Lodge Hotel, BANCHORY, Kincardineshire AB31 5HS
Tel: 01330 822625
• e-mail: enquiries@banchorylodge.co.uk
• website: www.banchorylodge.co.uk

B & B
Davaar B & B, Church Street, DUFFTOWN, Moray, AB55 4AR Tel: 01340 820464
• e-mail: davaar@cluniecameron.co.uk
• website: www.davaardufftown.co.uk

Self-catering
Newseat & Kirklea, FRASERBURGH, Aberdeenshire.
Contact: Mrs E.M. Pittendrigh, Kirktown, Tyrie, Fraserburgh AB43 7DQ. Tel: 01346 541231
• e-mail: pittendrigh@supanet.com

Golf Club
Moray Golf Club, Stotfield Road, LOSSIEMOUTH, Moray IV31 6QS
Tel: 01343 812018
• e-mail: secretary@moraygolf.co.uk
• website: www.moraygolf.co.uk

Self-Catering
Val & Rob Keeble, Lighthouse Cottages, RATTRAY HEAD, Peterhead, Aberdeenshire AB42 3HB Tel: 01346 532236
• e-mail: enquiries@rattrayhead.net
• website: www.rattrayhead.net

Self-Catering
Simon Pearse, Forglen Cottages, Forglen Estate, TURRIFF, Aberdeenshire AB53 4JP Tel: 01888 562918
• e-mail: reservations@forglen.co.uk
• website: www.forglen.co.uk

•ARGYLL & BUTE

Self-Catering
Ardtur Cottages, APPIN, Argyll PA38 4DD
Tel: 01631 730223
• e-mail: pery@btinternet.com
• website: www.selfcatering-appin-scotland.com

Inn
Mr D. Fraser, Cairndow Stagecoach Inn, CAIRNDOW, Argyll PA26 8BN
Tel: 01499 600286
• e-mail: cairndowinn@aol.com
• website: www.cairndow.com

Self-Catering
Catriona O'Keeffe, Blarghour Farm Cottages, Blarghour Farm, By DALMALLY,
Argyll PA33 1BW Tel: 01866 833246
• e-mail: blarghour@btconnect.com
• website: www.self-catering-argyll.co.uk

Guest House / Self-Catering
Rockhill Guesthouse & Self-Catering Cottages, DALMALLY, Argyll PA33 1BH
Tel: 01866 833218
• website: www.rockhill@lochawe.co.uk

Hotel
West End Hotel, West Bay, DUNOON, Argyll PA23 7HU Tel: 01369 702907
• e-mail: mike@westendhotel.com
• website: www.westendhotel.com

Self-Catering
B & M Phillips, Kilbride Croft, Balvicar, ISLE OF SEIL, Argyll PA34 4RD
Tel: 01852 300475
• e-mail: kilbridecroft@aol.com
• website: www.kilbridecroft.co.uk

Self-Catering
Robin Malcolm, Duntrune Castle, KILMARTIN, Argyll PA31 8QQ
Tel: 01546 510283
• website: www.duntrune.com

Caravans
Caolasnacon Caravan Park, KINLOCHLEVEN, Argyll PH50 4RJ Tel: 01855 831279
• e-mail: caolasnacon@hotmail.co.uk
• website: www.kinlochlevencaravans.com

Readers are requested to mention this FHG guidebook when seeking accommodation

WEBSITE DIRECTORY

Self-Catering
Castle Sween Bay (Holidays) Ltd, Ellary,
LOCHGILPHEAD, Argyll PA31 8PA
Tel: 01880 770232
- e-mail: info@ellary.com
- website: www.ellary.com

Self-Catering
Linda Battison,
Cologin Country Chalets & Lodges,
Lerags Glen, OBAN, Argyll PA34 4SE
Tel: 01631 564501
- e-mail: info@cologin.co.uk
- website: www.cologin.co.uk

Self-Catering
Colin Mossman, Lagnakeil Lodges,
Lerags, OBAN, Argyll PA34 4SE
Tel: 01631 562746
- e-mail: info@lagnakeil.co.uk
- website: www.lagnakeil.co.uk

Self-Catering
Mrs Barker, Barfad Farm, TARBERT,
Loch Fyne, Argyll PA29 6YH
Tel: 01880 820549
- e-mail: vbarker@hotmail.com
- website: www.tarbertlochfyne.com

Golf Club
Taynuilt Golf Club, TAYNUILT, Argyll
PA35 1JE Tel: 01866 822329
- website: www.taynuiltgolfclub.co.uk

•AYRSHIRE & ARRAN

Caravan Park
Laggan House Leisure Park, BALLANTRAE,
Near Girvan, Ayrshire KA26 0LL
Tel: 01465 831229
- e-mail: lhlp@lagganhouse.co.uk
- website: www.lagganhouse.co.uk

Farmhouse / B & B
Mrs Nancy Cuthbertson, West Tannacrieff,
Fenwick, KILMARNOCK, Ayrshire KA3 6AZ
Tel: 01560 600258
- e-mail: westtannacrieff@btopenworld.com
- website: www.smoothhound.co.uk/hotels/
westtannacrieff.html

Self-Catering
Bradan Road, TROON, Ayrshire
Contact: Mr Ward Brown
Tel: 07770 220830
- e-mail: stay@bradan.info
- website: www.bradan.info

•BORDERS

Self-Catering
The Old Barn, High Letham,
BERWICK-UPON-TWEED.
Contact: Richard & Susan Persse,
High Letham Farmhouse, High Letham,
Berwick-upon-Tweed, Borders TD15 1UX
Tel: 01289 306585
- e-mail: r.persse-highl@amserve.com
- website: www.oldbarnhighletham.co.uk

Self-Catering
Wauchope Cottages, BONCHESTER
BRIDGE, Hawick, Borders TD9 9TG
Tel: 01450 860630
- e-mail: wauchope@btinternet.com
- website: www.wauchopecottages.co.uk

Self-Catering / Caravan & Camping
Neuk Farm Cottages & Chesterfield Caravan
Park, Neuk Farmhouse, COCKBURNSPATH,
Berwickshire TD13 5YH Tel: 01368 830459
- e-mail: info@chesterfieldcaravanpark.co.uk
- website: www.chesterfieldcaravanpark.co.uk

Guest House
Ferniehirst Mill Lodge, JEDBURGH,
Borders TD8 6PQ Tel: 01835 863279
- e-mail: ferniehirstmill@aol.com
- website: www.ferniehirstmill.co.uk

Self-Catering
Mill House Cottage, JEDBURGH.
Contact: Mrs A. Fraser, Overwells,
Jedburgh, Borders TD8 6LT
Tel: 01835 863020
- e-mail: abfraser@btinternet.com
- website: www.overwells.co.uk

Hotel
George & Abbotsford Hotel, High Street,
MELROSE, Borders TD6 9PD
Tel: 01896 822308
- e-mail: enquiries@georgeandabbotsford.co.uk
- website: www.georgeandabbotsford.co.uk

Farm B & B/ Self Catering / Inn
Mrs J. P. Copeland, Bailey Mill, Bailey,
NEWCASTLETON, Roxburghshire TD9 0TR
Tel: 01697 748617
- e-mail: pam@baileymill.fsnet.co.uk
- www.baileycottages/riding/racing.com

Self-Catering
Mrs C. M. Kilpatrick, Slipperfield House,
WEST LINTON, Peeblesshire EH46 7AA
Tel: 01968 660401
- e-mail: cottages@slipperfield.com
- website: www.slipperfield.com

• DUMFRIES & GALLOWAY

Hotel
Hetland Hall Hotel, CARRUTHERSTOWN,
Dumfries & Galloway DG1 4JX
Tel: 01387 840201
• e-mail: info@hetlandhallhotel.co.uk
• website: www.hetlandhallhotel.co.uk

Farm
Celia Pickup, Craigadam,
CASTLE DOUGLAS, Kirkcudbrightshire
DG7 3HU Tel: 01556 650233
• website: www.craigadam.com

Self-Catering
Rusko Holidays, Gatehouse of Fleet,
CASTLE DOUGLAS, Kirkcudbrightshire
DG7 2BS Tel: 01557 814215
• e-mail: info@ruskoholidays.co.uk
• website: www.ruskoholidays.co.uk

B & B
Langlands Bed & Breakfast, 8 Edinburgh
Road, DUMFRIES DG1 1JQ
Tel: 01387 266549
• e-mail: langlands@tiscali.co.uk
• website: www.langlands.info

Farm / Camping & Caravans / Self-Catering
Barnsoul Farm Holidays, Barnsoul Farm,
Shawhead, DUMFRIES, Dumfriesshire
Tel: 01387 730249
• e-mail: barnsouldg@aol.com
• website: www.barnsoulfarm.co.uk

Guest House
Kirkcroft Guest House, Glasgow Road,
GRETNA GREEN, Dumfriesshire DG16 5DU
Tel: 01461 337403
• e-mail: info@kirkcroft.co.uk
• website: www.kirkcroft.co.uk

B & B
June Deakins, Annandale House,
MOFFAT, Dumfriesshire DG10 9SA
Tel: 01683 221460
• e-mail: june@annandalehouse.com
• website: www.annandalehouse.com

Camping & Touring Site
Drumroamin Farm Camping and Touring
Site, 1 South Balfern, Kirkinner, NEWTON
STEWART, Wigtownshire DG8 9DB
Tel: 01988 840613 or 077524 71456
• e-mail: lesley.shell@btinternet.com
• website: www.drumroamin.co.uk

www.holidayguides.com

Caravan Park
Whitecairn Caravan Park, Glenluce,
NEWTON STEWART, Wigtownshire
DG8 0NZ Tel: 01581 300267
• e-mail: enquiries@whitecairncaravans.co.uk
• website: www.whitecairncaravans.co.uk

• DUNBARTONSHIRE

Self-Catering
Inchmurrin Island Self-Catering Holidays,
Inchmurrin Island, LOCH LOMOND,
Dunbartonshire G63 0JY Tel: 01389 850245
• e-mail: scotts@inchmurrin-lochlomond.com
• website: www.inchmurrin-lochlomond.com

• EDINBURGH & LOTHIANS

B & B
Cruachan B&B, 78 East Main Street,
BLACKBURN, By Bathgate, West Lothian
EH47 7QS Tel: 01506 655221
• e-mail: cruachan.bb@virgin.net
• website: www.cruachan.co.uk

B & B
Mrs Kay, Blossom House, 8 Minto Street,
EDINBURGH EH9 1RG Tel: 0131 667 5353
• e-mail: blossom_house@hotmail.com
• website: www.blossomguesthouse.co.uk

Guest House
Kenvie Guest House, 16 Kilmaurs Road,
EDINBURGH EH16 5DA Tel: 0131 6681964
• e-mail: dorothy@kenvie.co.uk
• website: www.kenvie.co.uk

Guest House
International Guest House, 37 Mayfield
Gardens, EDINBURGH EH9 2BX
Tel: 0131 667 2511
• e-mail: intergh1@yahoo.co.uk
• website: www.accommodation-edinburgh.com

B & B
McCrae's B&B, 44 East Claremont Street,
EDINBURGH EH7 4JR Tel: 0131 556 2610
• e-mail: mccraes.bandb@lineone.net
• http://website.lineone.net/~mccraes.bandb

Holiday Park
Seton Sands Holiday Village, LONGNIDDRY,
East Lothian EH32 0QF Tel: 01875 813333
• website: www.touringholidays.co.uk

Self-Catering / Caravan & Camping
Drummohr Caravan Park, Levenhall,
MUSSELBURGH, East Lothian EH21 8JS
Tel: 0131 6656867
• e-mail: bookings@drummohr.org
• website: www.drummohr.org

WEBSITE DIRECTORY

• FIFE

Hotel
The Lundin Links Hotel, Leven Road,
LUNDIN LINKS, Fife KY8 6AP
Tel: 01333 320207
• e-mail: info@lundin-links-hotel.co.uk
• website: www.lundin-links-hotel.co.uk

Self-Catertring
Balmore, 3 West Road, NEWPORT-ON-TAY,
Fife DD6 8HH Tel: 01382 542274
• e-mail: allan.ramsay@ukgateway.net
• website: www.thorndene.co.uk

Self-Catering
Kingask Cottages, Kingask House,
ST ANDREWS, Fife KY16 8PN
Tel: 01334 472011
• e-mail: info@kingask-cottages.co.uk
• website: www.kingask-cottages.co.uk

B & B
Mrs Duncan, Spinkstown Farmhouse,
ST ANDREWS, Fife KY16 8PN
Tel: 01334 473475
• e-mail: anne@spinkstown.com
• website: www.spinkstown.com

• GLASGOW & DISTRICT

B & B
Mrs P. Wells, Avenue End B & B, 21 West
Avenue, Stepps, GLASGOW G33 6ES
Tel: 0141 7791990
• website: www.avenueend.co.uk

• HIGHLANDS

Accommodation in the HIGHLANDS.
• website: www.Aviemore.com

Self-Catering
Linda Murray, 29 Grampian View,
AVIEMORE, Inverness-shire PH22 1TF
Tel: 01479 810653
• e-mail: linda.murray@virgin.net
• website: www.cairngorm-bungalows.co.uk

Self-Catering
Pink Bank Chalets, Dalfaber Road,
AVIEMORE, Inverness-shire PH22 1PX
Tel: 01479 810000
• e-mail: pinebankchallets@btopenworld.com
• website: www.pinebankchalets.co.uk

Self Catering / Caravans
Speyside Leisure Park, Dalfaber Road,
AVIEMORE, Inverness-shire PH22 1PX
Tel: 01479 810236
• e-mail: fhg@speysideleisure.com
• website: www.speysideleisure.com

Self-Catering
The Treehouse, BOAT-OF-GARTEN,
Highlands
Contact: Mrs Mather Tel: 0131 337 7167
• e-mail: fhg@treehouselodge.plus.com
• website: www.treehouselodge.co.uk

Guest House
Mrs Lynn Benge, The Pines Country House,
Duthil, CARRBRIDGE, Inverness-shire
PH23 3ND Tel: 01479 841220
• e-mail: lynn@thepines-duthil.co.uk
• website: www.thepines-duthil.fsnet.co.uk

Hotel
The Clan MacDuff Hotel, Achintore Road,
FORT WILLIAM PH33 6RW
Tel: 01397 702341
• e-mail: reception@clanmacduff.co.uk
• website: www.clanmacduff.co.uk

Hotel
Invergarry Hotel, INVERGARRY,
Inverness-shire PH35 4HJ Tel: 01809 501206
• e-mail: info@invergarryhotel.co.uk
• website: www.invergarryhotel.co.uk

Self-Catering
Invermoriston Holiday Chalets,
INVERMORISTON, Glenmoriston,
Inverness, Inverness-shire IV63 7YF
Tel: 01320 351254
• website: www.invermoriston-holidays.com

Caravan & Camping
Auchnahillin Caravan & Camping Park,
Daviot East, INVERNESS, Inverness-shire
IV2 5XQ Tel: 01463 772286
• e-mail: info@auchnahillin.co.uk
• website: www.auchnahillin.co.uk

Self-Catering
Mrs A MacIver, The Sheiling, Achgarve,
LAIDE, Ross-shire IV22 2NS
Tel: 01445 731487
• e-mail: stay@thesheilingholidays.com
• website: www.thesheilingholidays.com

Self-Catering
Wildside Highland Lodges, Whitebridge,
By LOCH NESS, Inverness-shire IV2 6UN
Tel: 01456 486373
• e-mail: info@wildsidelodges.com
• website: www.wildsidelodges.com

B & B / Self-Catering Chalets
D.J. Mordaunt, Mondhuie, NETHY BRIDGE, Inverness-shire PH25 3DF Tel: 01479 821062
• e-mail: david@mondhuie.com
• website: www.mondhuie.com

Self-Catering
Crubenbeg Holiday Cottages, NEWTONMORE, Inverness-shire PH20 1BE
Tel: 01540 673566
• e-mail: enquiry@crubenbeg.com
• website: www.crubenbeg.com

Self-Catering
Mr A. Urquhart, Crofters Cottages, 15 Croft, POOLEWE, Ross-shire IV22 2JY
Tel: 01445 781268
• e-mail: croftcottages@btopenworld.com
• website: www.croftcottages.btinternet.co.uk

Hotel
Whitebridge Hotel, WHITEBRIDGE, Inverness IV2 6UN Tel: 01456 486226
• e-mail: info@whitebridgehotel.co.uk
• website: www.whitebridgehotel.co.uk

•LANARKSHIRE

Self-Catering
Carmichael Country Cottages, Carmichael Estate Office, Westmains, Carmichael, BIGGAR, Lanarkshire ML12 6PG
Tel: 01899 308336
• e-mail: chiefcarm@aol.com
• website: www.carmichael.co.uk/cottages

Guest House
Blairmains Guest House, Blairmains, HARTHILL, Lanarkshire ML7 5TJ
Tel: 01501 751278
• e-mail: heather@blairmains.freeserve.co.uk
• website: www.blairmains.co.uk

•PERTH & KINROSS

Self-Catering
Loch Tay Lodges, Remony, Acharn, ABERFELDY, Perthshire PH15 2HR
Tel: 01887 830209
• e-mail: remony@btinternet.com
• website: www.lochtaylodges.co.uk

Hotel
Lands of Loyal Hotel, ALYTH, Perthshire PH11 8JQ Tel: 01828 633151
• e-mail: info@landsofloyal.com
• website: www.landsofloyal.com

Self-Catering
Laighwood Holidays, Laighwood, Butterstone, BY DUNKELD, Perthshire PH8 0HB Tel: 01350 724241
• e-mail: holidays@laighwood.co.uk
• website: www.laighwood.co.uk

Self-catering
East Cottage, Roro Estate, GLEN LYON.
Contact: E. Thompson LLP, 76 Overhaugh Street, Galashiels TD1 1DP
Tel: 01896 751300
• e-mail: Galashiels@edwin-thompson.co.uk

B & B
Brochanach, 43 Fingal Road, KILLIN, Perthshire FK21 8XA Tel: 01567 820028
• e-mail: alifer@msn.com
• website: www.s-h-systems.co.uk/hotels/brochanach.html

Self-Catering
Gill Hunt, Wester Lix Cottage, Wester Lix, KILLIN, Perthshire FK21 8RD
Tel: 01567 820990
• e-mail: gill@westerlix.net
• website: www.westerlix.net

Hotel
Balrobin Hotel, Higher Oakfield, PITLOCHRY, Perthshire PH16 5HT Tel: 01796 472901
• e-mail: info@balrobin.co.uk
• website: www.balrobin.co.uk

Guest House
Jacky & Malcolm Catterall, Tulloch, Enochdhu, By Kirkmichael, PITLOCHRY, Perthshire PH10 7PW Tel: 01250 881404
• e-mail: maljac@tulloch83.freeserve.co.uk
• website: www.maljac.com

B & B
Mrs Ann Guthrie, Newmill Farm, STANLEY, Perthshire PH1 4QD Tel: 01738 828281
• e-mail: guthrienewmill@sol.co.uk
• website: www.newmillfarm.co.uk

B & B / Self-Catering
Ardoch Lodge, STRATHYRE, Near Callander FK18 8NF Tel: 01877 384666
• e-mail: ardoch@btinternet.com
• website: www.ardochlodge.co.uk

•STIRLING & TROSSACHS

Camping & Caravan Park
Riverside Caravan Park, Dollarfield, DOLLAR, Clackmannanshire FK14 7LX
Tel: 01259 742896
• e-mail: info@riverside-caravanpark.co.uk
• website: www.riverside-caravanpark.co.uk

WEBSITE DIRECTORY

Guest House
Croftburn Bed & Breakfast, Croftamie, DRYMEN, Loch Lomond G63 0HA
Tel: 01360 660796
- e-mail: enquiries@croftburn.co.uk
- website: www.croftburn.co.uk

• SCOTTISH ISLANDS

• SKYE

Hotel & Restaurant
Royal Hotel, Bank Street, PORTREE, Isle of Skye IV51 9BU Tel: 01478 612585
- e-mail: info@royal-hotel-skye.com
- website: www.royal-hotel-skye.com

• WALES

Self-Catering
Quality Cottages, Cerbid, Solva, HAVERFORDWEST, Pembrokeshire SA62 6YE Tel: 01348 837871
- website: www.qualitycottages.co.uk

• ANGLESEY & GWYNEDD

Self-Catering / Caravan Park
Mrs A. Skinner, Ty Gwyn, Rhyduchaf, BALA, Gwynedd LL23 7SD Tel: 01678 521267
- e-mail: richard.skin@btinternet.com

Caravan & Camping Site
Glanllyn Lakeside Caravan & Camping Park, Llanuwchllyn, BALA, Gwynedd LL23 7ST
Tel: 01678 540227
- e-mail: info@glanllyn.com
- website: www.glanllyn.com

Caravan Park
Parc Caerelwan, Talybont, BARMOUTH, Gwynedd LL43 2AX Tel: 01341 247236
- e-mail: parc@porthmadog.co.uk
- website: www.porthmadog.co.uk/parc/

Country House
Sygun Fawr Country House, BEDDGELERT, Gwynedd LL55 4NE Tel: 01766 890258
- e-mail: sygunfawr@aol.com
- website: www.sygunfawr.co.uk

Holiday Park
Greenacres Holiday Park, Black Rock Sands, Morfa Bychan, Porthmadog, CAERNARFON, Gwynedd LL49 9YF Tel: 01766 512781
- website: www.touringholidays.co.uk

Self-Catering / Caravans
Plas-y-Bryn Chalet Park, Bontnewydd, CAERNARFON, Gwynedd LL54 7YE
Tel: 01286 672811
- www.plasybrynholidayscaernarfon.co.uk

Self-Catering within a Castle
BrynBras Castle, Llanrug, Near CAERNARFON, Gwynedd LL55 4RE
Tel: 01286 870210
- e-mail: holidays@brynbrascastle.co.uk
- website: www.brynbrascastle.co.uk

Self-Catering
Mrs A. Jones, Rhos Country Cottages, Betws Bach, Ynys, CRICCIETH, Gwynedd LL52 0PB Tel: 01758 720047
- e-mail: cottages@rhos.freeserve.co.uk
- website: www.rhos-cottages.co.uk

Caravan & Chalet Park/ Self-Catering
Parc Wernol Parc, Chwilog, Pwllheli, Near CRICCIETH, Gwynedd LL53 6SW
Tel: 01766 810506
- e-mail: catherine@wernol.com
- website: www.wernol.com

Guest House
Mrs M. Bamford, Ivy House, Finsbury Square, DOLGELLAU, Gwynedd LL40 1RF. Tel: 01341 422535
- e-mail: marg.bamford@btconnect.com
- website: www.ukworld.net/ivyhouse

Guest House
Fron Deg Guest House, LLanfair, HARLECH, Gwynedd LL46 2RB Tel: 01766 780448
- website: www.bedandbreakfast-harlech.co.uk

Caravan & Camping
Mr John Billingham, Islawrffordd Caravan Park, Tal-y-Bont, MERIONETH, Gwynedd LL43 2BQ Tel: 01341 247269
- e-mail: info@islawrffordd.co.uk
- website: www.islawrffordd.co.uk

Golf Club
Anglesey Golf Club Ltd, Station Road, RHOSNEIGR, Anglesey LL64 5QX
Tel: 01407 811127 ext 2
- e-mail: info@theangleseygolfclub.com
- website: www.angleseygolfclub.co.uk

•NORTH WALES

Hotel
Fairy Glen Hotel, Beaver Bridge, BETWS-Y-COED, Conwy, North Wales LL24 0SH Tel: 01690 710269
* e-mail: fairyglen@youe.fsworld.co.uk
* website: www.fairyglenhotel.co.uk

Country House
Hafod Country House, Trefrin, Llanrwst, CONWY VALLEY, North Wales LL27 0RQ Tel: 01492 640029
* e-mail: hafod@breathemail.net
* website: www.hafod-house.co.uk

Guest House
The Park Hill / Gwesty Bryn Parc, Llanrwst Road, Betws-y-Coed, CONWY, North Wales LL24 0HD Tel: 01690 710540
* e-mail: welcome@park-hill.co.uk
* website: www.park-hill.co.uk

Guest House
Sychnant Pass House, Sychnant Pass Road CONWY, North Wales LL32 8BJ Tel: 01492 596868
* e-mail: bre@sychnant-pass-house.co.uk
* website: www.sychnant-pass-house.co.uk

Golf Club
Denbigh Golf Club, Henllan Road, DENBIGH, North Wales LL16 5AA Tel: 01745 816669
* e-mail: denbighgolfclub@aol.com
* website: www.denbighgolfclub.co.uk

Golf Club
North Wales Golf Club, 72 Bryniau Road, West Shore, LLANDUDNO, North Wales LL30 2DZ Tel:01492 875325 or 01492 876878
* e-mail: golf@nwgc.freeserve.co.uk
* website: www.northwalesgolfclub.co.uk

Hotel / Inn
The Golden Pheasant Country Hotel & Inn, Llwynmawr, Glyn Ceiriog, Near LLANGOLLEN, North Wales LL20 7BB Tel: 01691 718211
* e-mail: goldenpheasant@micro-plus-web.net
* website: goldenpheasanthotel.co.uk

Self-Catering Cottages
Glyn Uchaf, Conwy Old Road, PENMAENMAWR, North Wales LL34 6YS Tel: 01492 623737
* e-mail: john@baxter6055.freeserve.co.uk
* website: www.glyn-uchaf.co.uk

Holiday Park
Presthaven Sands Holiday Park, Gronaut, PRESTATYN, North Wales LL19 9TT Tel: 01745 856471
website: www.touringholidays.co.uk

•CARMARTHENSHIRE

Self-Catering
Maerdy Cottages, Taliaris, LLANDEILO, Carmarthenshire SA19 7BD Tel: 01550 777448
* e-mail: mjones@maerdyholidaycottages.co.uk
* website: www.maerdyholidaycottages.co.uk

•CEREDIGION

Holiday Village
Gilfach Holiday Village, Llwyncelyn, Near ABERAERON, Ceredigion SA46 0HN Tel: 01545 580288
* e-mail: info@stratfordcaravans.co.uk
* website: www.selfcateringholidays.com
        www.stratfordcaravans.co.uk

• PEMBROKESHIRE

Farm Self- Catering
Holiday House, BROAD HAVEN, Pembrokeshire.
Contact: L.E. Ashton, 10 St Leonards Road, Thames Ditton, Surrey KT7 0RJ Tel: 020 8398 6349
* e-mail: lejash@aol.com
* website: www.33timberhill.com

Hotel / Guest House
Ivybridge, Drim Mill, Dyffryn, Goodwick, FISHGUARD, Pembrokeshire SA64 0JT Tel: 01348 875366
* e-mail: ivybridge@cwcom.net
* website: www.ivybridge.cwc.net

Looking for holiday accommodation?
for details of hundreds of properties throughout the UK try:

www.holidayguides.com

WEBSITE DIRECTORY

Caravans & Camp Site
Brandy Brook Caravan & Camping Site,
Rhyndaston, Hayscastle, HAVERFORDWEST,
Pembrokeshire SA62 5PT
Tel: 01348 840272
• e-mail: f.m.rowe@btopenworld.com

Farmhouse B & B
Mrs Jen Patrick, East Hook Farm,
Portfield Gate, HAVERFORDWEST,
Pembrokeshire SA62 3LN
Tel: 01437 762211
• e-mail: jen.patrick@easthookfarmhouse.co.uk
• website: www.easthookfarmhouse.co.uk

Inn
The Dial Inn, Ridgeway Road, LAMPHEY,
Pembroke, Pembrokeshire SA71 5NU
Tel: 01646 672426
• e-mail: info@dialinn.co.uk

Hotel
Trewern Arms Hotel, Nevern, NEWPORT,
Pembrokeshire SA42 0NB
Tel: 01239 820395
• e-mail: info@trewern-arms-pembrokeshire.co.uk
• www.trewern-arms-pembrokeshire.co.uk

Self-catering
Ffynnon Ddofn, ST DAVIDS, Pembrokeshire.
Contact: Mrs B. Rees White, Brick House
Farm, Burnham Road, Woodham Mortimer,
Maldon, Essex CM9 6SR
Tel: 01245 224611
• website: www.ffynnonddofn.co.uk

Self-Catering
T. M. Hardman, High View, Catherine Street,
ST DAVIDS, Pembrokeshire SA62 6RJ
Tel: 01437 720616
• e-mail: enquiries@stnbc.co.uk
• website: www.stnbc.co.uk

Farm Guest House
Mrs Morfydd Jones,
Lochmeyler Farm Guest House, Llandeloy,
Pen-y-Cwm, Near SOLVA, St Davids,
Pembrokeshire SA62 6LL
Tel: 01348 837724
• e-mail: stay@lochmeyler.co.uk
• website: www.lochmeyler.co.uk

Holiday Park
Kiln Park Holiday Centre, Marsh Road,
TENBY, Pembrokeshire SA70 7RB
Tel: 01834 844121
• website: www.touringholidays.co.uk

•POWYS

Farm
Caebetran Farm, Felinfach, BRECON, Powys
LD3 0UL Tel: 01874 754460
• e-mail: hazelcaebetran@aol.com
• website: caebetranfarmhousebedandbreakfastwales.com

Guest House
Maeswalter, Heol Senni, Near BRECON,
Powys LD3 8SU Tel: 01874 636629
• e-mail: joy@maeswalter.fsnet.co.uk
   bb@maeswalter.co.uk
• website: www.maeswalter.co.uk

Self-Catering
Mrs Jones, Penllwyn Lodges, GARTHMYL,
Powys SY15 6SB
Tel: 01686 640269
• e-mail: daphne.jones@onetel.net
• website: www.penllwynlodges.co.uk

B & B
Annie McKay, Hafod-y-Garreg, Erwood, Builth
Wells, Near HAY-ON-WYE, Powys LD2 3TQ
Tel: 01982 560400
• website: www.hafodygarreg.co.uk

Self-Catering
Oak Wood Lodges, Llwynbaedd,
RHAYADER, Powys LD6 5NT
Tel: 01597 811422
• e-mail: info@oakwoodlodges.co.uk
• website: www.oakwoodlodges.co.uk

Self-Catering
Ann Reed, Madog's Wells, Llanfair
Caereinion, WELSHPOOL, Powys SY21 0DE
Tel: 01938 810446
• e-mail: madogswells@btinternet.com
• website: www.madogswells.co.uk

•SOUTH WALES

Narrowboat Hire
Castle Narrowboats, Church Road Wharf,
Gilwern, Monmouthshire NP7 0EP
Tel: 01873 832340
• info@castlenarrowboats.co.uk
• website: www.castlenarrowboats.co.uk

Guest House / Self-Catering Cottages
Mrs Norma James, Wyrloed Lodge, Manmoel,
BLACKWOOD, Caerphilly, South Wales
NP12 0RN Tel: 01495 371198
• e-mail: norma.james@btinternet.com
• website: www.btinternet.com/~norma.james/

WEBSITE DIRECTORY

Self-Catering
Cwrt-y-Gaer, Wolvesnewton, CHEPSTOW, Monmouthshire NP16 6PR Tel: 01291 650700
• e-mail: johnllewellyn11@btinternet.com
• website: www.cwrt-y-gaer.co.uk

Hotel
Culver House Hotel, Port Eynon, GOWER, Swansea, South Wales SA3 1NN Tel: 01792 390755
• e-mail: stay@culverhousehotel.co.uk
• website: www.culverhousehotel.co.uk

Guest House
Rosemary & Derek Ringer, Church Farm Guest House, Mitchel Troy, MONMOUTH, South Wales NP25 4HZ Tel: 01600 712176
• e-mail: info@churchfarmguesthouse.eclipse.co.uk
• website: www.churchfarmmitcheltroy.co.uk

Golf Club
St Mellons Golf Club, ST MELLONS, Cardiff, South Wales Tel: 01633 680408
• e-mail: stmellons@golf2003.fs.co.uk
• website: www.stmellonsgolfclub.co.uk

Hotel
Egerton Grey Country House Hotel, Porthkerry, Barry, VALE OF GLAMORGAN, South Wales CF62 3BZ Tel: 01446 711666
• e-mail: info@egertongrey.co.uk
• website: www.egertongrey.co.uk

• IRELAND

Self-Catering Cottages
Imagine Ireland
Tel: 0870 112 77 32
• e-mail: info@imagineireland.com
• website: www.imagineireland.com

CO. CLARE

Self-Catering
Ballyvaughan Village & Country Holiday Homes, BALLYVAUGHAN.
Contact: George Quinn, Frances Street, Kilrush, Co. Clare Tel: 00 353 65 9051977
• e-mail: sales@ballyvaughan-cottages.com
• website: www.ballyvaughan-cottages.com

• CHANNEL ISLANDS

GUERNSEY

Self-Catering Apartments
Swallow Apartments, La Cloture, L'Ancresse, GUERNSEY Tel: 01481 249633
• e-mail: swallowapt@aol.com
• website: www.swallowapartments.com

Looking for Holiday Accommodation?

for details of hundreds of properties throughout the UK visit our website on

www.holidayguides.com

Index of Towns and Counties

Abbotsbury	DORSET
Aberfeldy	PERTH & KINROSS
Abermawr	PEMBROKESHIRE
Aberporth	CEREDIGION
Abersoch	ANGLESEY & GWYNEDD
Alford	LINCOLNSHIRE
Alfriston	EAST SUSSEX
Allerford	SOMERSET
Alnwick	NORTHUMBERLAND
Ambleside	CUMBRIA
Appin	ARGYLL & BUTE
Ardgay	HIGHLANDS (NORTH)
Arisaig	HIGHLANDS (SOUTH)
Arlington	EAST SUSSEX
Ashbourne	DERBYSHIRE
Ashbrittle	SOMERSET
Ashburton	DEVON
Ashkirk	BORDERS
Askrigg/Wensleydale	NORTH YORKSHIRE
Auchtermuchty	FIFE
Aviemore	HIGHLANDS (SOUTH)
Aylesbury	BUCKINGHAMSHIRE
Ayr	AYRSHIRE & ARRAN
Badwell Ash	SUFFOLK
Bala	ANGLESEY & GWYNEDD
Ballantrae	AYRSHIRE & ARRAN
Ballyvaughan	CO. CLARE
Bamburgh	NORTHUMBERLAND
Barmouth	ANGLESEY & GWYNEDD
Barnstaple	DEVON
Bath	GLOUCESTERSHIRE
Bath	SOMERSET
Bath	WILTSHIRE
Beaminster	DORSET
Bedford	BEDFORDSHIRE
Belton-in-Rutland	LEICESTERSHIRE & RUTLAND
Betws-Y-Coed	NORTH WALES
Bicester	OXFORDSHIRE
Bideford	DEVON
Biggar	BORDERS
Biggar	LANARKSHIRE
Bishop Auckland	DURHAM
Bishop Wilton	NORTH YORKSHIRE
Blandford Forum	DORSET
Boat of Garten	HIGHLANDS (SOUTH)
Bodieve	CORNWALL
Bodmin	CORNWALL
Bodorgan	AMGLESEY & GWYNEDD
Bonchurch	ISLE OF WIGHT
Boscastle	CORNWALL
Bosherton	PEMBROKESHIRE
Bosley	CHESHIRE
Bowness-on-Windermere	CUMBRIA
Brampton	CUMBRIA
Brean	SOMERSET
Brechin	ANGUS & DUNDEE
Brecon	POWYS
Bredons Norton	GLOUCESTERSHIRE
Bridport	DORSET
Bridport/Nettlecombe	DORSET
Bristol	SOMERSET
Brixham	DEVON
Broadhaven	PEMBROKESHIRE
Broadstairs	KENT
Broughton-in-Furness	CUMBRIA
Buckingham	BUCKINGHAMSHIRE
Bude	CORNWALL
Burnham-on-Sea	SOMERSET
Burwash	EAST SUSSEX
Bury St Edmunds	SUFFOLK
Caernarfon	ANGLESEY & GWYNEDD
Caldbeck	CUMBRIA
Callander	STIRLING & THE TROSSACHS
Cambridge	CAMBRIDGESHIRE
Camelford	CORNWALL
Canterbury	KENT
Cardigan	CEREDIGION
Cardigan Bay	CEREDIGION
Carlisle	CUMBRIA
Castle Douglas	DUMFRIES & GALLOWAY
Cawsand	CORNWALL
Cerne Abbas	DORSET
Chard	SOMERSET
Charmouth	DORSET
Cheltenham	GLOUCESTERSHIRE
Chipping Campden	GLOUCESTERSHIRE
Church Stretton	SHROPSHIRE
Clacton-on-Sea	ESSEX

Index of Towns and Counties

Clitheroe	LANCASHIRE
Cockburnspath	BORDERS
Cockermouth	CUMBRIA
Cocklake	SOMERSET
Colchester	ESSEX
Colyton	DEVON
Comrie	PERTH & KINROSS
Congleton	CHESHIRE
Coningsby	LINCOLNSHIRE
Coniston	CUMBRIA
Conwy	NORTH WALES
Cornhill-on-Tweed	BORDERS
Coventry	WARWICKSHIRE
Coverdale	NORTH YORKSHIRE
Craven Arms	SHROPSHIRE
Criccieth	ANGLESEY & GWYNEDD
Croyde	DEVON
Culloden (By Inverness)	HIGHLANDS (SOUTH)
Cullompton	DEVON
Dalmally	ARGYLL & BUTE
Danby	NORTH YORKSHIRE
Dawlish	DEVON
Delabole	CORNWALL
Dent	CUMBRIA
Devizes	WILTSHIRE
Diss	NORFOLK
Dorchester	DORSET
Dover	KENT
Driffield	EAST YORKSHIRE
Dulverton	SOMERSET
Dunkeld	PERTH & KINROSS
Dursley	GLOUCESTERSHIRE
Eastbourne	EAST SUSSEX
Eccleshall	STAFFORDSHIRE
Ely	CAMBRIDGESHIRE
Ennerdale Bridge	CUMBRIA
Exeter	DEVON
Exmoor	SOMERSET
Eye	SUFFOLK
Fairford	GLOUCESTERSHIRE
Falmouth	CORNWALL
Felton	HEREFORDSHIRE
Fochabers	MORAYSHIRE
Forres	ABERDEEN, BANFF & MORAY
Fort William	HIGHLANDS (SOUTH)
Fowey	CORNWALL
Foxley	NORFOLK
Framlingham	SUFFOLK
Galashiels	BORDERS
Gartocharn/Loch Lomond	DUNBARTONSHIRE
Glaisdale	NORTH YORKSHIRE
Glossop	DERBYSHIRE
Gloucester	GLOUCESTERSHIRE
Goodwick	PEMBROKESHIRE
Grange-over-Sands	CUMBRIA
Haltwhistle	NORTHUMBERLAND
Hardraw	NORTH YORKSHIRE
Harlech	ANGLESEY & GWYNEDD
Harrogate	NORTH YORKSHIRE
Hartington	DERBYSHIRE
Haslemere	SURREY
Haverfordwest	PEMBROKESHIRE
Hay-On-Wye	POWYS
Helmsley	NORTH YORKSHIRE
Helston	CORNWALL
Henley-on-Thames	OXFORDSHIRE
Hexham	NORTHUMBERLAND
Holt	NORFOLK
Honiton	DEVON
Horncastle	LINCOLNSHIRE
Hyde (near Manchester)	CHESHIRE
Instow	DEVON

Visit the FHG website
www.holidayguides.com
for details of the wide choice of accommodation featured in the full range of FHG titles

FHG
K·U·P·E·R·A·R·D

Index of Towns and Counties

Invergarry	HIGHLANDS (SOUTH)
Invermoriston	HIGHLANDS (SOUTH)
Inverness	HIGHLANDS (SOUTH)
Inverurie	ABERDEEN, BANFF & MORAY
Isle of Seil	ARGYLL & BUTE
Ivybridge	DEVON
Johnshaven	ANGUS & DUNDEE
Keighley/Bronte Country	WEST YORKSHIRE
Kelso	BORDERS
Kendal	CUMBRIA
Kessingland	SUFFOLK
Keswick	CUMBRIA
Kettering	NORTHAMPTONSHIRE
Kilmarnock	AYRSHIRE & ARRAN
King's Lynn	NORFOLK
Kings Nympton	DEVON
Kingsbridge	DEVON
Kingsley	STAFFORDSHIRE
Kinlochleven	ARGYLL & BUTE
Kirkby Lonsdale	CUMBRIA
Kirkby Stephen	CUMBRIA
Kirkcudbright	DUMFRIES & GALLOWAY
Kirkoswald	CUMBRIA
Kirkwhelpington	NORTHUMBERLAND
Lamplugh	CUMBRIA
Lanchester	DURHAM
Langport	SOMERSET
Launceston	CORNWALL
Ledbury	HEREFORDSHIRE
Leek	STAFFORDSHIRE
Leighton Buzzard	BEDFORDSHIRE
Leominster	HEREFORDSHIRE
Leven	FIFE
Lighthorne	WARWICKSHIRE
Liskeard	CORNWALL
Little Asby	CUMBRIA
Llandrindod Wells	POWYS
Llangrannog	CEREDIGION
Loch Crinan	ARGYLL & BUTE
Loch Ness (Stratherrick)	HIGHLANDS (SOUTH)
Lochgilphead	ARGYLL & BUTE
Long Stratton	NORFOLK
Looe	CORNWALL
Looe Valley	CORNWALL
Louth	LINCOLNSHIRE
Ludlow	SHROPSHIRE
Lulworth Cove	DORSET
Luss	DUNBARTONSHIRE
Lydney	GLOUCESTERSHIRE
Lyme Regis	DORSET
Lymington	HAMPSHIRE
Lynmouth	DEVON
Mablethorpe	LINCOLNSHIRE
Machynlleth	POWYS
Malmesbury	WILTSHIRE
Malpas	CHESHIRE
Malvern	WORCESTERSHIRE
Malvern Wells	WORCESTERSHIRE
Market Rasen	LINCOLNSHIRE
Marlborough	WILTSHIRE
Matlock	DERBYSHIRE
Mawgan Porth	CORNWALL
Melbourne	DERBYSHIRE
Methven	PERTH & KINROSS
Mevagissey	CORNWALL
Middlesmoor	NORTH YORKSHIRE
Midhurst	WEST SUSSEX
Millport	AYRSHIRE & ARRAN
Minehead	SOMERSET
Minsterworth	GLOUCESTERSHIRE
Moffat	DUMFRIES & GALLOWAY
Morecambe	LANCASHIRE
Moretonhampstead	DEVON
Moreton-in-Marsh	GLOUCESTERSHIRE
Mullion	CORNWALL
Nantwich	CHESHIRE
Newcastleton	BORDERS
Newcastle-upon-Tyne	NORTHUMBERLAND
Newcastle-upon-Tyne	TYNE & WEAR
Newgale	PEMBROKESHIRE
Newport	SHROPSHIRE
Newquay	CORNWALL
Newton Stewart	DUMFRIES & GALLOWAY
Newtown	POWYS
Norfolk Broads (Neatishead)	NORFOLK
Northallerton	NORTH YORKSHIRE
Norwich	NORFOLK
Nottingham	NOTTINGHAMSHIRE
Oakamoor	STAFFORDSHIRE
Oban	ARGYLL & BUTE
Okehampton	DEVON
Oswestry	SHROPSHIRE
Otterburn	NORTHUMBERLAND
Oxford	OXFORDSHIRE

Index of Towns and Counties

Padstow	CORNWALL
Patterdale	CUMBRIA
Penrith	CUMBRIA
Pentraeth	ANGLESEY & GWYNEDD
Penzance	CORNWALL
Peterborough	LINCOLNSHIRE
Pickering	NORTH YORKSHIRE
Polperro	CORNWALL
Poole	DORSET
Porthmadog	ANGLESEY & GWYNEDD
Portland	DORSET
Portpatrick	DUMFRIES & GALLOWAY
Portree	ISLE OF SKYE
Redruth	CORNWALL
Robin Hood's Bay	NORTH YORKSHIRE
Rosewell	EDINBURGH & LOTHIANS
Ross-on-Wye	HEREFORDSHIRE
Ruthin	NORTH WALES
St Andrews	FIFE
St Austell	CORNWALL
St Davids	PEMBROKESHIRE
St Margaret's Bay	KENT
St Tudy	CORNWALL
Scarborough	NORTH YORKSHIRE
Seahouses	NORTHUMBERLAND
Sheffield	SOUTH YORKSHIRE
Shepton Mallet	SOMERSET
Sherborne	DORSET
Shillingstone	DORSET
Sidmouth	DEVON
Skegness	LINCOLNSHIRE
Skipton	NORTH YORKSHIRE
Solva	PEMBROKESHIRE
South Molton	DEVON
Southport	LANCASHIRE
Southwold/Walberswick	SUFFOLK
Staithes	NORTH YORKSHIRE
Stanley	PERTH & KINROSS
Stogumber	SOMERSET
Storrington	WEST SUSSEX
Stowmarket	SUFFOLK
Stow-on-the-Wold	GLOUCESTERSHIRE
Stratford-upon-Avon	WARWICKSHIRE
Sturminster Newton	DORSET
Swanage	DORSET
Tarporley	CHESHIRE
Taunton	SOMERSET
Taynuilt	ARGYLL & BUTE
Tenbury Wells	WORCESTERSHIRE
Tenby	PEMBROKESHIRE
Thirsk	NORTH YORKSHIRE
Thorpe Fendykes	LINCOLNSHIRE
Thropton	NORTHUMBERLAND
Tiverton	DEVON
Tolpuddle	DORSET
Tomatin	HIGHLANDS (SOUTH)
Tongue	HIGHLANDS (NORTH)
Torquay	DEVON
Totland	ISLE OF WIGHT
Totnes	DEVON
Truro	CORNWALL
Uppingham	LEICESTERSHIRE & RUTLAND
Uttoxeter	STAFFORDSHIRE
Wadebridge	CORNWALL
Wallingford	OXFORDSHIRE
Wareham	DORSET
Warminster	WILTSHIRE
Washford	SOMERSET
Wells	SOMERSET
Welshpool	POWYS
Weston-Super-Mare	SOMERSET
Weymouth	DORSET
Whitby	NORTH YORKSHIRE
Whitland	PEMBROKESHIRE
Winchcombe	GLOUCESTERSHIRE
Winchester	HAMPSHIRE
Windermere	CUMBRIA
Wiveliscombe	SOMERSET
Woodbridge	SUFFOLK
Woolacombe	DEVON
Worcester	WORCESTERSHIRE
Wymondham	NORFOLK
Yelverton	DEVON
York	NORTH YORKSHIRE

Readers are requested to mention this guidebook when making enquiries about accommodation.

CULTURE SMART!

a quick guide to customs & etiquette

THE SMARTER WAY TO TRAVEL

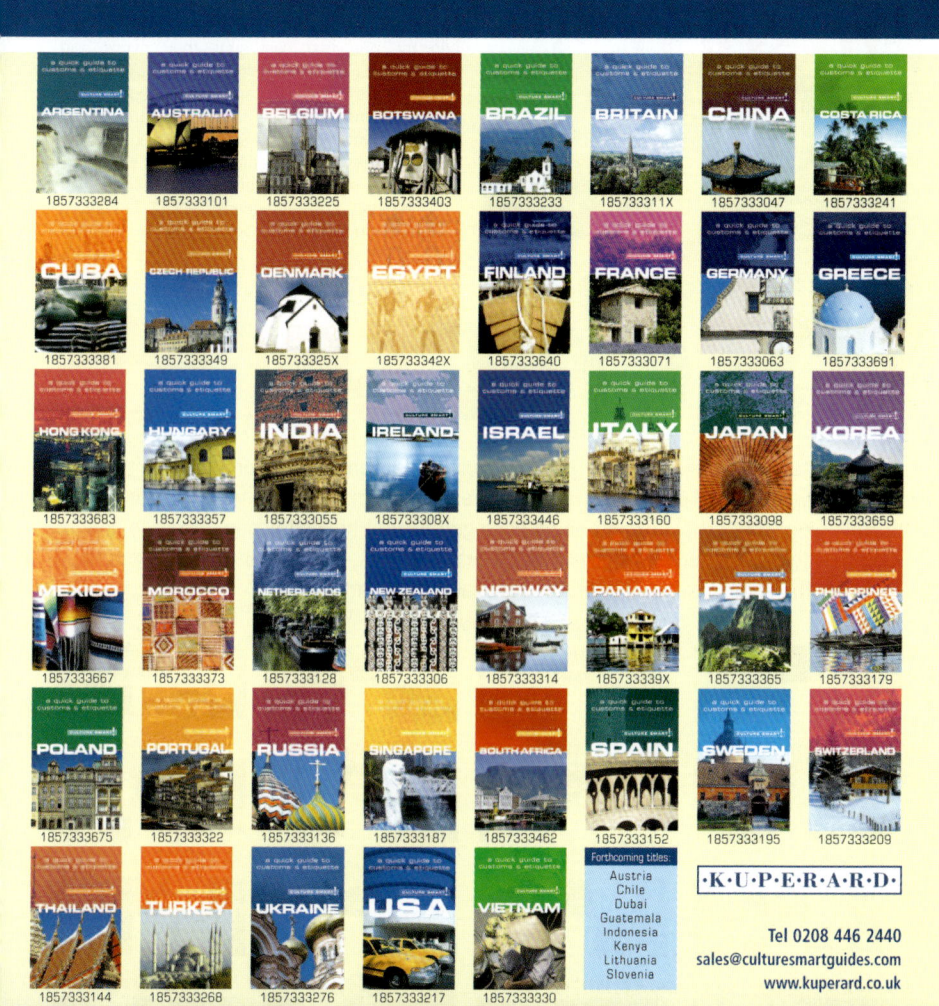

Title	ISBN
ARGENTINA	1857333284
AUSTRALIA	1857333101
BELGIUM	1857333225
BOTSWANA	1857333403
BRAZIL	1857333233
BRITAIN	185733311X
CHINA	1857333047
COSTA RICA	1857333241
CUBA	1857333381
CZECH REPUBLIC	1857333349
DENMARK	185733325X
EGYPT	185733342X
FINLAND	1857333640
FRANCE	1857333071
GERMANY	1857333063
GREECE	1857333691
HONG KONG	1857333683
HUNGARY	1857333357
INDIA	1857333055
IRELAND	185733308X
ISRAEL	1857333446
ITALY	1857333160
JAPAN	1857333098
KOREA	1857333659
MEXICO	1857333667
MOROCCO	1857333373
NETHERLANDS	1857333128
NEW ZEALAND	1857333306
NORWAY	1857333314
PANAMA	185733339X
PERU	1857333365
PHILIPPINES	1857333179
POLAND	1857333675
PORTUGAL	1857333322
RUSSIA	1857333136
SINGAPORE	1857333187
SOUTH AFRICA	1857333462
SPAIN	1857333152
SWEDEN	1857333195
SWITZERLAND	1857333209
THAILAND	1857333144
TURKEY	1857333268
UKRAINE	1857333276
USA	1857333217
VIETNAM	1857333330

Forthcoming titles:
Austria
Chile
Dubai
Guatemala
Indonesia
Kenya
Lithuania
Slovenia

·K·U·P·E·R·A·R·D·

Tel 0208 446 2440
sales@culturesmartguides.com
www.kuperard.co.uk

International travel is more than a different time zone – it's a different world. In China it's rude to be late. In France, it's rude to be on time. Never be unpleasant in Thailand but in Russia, smiling at strangers may be seen as a sign of stupidity. As flawless as your pronunciation might be, use the American sign for OK in Paris, and you've just used the gesture for "worthless". Unintended insults do more than make you cringe: At best they invite amusement, at worst a gaffe can jeopardize a business deal or even your personal safety. Make genuine efforts towards understanding the people and you've instantly enriched your experience.

Books are priced **£6.95** and are available from your wholesaler or ORCA Book Services.

'Order any Culture Smart! guide via the Kuperard website and receive free postage on any quantity of guides.

Visit www.kuperard.co.uk to see the full range in the series and type in the following promotional code on the payment page FHG01. Or call us on 0208 446 2440 and quote the same code'

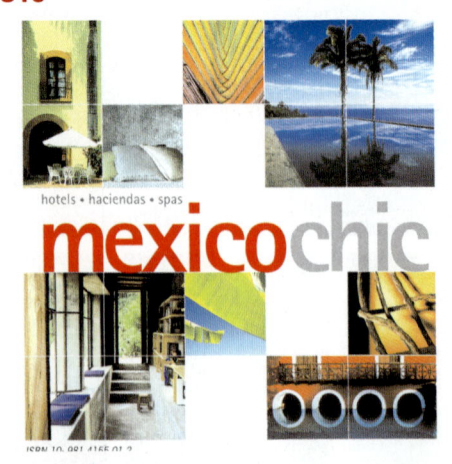

mexico chic

hotels · haciendas · spas

ISBN 10: 981-4155-01-2

Mexico Chic is the definitive guide to Mexico's most luxurious and alluring hotels. The properties featured—whether a city hotel, a beachside resort or a rustic hacienda—have been chosen for their individuality and chic appeal.

Over 40 hotels are featured in detail. Insights into the essence of each property help readers decide on the one that best suits their needs and preferences. A fact-packed panel summarises each hotel's facilities and nearby attractions. Seven regional chapters—Mexican Caribbean, Mayan Region, Central East and South Highlands, Pacific Coast, Mexico City, Central Western Highlands and Sea of Cortez—introduce major tourist destinations and attractions, giving readers a headstart in their exploration of Mexico.

the chic series

Extraordinary destinations. Incomparable accommodations. Exceptional advice. Join discerning travellers who have found everything they desire in the chic series travel guides: hot properties, stunning photography and brilliant tips on where to go and how to do it in some of the world's chicest locations. Now jetting off to Mexico, Bali, South Africa, Shanghai, Morocco, Thailand, India and Spain.

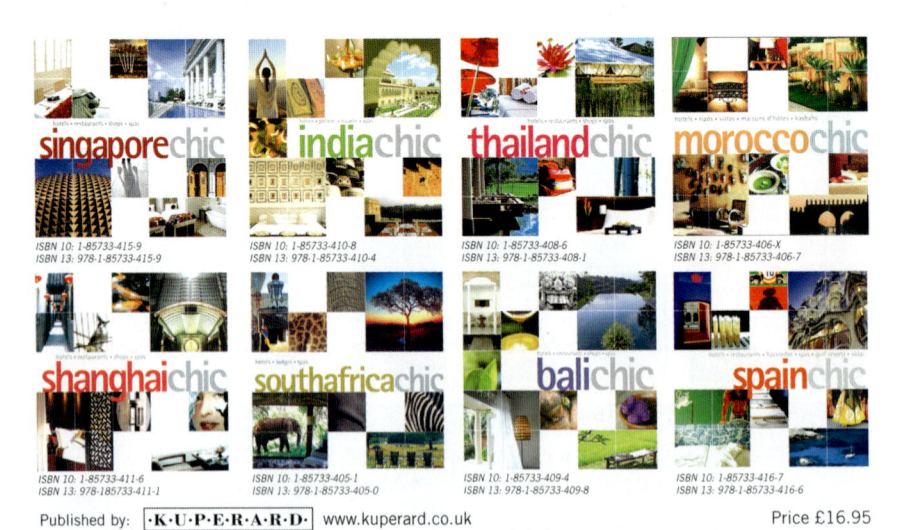

singapore chic
ISBN 10: 1-85733-415-9
ISBN 13: 978-1-85733-415-9

india chic
ISBN 10: 1-85733-410-8
ISBN 13: 978-1-85733-410-4

thailand chic
ISBN 10: 1-85733-408-6
ISBN 13: 978-1-85733-408-1

morocco chic
ISBN 10: 1-85733-406-X
ISBN 13: 978-1-85733-406-7

shanghai chic
ISBN 10: 1-85733-411-6
ISBN 13: 978-185733-411-1

southafrica chic
ISBN 10: 1-85733-405-1
ISBN 13: 978-1-85733-405-0

bali chic
ISBN 10: 1-85733-409-4
ISBN 13: 978-1-85733-409-8

spain chic
ISBN 10: 1-85733-416-7
ISBN 13: 978-1-85733-416-6

Published by: **·K·U·P·E·R·A·R·D·** www.kuperard.co.uk   Price £16.95

'Order any chic! guide via the Kuperard website and receive free postage on any quantity of guides. Visit www.kuperard.co.uk to see the full range in the series and type in the following promotional code on the payment page chic01. Or call us on 0208 446 2440 and quote the same code'

Ratings & Awards

For the first time ever the AA, VisitBritain, VisitScotland, and the Wales Tourist Board will use a single method of assessing and rating serviced accommodation. Irrespective of which organisation inspects an establishment the rating awarded will be the same, using a common set of standards, giving a clear guide of what to expect. The RAC is no longer operating an Hotel inspection and accreditation business.

Accommodation Standards: Star Grading Scheme

Using a scale of 1-5 stars the objective quality ratings give a clear indication of accommodation standard, cleanliness, ambience, hospitality, service and food, This shows the full range of standards suitable for every budget and preference, and allows visitors to distinguish between the quality of accommodation and facilities on offer in different establishments. All types of board and self-catering accommodation are covered, including hotels, B&Bs, holiday parks, campus accommodation, hostels, caravans and camping, and boats.

The more stars, the higher level of quality

★★★★★
exceptional quality, with a degree of luxury

★★★★
excellent standard throughout

★★★
very good level of quality and comfort

★★
good quality, well presented and well run

★
acceptable quality; simple, practical, no frills

VisitBritain and the regional tourist boards, **enjoyEngland.com**, **VisitScotland** and **VisitWales**, and **the AA** have full details of the grading system on their websites

enjoyEngland.com
visitScotland.com
visitWales.com
the AA.com

National Accessible Scheme

If you have particular mobility, visual or hearing needs, look out for the National Accessible Scheme. You can be confident of finding accommodation or attractions that meet your needs by looking for the following symbols.

- Typically suitable for a person with sufficient mobility to climb a flight of steps but would benefit from fixtures and fittings to aid balance

- Typically suitable for a person with restricted walking ability and for those that may need to use a wheelchair some of the time and can negotiate a maximum of three steps

- Typically suitable for a person who depends on the use of a wheelchair and transfers unaided to and from the wheelchair in a seated position. This person may be an independent traveller

- Typically suitable for a person who depends on the use of a wheelchair in a seated position. This person also requires personal or mechanical assistance (eg carer, hoist).

Looking for Holiday Accommodation?

for details of hundreds of properties throughout the UK visit our website

www.holidayguides.com

OTHER FHG TITLES FOR 2007

FHG Guides Ltd have a large range of attractive holiday accommodation guides for all kinds of holiday opportunities throughout Britain. They also make useful gifts at any time of year. Our guides are available in most bookshops and larger newsagents but we will be happy to post you a copy direct if you have any difficulty. POST FREE for addresses in the UK. We will also post abroad but have to charge separately for post or freight.

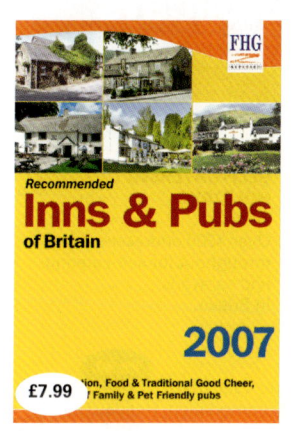

Recommended
INNS & PUBS of Britain.
Pubs, Inns and small hotels.

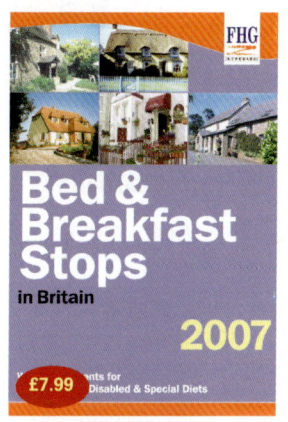

BED AND BREAKFAST STOPS
Over 1000 friendly and comfortable overnight stops. Non-smoking, Disabled and Special Diets Supplements.

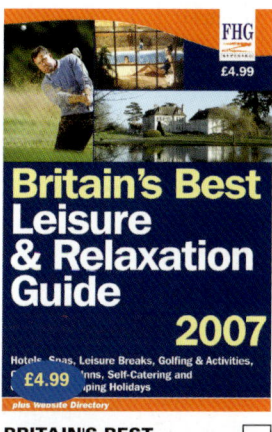

BRITAIN'S BEST LEISURE & RELAXATION GUIDE
A quick-reference general guide for all kinds of holidays.

The Original
PETS WELCOME!
The bestselling guide to holidays for pet owners and their pets.

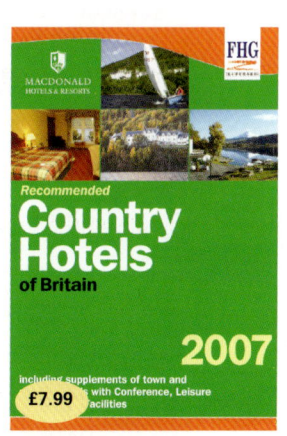

Recommended
COUNTRY HOTELS
of Britain
Including Country Houses, for the discriminating.

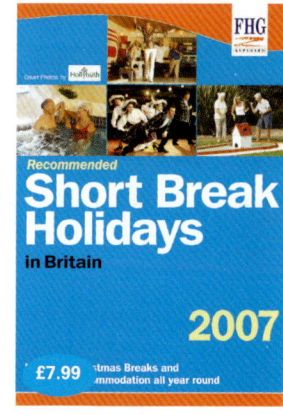

Recommended
SHORT BREAK HOLIDAYS IN BRITAIN
"Approved" accommodation for quality bargain breaks.

CHILDREN WELCOME!
Family Holidays and Days Out guide.
Family holidays with details of amenities for children and babies.

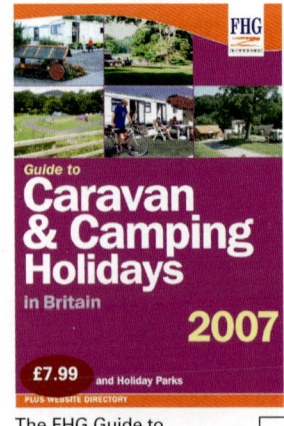

The FHG Guide to
CARAVAN & CAMPING HOLIDAYS,
Caravans for hire, sites and holiday parks and centres.

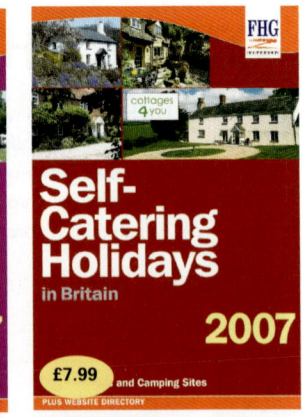

SELF-CATERING HOLIDAYS
in Britain
Over 1000 addresses throughout for self-catering and caravans in Britain.

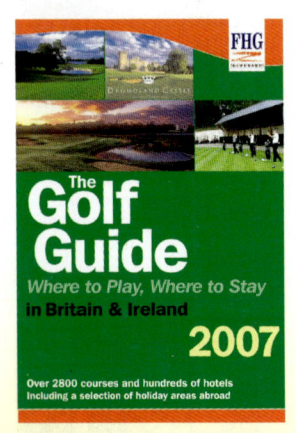

The GOLF GUIDE –
Where to play Where to stay
In association with GOLF MONTHLY. Over 2800 golf courses in Britain with convenient accommodation. Holiday Golf in France, Portugal, Spain, USA, South Africa and Thailand.

£9.99

Tick your choice above and send your order and payment to

**FHG Guides Ltd. Abbey Mill Business Centre
Seedhill, Paisley, Scotland PA1 1TJ
TEL: 0141- 887 0428 • FAX: 0141- 889 7204
e-mail: admin@fhguides.co.uk**

Deduct 10% for 2/3 titles or copies; 20% for 4 or more.

Send to: NAME ....

ADDRESS ....

....

....

POST CODE ....

I enclose Cheque/Postal Order for £ ....

SIGNATURE..DATE ....

Please complete the following to help us improve the service we provide.
How did you find out about our guides?:

☐ Press   ☐ Magazines   ☐ TV/Radio   ☐ Family/Friend   ☐ Other